INDISPENSABLE FOR EVERY HOMEOWNER

Do you know what to look for when you buy lumber? The newest products for your kitchen and bathroom? What paint colors streak and fade? Which tools and products to have on hand . . . and which to rent? Bob Vila gives you all the information you need to plan your project, make estimates, go to the lumber yard or building supply store (with this guide in hand!), and avoid confusion and costly mistakes. In this book Bob Vila and his expert co-authors show you how to get the best quality, the right product, the right size, the right amount, and the right price with—THIS OLD HOUSE GUIDE TO BUILDING AND REMODELING MATERIALS.

About the Authors

BOB VILA has been the host of the Emmy Award winning PBS series *This Old House,* a program seen by over 5 million viewers every week, since 1979. A specialist in residential remodeling and design, he is both a top expert in home restoration and a professional commercial builder. His restoration of a Victorian Italianate house in Boston was selected as "Heritage House of 1978" by *Better Homes and Gardens.*

NORM ABRAM, *This Old House* master carpenter has worked as a carpenter and contractor in the home improvement industry for more than 20 years. Growing up in Milford, Massachusetts, he learned his trade from his father, who was also a carpenter. Subsequently, Norm attended the University of Massachusetts at Amherst, where he studied Mechanical Engineering and Production Management. In between filming episodes of *This Old House* and lecturing at home centers across the country, Abram directs his firm's residential remodeling business in the Massachusetts area.

STEWART BYRNE, inventor and author, is a technical liaison on *This Old House.* His book, *Arkansas Story* contributed to the trend in building energy saving homes. During his forty years of marketing communication experience he has helped introduce dozens of new products for Owens-Corning Fiberglas and has been deeply involved in the development of Super Insulated Homes.

LARRY STAINS, founding editor of *New Shelter* magazine and a contributing editor of *The Family Handyman,* is a writer specializing in homes and their improvement. His articles have also appeared in *Better Homes and Gardens, Money,* and *Woman's Day Home Ideas.*

THIS OLD HOUSE™ GUIDE TO BUILDING AND REMODELING MATERIALS

By Bob Vila

with Norm Abram, Stewart Byrne and Larry Stains

WARNER BOOKS

A Warner Communications Company

Special Thanks To:

Bryan Earl for the book concept . . .
Russ Morash for THIS OLD HOUSE
. . . Fritz Lalendorf for editing . . .
Joseph Doherty for making it possible
. . . Marge Schwartz, Arnold Knipp and
Rob Sweney for production . . . and a
very special thanks to Traci Martineau
for hours and patience at the word
processor.

Printed in the United States of America
First Printing: November 1986
10 9 8 7 6 5 4 3 2 1

Library of Congress Cataloging-in-Publication Data

Vila, Bob.
    This old house guide to building and remodeling
materials.

    1. Dwellings—Remodeling—Equipment and supplies.
2. Building materials. I. Title.
TH4816.V539 1986   643'.7   86-22391
ISBN 0-446-38246-9 (U.S.A.) (pbk.)
        0-446-38247-7 (Canada) (pbk.)

Acknowledgments

The editors are grateful for the assistance provided by the following individuals, manufacturers and organizations:

Abrasives Manufacturers Institute
ACE
ADM Chemicals Division
American Brush Manufacturers Association
American Plywood Association
American Wood Preservers Association
Ashland Chemical Company
ASHRAE
Asphalt Roofing Manufacturers Association
Barnes and Noble Books—Harper & Row Publishers
Beecham Home Improvement Products, Inc.
Blackwell Scientific Publications Ltd.
Borden Chemical Division of Borden Inc.
Bostwick-Braun
Certified Ballast Manufacturers
Champion International
Coated Abrasives Manufacturers Institute
Contech Brands
Convenience Products Inc.
Crown Publishing Group
D.A.P. Inc.
Darworth Company
DIY Retailing
Dow Corning Corporation
Dri Industries
Emhart Chemical Group (Bostik Construction Products, Division)
Flat Glass Marketing Association
The Flood Company
Forest Products Lab, U.S. Department of Agriculture
Garrett Wade Company
General Electric
Geocel Corporation
Georgia Pacific
Gloucester Company
Goodyear Tire & Rubber Company
Hardware Age
Hardware Retailing
Harold B. Olin, AIA
H.B. Fuller Company
Henkel
Insta-Foam
International Staple, Nail & Tool Association
International Steel Wool
Jack R. Lewis
John-Ferrier—Western Michigan University
Kool Seal
Lucas Group—Tiger Grip
Macco Adhesives
Macklanburg-Duncan
Mameco International
McGraw-Hill Book Company
Miracle Adhesives Corporation
Muralo Company
NAHB
Nankee
National Fire Protection Association
National Paint & Coatings Association
Nicholson File Company
Oak Flooring Institute, affiliate of National Oak Flooring Manufacturers Association
Ohio Sealants, Inc.
Pecora Corporation
Pella Rolscreen Company
Phifer Wire Company
Plumbing, Heating, Cooling Information Bureau
Polycel Products, W.R. Grace & Company
Portland Cement Association
Prentice-Hall, Inc.
Products Research & Chemical Corporation
Red Cedar Shingle & Handsplit Shake Bureau
Red Devil, Inc.
Regal Industries
Remodeling Magazine
Rexnard, Contech Division
Rodale Press
Ross Chemical Company
Safety Glazing Certification Council
Scott-Page
Shakertown Corporation
Sherwin-Williams
Skeist Laboratories Inc.
Southwall Technologies
Stanley Tools/Division of the Stanley Works
Stauffer Chemical Company—Specialty Chemical Division
Stauffer-Wacker Silicones Corporation
Stonesong Press Inc.
Synkoloid Company, Inc.
Therma-Tru Corporation
3M
Tremco
Tremont Nail Company
U-G-L United Gilsonite Labs
Van Nostrand Reinhold Company
William Zinsser & Company, Inc.
Willis H. Wagner
W.J. Ruscoe
Woodmont Chemical

Contents

Introduction

BOB VILA
Host of *This Old House*

Hi. I'm Bob Vila. As host of WGBH-TV's *This Old House,* I've helped millions of people—do-it-yourselfers and professionals alike—plan, design and undertake home improvement projects.

There is, however, one important step that I never seem to have time to talk about on the show: choosing the right tools and materials for the job. Whether you are an ambitious do-it-yourselfer or a professional remodeler, the right tools and materials make a remodeling project go smoothly. And in the end, they can make the difference between a high-quality investment of your time and dollars and an amateur, slightly slapdash appearance.

This book is designed as a convenient one-source reference that lists all the tools and materials used in most remodeling projects, what they look like, where to get them, what quality and quantity to buy and, most importantly, which ones to use.

As you may already know and I have learned, choosing the right tools and materials is not always easy. There are a multitude of products available—and until now—no one source that tells which is best to use when. The point is best illustrated on a Saturday morning in any home center when enthusiastic remodelers, anxious to undertake a weekend project, stand perplexed before shelf after shelf of what appears to be the same product, just slightly different in each case.

It is with this scene in mind, as well as hundreds of less than perfect remodeling projects due to the wrong materials and tools, that we have created this Guide.

Introduction

NORM ABRAM
Master Carpenter of *This Old House*

During my years as a professional carpenter with my own remodeling business and as master carpenter on WGBH-TV's *This Old House,* I wished many times for a reference like this. I looked for such a book, but could not find one. So, when the opportunity came up to help create such a guide, I was glad to share what I'd learned the hard way all these years.

I think you will find this guide to be the single best source for home improvements and rehabbing. There isn't another like it.

This is an up-to-date reference that answers questions both big and small. It teaches you major things, like how to estimate the number of shingles for a roofing job, and which kind offers the longest warranty and greatest fire resistance. You'll learn how to evaluate kitchen cabinets for quality and value, how much insulation you really need, and just what the difference is between latex and oil-based paint. You'll learn how to sort through a pile of lumber for wood that won't warp. You'll see the varieties of labor-saving plastic plumbing available these days, and you'll read about a life-saving electrical device called a ground-fault circuit interrupter.

You'll also learn about little things—the details that can make a big difference. Like the difference between plywood siding that is graded 303-NR and 303-30. You'll learn how to turn your electric drill into a labor-saving

paint remover, and how to mix mortar when repointing old brickwork. You'll learn how to eyeball a door or a window for the little features that mean the most energy-savings and security. You'll find out when to rent a cement mixer, rather than mix by hand. You'll be able to look up everything from hasps to piano hinges, washers to wall anchors, ColorCore to siliconized caulk. You'll also learn about tools to rent instead of buy, be it a paint sprayer, pneumatic stapler, or a belt sander.

Consult this book before you wander down to the home center, hardware store or lumber yard, and you'll be able to buy your tools and materials with confidence. You won't have to rely on a salesperson whose knowledge might be limited, partial to a particular product, or just plain wrong. You'll save yourself time, money, trouble and frustration.

Bob Vila, myself, Stewart Byrne and Larry Stains all welcome this chance to spare you headaches by sharing what we know with you. If you can't find something you need in this book, please write to us in care of Warner Books, 666 Fifth Avenue, New York, NY 10103. We'll respond directly and will consider your information in the next update of the book. We plan to stay abreast of all the new products that will improve your next home improvement project.

THIS OLD HOUSE GUIDE TO BUILDING AND REMODELING MATERIALS

Your Workshop

1

There are people who approach construction projects with fear and loathing. For them, such projects produce only frustration, bad results, and blisters. Odds are, these people own ill-equipped workshops. They need the right tools and a better place to do their work than the kitchen table. So do you. Whether you work with building materials for fun or profit, a good workshop can spell the difference between success and failure, pleasure and pain, safety and danger.

This chapter lists all kinds of tools: hand tools, power tools, the familiar and the bizarre. It also lists the oils, cleaners, and other miscellaneous things that ought to be within arm's reach of your workbench.

Most of the common hand tools are worth buying. But don't go out and buy them all at once; buy them as the need arises. Before you know it you'll be well stocked. Some of the portable power tools are also worth buying, but it may be more to your advantage to rent others from a local tool rental outlet. (Specialized tools, such as cement mixers and paint sprayers, are listed in the corresponding chapters on materials.)

Here are my three rules of tools:

1. Buy quality.

When buying tools, you generally get what you pay for. A quick scan of your home-center shelves will reveal a wide range of prices. When buying hand tools, avoid the bargain racks. Shop for name brands. Shop also for commonsense quality: hammers that won't break as you're yanking a nail, screwdrivers that won't slip out of screw slots and wreck the heads, socket sets that won't lose their grip. If the tool is made of steel, look for steel that is tempered and drop-forged.

When shopping for portable power tools, also look for quality, brand names, and a good warranty. If you're a home handyman, you don't necessarily need to buy the most expensive models sold to professionals. Those models are usually built to withstand the abuse of construction sites. Professional-quality electric drills, for example, can be dropped from the roof of a two-floor building and still keep on drilling.

Remember the adage: Good tools do work; bad tools make work.

2. Maintain quality.

Be careful with your tools, especially cutting tools. Protect sharp edges of chisels, retract plane blades when not in use, and hang up handsaws. Oil metal parts to prevent rust. Sharpen what's dull, and use tools wisely to keep them sharp. There's nothing duller than a ripsaw that has hit a few nails in its day and nothing aches worse than your arm after using it.

A well-organized workshop keeps your tools in good shape. Stay organized so you won't be tempted to leave your tools in a pile at day's end.

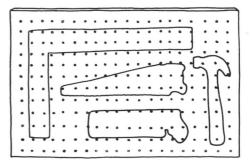

3. Think safety.

Sharp, high-quality hand tools keep you from using excessive or reckless force on a project. Hence the saying "A dull tool is a dangerous tool, a sharp tool is a safe tool."

Your Workshop

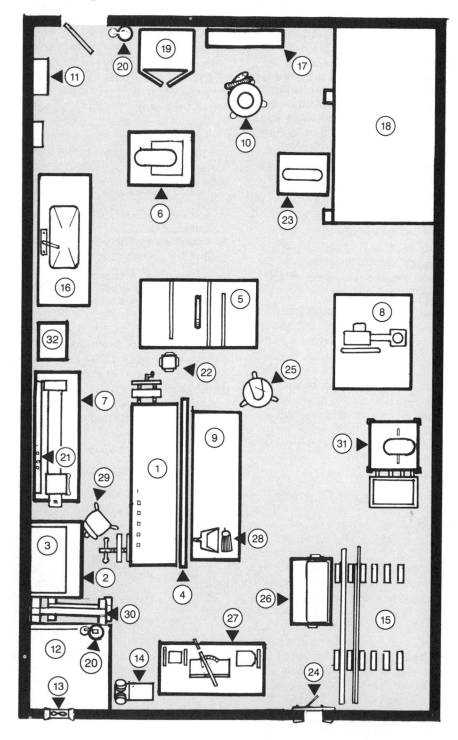

You may not have the leeway of this 18′ × 24′ room, but whatever the size, your shop should be designed around your main power saw (table, band, or radial) so enough space is provided for cutting a 4′ × 8′ plywood panel and so other tables or equipment of equal table height will support the work while cutting. Fold-down tables, hanging cabinets, and a portable workbench can save space.

1. Workbench with vices
2. Hand-tool cabinet on casters
3. Hanging supply cabinet
4. Two-sided pegboard for tools
5. Table saw or band saw
6. Drill press
7. Lathe
8. Radial saw
9. Worktable with electric hand-tool storage space underneath
10. Shop vacuum
11. Abrasives, paint, and thinner storage
12. Spray booth
13. Power ventilator
14. Compressor
15. Vertical panel storage
16. Sink
17. Plumbing and electrical parts storage
18. Lumber storage
19. Clothing, safety equipment, and first-aid storage
20. Fire extinguishers
21. Lathe tool rack
22. Electric outlets dropped from ceiling on 4″ × 4″s
23. Jigsaw
24. Insulated pass-through door for plywood
25. Metal garbage can with latch-down lid for rags
26. Portable power-tool chest (may contain electric drill, power sander, saber saw, and router)
27. Miter saw
28. Dustpan and brush
29. Castered chair
30. Sawhorse storage
31. Jointer
32. Dehumidifier

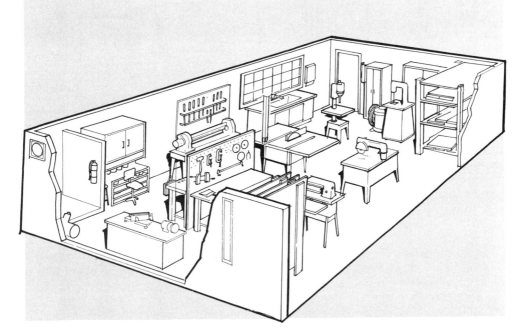

Your Workshop

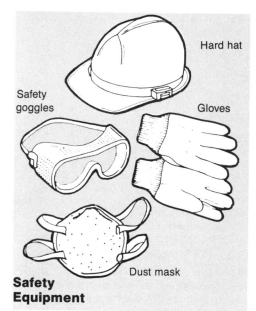

Hard hat

Safety goggles

Gloves

Dust mask

Safety Equipment

Power tools, which are far faster than hand tools, are also potentially more dangerous. Wear safety goggles, don't remove blade guards, and don't snip off the ground-wire prong of a three-prong plug. Learn and practice the tricks of using power tools when working on sawhorses. Finally, remember that in your entire workshop, there are two pairs of tools that can never be replaced: your hands and your eyes.

Abrasives

The term *sandpaper* is commonly used to describe several different kinds of abrasive paper. Generally, the man-made silicon carbide (the hardest) and aluminum oxide papers outperform emery and flint papers, although emery is good for polishing. Garnet is brittle and fractures with use, forming new cutting surfaces. The backing consists of paper of various thicknesses or, in the case of aluminum oxide, cloth. Emery is always cloth-backed.

Sandpapers are rated by their coarseness, as shown on the chart on page 9, from *Super-Fine* (600 screen) to *Extra-Coarse* (12 screen). Each is recommended for particular jobs, but your own experience will guide you best.

To reduce clogging, many open-coat papers are available. Also, wet-and-dry sandpaper can be used with light machine oil or water to flush out shavings. Sanding sponges can be squeezed out in water. Regular sandpaper is closed-coat, but it is also available with an antistatic surface to reduce clogging. Since the coating used is zinc stearate, these are called "stearated papers."

Sandpaper is now available in a two-sided form, with peel-and-stick backing, even with a Velcro attachment for sanding discs. Some sandpaper has a textured back that helps it cling to the block without adhesives.

Sandpaper And Garnet Paper

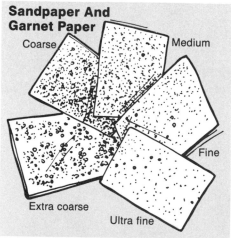

Coarse

Medium

Fine

Extra coarse

Ultra fine

Steel wool will perform many of the same tasks as sandpaper and is excellent for adding luster to furniture (see chart, facing page). Pumice is also good for fine finishing though many prefer crocus cloth (iron oxide), otherwise known as rouge cloth.

While sandpaper abrades, coarse steel wool cuts or chisels and fine steel wool tends to burnish. Furniture manufacturers use 0000 steel wool to apply rubbing stains and the final coat of wax or oil. Generally, steel wool is used between coats of paint, lacquer, varnish, or shellac and for the finishing operation.

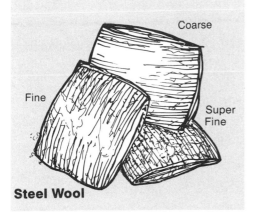

Steel Wool

Use 0 Medium-Fine then 00 Fine to clean aluminum window frames. Professional window cleaners use 0 Medium-Fine to remove the soot and grime from glass and 1 Medium to remove paint from glass.

On any object that will be outdoors or in the water—for example, a boat hull—use bronze wool. Should any particles embed themselves, the bronze wool will not cause a rust streak.

To protect your skin, wear gloves when using steel or bronze wool.

A couple of useful tips. When the surface of the steel wool gets loaded, you can open the pad and refold it to provide a newly usable surface. Thrifty craftsmen cut their pads into three sections for use when they don't require a whole pad.

Steel Wool—Choose the Right Grade

0000 Super Fine	
Buffing	Final finish on fine woodwork, shellacs, lacquers, varnishes (use to apply final wax or oil)
Cleaning	Delicate instruments
000 Extra Fine	
Buffing	Cabinetwork and auto finishing; new wax finish
Polishing	Aluminum, copper, brass, and zinc
Removing	Minor burns from wood and leather; paint spots and splatters
00 Very Fine	
Buffing	For final finish on painted trim
Cleaning	Golf clubs, screens, and frames
Cutting	To cut gloss finishes to semigloss
Removing	Old finishes from antiques (use with varnish remover)

Your Workshop

Steel Wool—Choose the Right Grade (Concluded)

0 Medium: Fine

Cleaning	Barbecue grills, aluminum, copper, brass, zinc, and other metals
Removing	Rust from metal tools

1 Medium

Cleaning	Linoleum, rubber asphalt, and other resilient floors; white sidewalls, bowling balls, and soles of bowling shoes
Prepare	Preparation of wood for first coat of paint

2 Medium: Coarse

Cleaning	Glass brick, rough metal, or stone surfaces
Removing	Rust and dirt from garden tools and machinery, scuff marks and old wax from floors.

3 Extra Coarse

Removing	Old paint and varnish

Source: International Steel Wool, Springfield, OH 45501.

Abrasive blocks are essentially sponges wrapped on four sides with an abrasive coating. They are springy and flexible for sanding moldings and other complex shapes. They can be rinsed out to unclog the abrasive. Foam glass blocks are similar but are rigid and crumble easily. The glass blocks are also less suitable than the sponges because they wear away rapidly when used and sometimes give off the odor of rotten eggs. However, their abrasiveness makes them handy for removing scale or peeled paint.

Most models are available with handles and in a variety of abrasive grades somewhat similar to sandpaper. The Medium to Coarse grits perform like sandpaper but normally last much longer and don't clog as often. They can be used for scraping or sanding wood, metal, or brick.

Sandpaper substitutes are made from nylon mesh, steel wool, a tough polyester cloth coated with an abrasive, or thin sheet metal punched with ragged holes. Their flexibility allows them to reach places that rasps and scrapers cannot. *One good tip:* The mesh or cloth sanders can be wrapped around a dowel to sand a convex surface. The Hempe flexible sander will sand concave surfaces.

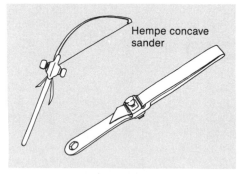

Hempe concave sander

Abrasives

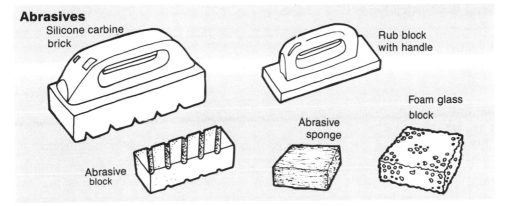

Silicone carbine brick

Rub block with handle

Foam glass block

Abrasive sponge

Abrasive block

Comparative Abrasive Grades

Technical Grades				Simplified Grades	Other Grades
Aluminum Oxide, Silicon Carbide, Garnet & Flint					
Mesh	Symbol	Flint	Emery	Flint Finishing	Emery Polishing
600					4/0
500					3/0
400	10/0				0
360					
320	9/0			7/0	½
280	8/0			6/0	
240	7/0			5/0	1/2
220	6/0			4/0	2
180	5/0	Extra Fine		3/0	3
150	4/0		Fine	2/0	
120	3/0	Fine			
100	2/0		Medium		
80	0	Medium	Coarse		
60	1/2				
50	1		Extra Coarse		
40	1½	Coarse			
36	2				
30	2½	Extra Coarse			
24	3				
20	3½				
16	4				
12	4½				

Your Workshop

Abrasive Selection Guide

Abrasives Key: EC-Extra Coarse;MC-Medium Coarse;

ABRASIVE	Silicon Carbide	Aluminum Oxide	Garnet
METAL			
Scale Removal (Ferrous)		EC, C	
Rust Removal (Ferrous)			EC, C
Corrosion Oxidation Removal (Alum.)			
Paint Removal	EC, C		
Light Stock Removal High Tensile	EC, C		
Light Stock Removal Low Tensile	M (dry)		
Priming Preparation	VF (dry)	M, F	
After Priming	EF SF (wet)	EF	
Between Coats	SF (dry) SF (wet)		
After Final Coat	VF (wet)		
Finishing and Polishing	VF, EF, SF, UF (wet)	EF	
For High Luster		EF	
Electrical Contacts		EF	
WOOD			
Heavy Stock Removal			
Soft Woods	EC, C (wet)		M
Hard Woods		EC, C	C
Moderate Stock Removal			
Soft Woods	M (wet)		M
Hard Woods		M	C
Removing Paint		EC, C	
Preparing for Sealing		F	M
After Sealing	EF (wet)	EF	EF
Between Coats	EF, SF (wet) EF (dry)		
After Final Coat	SF, UF (wet)		
Polishing for High Luster			

FOOTNOTES:
*Use bronze wool on items subject to wetting to avoid rust stains.
Sanding sponge has fine one side, medium other, or medium one side and coarse on other. Open coat has less abrasive but has less tendency to clog up. Use on tacky surfaces.
NOTES:
Wet sandpaper has an abrasive attached and coated with resin. It is used with water or light machine oil to flush out shavings. Outlasts dry paper.
BACKING:
Sheet materials 9″ x 11″ have paper backing: Graded A (light and flexible) through F (heavy and stiff). Aluminum oxide is also available with cloth backing. Emery only comes with cloth backing.
DURABILITY:
Except for low-cost flint paper, the durability of all others is good, with wet and dry being excellent.

C-Coarse; M-Medium; F-Fine; EF-Extra Fine; VF-Very Fine; SF-Super Fine; UF-Ultra Fine

Flint (Silicon Dioxide)	Emery	Steel Wool*	Pumice (Rotten stone)	Crocus (Rouge) Cloth	Wire Brush or Perforated Metal	Sanding Sponge
	C	C			X	
	C	C			X	
		EF, F, F				
		C, VF, F			X	C
	C					
	C	C				
M or F	M	F				M
		VF				M
	M	EF				M
	F	EF	X			F
	F, EF, UF	SF	X	X		
		SF		X		
					X	
					X	
		C			X	C
M		M				M
EF						M
						F
		VF	X	X		F
		EF, SF	X	X		

11

Your Workshop

Abrasive Selection Guide (Concluded)

Abrasives Key: EC-Extra Coarse;MC-Medium Coarse;

ABRASIVE	Silicon Carbide	Aluminum Oxide	Garnet
GLASS, TILE, FIBERGLASS AND PLASTIC			
Removing Paint			
Removing Soot and Grime (Glass)			
Shaping	1	EC, C	
Light Stock Removal (Fiberglass & Plastic)		M	
Finishing, feathering edges, scuffing	VF (wet) VF (dry)	F, EF	
Removing "chalking"			
Removing Grease			
Removing Dirt and Grime			

FOOTNOTES:
*Use bronze wool on items subject to wetting to avoid rust stains.
Sanding sponge has fine one side, medium other, or medium one side and coarse on other. Open coat has less abrasive but has less tendency to clog up. Use on tacky surfaces.
NOTES:
Wet sandpaper has an abrasive attached and coated with resin. It is used with water or light machine oil to flush out shavings. Outlasts dry paper.
BACKING:
Sheet materials 9″ x 11″ have paper backing: Graded A (light and flexible) through F (heavy and stiff). Aluminum oxide is also available with cloth backing. Emery only comes with cloth backing.
DURABILITY:
Except for low-cost flint paper, the durability of all others is good, with wet and dry being excellent.

Nylon abrasive mesh

Flexible Abrasives

Awls

These are used for marking or starting holes for brads, nails, or screws in wood, plastic, or aluminum. The four most useful are:

Brad awl

Screw starter

Scratch awl

Striking knife

Brad awl (often called a brad driver). This magnetically holds small brads so that they can be driven into hard-to-reach places.

C-Coarse; M-Medium; F-Fine; EF-Extra Fine; VF-Very Fine; SF-Super Fine; UF-Ultra Fine

Flint (Silicon Dioxide)	Emery	Steel Wool*	Pumice (Rotten stone)	Crocus (Rouge) Cloth	Wire Brush or Perforated Metal	Sanding Sponge
	F, VF	C			X	M
		M, C				M
						C
						F
		F			X	F
		F				F
		VF, F, M			X	F

Scratch awl. Marks location of nails or screws in wood or soft nonmetal material. Blade length 3″ to 4.″ Starts hole for fastener.

Screw starter. Similar to a scratch awl but with threaded tip for making screw starting holes in wood or soft metal.

Striking knife. A little-known but useful tool. One end is an awl, the other is a blade cut at a 135° angle for inscribing very thin lines for layout work.

Boring Tools

The conventional hand braces are now often supplanted by wood bits and hole saws having drill shanks suitable for use in electric drills. These permit you to cut larger diameter holes and save time.

Use of a combination drill-countersink bit will allow you to drill the pilot hole, shank hole, and countersink for the screw head in one operation rather than three. New bits for electric drills enable you to cut holes up to 1½″.

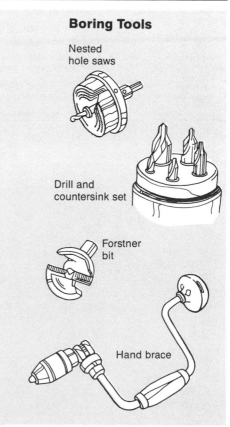

Boring Tools

Nested hole saws

Drill and countersink set

Forstner bit

Hand brace

Your Workshop

Boring Tools

Type	Use	Size/Capacity	Comments
Ratchet Bit Brace	Normally used for drilling ¼" or larger holes in wood or soft metal. Ratchet brace allows drilling in close quarters. Square tapered shank auger bits can be used for holes up to 1." Expansion bits can be used for holes up to 3" in diameter. Screwdriver bits and countersink bits can be used. Some chucks will hold straight shank drills up to ½" diameter.	Size classifications are 10" & 12." Will take expansion bits up to 3" diameter.	See below for bits to fit bit brace.
Hand Drill Also called: Eggbeater drill	Drills holes under ¼" in diameter. Uses straight shank twist drills. Operates similar to an eggbeater.	Takes drill bits up to ¼" diameter.	Hollow handle normally contains up to 8 drill bits.
Push Drill Also called: Yankee drill	Best used to drill small pilot holes or holes up to 11⁄64" diameter. Pushing on handle rotates drill's mechanism to drill holes.	Takes 8 sizes of drill bits up to 11⁄64" diameter.	Hollow handle holds drill bits normally supplied with drill.
Auger Bit	Used with bit brace to drill holes in wood up to 1½" diameter.	Purchase in sets: from ¼" diameter to 1" diameter. Larger bits normally purchased separately. Available sizes: 1⅛", 1¼" and 1½".	

Boring Tools (Continued)

Type	Use	Size/Capacity	Comments
Pole Bit	For boring through creosoted poles or railroad ties without clogging or binding.	$\frac{9}{16}''$, $\frac{11}{69}''$, $\frac{13}{16}''$, $\frac{15}{16}''$.	
Arbor and Pilot Drill	This is the arbor and pilot drill used in the center of hole saws.	For chuck sizes $\frac{1}{4}''$, $\frac{1}{2}''$, $\frac{3}{4}''$. Shank diameters: $\frac{1}{4}''$, $\frac{7}{16}''$, $\frac{5}{8}''$. Uses $\frac{1}{4}''$ high speed pilot drill.	Hole saw attaches to threads on arbor.
Spade Bit Also called: Speed Bore Bit Electric Drill Wood Bit Power Bit Wood Bit	Used with electric hand drill to bore larger holes in wood. Often used to countersink washers and bolt heads. Can be used on drywall or plastic. Chatters and makes rough hole.	$\frac{1}{4}''$ up to $1''$ by 16ths; $1\frac{1}{8}''$ to $1\frac{1}{2}''$ by 8ths. Round Head Sizes: $\frac{3}{8}''$ to $1''$.	Normally sold in sets, although could be purchased separately as needed. Round head type also available. Good for rough construction or boring holes for cable or pipe.
Door Lock Bit	For drilling holes for door handle in doors. Can be used with brace or electric drill.	$5\frac{1}{4}''$ overall length. $2\frac{1}{8}''$ diameter.	
Power Bit Extension	Extends drilling depth of straight shank drills.	Length $12''$ Fits most $\frac{1}{4}''$ shank or larger chucks.	

Your Workshop

Boring Tools (Continued)

Type	Use	Size/Capacity	Comments
Expansion Bit	Bit cuts holes from 1″ diameter to 3″ diameter by adjusting the extension of the cutters. Cutters are interchangeable.	Available in two sizes: $5/8$″ to $13/4$″. $7/8$″ to 3″.	
Countersinks Taper Shank Straight Shank	Used to countersink materials for flush head screws.	Taper shank: $3/4$″ cutting edge; Straight shank: $1/2$″ or $3/4$″ cutting edge.	Square taper shank for braces. Straight shank for hand or electric drills.
Forstner Bits	Has a disc-shaped head wider than its shank with sharp spur cutting rim. Indispensible for shallow holes and angular cuts into wood or cutting into end grain, particularly when you want to drill only partway into the board. Unlike standard bits it does not have a large lead point and provides a flat bottom hole.	$3/8$″, $1/2$″, $5/8$″, $3/4$″, 1″, $11/4$″, $11/2$″, $13/4$″, 2″, $21/8$″.	Excellent for hardwoods. Must be tapped into wood before starting to drill. Never touch the outside or rim–skin acids will corrode cutters. Will cut cleanly through knots. Cuts slowly.

Boring Tools (Continued)

Type	Use	Size/Capacity	Comments
Combination Drill & Countersink Combination drills are available in most of the common wood screw sizes. 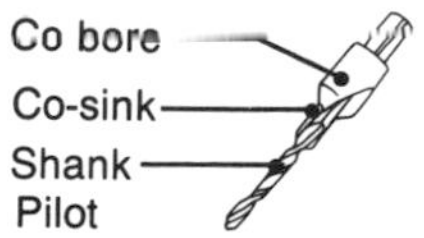 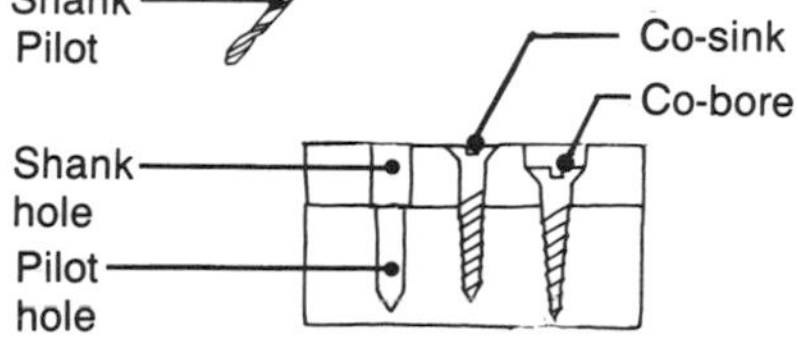 Co bore Co-sink Shank Pilot Co-sink Co-bore Shank hole Pilot hole	Drills, countersinks, and sometimes counterbores holes in one operation. Those with set-collar provide variable counterbore for plugging.	Available in screw sizes from #6 to #12 and lengths from ¾" to 2". Adjustable tools available for screw sizes: #5, 6 & 7; #7, 8, & 9; #10, 11, & 12; #11, 12, & 14.	Pilot hole & shank clearance-hole depths are adjustable on some makes. Normally used with ¼" or larger electric drills.
Hole Saw 	Used with portable hand drills or drill presses to cut holes up to 6" in diameter in wood, plastic or soft metal. Uses an arbor with high-speed drill bit to locate hole center.	Available arbor chuck sizes: ¼", ½", & ¾". Arbor shank size: ¼", ⁷⁄₁₆", & ⅝". Hole saw sizes: from ⁹⁄₁₆" to 6". Hole saw depth of cut: 1⅛".	Saws with integral arbors are available in size range ⅝" to 4". Nested saws available, are cheaper but less accurate.
Nail Setters Stop Collars Set Collars 	Attaches to drill bit to limit drilling depth. Has set screw or radial clamping.	For ⅛" to 1" drills.	Handy and inexpensive.
Power Bore Bits 	For precision cutting of larger holes with electric drill. Single-spur blade does the cutting.	⅜" through 1".	Less friction than with twist drill of same bore. Prevents burning of wood and motor stalling.
Masonry Drill 	Uses carbide tip and wide flutes to drill holes in masonry. Requires electric or air drill.	Hole diameter: ¼" to 1". Shank diameter: ¼", ⅜", & ½". Bit length: 4", 6", & 13".	Sold individually or in sets.
Plug Cutter 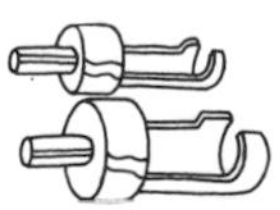	Specially designed drill bit used to cut plugs for covering recessed screws in cabinetry and furniture.	Plug sizes: ⅜", ½", ⅝", & ¾".	

Your Workshop

Boring Tools (Concluded)

Type	Use	Size/Capacity	Comments
Single Spur	Provides clean cut in wood.	Bit sizes: ½" to 1".	Accurate and clean cutting but difficult to sharpen.
Twist Drill	For use in drill press or electric hand drill to drill holes in all hardwoods and metal except hardened steel.	Normally sold in sets. ¼", ⅜" or ½" shanks for holes from 1/16" to ½" diameter.	Hard to sharpen without a sharpening jig. Available with stepped shanks to permit use of larger diameter bits in smaller drill chucks—example—a stepped ½" drill bit can be used in a ⅜" or ¼" drill motor chuck.
Brad Point Drill	Better than twist drill for wood—has larger flutes to clear chips. Don't use on metal.	Bit sizes: ⅛" to ½".	Center point provides accuracy. Less likely to split wood. Cheaper than a twist drill. Reduced shanks available.

Chisels

A chisel should be kept razor-sharp so you can concentrate on the line you are cutting instead of the force you have to apply. A sharp chisel will be less likely to jump out of the cut and is therefore safer to use. Craftsmen make a practice of sharpening their chisels before they put them away. They store them on the wall, not in a tool chest, where the edge will get damaged. A chisel is sharpened *on the bevel side only,* and a leather strap is used to apply a razor edge.

Chisel blades vary in shape. Straight chisels are ground across the face; skew chisels are ground at about 23°, so they have a flat but angled cutting edge. Parting chisels are narrow and thin, designed for hand pressure only. Those used for mortise cuts are perfectly flat and straight and usually thicker than those with beveled sides used for cabinetwork. Boxwood or beech handles are preferred, these being less likely to split from mallet blows. Brass caps are available to protect the handles. If you don't have a mallet and plan to use a hammer, the chisel should have a plastic handle.

In using a chisel the work should be firmly attached or secured in a vise.

Blade length and balance (heavy handle or heavy blade) is a matter of personal choice.

Chisels

Type	Use	Size	Comments
Wood Chisels	Used to remove wood for door locks, hinges and other recessed items.	Available with blade widths from ¼" to 2".	Purchase a set of 4 chisels with ¼", ½", ¾" & 1" blade widths to handle most home-handyman jobs.
Woodworking Tools	Used for carving wood for decorative purposes. Special sets available for wood lathes. Sets consist of various widths of skews, gouges, parting tool, spear and round-nose tools.	Sets of 6 or 8 tools are available. Size or width of tips ¹⁄₁₆" up to 1". V bent gouges are available from 40 degrees to 90 degrees.	Normally purchased as a set.
Cold Chisel	Cold chisels are used to cut off nails, bolts & nuts or cut light sheet metal. Special-use chisels include ripping chisels for tearing through studding, brick chisels with broad blade and stone cutters chisels with serrated broad blade.		Normally purchased in sets with punches and nail set.
Punches	Drift punches are for aligning bolt holes in two adjoining surfaces. Used to drive pins or bolts into or out of metal parts. Prick punch marks metal for drilling holes. Center punch provides a center point for drilling holes.	Pin punches come in various diameters to match drill sizes.	Normally purchased in sets with cold chisels and nail set.

Your Workshop

Chisels (Concluded)

Type	Use	Size/Capacity	Comments
Nail Set	Use to recess nail heads so that they are not visable. Tip is accurately cupped to fit nail or brad heads.	$\frac{1}{32}''$, $\frac{1}{16}''$, & $\frac{3}{32}''$ points	Normally part of cold chisel set.
Tack Claw	Used to pull up tacks and small brads.	Approximately 7″ long.	Should have a long-shouldered, broad claw to prevent surface damage.
Caps	Brass caps are available to attach on your chisel handles to protect them from mallet blows.		
Brick Chisel Also called: Plumber's chisel Nail Chisel Long Brick Chisel	For trimming brick, also used by carpenters, electricians and plumbers to tear through studding joists and other thick material.	Cutting edges: $\frac{5}{8}''$ to 1″. Tool lengths 12″ to 18″. Have target head.	Look for drop-forged tool steel hardened and tempered with blue enamel finish and polished taper.
Stone Cutters Chisel	For trimming and carving stone. Similar to brick chisel but different in size and some have a tooth cutting edge.	Cutting edges: $1\frac{1}{4}''$, $1\frac{3}{4}''$, $2\frac{1}{4}''$. Length: 10″.	Should be forged from tool steel, hardened and tempered with blue enamel finish.
Clapboard Chisel	For splitting shingles and clapboard.	Cutting edge: 2″. Length: 18″.	Octagon forged tool steel with 5″ polished blade 2″ wide.
Star Drill	Used to manually drill a hole for expansion anchors in masonry.	Diameters: $\frac{1}{4}''$ to $1\frac{3}{8}''$. Length: 12″.	Drive with a hammer.

Clamps and Vises

Think of a clamp or vise as an assistant, one with superhuman strength and endless patience. A vise will equip you for jobs you couldn't otherwise undertake. A good vise will ensure greater safety for both you and your work and enable you to work with greater speed and flexibility. Eventually you'll need a variety of clamps and at least one solid woodworker's vise and a bench vise for metalwork. It may be better to wait until you have a specific need before making your purchase, as the types of vises and clamps necessary will depend on the nature of the projects you undertake.

Flimsy vises will not last and can be hazardous if they let go at the wrong moment. Vises must be attached to a solid, secure surface such as the top of a workbench. They need to be located away from a wall or other obstruction. A good woodworker's vise attaches under the workbench and has a large threaded spindle and two ¾" steel guide rods. Wood vise faces should be at least 10" long and 2½"

deep and have a sturdy handle with knobs. A tail vise, which attaches to the end of the workbench, or a shoulder vise, which attaches to the front, may suit your needs best. It is possible to buy a quality workbench with both types preattached.

A metal vise can be smaller and is portable, but it must have two strong guide rods and at least a ½" threaded spindle and thick handle. It will be more versatile if it is equipped with pipe grips. Fiber grips are available to protect softer materials from being damaged by the metal faces. Get a metal vise large enough to attach to secure surfaces up to 1½" thick. It should open to at least 2". The jaws should be wide and deep to avoid scarring work and to prevent movement.

You'll find dozens of uses for C clamps, but you'll need pairs in two or three different sizes. Other clamps—for example, frame clamps—are essential for specific jobs. You'll find their uses and descriptions in the table below.

Clamps and Vises

Type	Use	Size/Capacity
C-Clamp Square Throat Regular Heavy Duty Deep Throat	C-Clamps can be used to hold two or more pieces together when gluing or nailing. The amount of pressure required normally dictates the clamp size required. You'll find dozens of uses for these—they're an essential component of the standard tool kit.	C-Clamps are sized according to throat opening and depth. Sizes range from 1" opening with a 1" depth to an 8" opening and 4" depth. Deep throat clamps are available with throat depths to 5¾".

Regular C-Clamp

Square Throat Clamp

Deep Throat Clamp

Your Workshop

Clamps and Vises (Continued)

Type	Use	Size/Capacity
Pipe Clamp (also called cabinet or furniture clamps)	Used to clamp large stock such as tabletops when doweling or gluing. Sets of clamping feet can be purchased separately and attached to lengths of pipe to make clamps up to 20 feet long.	Capacity limited only by length of pipe.
Adjustable Handscrews Also called: Woodworkers Clamps	Used to assemble woodwork, furniture, cabinets, etc., when gluing or attaching with fasteners. Jaws can be closed irregularly by tightening or loosening one screw more than the other, to clamp tapared or odd-shaped material.	Jaw lengths: 6" to 12". Jaw openings: 3" to 8½".
Spring Clamps	Spring clamps work like large clothespins providing quick clamping pressure for jobs requiring minimal pressure.	Jaw lengths: 4" to 9". Jaw openings: ⅞" to 3".
Band Clamp Also called: Web Clamp	Clamp large or unwieldy material such as chair-leg/rung assemblies or bracing large boxes or oddly shaped containers.	Webbing lengths: 12' to 15'.
Frame Clamps	Clamps corners of picture frames, doors or screens.	Several sizes available.

Clamps and Vises (Continued)

Type	Use	Size/Capacity
3-Way Edging Clamp	Provides a method of applying "right-angle" pressure to the edge or side of work. Unique "3-screw" design permits the "right-angle" screw to be centered or positioned above or below center, on varying thicknesses of work, and also permits clamping over and around "returns" or other obstructions on countertop edges.	2½" opening capacity with 2½" throat depth.
Vise-Grip Clamps	Specialized clamping jaws attached to vise-grip handles for gripping metal during welding, sheetmetal or woodworking. Provides quick application/removal for repeat jobs.	Jaw adjustment normally 1⅝" to 3¾", Jaw configuration as required by job.
Woodworker's Vise	Attached to underside of workbench with carriage bolts and screws, this vise has a long spiral screw opener so it can be used to hold boards up to 12 inches wide.	Variety of sizes available.
Clamp-On Vise	The clamp-on vise holds lumber horizontally on top of workbench. Set back and bolted to bench, the tightening screw holds lumber against bench top.	Various sizes.
Cam-Action Clamp	Wood jaws with steel bar. Clamp has cam-tightening action—exerts up to 300 pounds pressure. Excellent for light gluing or veneering.	Lengths: 7¾", 15¾", 23¼". Depths: 4¼" and 7¾".

Clamps and Vises (Concluded)

Type	Use	Size/Capacity
Bar-Clamp	Bar clamp has ratchet stop on one end, screw tightener on fixed end.	24″, 36″ and 48″ aluminum bars.
Bench Vises	Clamp-on vise is portable. Swivel-base vise is bolted through top of workbench. Vacuum-based vise (gasketed bottom and lever to raise and cause vacuum) can be attached to any firm, hard smooth surface. Multi-angle bolt of vises that swivel horizontally and can tilt vertically are also available.	Swivel-base vise has exchangeable regular and pipe jaws. Look for a minimum jaw opening of 3½″ to 4″.

Swivel-Base
Bench Vise

Clamp-On
Bench Vise

Vacuum
Bench
Vise

Motor Carvers

Small battery-driven or cord motors are available with dozens of different bits to make carving quick and easy.

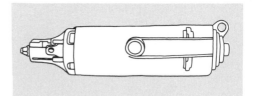

Your Workshop

Because many of the projects you will be doing in your workshop demand cleanliness—varnishing, for example—the first item to buy is a shop vacuum cleaner. This deposits dust directly into a drum. Shop cleaners have attachments to take the sawdust directly from the blade of your arbor saw or electric sander but also have all the regular attachments to keep your shop shipshape.

For other cleaning jobs you'll need a plentiful supply of cleaning cloths, sponges, and brushes. You will also find a box of Wash-n-Dri handy if the sink is upstairs. And if you are using thinners or cleaning chemicals, you will need plastic or rubber gloves. (All chemicals should be kept in appropriate sealed containers and out of the reach of children.)

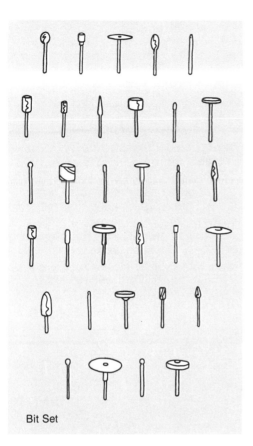

Bit Set

Cleaning Aids

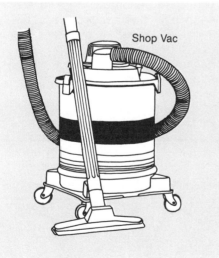

Shop Vac

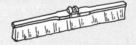

Floor Brush

"Desk" Brush

Soft Bristle Scrub Brush

The cleaning aids you will need will vary by project. A review of items available may help you in your selection.

Your Workshop

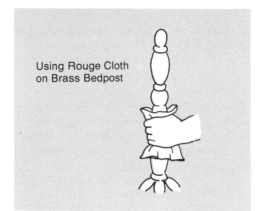

Using Rouge Cloth on Brass Bedpost

Special *metal cleaners* are available for each metal. A solution is available for removing black oxides from silver. Or you can use abrasive cleaners containing pumice. An aluminum cleaner is ideal for screen and window frames. Separate brass and copper cleaners are available, including one that will remove verdigris from battery terminals, a solution to speed up the greening of copper, and a special solution for cleaning electrical contacts.

Navy jelly will remove rust. For cleaning mower and other engine parts there are degreasers and engine cleaners. Penetrating oil is available for loosening rusted nuts.

Various *paint removers* are good to have on hand. You don't have to throw away that paintbrush someone forgot to clean. There are paint strippers that will soften the paint or varnish so you can then wash the paint out in commercial thinner.

Often Sold With Spray Nozzles

Paint strippers and liquid sandpaper will help you strip paint back to the bare surface of wood or metal.

Before you paint over existing finishes, you may want to use a wax remover or household detergent. Before painting or coating a concrete floor, you will need a concrete cleaner, and there is also a blacktop cleaner available for removing oil before you recoat your driveway.

Although these are not cleaners, you will need light machine oil, silicone spray, or petroleum jelly to protect steel tools from rusting. (But never use silicone spray near items you intend to stain, spray, or paint. Silicone is a "release agent" and will prevent the coating from adhering.)

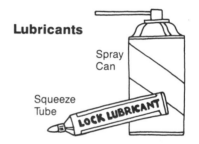

Lubricants

Spray Can

Squeeze Tube

LOCK LUBRICANT

You'll also need graphite solution to keep locks free and working. This includes padlocks, which most people forget.

Solvents and thinners are highly combustible. Always air out and carefully dispose of, preferably outdoors, any paper or rags you've used for cleaning. Common solvents are commercial thinner, kerosene, methylated spirits, MEK (methyl-ethyl-ketone) toluene, xylene, and alcohol. Never use gasoline for cleaning. *(Have you installed a Class B or C fire extinguisher in a handy location?)*

Hand cleaners are indispensable for quickly removing grease, grime, and paint. Some of these cleaners can be used without water. Cleaners with lanolin can be applied before you do a job, such as installing insulation, making it easier to clean up afterward. Others contain pumice for removing tar and stubborn materials.

As far as *stain removal,* always follow the manufacturer's directions. If you don't know the manufacturer, you can try the suggestions below. But first, always test on a hidden part of the material and wait a day or two to make sure there is no ill effect. Remove a stain as soon as you notice it. Never use hot water; it may set the stain.

Brick and stone. Most soot and dirt stains can be removed with detergent and water. On stubborn stains use one part muriatic acid to five parts water or a half-and-half solution of water and muriatic acid.

Carpets. If badly stained, call a professional carpet cleaner immediately. Two products promoted for small stains are Stain-X and Up & Out. The latter removes all water-based stains, soft drinks, tea, and coffee from all but wool carpets. Stain-X will remove oil, ink, coffee, wine, grease, and blood. Put a sheet of poly or foil under the carpet before applying a cleaner. To dry the carpet, place towels between the poly or foil and carpet backing. Then place towels on top of carpet and weight down with heavy books or boards. For pet stains or fruit stains, wash with a solution of water (1 pint) and white vinegar (1 teaspoon). For bloodstains use a drop of ammonia in a cup of water or a paste of laundry starch. Let it dry and brush off. For scorch marks, use glycerine or one ounce of borax in a pint of water. Mildew, use lemon juice. Oil, tar or grease, use turpentine.

Leather and vinyl. Apply saddle soap with damp sponge or soft cloth.

Marble. Wine and coffee stains may not come out, so rinse immediately. For other stains, try a tablespoon of borax in a pint of water and rub with a cloth. Dab with white vinegar and rinse immediately.

Melamine (normal countertop material and used on some cabinet doors). Never use ammonia or window cleaner that contains ammonia. Rub with a nonabrasive paste cleaner.

Tile. Spills should be removed promptly. If a stain sets, try household bleach, white vinegar and water, hydrogen peroxide, rubbing alcohol, household ammonia, damp bicarbonate of soda, or, as last resort, nail polish remover.

Upholstery and fabrics. Try a dry upholstery cleaner, then brush or vacuum. Before using any liquid cleaners consult manufacturer. If tested in a hidden spot, foam cleaners may help but must be wiped off quickly. Never wet or soak fabric.

Heat or water marks on waxed or polished wood. Rub with a solution of turpentine ($\frac{1}{2}$ pint) and linseed oil (1 pint) and let set for a day. Polish after removing cleaning solution. As a last resort use pumice stone and linseed oil or very fine 0000 steel wool.

Drills and Attachments

A portable electric drill is one of the most useful tools that you can purchase. The most popular size is $\frac{3}{8}''$ because it is light enough for easy handling and offers features such as a reversing switch and variable speed control for use with hole saws and power-bore bits up to $2\frac{1}{2}''$ in diameter. Drill sets are available for holes from $\frac{1}{16}''$ to $\frac{1}{4}''$ and reduced shank from $\frac{5}{16}''$ to $\frac{1}{2}''$.

You can do much more than just drill holes. For instance, a screwdriver bit

Your Workshop

combined with the zero to 2500 rpm
variable-speed capacity of a ⅜″ drill
can drive screws faster than by hand.
The reversing feature can also allow
you to withdraw screws. Normally the
drilling torque will increase as the
rpm's decrease.

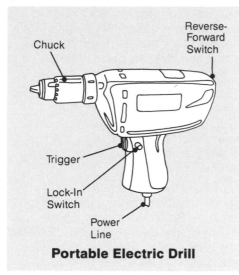

Portable Electric Drill

Portable electric drills are available
in four basic sizes: ¼″, ⅜″, ½″, and
¾″, as determined by the largest-size
drill shank that will fit into the drill
chuck. Normally a ¼″ or ⅜″ drill motor
will perform most of the tasks required
by the homeowner.

When running free (no-load
condition), ¼″ and ⅜″ drills have a
top speed ranging from 750 to 2500
rpm, while ½″ drills are geared down
for lower speed (500 to 1000 rpm) but
provide the greater torque required to
keep their larger bits turning. The lower
speed also keeps the larger bits from
overheating and quickly dulling.
Designed for continuous use, ¾″ drill
speeds are 250 to 475 rpm, but these
larger drills are heavy and somewhat
awkward to use. Variable-speed drills
will operate at any speed from 1 rpm
to their maximum speed. Reversing

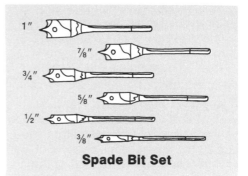

Spade Bit Set

drills with a screwdriver bit save time
in removing screws and are handy
when using a sanding disc.

Cordless drills (operating on
rechargeable batteries) are convenient
for some projects, but should be used
only for light- to medium-duty jobs
since their maximum speed under load
drops considerably from the "no-load"
speed.

An electric drill should have a double-
insulated housing, and while designed
to allow safe operation with an
ungrounded, two-prong power cord, it
is much wiser always to use a three-
prong cord. (This is true with all power
tools). Also look for a safety trigger,
which disengages when released to
prevent the drill from running out of
control.

Some ½″ drills have a feature that
allows the drill to be used as a
hammerdrill or hammerchisel. The
"triple-action" feature provides a rapid
reciprocating hammer stroke that
speeds up masonry drilling (with a
masonry bit) and wood chiseling. A ⅜″
adjustable hammerdrill will operate at
40,000 blows per minute. It can be
used as a hammerchisel to mortise,
chisel, gouge, or scrape paint,
wallpaper, tile, etc.

A triple-action drill is much more
expensive than standard drills and very
noisy when operating in the hammer
or chisel mode.

People who love their power drills sooner or later discover the world of drill attachments. Some of the most popular and/or inventive examples follow. Wear goggles in using any of these tools.

Grinding wheel. Used for sharpening tools. Drill must be locked firmly in a stand.

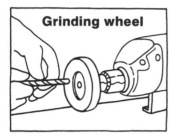

Grinding wheel

Grinding disc. A rotary surform tool for removing paint.

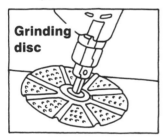

Grinding disc

Grinding stones. Various sizes and shapes attached to ¼″ shank for grinding and sharpening chores.

Grinding stones

Disc sander. Only use for rough sanding and removing paint, as it is easy to tip too much and gouge circles.

A ball-joint sander is also available that is self-leveling.

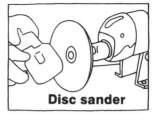

Disc sander

Drum rasp. Surface-forming drum on a ¼″ shank.

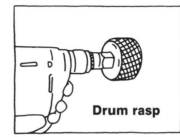

Drum rasp

Wire brush. Speeds the tedious work in removing paint and rust. Since this applies side pressure, make sure the chuck is well tightened and wear gloves and goggles.

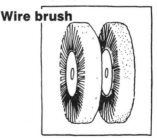

Wire brush

Hole saw. Each cuts one size hole from ¾″ to 2½″ and ¾″ deep.

Hole saw

Your Workshop

Drum sander. Good for sanding edges; comes in a variety of grits.

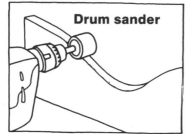

Drum sander

Cut-off disc. Carbide-impregnated disc for cutting metal. Drill must be locked in a stand.

Circle cutter. Inserted in predrilled centerhole, this adjustable attachment swings drill in prescribed diameter circle.

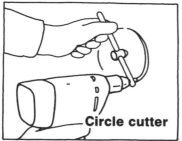

Circle cutter

Chipping wheel. Chips paint from concrete.

Chipping wheel

Paint stirrer. Double-bladed rotating paint blender.

Paint stirrer

Stop collar. Locks on shaft of drill to control depth of hole.

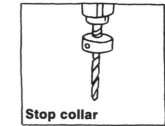

Stop collar

Buffing wheel. Made of multiple layers of cloth in sizes 3″ to 6″ in diameter for waxing and polishing.

Buffing wheel

Flexible shaft attachment. A 40″ flexible extension that accommodates all drills and accessories to allow working in tight quarters.

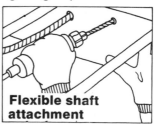

Flexible shaft attachment

Auger. A 1″ or 1½″ auger can be used for drilling holes in ground to accommodate tomato posts or to aid in planting bulbs.

Auger

Screw bit. Drills pilot hole, shank hole, and countersink all in one operation.

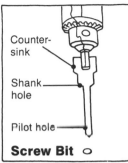

- Counter-sink
- Shank hole
- Pilot hole

Screw Bit ○

Stands. These allow electric drills to be used as drill presses.

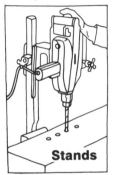

Stands

Paint sprayer attachment. The drill powers a compressor. The attachment comes with spray gun, paint cup, and rubber hose.

Pump. This rotary pump attaches to a drill and can be used with piping to run a fountain, drain tanks, etc.

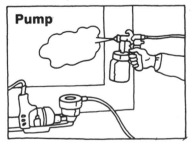

Pump

Drill guide. Available with a rubber backing that grips the surface. This prevents the drill from traveling.

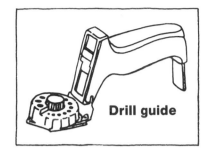

Drill guide

Drill Press

This stationary power tool enables you to do precise and repetitive drilling at any angle in about any material—wood, metal, or plastic. The chuck can be fitted with a hole saw, fly cutter, or drum sander. A variable speed control is essential.

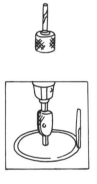

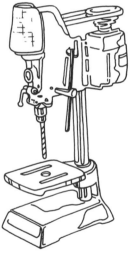

It's ideal for quick, accurate drilling, such as when making screw holes in paneling all at the same distance from the edge. Also, it's more accurate than a hand-held electric drill when boring through thick materials or multiple pieces.

Files and Rasps

There are four types of files: single-cut, double-cut, rasp-cut, and curved-tooth. *Single-cut files* run in one direction only for slow, careful filing. *Double-cut files* have rows of opposing teeth for quick, coarse work, usually on metal. *Rasp-cut files* have straight rows of individual teeth for use on soft metal or wood. The teeth are not connected and cut coarser than those on other files but are less likely to clog. The *curved-tooth files* are milled in an arc for use on flat metal to provide a fairly good finish and rapid stock removal. They are available in 10″ and 12″ lengths without handles, which are bought separately. (File length is measured from the point to the shoulder.)

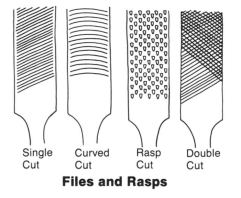

Single Cut   Curved Cut   Rasp Cut   Double Cut

Files and Rasps

The longer the file, the coarser the cut. And the longer the stroke distance, the greater the rate of stock removal. For more delicate work, cabinet files are available in 8″ lengths.

Files in order of abrasiveness from coarsest to smoothest: coarse, bastard-cut, second-cut, and smooth. Rasps: wood rasp, cabinet rasp, bastard-cut, and second-cut. A *four-in-hand* is a two-sided flat file with two different cutting surfaces on each side.

Files and rasps come in flat, triangular, half-round, and half-flat as well as round shapes, and they are either tapered or blunt (same width the entire length).

A cousin of the file is the *surface-forming tool.* Instead of solid teeth, as in a file, these tools have an array of cupped, edge-sharpened open teeth through which scrapings can escape. Amazingly versatile and easy to use,

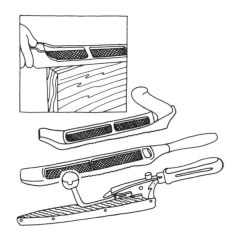

Surform Tools

File Procedure for Degree of Finish Using Surform Tool

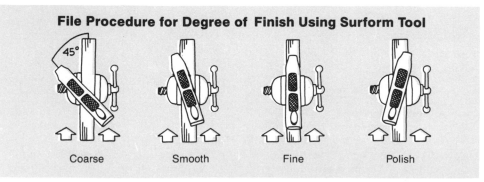

Coarse   Smooth   Fine   Polish

they shape, file, or smooth merely by changing the angle of stroke. (See diagram below.) These tools can be used to chop, shape, file, or polish wood, aluminum, plywood, and plastics. The blades can't be resharpened but are durable and replaceable. The tools come in shapes for planing, shaving (you pull it), filing, and in a round form for enlarging holes.

Italian needle files are used by machinists. Italian needle rasps, which are only 6″, 8″, and 10″ long, are for woodworking. They are narrow files for keyhole and detail carving work and are sold in sets of six.

Italian rifflers are two-ended rasps used chiefly for wood carving. Both ends are the same. They are sold in packs of eight. Blades are generally 2″ to 3″ long with 6″ handles.

German rifflers are larger than their Italian cousins, with curved cutting edges in flat, triangular, square, half-round, round, and tapered shapes. Unlike the Italian rasps, the German rasps have one end file-cut, the other end rasp-cut. Blades are 4″ to 5″ long with 5″ to 6″ handles.

German Rifflers

Italian Rifflers

Files and Rasps

Type	Use	Size
Taper Saw File	Taper saw/files are primarily used for filing handsaw teeth. Available in regular, slim, extra-slim. The finer the sawteeth the finer the file you'll need.	Flat, mill, half-round, square, and round files are supplied in lengths of 4″, 6″, 8″, 10″, 12″, & 14″. 10″ for bastard files and up to 12″ for 2nd-cut and smooth files.
Triangular File	Triangular files are for reaching sharp corners.	Taper saw/files are available up to 10″ long for the coarse files and 8″ for finer files.
Cant or Lightning File	Cant or lightning files are for sharpening crosscut saws with "M"-shaped teeth and circular saws with less than a 60° angle.	Bastard-cut in 6″, 8″, and 10″ lengths.

Your Workshop

File and Rasps (Continued)

Type	Use	Size
Knife or Crosscut File	Knife files are for sharpening crosscut saws.	Like a mill bastard with rounded back and knife edge, both cut. Sizes: 8″ and 10″
Flat File	Flat files are for general machinist or mechanical work and rapid removal of metal.	Double-cut file on both sides with edges single-cut. Sizes: bastard—4″, 6″, 8″, 10″, 12″, 14″, 16″; second-cut—6″, 8″, 10″, 12″, 14″; smooth—4″, 6″, 8″, 10″, 12″, 14″
Half-Round File	Half-round files are for general machine-shop work.	Half-round backs of all bastard files are double-cut, as are half-rounds over 8″ on second-cut files. Half-round backs of smooth files are single-cut. Flat sides of all half-rounds are single-cut. Sizes: bastard—4″, 6″, 8″, 10″, 12″, 14″, 16″; second-cut—4″, 6″, 8″, 10″, 12″, 14″; smooth—4″, 6″, 8″, 10″, 12″, 14″
Round File	Round files are for enlarging holes and filing circular openings or concave surfaces.	Single-cut: 5″, 6″, 8″, 10″; bastard- and second-cut— 12″, 14″. Bastard- and second-cut are double-cut 12″; smooth is single-cut. Bastard in 4″, 6″, 8″, 10″, 12″, and 16″ lengths. Second-cut and smooth: 4″, 6″, 8″, 10″, 12″ lengths
Square File	Square files are for filing or dressing square corners and smoothing slots in keyways.	All sides are double-cut. Bastard-cut in 4″, 6″, 8″, 10″, 12″, and 16″ sizes. Second- and smooth-cuts in 4″, 6″, 8″, 10″, and 12″ sizes
Equaling File	Equaling files are parallel in both width and thickness for their entire length, double-cut on the two sides, and single-cut on both edges.	$\frac{19}{32}″ \times \frac{7}{64}″$ or $\frac{3}{4}″ \times \frac{9}{64}″$

File and Rasps (Concluded)

Type	Use	Size
Pillar File	Pillar files have a rectangular cross section. They are like equaling files in general shape illustration looks identical to equaling file— should be narrower. They have one edge safe or uncut.	$^{19}\!/_{32}$" × $^{7}\!/_{64}$" or $^{3}\!/_{4}$" × $^{9}\!/_{64}$"
Die Sinkers or Needle File Sets	As their name indicates, these are small files for intricate finishing work. They are usually sold in sets of 12.	Die sinker files are $3\frac{1}{2}$" long in #0 to #2 cuts. Needle files have round handles and are $5\frac{1}{2}$" & $6\frac{1}{4}$" long in #1 & #2 cuts
Wood Rasp— Half-Round	Rapidly remove material. Replace spokeshave or draw knife.	8", 10", & 14" long
Combination Shoe Rasp— Half-Round (4-in-hand)	Has rasp and file on flat side and rasp and file on half-round side.	14" long
Bastard File	Flat rough-cut file, diagonal rasp. Flat one side, half-round on the other.	10" long

Your Workshop

Hammers

Hammers are among the most used and abused tools in your toolbox. By far the most common is the claw hammer, pictured in the illustration. It has a pronged claw for pulling nails or for ripping apart fastened pieces. (You should always cushion the head with a flat piece of wood when pulling nails or you'll damage the surface you're working on.)

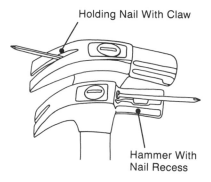

Holding Nail With Claw

Hammer With Nail Recess

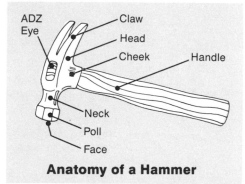

Anatomy of a Hammer

Hammers are sized according to the weight of their heads. Perhaps because people are getting healthier, taller, and stronger, popularity has switched from the 16 oz., 15″ hammer to the 24 oz., 16″ hammer. The hammer face can be either flat or bell-shaped (slightly convex). Bell-shaped faces are less likely to leave hammer marks in the wood but require more precise handling.

Quality hammers have heads made of drop-forged steel and either steel, fiberglass, or hickory (wood) handles. Cast heads and soft-wood handles are dangerous and should not be purchased. *One caution:* When buying your hammer make sure the head is mounted straight—a surprising number are not.

The Cheney hammer has spring-loaded ball bearings on the shaft behind the claw to hold the nail. This gives you a free hand for positioning the lumber. Better yet, a new hammer from Europe has a nail recess in the head, so you can set the nail and keep driving without having to reverse the shaft.

Hammers

Type	Uses	Size or Weight	Remarks
Curved Claw Hammer Also called: Carpenter's hammer Nail hammer	Drive and pull nails in general construction work.	7 oz. to 20 oz. head; 12″ to 13″ length	16 oz. hammer best for normal home repair, smaller sizes for light-duty work.

Hammers (Continued)

Type	Uses	Size or Weight	Remarks
Framing Hammer Also called: Flooring hammer Straight claw hammer Ripping claw hammer	The straight claw is used as a wedge to pry apart boards or open boxes and crates. Also drives and pulls nails. Has checkered face to prevent glancing off of nail heads.	16 oz. to 28 oz. head; 12″ to 18″ length	Similar to curved claw hammer but with straighter claw, which functions as a wedge. Larger poll and face for heavy-duty work. Sometimes longer handles. The 16″ 24 oz. is now the most popular.
Ball Peen Hammer Also called: Machinist's hammer	Used for shaping iron and working on machinery.	4 oz. to 40 oz. head; 10″ to 16″ length	Claw replaced with peen. Has larger poll and face similar to framing hammer. Hickory (wood) or fiberglass handles.
Brick Hammer Also called: Mason's hammer Tile setter's hammer Rock hammer	Used to set bricks or tile in place. Single claw used to cut bricks or chip mortar from bricks or tiles.	18 oz. to 24 oz. head; 11″ to 12″ length	Has square face and poll with long, straight, single claw for splitting bricks. Handles are wood, steel, or fiberglass; cushioned available.
Double-Face Hammer Also called: Engineer's hammer	Used for driving retaining pins and bolts.	Head: 40 oz. to 48 oz. Length: 14″ to 15½″	
Blacksmith Hammer	Used for wrought-iron work and forging.	Head: 40 oz. to 48 oz. Length: 15″ to 16″	Similar to double-face hammer but with cross peen on one face of head. Hickory handles.

Hammers (Continued)

Type	Uses	Size or Weight	Remarks
Hand Drilling Hammer	Used to drive stardrills in masonry work.	Head: 48 oz. to 64 oz. Length: 10″	Similar to double-face hammer but with heavier head for increased driving power and shorter handle for better control. Handles are normally wood.
Tack Hammer	Used to drive and pull tacks for upholstery operations.	Head: 4 to 5 oz. Length: 10″ to 12″	Head is normally magnetized to hold tacks when driving. Claw is split and sharply tapered for removing tacks in corners. Handles are normally wood.
Riveting Hammer	Driving rivets.	Head: 12 oz. Length: 12″	Ground and polished head with wood handle.
Tinner's Hammer	Bending sheet metal over hard edge.	Head: 18 oz. Length: 12″	One-piece forged head and handle or wood handle with forged head.
Welder's Hammer	For chipping metal and wedging parts apart.	Head: 14 oz. Length: 12″	Heat-treated high-alloy steel heavy-duty tool. One pointed pick end, one ¾″ chisel end. Plastic handle.
Pick Hammer	Used as driving wedge with standard ball peen hammer and for disassembling crates.	Head: 9 oz. Length: 12″	

Hammers (Continued)

Type	Uses	Size or Weight	Remarks
Rubber Mallet	Assembling joints in furniture. Beating dents out of metal.	Head: 16 oz. to 22 oz. Length: 13″ to 14″ Head size: 1¾″ diameter × 2¾″ length to 2½″ diameter × 5″ length	Uses wood handles or steel tube handles with cushion grips. Barrel-shaped head.
Malleable Head Hammer Also called: Copper hammer Brass hammer Babbet hammer Compo-cast hammer (Stanley)	For working malleable metal sheet and removing dents in sheet metal.	Head: 1 to 5 lbs. Handle Length: 10″ to 15″	Heads are normally barrel-shaped with wood or steel tube handles. Steel handles normally have cushion grips. Compo-cast hammers have head and handle molded as one-piece urethane composite. Head is filled with "shot" to increase striking power and handle is reinforced with steel rod.
Wood or Rawhide Mallets	Used with wood chisels or to shape soft material without damaging or marking it.	Head size: 1½″ diameter × 3″ length; 2¾″ diameter × 5½″ length Handle length: 11″ to 12″ Head weights: 6 oz. to 24 oz.	
Split-Head Hammer Also called: Jaw-head hammer Replaceable-face hammer	Used for driving trim with clips into holes in painted surfaces without damage.	Face diameters: 1½″ to 2¾″	Metal heads with wooden handles. Available with rawhide or nylon face inserts.

Hammers (Concluded)

Type	Uses	Size or Weight	Remarks
Soft-Face Hammer Also called Replaceable-tip hammer	For bending, joining, seaming soft or finished surfaces without damage.	Head weight: 4 oz. to 20 lb. Normally: 1″ to 4″ diameter tips Handle length: 11″ to 14″ Normal head weight: 4 oz. to 16 oz.	Interchangeable, screw-in type tips in dome, wedge, conical, and square shapes. Wood or fiberglass handles with metal tip holders.

Lathe for Woodturning

This bench-mounted electrically driven tool enables you to turn chair and table legs, balusters, dowels, lamp columns, knobs, and anything else round, such as bowls, medallions, or tabletops. For large round objects you'll need a lathe with special chucks and a headstock spindle that can be turned 90° to the bed. This allows you to turn large, short pieces too deep to fit over the bed. Some lathes are available with a spiral cutting attachment and a duplicator for copying existing spindles or patterns.

Besides the lathe and its equipment, a set of chucks, a tool rest, and face plate, you'll also need a set of at least eight, long-handled, scraping tools. A variable speed control is essential.

The distance between spindle heads and the distance above the bed will dictate the length and thickness of stock you can shape on most lathes. You'll probably want a minimum of 24″ between spindles.

Always wear goggles and a short-sleeved shirt without a tie and stand to one side when working the lathe. Keep cutting tools razor-sharp.

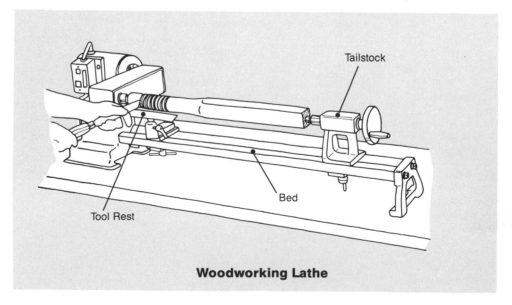

Woodworking Lathe

Lubricants

The selection chart below gives a few of the typical lubricating needs and the type of lubricant to use for each job.

Lubricants

A. Automobile grease
B. Belt lubricant
C. Chain saw oil
D. Graphite (and lock lubricant)
E. Light machine oil
F. Paraffin wax
G. Petroleum jelly
H. Penetrating oil
I. Silicone
J. Soap
K. Engine oil
L. Hydraulic oil
M. White lubricant
N. Stroke oil
O. Dry lubricants
P. LPS film lubricants and WD40
Q. Lubricant with Teflon

Lubricating Needs

Lubrication Need	Comments	Lubricant
Power tools and electric motors:	Today these generally have sealed-in lifetime lubricants. Only oil those that have an oil cap or indicated oil hole.	E
Fan belts		B or I
Fan bearings		E
Electric drills/saber saws, etc.	Change grease in gear case.	A
	Oil bearings.	E
	Oil drills while drilling metal.	E
	Protect saw blades.	E
Circular saws/routers, etc.	Oil holes and caps.	E
Cutting tools	To protect blades mix with gas: special 15-to-1 and 50-to-1 oils.	E or G
		N
Chain saws	Oil chain (can use filtered used auto-engine oil).	C
Windows and sliding doors		
Awning or casement	Oil crank and sliding hinge.	E or I
Wood against wood	Lubricate sliding tracks.	J or F
Aluminum	Lubricate tracks.	I, J, F
Garage doors		
Rollers		E or I
Tracks		A or M
Hinges		E or I
Door		
Locks		D or I
Hinges		I
Bolts		I
Sharpening stones		E
Squeaking floors	(This is only a temporary expedient until you have the time to install additional wedges or fasteners.)	D
Bottom of planes		F
Rusting nuts and bolts		H
Mold release		I

Your Workshop

Lubricating Needs (Concluded)

Lubrication Need	Comments	Lubricant
Drawer glides		I
Garden tools and construction tools	Treat to prevent rusting.	O or P
Gears and other moving metal parts	Lubricate those that get hot in operation.	Q
Drive chains		D or Q
Battery terminals		I
Sliding parts in precision equipment		D
Attaching rubber hoses to tubing or piping		G
Hydraulic jacks		L

NOTE: Petroleum jelly is indispensable as a temporary metal protective coating, as a lubricant to aid in squeezing rubber hoses over fittings, and as a protective coating for your hands when working in the garden, on your car, installing insulation, waxing, staining, or painting. However, other creams are available at your drugstore that are not as tacky.

Measuring Tools

Without specific dimension and form, construction is chaos. Fortunately, some creative people have made the skill of measuring dimensions and angles fun and have provided us with tools of great accuracy. For example, the four-function rule and compass tape, in addition to providing a straightforward, lockable 10' rule, combines a spirit level and draws perfect circles. The radius is read in the top window and the tape gives a direct reading on inside measurement. It is surprisingly cheap!

On the pricey side is the builder's combination tool—seven tools in one. It is a professional 24" rule, a level, a square, a protractor, a bevel, a plumb, and a pitch-to-foot indicator. Expect to pay $200 or so. (You may want to ask for this on your birthday.)

It is essential you keep these tools dry, clean, and free of rust. And you will save yourself grief and materials if you remember the maxim "Measure twice, cut once!"

Measuring Tools

Multipurpose Types	Use	Size/Capacity	Comments
4-Function Rule And Compass Tape	Lockable 10' rule. This tape unit draws perfect circles, giving the radius in its top window. It also gives you direct readings for inside measurement and has a built-in level.	3½" square × ½" deep	Graduated in inches and mm. Relatively low cost. We discovered this in the Garrett Wade catalog.

Measuring Tools (Continued)

Multipurpose Types	Use	Size/Capacity	Comments
Builder's Combination Tool	This tool performs 7 functions. It's a 24" rule, a square, a bevel, a level, a protractor, a plumb, and a pitch-to-foot indicator.	24" × 4¼"	A perfect gift for the serious remodeler. It's very expensive.
Framing Square Also called: Rafter square Carpenter's square Builder's square	Used to square stock accurately and guide layout lines. Legs of framing square are conveniently sized: 24" body and 16" tongue—standard stud spacing dimensions. Several scales including a protractor, printed on the tool to assist in making angle layouts.	Legs are 24" × 16"	Here are the calculations that a framing square scale will solve at a glance: 1) Table of board measurements gives content in board measure of any size board or timber. 2) Helps determine length of common, hip, valley, and jack roof rafters. 3) Brace scale—gives lengths of braces. 4) Determines top, bottom, and side cuts of rafters. 5) Octagon scale gives measurements necessary to shape a square piece of lumber into an eight-sided one.
Tri-Square	Checking squareness of boards and laying out straight lines perpendicular to an edge.	Blade length 4" to 12"	Rigid connection between handle and blade provides very accurate measurements.

Your Workshop

Measuring Tools (Continued)

Multipurpose Types	Use	Size/Capacity	Comments
Combination square	Performs same operations as a tri-square. Square head includes a spirit level for leveling operations and 45° surface for making miter cuts. Often has awl in bottom of handle for scoring mark.	Blade length 12″	Sets available with center head and/or protractor head in addition to square head.
Electronic Level	Snaps into wide base, 3′ extruded aluminum rail. Very sensitive and accurate. Signals with flashing red and green lights and emits even tone when level is reached.	7.8″ × 2.4″ × 1″ weighing 8 oz.	Will determine unknown angle or preset one. Appears in Fine Tool Shops Inc. catalog.
T Bevel *Also called:* Bevel gauge	Handle swivels on blade and can be locked at any position so that any angle can be measured and transferred. Often used in hip-and-valley rafter layouts.	Bevel lengths 8″, 10″, 12″. Combination bevel has two 4″ bevels joined by slotted blade.	Use protractor on framing square to measure angles. Combination bevel allows an angle to be transferred from one surface to another.
Marking Gauge	Used to scribe lines parallel to an edge.	Length 8″	Use a rule to set gauge dimensions, as gauge markings may be inaccurate. Most accurate when scribing parallel to the grain.

Measuring Tools (Continued)

Multipurpose Types	Use	Size/Capacity	Comments
Dovetail Marking Gauge	Marks out pins and tails for accurate jointing. Or you can use clamping templates to guide router.	3″ × 3½″	A less expensive double-angle model is available for simple 6-to-1 and 8-to-1 dovetails.
Folding Rule Also called: Carpenter's rule "Zig-zag" rule	Used for laying off long measurements where rigid rule is required, such as on vertical surfaces or across gaps in flooring or roofing.	Lengths: 6′ and 12′	Graduated in inches and fractions thereof. Some rules have special markings every 16″ or 24″ for stud layout. Some rules have extensions for inside measurement.
Flexible Tape Also called: Steel tape Push-pull tape Tape rule	"Pocket-type" tapes are used to lay off measurements up to 12′ long. "Reel-type" tapes are for longer distances usually requiring 2 people to make measurement. Also available for measuring pipe diameters and ⅛″, ¼″, and ½″ to the foot scales for measuring lengths on plans and blueprints.	Available lengths: 6′, 8′, 10′, 12′, 16′, and 25′ Pocket tapes: 25′, 50′, and 100′ Reel type: usually 36′	Easier to carry and use than folding rules. Some tapes have metric scales alongside the inch markings. Dome tapes highlight dimensions every 16″ or 24″. 12′ tape is best buy for homeowner!
Line Level	Suspend level on taut line between two points to check horizontal trueness. Used in masonry, excavation and grading work.	Body length: 3″ to 3¼″ ⅜″ or ⁷⁄₁₆″ round or hex tubing	

Your Workshop

Measuring Tools (Continued)

Multipurpose Types	Use	Size/Capacity	Comments
General Protractor	Measure and lay out angles. Arm swivels to desired angle and is locked in position with knurled nut.	6″ long arm graduations 0–180° range in both directions	Large 5″ protractor is easy to read and can be set in half degrees.
Doweling Jig	Acts as a template to locate dowel holes accurately. Suitable for edge-to-edge, edge-to-end, and edge-to-surface locating.	For ¼″, ⁵⁄₁₆″, and ³⁄₈″ dowels.	You will also need brad-point drill bits, drill stops, and dowels.
Carpenter's Level Also called: Magnesium level Aluminum level Urethane level Wool level	Check horizontal surfaces for level and vertical surfaces for plumb.	Body lengths: 24″ to 48″	Normally has three replaceable spirit level vials. Center for horizontal leveling; end vials for plumb— one for each side of body. One end vial set at 45° on some levels. Available with 3, 4, or 6 vials.
Mason's Level	Check level and plumb of foundations and masonry walls.	Body lengths: 48″ and up	Similar to carpenter's level but longer. Usually has 6 matched vials.
Torpedo Level	Similar to carpenter's level but shorter. Two or 3 level vials for checking level, plumb, and 45° angle. One surface of level with V groove for pipe or conduit work.	Body length: normally 9″ long	

Measuring Tools (Continued)

Multipurpose Types	Use	Size/Capacity	Comments
Flexible Tube Level	Transparent tubing filled with colored liquid with air space and stopper at each end. Ideal for establishing dropped ceiling level or chair rail level across room.	24' to 30' long	Also available with dyed water reservoir so level line can be chalked around room and a rule can be used to measure and mark desired height of ceiling suspension system.
Circular Levels	Used to level flat surfaces in all directions by centering bubble in round body.	1¾" diameter	
Angle Finder	Finds level or angles. Dial needle swings from 0° to 90° in any quadrant for fast, accurate readings. Accurate to ½ of 1°. Made of high-impact ABS plastic: resists heat, cold, shock. Needle and face protected by clear, tough acrylic plastic cover.	Approximate size: 2⅝" diameter	Some models magnetically attach to any magnetic surface-square or straightedge.
Contour Gauge	Enables you to make template of complex curves from drawings or existing moldings.	6" long × ¾" wide × ⅜" high	Has multiple stainless-steel probes. Low profile facilitates transfer from shop drawings.
Plumb Bob	Suspend bob from cord to indicate vertical plane accurately. Useful in framing, painting, and wallpapering.	Weights: 4 oz., 8 oz., and 12 oz.	

Your Workshop

Measuring Tools (Concluded)

Multipurpose Types	Use	Size/Capacity	Comments
Chalk Line	Used to mark long, straight lines on horizontal or vertical surfaces.	Supplied with 50' or 100' line lengths	Supplied on reels in metal or plastic housing which contains chalk and line. Reel housing can be used as a plumb bob.
Magnetic and Electronic Stud Finders	Locate studs through wallboard/paneling by moving stud finder along surface until pointer centers when it is opposite an attaching nail. Electronic stud finder measures mass, not nails, and is more versatile, accurate and expensive.	$3\frac{1}{2}'' \times 3\frac{1}{2}'' \times 1''$	To avoid putting pencil lines on a finished wall use 3M (Scotch) Post-its® at stud locations. They can be removed without leaving a mark.
Calipers Inside-outside vernier type inside outside	Outside calipers measure the outside diameters of tubing and pipes. Inside calipers measure inside diameters. Use vernier calipers for more accurate work.	Normally 6" legs on spring calipers. Vernier caliper approximately 9" long, and reads inside or outside dimension up to 6"	Vernier calipers are available with combination inside and outside measurements. A vernier is an auxiliary scale with either dial or electronic readout accurate to ± 0.0005".
Dividers Also called: Compass scriber	Used to scribe small areas or steps of a series of equal increments along a line.	Normally 6" legs	A compass has a pencil attached to one leg.

Planes

If you do enough carpentry, you'll want to purchase top-quality planes, the prize possession of the master carpenter. The parts should be made to close tolerances, and the blade should have a high carbon cutting face or you'll forever be having to disassemble the parts and resharpen the blade.

To keep the blade razor-sharp, you'll need a good-quality, carefully maintained sharpening stone. Waxing the bottom of a steel plane with candle wax makes it move more freely.

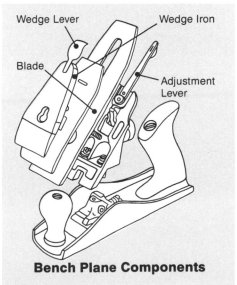

Bench Plane Components

Remember to buy a spare blade so you can start with two sharp blades and avoid work interruption.

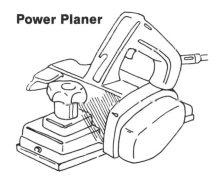

Power Planer

If you are heavily into constructing tables, benches, or similar furniture, you may want to buy or rent a *power planer.* This hand-operated electrical tool operates at 20,000 rpm, driving a spiral cutter. An adjustable front shoe controls the depth of cut. When using this speedy device, the work must be firmly anchored and the tool firmly controlled with both hands. This tool can be used to resurface properly installed hardwood floors if you first make sure there are no surface nails. You'll damage the machine if you hit a nail, so you may decide it's wiser to use a power sander. Always wear gloves, goggles, and a dust mask when operating this tool.

Bench Planes

Type	Use	Size/Capacity	Comments
Block Plane Also called: Trimming plane	Designed for cutting end grain and making finishing cuts where woodworking chisels have made preliminary cuts.	Normally 6″ to 7″ long	Blade set at lower angle (12°). Low-profile block plane with *lower* angle is available. Used for planing end grain.

Your Workshop

Bench Planes (Continued)

Type	Use	Size/Capacity	Comments
Jack Plane	Trues long boards or doors. Shorter than jointer plane.	Size range: 14″ to 18″	Good home workshop tool. Can be used for the majority of planing tasks. The blade can be set for even or slanted cuts. The blade is retained with metal cap that curbs cut wood shavings and prevents splitting and splintering of wood.
Rabbet Plane	Cuts plows, rabbets, dadoes, and beads for cabinetmaking.	Size: 6¾″ long with 1½″ blade	This plane is equipped with a fence, depth gauge, and lever adjustment. Chiefly used for edge planing.
Cabinetmaker's Rabbet Plane	Cabinetmaker's plane can cut small mortises, gains, rabbets, and short splices and can remove glue and excess wood in corners.	Size: 6″ long with ¾″ cutter or 4⅛″ with 1″ blade	Designed to cut right to the edge of the plane body.
Butt Mortise Plane	Enables you to cut mortises for hinge butts, lock fronts, and strike plates clearly, accurately, and quickly.	Approximately 10″	Provides a clear view of the work and does a job no other plane can do.
Spokeshave	A two-handled plane used to smooth curved surfaces and spindles. Those with adjustable throats can be set to plane convex and concave surfaces.	Tip to tip 10″, base 1⁵⁄₁₆″ × 1⁵⁄₁₆″, blades 1⁵⁄₁₆″ up to 2⅛″ on some models	Depth of blade is controlled by two screws. Interesting variation is dual use combination spokeshave with both flat and concave blades.

Bench Planes (Concluded)

Type	Use	Size/Capacity	Comments
Jointer Plane	Used to true long boards or doors. Extended heel and toe plates provide a more level cut.	Size range: 20″ to 24″	Longest of bench planes, used for specialized work.
Smoothing Plane	Shorter than jack plane, can perform majority of home workshop planing tasks. Used for finishing cuts after longer planes have made rough cuts.	Size range: 4″ to 9″	Good home workshop tool. Angle set at 20°.
Combination Plane	This plane has a fence that can be attached to either side and interchangeable cutters so you can cut dadoes, grooves, beads, flutes, fillisters, multiple reeds, tongue and groove joints, and sash moldings.	Cuts 1/8″ to 1 3/4″ grooves. A choice of 30 cutters. Side fence version cuts 5/8″ up to 5 1/2″ from edge of workpiece.	If the cutters are kept properly honed, the plane will produce cuts that need no further finishing.

Pliers

You'll need pliers for a variety of jobs. Some, such as the locking pliers, are small portable vises for holding a bolt while you wrench off the nut. (You use the wrench for turning, not the pliers.) Many types of pliers are for cutting wire, cable, or excess lengths of small bolts. Prime among these are the end cutting pliers or "nippers." For cutting a large bolt you'll need long-handled bolt cutters. For working on electric circuits you'll appreciate a pair of long-nose pliers with insulated handles having a side wire cutter.

Working with sheet metal? There are snips for every purpose and several with curved cutters that help bend the cut strips away from your hand.

Four types of hand snips are available. *Regular* snips are used for straight cutting; *Combination Pattern* can cut straight and moderately irregular cuts; *Duckbill* snips can cut curved designs; and *Aviation* snips come in straight, or right- or left-hand cutting versions and also provide compound leverage for easier cutting.

Quality snips are hot-forged with precise-fitting pivot bolts and hand-

Your Workshop

contoured handles; often protected with plastic grips. Some snips have replaceable blades.

A selection is illustrated below. Consider power snips when cutting more than a few inches on heavy-gauge material. Hand snips can be very bruising to your hands.

If you have a frequent need for this type of tool, consider electrical nibblers or shears. They can be used to cut plastic, metal, or wood.

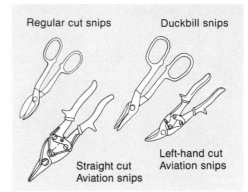

Regular cut snips

Duckbill snips

Straight cut Aviation snips

Left-hand cut Aviation snips

Pliers

Type	Use	Size/Weight	Remarks
Slip-Joint Pliers Also called: Combination pliers		5″, 6″, 8″, and 10″ lengths Holding capacities: ¾″ to 1¼″	Most jaws have a wire cutter. Handles are knurled and/or have vinyl grips for electrical work. Nose is bent 30° on some.
Tongue and Groove Pliers Also called: Channellock pliers Utility pliers Multipurpose pliers Joint pliers Rib-joint pliers Knurled hand pliers Groove pliers		Wrench size: 7″, 9½″, 10″, 12″, 14″, and 16″ Jaw capacity: ³⁄₁₆″ to 4½″	Smooth jaws available for plated fittings. Curved jaws for gripping rounded objects. Plastic handle grips on most.
Long-Nose Pliers		Lengths: 4″ to 7″	Usually has side wire cutter. Normally has vinyl-covered grips. Curved long nose available 30°, 45°, or 90°.

Pliers (Continued)

Type	Use	Size/Weight	Remarks
Needle-Nose Pliers		Lengths: 4″ to 7″	Normally doesn't have side cutters. Normally has vinyl-covered grips. Curved needle nose available 45° and 90°.
Duckbill Pliers		Lengths: 6″ or 7″	Duckbill pliers and snips are preferred by professionals for sheet metal work as the duckbill makes the tips stronger and more durable.
Retaining Ring Pliers Also called: Snap ring pliers	Points fit into holes in snap rings to allow their installation or removal.	¼″ to 3″ capacity shaft diameter	Some pliers have replaceable tips.
Locking Pliers Also called: Vice grips Lever wrench	Designed for gripping hard-to-reach nuts, bolts, or fittings. Jaw tension can be preadjusted to provide enough tension to clamp wrench to job.	Jaw capacity range: 1″ to 1⅞″ opening	Pliers available with and without wire cutters. Long-nose pliers available. Special flat-noses available for welding or other specialty work.
End-Cutting Pliers Also called: Nippers	Used to cut off screws, bolts, or wire that has penetrated a surface.	7″ and 8″ lengths for normal duty; 10″ and 14″ lengths for heavy duty	Cushion or insulating grips available.

Your Workshop

Pliers (Continued)

Type	Use	Size/Weight	Remarks
Side-Cutting Pliers Also called: Lineman's pliers High-leverage pliers Fence pliers		6" to 9" lengths for normal duty; 10" length for heavy duty	Fence pliers have two or more wire-cutting slots instead of diagonal side cutter.
Flat-Nose Side-Cutting Pliers		6½" and 8" lengths	Useful as wire cutter, metal bender, and holding nuts.
Fence Pliers Also called: Prong and hammerhead pliers	Fence plier and staple puller. No other tools needed in fence building and repair. Equipped with staple pulling point and lifter for bent lugs on steel posts, wire splicer, two wire cutters, wire stretcher, and corrugated hammerhead for driving staples and bending down lugs on steel posts.	10" to 11" lengths	Due to outdoor use, stainless steel unit is recommended.
Frame Brad/ Point Driver	The only easy way to insert the small brads or points that hold mats in place on picture frame.	Works or any molding up to 3⅜" wide and 1¾" deep.	This simple tool allows you to squeeze in the brad safely. Rubber pads protect the frame.
Hose Clamp Pliers	Notched jaws hold wire hose clamps open to allow installation or removal.	8" length	

Pliers (Concluded)

Type	Use	Size/Weight	Comments
Hog-Ring Pliers	Closes "hog rings" used in upholstery work.	7" lengths	
Diagonal Cutting Pliers Also called: "Dikes" Automotive Pliers	Used for cutting wire and cable. Can be used for narrow widths of thin-gauge sheet metal.	4", 5", 6", and 7" lengths	Cushion or insulating grips available.
Bolt Cutters	For general cutting of medium-hard rods, bolts, etc; cold-drawn spring wire, stranded guy wire, alloy wire and rods not heat treated, and other medium-hard steel up to Brinell 300, Rockwell C31 Hardness. The cutting edge is in the middle of the blade with an equal bevel on each side.	Tool lengths from 14" to 42" Cuts bolts from $5/16$" diameter to $3/4$" diameter.	Some cutters available with interchangeable jaws. Uses steel or fiberglass handles.

The Router

The router is a simple portable tool consisting of a high-speed electric motor (22,500 to 27,500 rpm) mounted vertically on a horizontal base plate. A chuck on the lower edge of its shaft holds keen-edged cutting bits that can be extended below the base to cut grooves, round off edges, form recesses, produce moldings, and otherwise shape wood in a variety of handy ways.

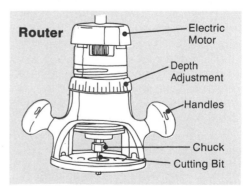

Router — Electric Motor, Depth Adjustment, Handles, Chuck, Cutting Bit

Your Workshop

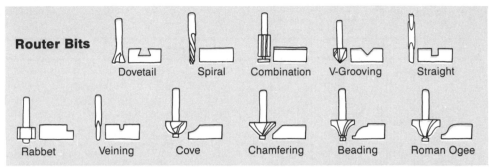

Router Bits

Dovetail   Spiral   Combination   V-Grooving   Straight

Rabbet   Veining   Cove   Chamfering   Beading   Roman Ogee

The power of router motors is rated in horsepower, amps, and rpms. They are sized by the largest bit they will hold. The horsepower, from ¼ to more than 3½ horsepower (for professional models), determines how deep and how fast the tool can cut through work and what it costs. The ¼ to ⅝ horsepower models are strictly for cutting laminates.

A low-powered (1 horsepower) router, however, can do many of the jobs a high-powered router can do, although in stages. It can make a deep cut, for example, by means of a number of shallow passes. So, for the do-it-yourself carpenter, a 1 horsepower is usually adequate. If you have frequent use for a router, you may want to move up to the 1¼ horsepower model. Rpms range from 15,000 to 30,000 (The lower the rpm, the greater the cutting power.)

A trigger switch is a convenient feature, since reaching around for a slide or toggle switch can be difficult.

The router, with its cutter bit operating, may be lowered into the work from above and then moved along the path to be shaped or cut, or it may move into the work from the edge. For repetitive work it pays to cut a template for the router to follow. The bits are set for depth of cut by an adjustment on the router body. Some types of bits are shown above, but there are others. In fact, a collection of bits can easily

exceed the cost of the router itself!

When using a router, set the depth of the bit so your router base rests flatly on the wood surface. When cutting, move the router from right to left.

Power Sanders

Sanding any large, flat surface by hand is sheer drudgery. An electric sander will do the job for you in much less time and often with better results. There are two types: belt sanders for rough work and finish sanders for (you guessed it) fine finishing. Most homeowners buy a finish sander and rent a belt sander on the odd occasion when they need one.

Finish Sander

Finish sander. This type of sander is sometimes called an orbital sander and is used for fine finishing after the project has been assembled or is ready for a coat of paint, stain, or varnish. The abrasive paper is cut the width of the pad and normally held in place by clamps at the front and rear

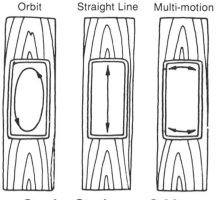

| Orbit | Straight Line | Multi-motion |

Sander Strokes or Orbit

of the pad. Sanding motion is "orbital" for more rapid stock removal and "straight line" for less removal and smoother finishes. A "multi-motion" sanding action, which moves the pad in a "twisting" motion, is available on less expensive sanders. Finish sanders operate from 8,000 to 10,000 rpm.

Best purchasing bet for the homeowner is a sander that will operate with both orbital and straight-line motions. Orbital sanding can leave swirls in the wood, so use straightline motion in the direction of the grain on your final passes.

Belt sander. Use this for rough finishing operations such as removing the finish from a painted or varnished surface or smoothing rough-cut lumber. Belt sanders are sized by their belt size, which ranges from 15″ to 21¾″ long. Belt widths are usually proportional to

Belt Sander

their lengths and range from 2½″ to 4″. Belt sanders operate with belt speeds of approximately 600 sfpm to 1350 sfpm.

The 3″ × 21″ model is good for the occasional user, while the 3″ × 24″ and 4″ × 24″ belt sanders will probably be the choice of the professional carpenter or painter. Dust catchers can be attached to belt sanders, which greatly simplify cleanup. A sander with a "flat-top" design will allow you to secure it upside down as a stationary sander. A quick belt release and control to keep the belt on track are worthwhile features. A front handle or knob is essential for control.

Be aware that belt sanders cut fast and require skill to operate since they must be kept moving constantly.

Handsaws

There is no escape from having a variety of saws. Each is designed by shape, size, or teeth spacing and set to be best for a given chore. While most of us would prefer to use power saws, some jobs will pop up that make a power saw impractical or an expensive way to go for a single application. If you are only doing a small molding or picture framing job, a backsaw and miter box will work fine.

Among the special handsaws to consider are:

Crosscut saw. For cutting across grain. The longer and deeper the saw, the faster it will cut and the easier it will be to maintain a straight cut. The more teeth to the inch, the finer the cut.

Ripsaw. This has teeth that are perpendicular at the front so they cut as chisels in cutting with the grain.

Backsaw. Has a rigid back, thin blade, and fine teeth for cutting joints.

Compass saw. Swordfishlike blade enables you to cut a shape out of the center of a board, starting with a bored

Your Workshop

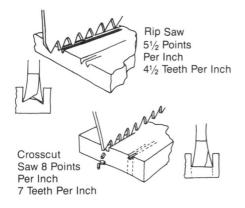

Rip Saw
5½ Points
Per Inch
4½ Teeth Per Inch

Crosscut
Saw 8 Points
Per Inch
7 Teeth Per Inch

hole. A *keyhole saw* is for smaller cutouts.

Hacksaw. Essential for cutting pipes, rods, bolts, or other metal objects.

Coping saw. Used for fretwork. It has a thin blade for cutting complex shapes.

When buying a saw, look for a tempered steel or stainless steel blade, preferably one that has a Teflon-S finish, to reduce corrosion and prevent binding. Carbide-tipped or "hard point" teeth reduce the need for frequent sharpening.

In using a saw there are some points to remember. A saw handle should be grasped in a relaxed fashion with one's forefinger extended along the blade. This is to avoid pressing as you cut, which makes it difficult to guide the saw. The blade should cut from its own sharpness and weight as you push it forward and cut faster and truer if held lightly. Teeth should be checked for sharpness and set when you finish a job, not when you need the saw. Keep the blade clean and lightly oiled.

Buying a cheap miter box is as unwise as buying one-size-fits-all shoes. For accurate jointing, you need a miter-saw combination made with precision and having guides front, back, and top to prevent play in the blade. Since the keenness of the sawteeth is essential for finished joints, a unit with exchangeable blades, similar to hacksaw blades but deeper, is desirable. Signs of quality include the presence of roller bearings in the saw guides and a grip to hold up the saw while you position the wood. Keep the sawteeth sharp.

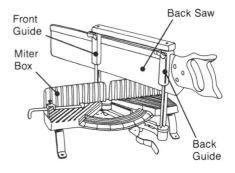

Front
Guide

Miter
Box

Back Saw

Back
Guide

Handsaws

Type	Use	Size/Weight	Remarks
Crosscut Saw	Cutting across grain of wood. Used for 80% of woodcutting requirements.	Lengths between 20″ and 26″	Teeth are pointed and slice wood fibers leaving V-shaped tracks. Teeth score wood on back stroke. Forward stroke cuts groove deeper and expels sawdust from kerf.

Handsaws (Continued)

Type	Use	Size/Weight	Remarks
Ripsaw	Cuts with the grain of wood (ripping).	Lengths between 24" and 26"	Chisellike teeth chop wood into minute chips. Forward stroke cuts wood into particles; return stroke pulls sawdust from kerf. Cuts only on forward stroke.
Tenon and Dovetail Saws	For making joints.	Lengths: 6", 8", 10", 12" and 14"	
Backsaw	Makes precise cuts in moldings. Usually used with miter boxes.	Lengths between 10" and 20"	
Rodsaw	For really tough jobs such as cutting through spring and stainless steel, chains, glass, brick, and tile. Designed to fit hacksaw frames.	Round, 8" to 12" long	Hacksaw-type blades with round rods having permanently bonded tungsten carbide surface.
Compass Saw	Cuts holes or inside pockets in installed panels where only one side is accessible. Usually used for odd-shaped cutouts.	Various lengths 6" to 14"	Normally requires drilling a hole or holes in panel for a starting point. Cuts where a larger saw will not fit and cuts curves.
Keyhole Saw	Normally used to cut small, round holes.	Lengths: 4" to 8"	Similar to compass saw but with thinner blade with finer teeth.
Nesting Saw	Used like compass and keyhole saws. Also used to cut light metal.	Blade lengths: 4" to 8"	Consists of one handle with interchangeable compass, keyhole, and metal-cutting blades.

Your Workshop

Handsaws (Concluded)

Type	Use	Size/Weight	Remarks
Hacksaw	Cuts light metals, piping, and PVC tubing.	Frame adjusts to accept 8" to 12" long blades. Blades have 16 to 32 teeth per inch	Interchangeable blades for different types and thicknesses of material.
Coping Saw	Normally used to cut odd shapes in thin plywood, paneling, or hardboard. Blade can be turned at various angles to frame to permit circular cuts.	Holds 8" to 10" thin blades	Similar to hacksaw but with thinner blades with larger teeth and larger throat.
Bow Saw	Tree trimming and cutting firewood.	3 to 6 teeth per inch	Sawteeth are measured by: Pitch: The angle at which the teeth are set. Set: The alternate angles at which the teeth are bent. Tooth size: The number of points per inch.

Power Saws

Power saws have replaced handsaws as the primary way to cut wood. For straight-line cuts they are far faster and often more accurate. Below is information on the circular saw, saber saw, reciprocating saw, chain saw, band saw, table saw, radial-arm saw, and power miter box, along with a review of saw blades.

Portable power saws, also known as portable circular saws, are primarily used for straight cutting on lumber and plywood. Many types of blades are available for cutting lumber, plywood, plastic laminates, and nonferrous metals. The size of a portable power saw is governed by the blade diameter, which ranges from

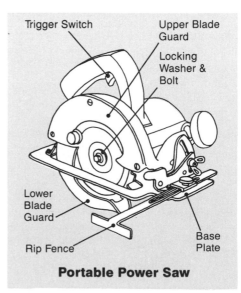

Portable Power Saw

4½" to 10¼". Motor horsepower ranges from 1¼ to 2½.

An acceptable size for most homeowner operations is a 7¼" diameter blade with a 1¾ to 2 horsepower, 10 amp ball bearing saw. The saw consists of a motor, a handle, a base plate or shoe, a fixed and a movable guard, a blade, and a switch. Blades used are the same type as for the table saw. Be certain that the blade is of the correct diameter and well sharpened and that the arbor hole in the blade is of the right size and shape. The saw should have an electric brake and slip clutch to prevent kickbacks. The retractable blade guard should slide up smoothly and close quickly. *Never remove it.*

On major jobs, such as cutting the T's for a suspended ceiling, you can really speed up production by using a *motorized miter box.* This is a heavy, secured miter box with a pivoting circular saw. It can be set to cut any angle, and the saw swings down to do the cutting. It has an attachment for your workshop vacuum. A lighter model suitable for cutting wood, plastic, or metal is available for taking to job sites.

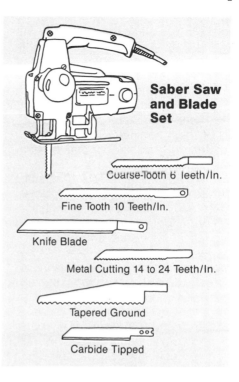

Saber Saw and Blade Set

Coarse-Tooth 6 Teeth/In.

Fine Tooth 10 Teeth/In.

Knife Blade

Metal Cutting 14 to 24 Teeth/In.

Tapered Ground

Carbide Tipped

Motorized Miter Box

Saber saw. The *portable jigsaw,* often called a *saber saw,* is capable of cutting glass, wood, plywood, hardboard, laminates, plastics, leather, rubber, light metal, and ceramics by using the appropriate blade. Unlike a circular saw, it can make curved cuts.

It's terrific for making rounded cutouts, such as a hole for a sink in a kitchen countertop. Due to the thin, narrow blade, it is not very reliable for cutting through materials thicker than ¾", but recently some wider and longer blades have become available, though their use may cause a saw to overheat.

Saber saws are classified for light duty and standard duty. Light-duty saws have double-insulated ⅕ to ⅓ horsepower motors that draw 2.5 to 3.2 amps. These are available in either single speed (3500 strokes per minute) or variable speed (0 to 3500 strokes per minute). Most are capable of cutting 1⅝" softwood, 1" hardwood, ¼" aluminum, and ⅛" mild steel. The ⅓ horsepower model with a 1" stroke length is probably the best tool for the average do-it-yourselfer.

Standard-duty saws usually have more or larger bearings and are rated

Your Workshop

up to ⅝ horsepower. Saws have chucks for ¼" wide blades as standard, with ⅜" and ½" shanks available. Some models have fans to blow the sawdust away from the cut.

Blade lengths vary from 2¾" to 3⅝". Woodcutting blades have 6 or 10 teeth per inch; metal-cutting blades 14 to 24 teeth per inch. Scroll-sawing blades are available for making fine cuts and tight circles.

An adjustable shoe that enables you to cut at an angle is a valuable feature. Avoid saws that will only accommodate narrow shank or special blades. The weakest part of a saber saw is the blade clamp. It tends to work loose, as does the shoe adjustment screw. Make sure this clamp starts out tight and snug, and don't overtighten the screw. Avoid hex-head screws. It's easier to find a screwdriver in your overall pocket than a small hex wrench.

When cutting wood, place the good side down to avoid splintering.

The **reciprocating saw** is an adaptation of the saber saw, or jigsaw, for heavy-duty construction work. Basically, this is a tool for professionals only, but if you are renovating an old home, it may prove to be absolutely essential. This tool can normally be rented from a tool rental outlet.

Reciprocating Saw

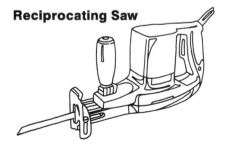

Blades, largely interchangeable among different makes, are available in lengths from 2½" to 12". Heavier than saber saw blades, they range in

Reciprocating Saw Blades

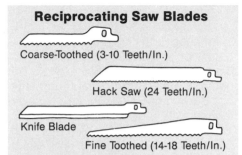

Coarse-Toothed (3-10 Teeth/In.)

Hack Saw (24 Teeth/In.)

Knife Blade

Fine Toothed (14-18 Teeth/In.)

purpose from cutting metal to cutting wood up to 6" thick.

In many models, blades may be mounted to cut up, down, or horizontally and flush with an adjoining surface. In structural work and remodeling, long blades are sometimes used to cut right through a wall (after making sure wiring or plumbing won't be endangered). These blades can cut through any nails they may encounter. Blades made specifically for cutting metal—such as pipe or bar stock—should be lubricated during use with light oil. *Always wear goggles when using reciprocating saws.*

These saws are made in both single-speed (about 2300 strokes per minute) and variable-speed (0 to 2000 strokes per minute) models. The lower speeds are more efficient for cutting steel and plastic which may melt from the friction of higher speeds.

For average use, a **gasoline-** or **electric-powered chain saw** with a 14" or 16" bar (blade body) is a good choice. While 10" and 12" blade bodies are available, the shorter chain saw length means each tooth has to cut at a shorter interval and there is more chance of overheating. Also, the sawteeth get blunt faster, a great aggravation.

A typical 14" model can cut through a 6" hardwood log in seconds. Gasoline-powered saws have a special clutch that prevents the chain from moving while the motor is idling. When

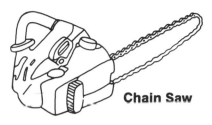

Chain Saw

a belt, and a $6/10$ horsepower motor provides about 1700 rpm. The professional model has a 20″ throat and can cut stock up to 8″ thick or, with an extension, up to 10″ thick. There is a wide selection of blades and some models are available with three speeds.

the throttle is opened, the clutch engages and drives the chain. (A safety handle that stops the saw instantly is essential.) On gasoline models, always premix the oil and gas in the recommended quantities in a separate can. Never add the oil to the gas tank on the saw, or you'll foul the plug. Never stand behind the saw when operating, and never let the saw cut into the ground. Keep the cutting edges sharp or you'll overheat your engine.

Band saws are a special breed of stationary saws. They have narrow $1/4$″ to $1/2$″ blades that can cut curves. The table is usually about 20″ square, and the throat, being 10″ deep, enables you to cut or rip lumber up to 6″ thick. The better models use ball bearing blade guides. The blade is driven with

Jigsaw

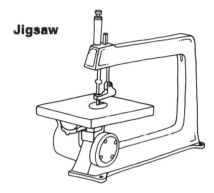

With the renaissance in millwork and Victorian homes, the **jigsaw** is making a comeback. It is very versatile, permits cutting out complex designs, and is fun to use. It is chiefly designed for cutting boards up to 2″ thick. The better models have a blower system to keep sawdust off the cutting area and have a tilting table and precision parts to reduce blade breakage.

A **table saw** is so versatile, it's usually the first stationary power tool added to the homeowner's workshop. It consists of a frame that supports a table, motor, and the blade arbor. The blade, secured to the arbor with a nut and washer, is driven by the motor via a belt and pulleys. You can raise or lower the arbor with a handwheel crank to adjust the height of the blade. A second crank controls the tilt angle of the arbor, from 0 percent to 45 percent, to permit bevel cuts.

The rip fence slides from side to side on support bars located at the front and rear of the table. A locking

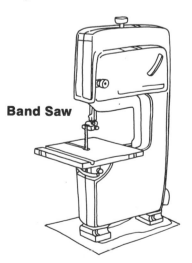

Band Saw

Your Workshop

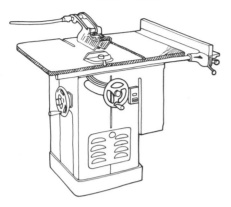

handle secures the fence parallel to the blade after it has been adjusted for the width of cut.

The miter gauge guides the work crosswise past the blade (crosscutting). It is supported on a bar that rides in a groove in the tabletop. The gauge can be adjusted to make angled cuts between 30° and 90°, including precise 45° miter cuts.

Although the many different models of table saws are similar in function, they differ in quality, cutting capacity, and operational features. A given blade diameter will have a different cutting capacity from one saw to the next, due to the type of drive (direct or belt) and the design of the mechanism under the table. Normally a belt-driven saw will have a larger cutting capacity. Home workshop-type table saws are available with blade diameters of 8", 9", 10", and 12". The larger the diameter, the greater the depth of cut. For most home applications the blade should be large enough to cut a 2" x 4" piece of lumber on a 45° angle. Generally a 10" diameter blade is adequate.

Ripping capacity is governed by the distance the "rip fence" can be moved laterally from the blade. Normally, a minimum dimension of 24" is preferred

so that a 4' wide panel can be cut down the middle. Crosscut capacity is governed by the length of table in front of the saw blade. The stock is moved into the blade along the miter gauge.

Look for a saw with sturdy construction details. The table should be smooth-ground with adequate ribs (90° structural members) below to prevent tabletop warping. The better saws have rack-and-worm gear blade elevation and tilting mechanisms rather than a screw and nut.

The blade guard should function with minimal interference and provide clear visibility of the cut. The guard, splitter, and anti-kickback assembly should be easy to remove and reinstall when necessary. The rip fence should lock securely and be self-aligning. The blade-elevating and tilting controls should be located within easy reach for fast, safe operation. And—very important—the on/off switch must be designed to prevent accidental starts and should be lockable. The safest models require a key to operate the saw.

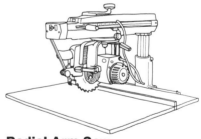

Radial-Arm Saw

The **radial-arm saw** can be used for ripping, crosscutting, dadoing, grooving, mitering, and rabbeting. Although this saw has some width limitations, it has some advantages over the table saw. For instance, crosscutting large stock can be handled easily because the stock remains stationary on the table while the saw blade is pulled through. Another advantage is that the cut is always in sight, since the saw blade is on top of the work when cutting dadoes, grooves, and stop cuts.

About Blades

All saw blades, except for hollow-ground and carbide-tipped blades, have set teeth, meaning they are alternately bent to the right and left. This makes the kerf cut wider than the body thickness of the blade so the blade can move freely through wood.

The most common blades are:

Rip. Used to cut lumber in the same direction as the grain. It has a relatively small number of large teeth filed straight across the top to form chisel-like points. Use with a rip fence.

Crosscut or cutoff blade. Designed to cut wood across the grain, it has more and smaller teeth than a rip blade. Teeth are filed to a bevel on both the front and back edges. Suitable for cutting hardwood, framing, veneers, and plywood. Do not use for ripping.

Plywood. This fine-tooth blade cuts face veneers with minimal splintering. Also good for finish cuts. Always cut with the face-side down.

Hollow ground or planer. Ground hollow on both sides, it has no set teeth and is for fine cutting, leaving smooth faces. Keep blade sharp to prevent scorching.

Carbide-tipped. Available in standard blade designs, these blades hold a sharp edge longer but cost more.

Abrasive blade. Used for cutting masonry, metal, plastic, and other hard-to-cut materials. Can be used for scoring bricks and blocks prior to breaking. Separate blades are sold for each material.

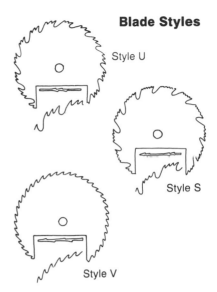

Blade Styles

Style U

Style S

Style V

Combination blades These blades are convenient when it is impractical to change blades frequently. Style S teeth are recommended for bench saws, which require a fine cut. Style U teeth are recommended for radial-arm saws. Style V teeth are the fastest cutting of the various combination saws and can be used on all types of machines.

Dado Head

Dado head. The dado head provides the safest and fastest method of cutting grooves. It consists of two outside cutters with chippers placed between them. Varying the number of chippers will vary the width of the cut. Blades

Your Workshop

are normally $\frac{1}{8}$" wide with chippers supplied in $\frac{1}{16}$", $\frac{1}{8}$", and $\frac{1}{4}$" widths. With the combination of blades and chippers shown, grooves from $\frac{1}{8}$" to $\frac{13}{16}$" width can be cut.

Dado Head Components

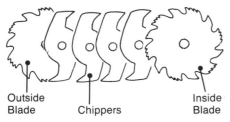

Outside Blade   Chippers   Inside Blade

Cut thickness desired dictates the number and thickness of chipper blades that should be used.

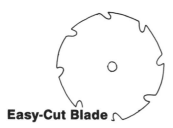

Easy-Cut Blade

Easy-cut blade. The easy-cut blade is designed for ripping or cutoff and rough combination work. The high back of the tooth prevents overfeeding. Kickback tendency is minimized and relatively little power is needed. For use on all types of machines.

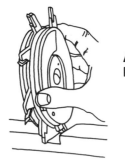

Adjustable Dado Head

Adjustable dado head. The adjustable dado head is easy to use and will give a clean cut. The width can be set by loosening the arbor nut and rotating the center section of the head until the width mark on this part is opposite the desired dimension. The cut can be easily and accurately varied to any width from $\frac{1}{4}$" to $\frac{13}{16}$"

Screwdrivers

A set of good manual screwdrivers is essential to any serious do-it-yourselfer's toolbox. These four screwdrivers will handle most screws for construction work:

- $\frac{3}{16}$" × 4" straight blade, round shank
- $\frac{1}{4}$" × 4" straight blade, round shank
- $\frac{5}{16}$" × 6" straight blade, square shank
- #2 Phillips screwdriver with 4" round shank.

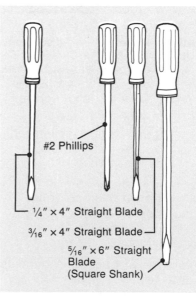

#2 Phillips

$\frac{1}{4}$" × 4" Straight Blade

$\frac{3}{16}$" × 4" Straight Blade

$\frac{5}{16}$" × 6" Straight Blade (Square Shank)

A good screwdriver performs under normal use without deforming or breaking the tip or screw. Ideally, the screwdriver tip must be heat-treated so that the outside metal is hard enough to resist wear while the inside metal retains enough flexibility to prevent the tip from deforming or breaking. The square shank is designed for stiff turning; you can use a wrench to help you turn.

You should always use a screwdriver with a tip a fraction narrower than the length of the slot in the screwhead and a snug fit in the slot.

Never use a screwdriver for leveraging open paint cans or as a pry bar.

Purchase screwdrivers in sets of 6 or 7. Screwdrivers should have full-size, insulating handles. A typical set includes: 4″ and 6″ standard, 3″ and 6″ cabinet, #1 and #2 Phillips, and plastic rack.

It's handy to magnetize the tip of small screwdrivers so they will hold the screw while being inserted in access holes.

Screw holders attach to the tip of the screwdriver. One type of holder uses two small spring-steel jaws to hold screw head tightly to screwdriver. Another type uses a split-bladed screwdriver with sliding handle that expands the blade thickness to hold slotted-head screws.

If using an electric drill to drive or remove screws, always use a shield to prevent scarring work. A ⅜″ variable speed, reversing drill works best and is a real time saver on rough work.

Screwdrivers

Type	Use	Size
Standard Tip, Round Blade **Standard Tip, Square Blade** **Cabinet Tip, Round Blade** **Phillips Tip, Round Blade**	All screwdrivers should be used for same purpose: *drive and withdraw screws.* Don't use them as pry bars, drift pins, or gouges. Round-blade screwdrivers are for normal or light-duty work, while square blades are for heavier-duty work. Wrenches may be applied to square blades to provide additional torque.	*Standard type* Tip width: 7/32″ to 7/16″ Blade length: 3″ to 28″ *Cabinet type* Tip width: 3/16″ Blade length: 3″ to 10″ *Phillips type* Tip size Screw size #1 #1-#4 #2 #5-#9 #3 #10-#16 Blade lengths: 2¾″ to 8″
Standard or Phillips Tip, Stubby		*Stubby* Lengths: Approximately 3¾″ Standard tip: ¼″ Phillips tip #2
Clutch Head		*Clutch head* Blade lengths: 3″ to 5″ O.A. lengths: 6½″ to 10″

Your Workshop

Screwdrivers (Continued)

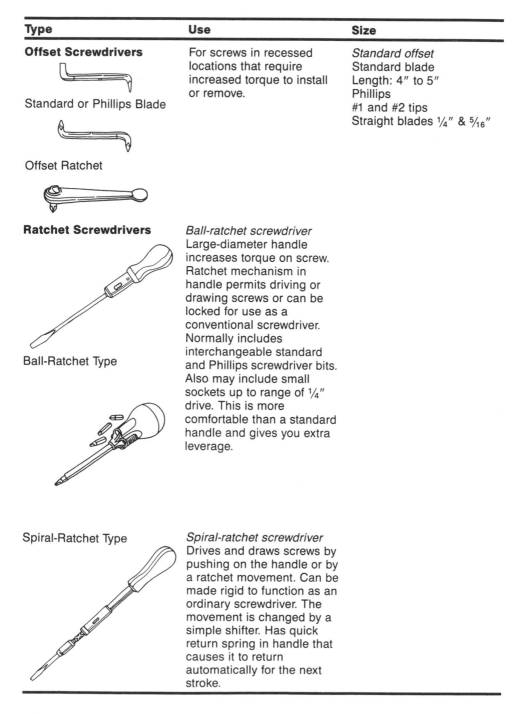

Type	Use	Size
Offset Screwdrivers Standard or Phillips Blade Offset Ratchet	For screws in recessed locations that require increased torque to install or remove.	*Standard offset* Standard blade Length: 4″ to 5″ Phillips #1 and #2 tips Straight blades ¼″ & ⁵⁄₁₆″
Ratchet Screwdrivers Ball-Ratchet Type	*Ball-ratchet screwdriver* Large-diameter handle increases torque on screw. Ratchet mechanism in handle permits driving or drawing screws or can be locked for use as a conventional screwdriver. Normally includes interchangeable standard and Phillips screwdriver bits. Also may include small sockets up to range of ¼″ drive. This is more comfortable than a standard handle and gives you extra leverage.	
Spiral-Ratchet Type	*Spiral-ratchet screwdriver* Drives and draws screws by pushing on the handle or by a ratchet movement. Can be made rigid to function as an ordinary screwdriver. The movement is changed by a simple shifter. Has quick return spring in handle that causes it to return automatically for the next stroke.	

Screwdrivers (Concluded)

Type	Use	Size
Split-Blade Screw-Holding Screwdriver		

Screwdriver Bits Fit These Screw Heads

Slotted   Phillips   clutch

Torx® Tamper Resistant   Torx® Wedge fit

Posidrive®   Frearson   Hexagon   Torq-Set®   Torx®   Hex socket   Square recess

Medium-hard bits are for driving standard (soft) screws and for impact use; they have a 118° point. Extra-hard bits are for heat-treated or case-hardened screws, for use in sheet metal, self-tapping, and self-drilling screws. These have a 135° point.

Blade sizes to fit all types and sizes of heads or slots.

Sharpening Stones

The most common whetstone costs about $10 and is usually about 2" wide by 4" or 8" long. Use the coarse side for rapid initial sharpening, then the smooth side to get an even keener edge. Keep the stone well oiled with machine oil as you work, to reduce friction and wash away fine particles of metal.

Sharpening Stone Selection Guide

	Coarse Crystolon	India Combo.	Multistone	Soft Ark.	Hard Ark.	Bl. Hard Ark.	#800 Jap.	#1000 Jap.	#1200 Jap.	Jap. Finish	Jap. Super.	Large Grind.	Gear Grind.	Jap. Grind.	Strops/Wheels
Basic Grinding or Shaping an Edge	●		●									●	●	●	
Initial Sharpening		●	●	●			●	●							●
Middle Level Sharpening		●	●	●	●			●	●						●
Final Sharpening			●		●	●				●	●				●
Honing or Polishing			●			●				●	●				●
Stropping															●

69

Your Workshop

Sharpening Stones

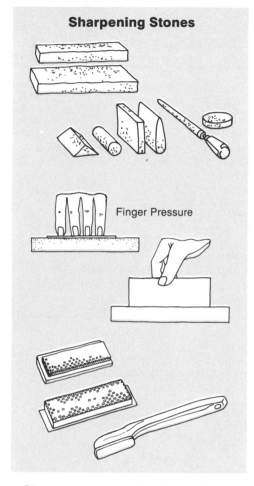

Finger Pressure

Slipstones are hand-held and shaped for sharpening hand-cutting tools such as scythes.

Hard to find but worth their weight in gold are diamond files and hones. Their higher price is justified by their faster cutting and long life. Diamond files are available flat and round and as sharpening stones.

The job at hand dictates which type of sharpening stone you should use—a hard-block Arkansas, coarse Erystolon, or fine-grit Japanese water stone.

The finer the grit, the slower but sharper the stone will cut. Use plenty of oil or water, depending on what is called for, and wipe off sludge to keep the stone from becoming glazed.

Grinding wheels are used for shaping, not sharpening, because they are very coarse. You'll only need one of these if your are engaged in metal-fabricating, wrought-iron, or black-smith work. Always wear goggles when grinding. You may need to grind when you break the tip of a tool or nick a blade on a hidden nail. The angle or the bevel needs to be exact for its intended purpose.

Grinding wheels may be operated by hand or electric motor.

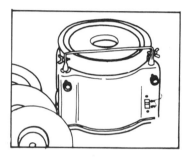

Horizontal Blade Grinder

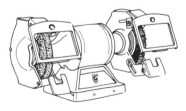

Bench Grinder

Soldering Tools

Used primarily for plumbing and electrical work, *soldering irons* come in three basic groups. The first two, line-voltage and low-voltage pencils, have built-in electrical heating elements. Low-voltage pencils operate from car batteries. Temperature-controlled irons operate off line voltage. Copper irons have to be heated on hot

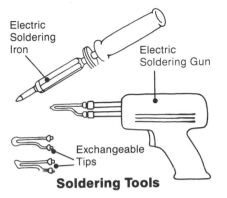

Electric Soldering Iron

Electric Soldering Gun

Exchangeable Tips

Soldering Tools

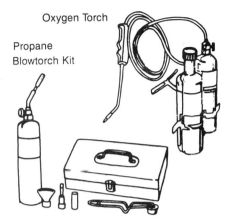

Oxygen Torch

Propane Blowtorch Kit

coals or in a flame. Irons are rated by watts and are slower at both heating and cooling than soldering guns.

Turned on and off by a trigger switch, *soldering guns* heat and cool rapidly and have a choice of heat levels. Some feature built-in lights to illuminate work. Battery-powered models are also available. Solder with an acid-core flux is used for plumbing and general applications. Solder with a plastic resin-core flux is used on electrical work.

Propane, Mapp Gas, and Oxygen/ Propane Torches. Most do-it-yourselfers have replaced the gasoline-fired blowtorch with safer, cleaner-burning gas-fired torches. These hand-held torches can be used to solder, remove paint, melt ice on steps and walks or anything that requires localized heat.

Torches are available in kits which include a disposable fuel tank, burner head, interchangeable burner tips, sparking striker, and carrying case. The burner head, which screws onto the top of the fuel tank, contains a manually operated valve which turns the gas flow on and off and regulates the size of the flame. The tips screw into the burner head and can be used for a variety of projects.

One new model has the striker-action built into the burner head so that squeezing a triggerlike mechanism lights the torch, without using a separate striker.

Another model clips the tank to your belt while connecting the pistol-shaped nozzle assembly to the tank with a small hose. The nozzle assembly also contains the striker mechanism. This unit permits one-hand operation and access to tight places.

Propane and Mapp gas are commonly used as fuel. Propane torches burn hot enough for heavy-duty soldering, removing paint, and other utility operations. Mapp gas, which can generate temperatures up to 3600°F, can perform light brazing jobs up to 1/8″ sheet metal and 5/8″ steel rod and is excellent for operations requiring silver solder.

Oxygen/Propane torches generate temperatures in excess of 5000°F. The oxygen for these torches is generated either from a separate fuel cylinder or by burning a solid oxygen pellet, called solid ox pellets, in a small cylinder, similar in size to a propane cylinder. A standard propane cylinder supplies the propane which is combined with the oxygen at the torch tip and ignited with a striker. The oxygen/propane torches

Your Workshop

can be used to braze, weld, and cut mild metal up to ¼" thick. These torches weigh about 6 pounds and are supplied in kits containing all necessary accessories.

Portable Workbench Vise

The portable workbench serves as a worktable and large-scale vise. It folds flat for compact storage and is light enough to be carried almost anywhere. The flat, viselike wooden top is controlled by two hand cranks. When cranked fully open the jaws will hold items approximately 5" thick.

Portable Worktable & Storage Cabinet

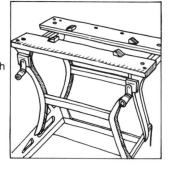

Portable Workbench

Special bench stops, which can be attached to the work top, permit clamping stock up to a foot thick. The inner edges of the jaws are grooved to

permit holding pipe and tubing. And the cranks operate independently to permit odd-shaped objects to be clamped.

Various accessories permit making accurate cutoff and miter cuts; other models hold portable circular or sabre saws and routers.

Several different manufacturers make essentially the same product, which is marketed under different trade names.

A portable workbench is an excellent buy for field use or for a homeowner with little or no room for a conventional workshop or workbench. Its portability allows it to be quickly moved to the work area, then easily dismantled and stored after use.

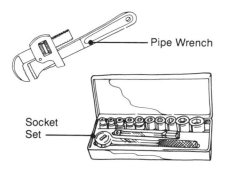

Pipe Wrench

Socket Set

Wrenches

Since so many imported products are fastened with metric-scale nuts and bolts, adjustable wrenches have become indispensable. You can also buy wrenches sized according to the metric scale. Some imported wrenches are made from malleable mild steel. Avoid them. Look for good-quality wrenches made from hardened or tempered fine-grade tool steel.

A wrench should be pulled, not pushed. And never use a "cheater" extension; the excessive torque created will damage the nut or threads you are working on. Tap the bolt or use a rust solvent if the nut is bound.

Wrenches

Type	Use	Size/Capacity	Remarks
Pipe Wrench	For tightening or loosening pipe fittings.	Length: 6″ to 48″ Stock capacity: ¾″ to 6″ diameter	
Offset Pipe Wrench	Offset jaw configuration available for use in tight places. Offset hex wrench has extra-large opening offset jaw for use on sink and tub drain nuts and all other hard-to-get-at nuts and fittings.	Lengths: 6″ to 24″ Stock capacity: ¾″ to 3″ diameter	
Strap Wrench	Use in place of chain wrench on polished pipe or tubing to prevent marring surface.	Capacity range: ⅛″ to 8″ Handle lengths: 6″ to 18″	
Chain Wrench	Use on heavy pipe or large, irregularly shaped fittings. The chain wrench comes with a smooth side and a side with teeth. Use the smooth side down on pipes and round objects. Place the teeth down when using on hex nuts or other irregularly shaped objects.	Capacity range: ¾″ to 6″ diameter Handle lengths range from 8″ to 12″ Chain lengths range to 44½″	
Monkey Wrench Also called: Auto wrench Ford wrench	An adjustable wrench with sliding jaw that can apply nonslipping pressure to small or large nuts. Use on nuts and bolts beyond the capacity of open-end or box-end wrenches.	Wrench sizes: 9″ to 18″ Capacity range: 2¾″ to 4⅜″	

Your Workshop

Wrenches (Continued)

Type	Use	Size/Capacity	Remarks
Socket Wrench Sets	Rapid removal or installation of standard U.S. or metric nuts and bolts. $1/4''$ drive sockets are for small household appliances. $3/8''$ drive sockets are for normal-sized bolt/nuts up to about $7/8''$. $1/2''$ drive sockets are mostly for automotive use or larger nuts/bolts. $3/4''$ drive sockets are for trucks and other heavy items. Spark plug sockets have greater depths. Now available in sets at very reasonable prices.	Socket sizes: $1/4''$ drive: $3/16''$ to $1/2''$ $3/8''$ drive: $1/4''$ to $7/8''$ $1/2''$ drive: $7/16''$ to $11/4''$ $3/4''$ drive: $7/8''$ to $2''$	A set consists of the following: Ratchet Extension bar Universal swivel joint Sockets either U.S. or metric or both Look for those made with hardened or tempered steel.
Allen Wrench Sets	Hexagonal L- or T-shaped keys that fit into machine screws and plumbing plugs.	$1/8''$ to $1''$ and in metric sizes. Sold in multisized sets of 8 or 12.	Make sure they are made of hardened or tempered steel.
Hexagon Wrenches	Designed for plumbing taps.		
Flare Nut Wrenches	These cover 5 of the 6 faces on copper tubing fittings and are positioned by sliding down tubing over hex fitting. They are designed to prevent tearing corners off of fittings. One end has a sided grip, the other a circular knuckled grip.		Sold in sets. The only type of wrench to be used on copper or brass fittings.

Wrenches (Continued)

Type	Use	Size/Capacity	Remarks
Adjustable Wrench Also called: Crescent Wrench 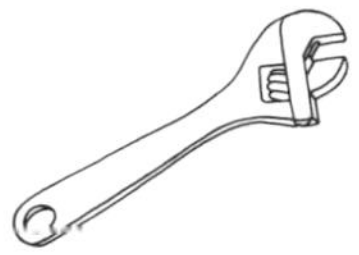		Length range: 4″ to 24″ Jaw capacity range: ½″ to 2⁷⁄₁₆″	It is usually best to purchase a 3-wrench set—4″, 8″, and 12″ lengths.
Open-End Wrench (Double End) 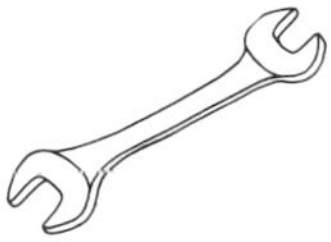	Designed to loosen or tighten standard-size nuts and bolts. Different nut size on each end of wrench (for example, ⁹⁄₁₆″ and ⅝″). Use where socket wrench or box-end wrench will not fit.	Size range: ¼″ to 2″ U.S.; 6 to 21 metric. Lengths vary.	Purchase as a 10-wrench set with sizes from ¼″ to 1⅛″
Box-End Wrench  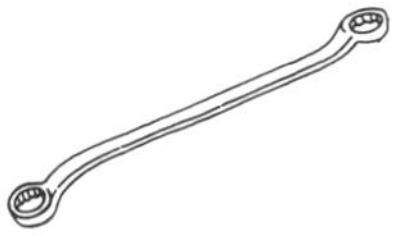	Closed-end wrench designed to hold nut/bolt without slipping. Must have enough clearance to slip wrench over nut/bolt. Different nut size on each end of wrench. (Example: ½″ and ⁹⁄₁₆″). Normal 45° offset head. Normally 12-pt. openings.	Size range: ⅜″ to 1½″ U.S.; 6 to 27mm Metric Short lengths for close-quarter work. Longer lengths for more leverage.	Available as a set with sizes from ⅜″ to 1″. Optional 15° offset head available.
Combination Wrench 	Provides open end and box end of same size on one wrench. Heads angle at 15°.	Size range: ⅜″ to 1½″ U.S.; 6 to 50 metric.	Purchase as a 10-piece set with sizes ⅜″ to 1″. Suggest purchasing one combination set in place of separate box-end and open-end sets.

Your Workshop

Wrenches (Concluded)

Type	Use	Size/Capacity	Remarks
Ratcheting Wrenches 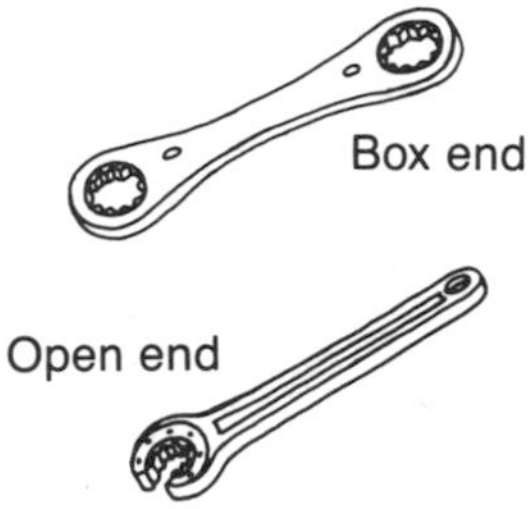 Box end Open end		*Open-end sizes:* Size ½", length 5⅜" Size ⅝", length 6¾" *Box-end sizes* 6-pt. opening in both ends Nominal opening Length ¼" × ⁵⁄₁₆" 4½" ⅜" × ⁷⁄₁₆" 5½" ½" × ⁹⁄₁₆" 6¾" 12-pt. opening in both ends Nominal opening Length ⅝" × ¹¹⁄₁₆" 8" ⅝" × ¾" 8" ¾" × ⅞" 9¼"	
Multi-Wrench 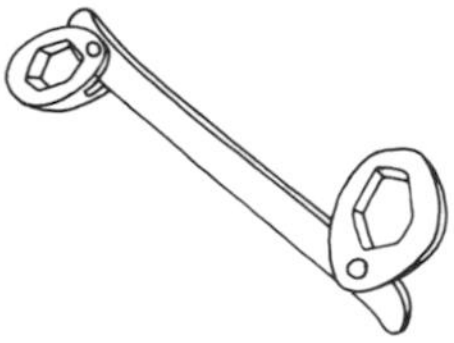	For tightening and loosening nuts and bolts of indeterminate size.	Various sizes to accommodate nuts and bolts between: ⅜" to ¹³⁄₁₆" ⅞" to 1½"	Automatically adjusts itself and grips harder the more it is turned. Useful if you do not own both metric and English-sized wrenches.

Lumber

2

2. Lumber

Wood is wonderful. Its beauty endures beyond all fashion. It can last for centuries, whether in the form of a New England home or a twelfth-century table. It is strong yet light, possessing one of the best "strength-to-weight ratios," as engineers say, of all known materials. It is flexible enough to be curved into laminated arches. It is easily shaped, smoothed, fastened, repaired. And as most things go, it's still a relative bargain.

That's why wood is our number-one building material. But the more you buy and use wood in various projects, the more you know it like a spouse—its foibles, as well as its strengths. It shrinks and expands with the weather. It can get all bent out of shape as it's drying. It can be eaten by termites and ravaged by dry rot.

Worse yet, a good piece of wood seems harder to find these days. Lumber is seldom fully dried when you buy it. Some pieces are straight; others are twisted, bowed, or cupped. Still others have knots, checks, or splits. Some lumberyards let you paw through a pile to pick out the best, others don't.

Lumber isn't all the same. It's up to you to get the best quality, the right product, the right size, the right amount, and the right price.

First let's get some terms straight. Trees come in two flavors: hardwoods and softwoods. *Hardwoods* come from deciduous trees, the kind that lose their leaves every winter (bald cypress and larches excepted). Deciduous trees take up more growing space in the forest, take longer to grow, and rarely grow straight, so the wood is expensive. Hardwoods are most often cut for use as strip flooring, furniture, fine board stock, cabinetry, and veneers (very thin sheets). The most common are oak, maple, walnut, cherry, and birch.

Softwoods come from conifers (trees with needles). They grow straighter, faster, and taller than hardwoods, so are less expensive. The common softwoods—pines, firs, hemlock, and spruces—are used to make construction lumber. Redwood and cedar are also softwoods, but they are slower growing and therefore more expensive. Fortunately their resistance to weather provides cost justification for their use as siding and for other exterior projects.

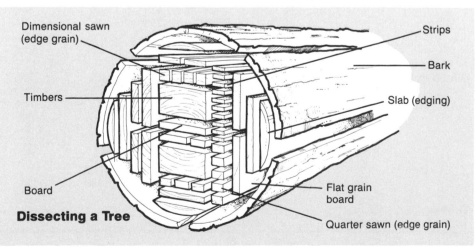

Dimensional sawn (edge grain)

Strips

Bark

Timbers

Slab (edging)

Board

Flat grain board

Dissecting a Tree

Quarter sawn (edge grain)

Lumber

Construction lumber is separated by size into three categories: timbers, dimension lumber, and boards. *Timbers,* the biggest, are at least 5″ in their smallest dimension. They are used as beams, stringers, posts, and heavy structural members and are graded for strength. *Dimension lumber* is what you're most familiar with: 2 x 4's, 2 x 6's, 4 x 4's, and the like. Such lumber may be called studs, framing, joists, or planks, depending on likely use. *Boards* are less than 2″ in nominal thickness. The cheaper grades are used for fencing, sheathing, shelves, subflooring, and concrete forms; the better grades are used in finish carpentry.

When lumber is milled into particular shapes, it's called *pattern lumber.* Pattern lumber is used for sheathing, siding, flooring, and moldings, including window and door trim.

Finally, there are the lumber products where man has improved on nature. These include plywood, pressure-treated wood, chipboard, and oriented-strand board. They'll be covered later in the chapter.

American Standard Softwood Lumber Sizes[1]

Item	Thickness			Face width		
	Actual size Minimum dressed			Actual size Minimum dressed		
	Named Size	Dry	Green	Named Size	Dry	Green
	(in.)	(in.)	(in.)	(in.)	(in.)	(in.)
Board	1	$3/4$	$25/32$	2	$1\frac{1}{2}$	$1\frac{9}{16}$
	$1\frac{1}{4}$	1	$1\frac{1}{32}$	3	$2\frac{1}{2}$	$2\frac{9}{16}$
	$1\frac{1}{2}$	$1\frac{1}{4}$	$1\frac{9}{32}$	4	$3\frac{1}{2}$	$3\frac{9}{16}$
				5	$4\frac{1}{2}$	$4\frac{5}{8}$
				6	$5\frac{1}{2}$	$5\frac{5}{8}$
				7	$6\frac{1}{2}$	$6\frac{5}{8}$
				8	$7\frac{1}{4}$	$7\frac{1}{2}$
				9	$8\frac{1}{4}$	$8\frac{1}{2}$
				10	$9\frac{1}{4}$	$9\frac{1}{2}$
				11	$10\frac{1}{4}$	$10\frac{1}{2}$
				12	$11\frac{1}{4}$	$11\frac{1}{2}$
				14	$13\frac{1}{4}$	$13\frac{1}{2}$
				16	$15\frac{1}{4}$	$15\frac{1}{2}$
Dimension	2	$1\frac{1}{2}$	$1\frac{9}{16}$	2	$1\frac{1}{2}$	$1\frac{9}{16}$
	$2\frac{1}{2}$	2	$2\frac{1}{16}$	3	$2\frac{1}{2}$	$2\frac{9}{16}$
	3	$2\frac{1}{2}$	$2\frac{9}{16}$	4	$3\frac{1}{2}$	$3\frac{9}{16}$
	$3\frac{1}{2}$	3	$3\frac{1}{16}$	5	$4\frac{1}{2}$	$4\frac{5}{8}$
	4	$3\frac{1}{2}$	$3\frac{9}{16}$	6	$5\frac{1}{2}$	$5\frac{5}{8}$
	$4\frac{1}{2}$	4	$4\frac{1}{16}$	8	$7\frac{1}{4}$	$7\frac{1}{2}$
				10	$9\frac{1}{4}$	$9\frac{1}{2}$
				12	$11\frac{1}{4}$	$11\frac{1}{2}$
				14	$13\frac{1}{4}$	$13\frac{1}{2}$
				16	$15\frac{1}{4}$	$15\frac{1}{2}$
Timbers	5 and greater		$\frac{1}{2}$ less than named size	5 and greater		$\frac{1}{2}$ less than named size

[1]From American Softwood Lumber Standard PS 20.70.

How to Estimate Your Needs

Lumber is usually sold by the board foot. A board foot is based on a piece of wood 1″ thick, 12″ wide, and 12″ long. The actual dimensions of lumber will be less than these measurements (see the tables that follow), but you must pay for the volume of wood before it is dried and surfaced.

Here's how to figure the board feet of a piece of lumber:

$$\frac{\text{thickness (inches)} \times \text{width (inches)} \times \text{length (feet)}}{12}$$

Thus the board feet of a piece 2″ thick, 6″ wide, and 12′ long is:

$$\frac{2 \times 6 \times 12}{12} = 12 \text{ board feet}$$

As you can see, a board foot can be a 3′-long piece of 1 × 4, a 1′ piece of 2 × 6, or a 6″ piece of 2 × 12, among other things.

Construction lumber is usually sold in multiples of 2′ lengths from 6′ up to 24! The longer lengths are not available in many types of wood. You may be able to obtain lengths under 10′ in 1′ multiples, as with 7′ and 9′, since these are often cut without waste from longer lengths. Some items, like sheathing and finish flooring, are more commonly sold in random lengths, a reasonable assortment that can be fully used with little waste.

Studs often are sold in specified lengths from about 7′ up to 10! They may be 2 × 4's or 2 × 6's. When buying 2 × 6's be sure you get stud grade or the yard may cut long, better quality, No. 2 structural framing down to stud length and charge you a higher price. (More on lumber grades coming up.)

Hardwood is sold in 1′ increments from 4′ to 16! Not more than 50 percent odd lengths are allowed in any one shipment. But note well: With this 50 percent leeway you'll have to expect a lot of variation. You should only pay for the board footage you actually get.

Buying and using lumber efficiently, with the least amount of waste, requires planning. Sit down and figure out what you need. Get a piece of graph paper and lay out your project to scale. Find out how best to assemble the pieces and how long they need to be. Change your project dimensions, if necessary, to accommodate standard lumber sizes. When you are satisfied with your layout, count up the pieces of each length you need. Some may be short enough to be cut from longer lengths with less net waste. Don't forget to include essential but often forgotten needs such as the cross bracing for floor joists.

Lumber Sizes

As already mentioned, lumber is sold in sizes greater than actual size. This is because (a) it shrinks as it dries, and (b) it is run through a planer to convert it from "rough" to "surfaced" (or "dressed") lumber. So a softwood 2 × 4 is not 2″ by 4″. It is about $1\frac{9}{16}″ \times 3\frac{9}{16}″$ when surfaced green, and about $1\frac{1}{2}″ \times 3\frac{1}{2}″$ when surfaced dry. (See the accompanying tables for standard sizes for softwood lumber.)

Hardwood is also sold at less than its nominal size, but in most species it does not shrink as much as softwood (see table).

Hardwood Lumber Minimum Widths S-2-S (smooth 2 sides)
All Measures in Inches

Rough	Surfaced	Rough	Surfaced
3/8	3/16	1½	1 5/16
1/2	5/16	1¾	1½
5/8	7/16	2	1¾
3/4	9/16	2½	2¼
1	13/16	3	2¾
1¼	1 1/16	3½	3¼
		4	3¾

Lumber

Finished width over 4" or S-1-S (smooth 1 side) is not specified by rules. Thickness is subject to special contract. For example, if you order 1" hardwood, 7" wide, its actual thickness should be $13/16$" but its width may be $6\frac{1}{4}$" to $6\frac{3}{4}$".

When ordering hardwood wider than 6" things get really confusing. You'll go to the lumberyard and order 8" oak for shelving. What you get the first time may be $7\frac{1}{2}$". Running short, you go back and ask for 8" oak, only this time it is $7\frac{1}{4}$". The reason is that the standards only go up to 4" widths on select or common grades and 6" on Firsts and Seconds. Mills can choose a different width to make best use of lumber. Your best bet is to call a friendly lumberyard manager a few weeks ahead, tell him what you are looking for, and ask him to set it aside if any of the desired dimension comes in.

Lumber Grades

The lumber industry, together with the federal government, has established uniform lumber grades as a guide to quality. Grading is different for hardwoods and softwoods.

The grading system for softwoods breaks down into two basic categories: *select* and *common.*

Select grades are "B and better," "C" and "D." The "B and better" grade is used for trimwork, moldings, and finish woodwork where appearance is highly important. Grade C has minor defects, and Grade D has minor defects on one side but larger defects on the other side. Grade D is often used for interior woodwork that will be painted.

Common grades are ranked, in descending order of quality, from No. 1 to No. 5. No. 1 is also known as "Select Merchantable," No. 2 as

Grade Categories of Visually Stress-Graded Lumber Available Commercially[1]

Category	Grade	Thickness	Width
		(In.)	(In.)
Structural	Select Structural	2-4	2-4
Light	No. 1	2-4	2-4
Framing	No. 2	2-4	2-4
	No. 3	2-4	2-4
Light	Construction	2-4	2-4
Framing	Standard	2-4	2-4
	Utility	2-4	2-4
Stud	Stud	2-4	2-5
Structural	Select Standard	2-4	6 & wider
Joist and	No. 1	2-4	6 & wider
Plank	No. 2	2-4	6 & wider
	No. 3	2-4	6 & wider
Beams and Stringers		5 & thicker	8 & wider
Posts and Timbers		5×5 and greater, approximately square	

[1]All grades described in all United States rules in accordance with the American Lumber Standard. Allowable stresses assigned to Structural Light Framing are not the same as those assigned to the Structural Joists and Planks of the same grade name. Allowable stresses also vary with kinds of wood. Names are examples of some grades, but various grading rules may use other terms.

"Construction," No. 3 as "Standard," No. 4 as "Utility," and No. 5 as "Economy." Common wood ranges in quality from having a few small, tight knots to having large knots, holes, and large pitch pockets.

The accompanying tables list the commonly used grades of lumber for typical uses in home construction. Grades for engineering use, as in trusses, joists, and rafters, are not fully covered in these tables. You should consult a professional designer or applicable codes to determine grades and sizes required for these uses.

By the way, there is nothing wrong with selecting the lowest grade that satisfies your requirements. In fact, it will save you money, since higher grades cost more. So use the least quality that will do the job. That doesn't mean accepting warped or damaged wood; it simply means choosing the best wood of the lowest grade required for your application.

Hardwoods have a different grading system. The highest cutting grade is termed Firsts, followed in order by Seconds, Select, No. 1 Common, and No. 2, No. 3A, and No. 3B Common.

Little differentiates Firsts and Seconds, which are often combined as one grade: FAS (Firsts and Seconds). The highlights are these:

FAS. Not more than $8\frac{1}{3}$ percent may be waste material. Miminum size: 4" by 5' or 3" by 7'. Must contain 4 square feet of acceptable surface area and 70 percent must be 8' to 16' long and 6" wide. Over $91\frac{2}{3}$ percent of face must be clear for Firsts, $83\frac{1}{3}$ percent to $91\frac{2}{3}$ percent for Seconds.

Seconds. Minimum pieces must be over 3" by 7' or 4" by 5'.

Select. As above, except 30 percent can be 6' to 11' long and 4" widths are acceptable.

No. 1 Common. Allows 10 percent to be 4' to 7' long, and 3" widths are acceptable. Clear surface varies from $66\frac{2}{3}$ percent clear to 100 percent clear. Minimum pieces must be 4" by 2' or 3" by 3'.

No. 2 Common. Allows 30 percent to be 4' to 7' long and 3" widths. Surface varies from 50 percent to $66\frac{2}{3}$ percent clear. Minimum pieces must be 3" by 2".

Softwood Grading Stamps

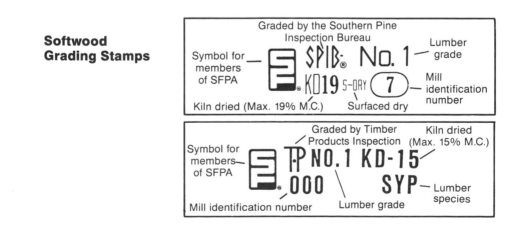

83

Lumber

No. 3A Common. The same as No. 2 but allows 50 percent to be 4' to 7' long and only 33⅓ percent has to have clear face.

No. 3B Common. Same as No. 3A except only 25 percent has to be clear-faced and smallest piece can be 1½" by 2'.

Solid dimension stock, which will be used virtually in mill-cut size, is graded Clear—Two Faces; Clear—One Face; Select; Paint; and Second. Flooring lumber (see Chapter 11) has separate grading classifications for oak, maple, and pecan.

Moisture Content

Up to half a tree's weight is water. For most uses, some of this water must be removed to improve the quality of lumber and, incidentally, reduce its weight. Lumber is mechanically dried in a kiln or naturally dried in a stack. Either method is satisfactory, although kiln drying is much more common.

Moisture affects wood quality in many ways. Wood can decay at high

Commonly Used Grades for Construction Lumber

Item	Grade
Framing	
Wall framing	Stud
Sills on foundation walls or slab on ground	Utility
Sills on piers—built up[1]	No. 2
Joists, rafters, headers[2]	No. 2
Plates, caps, bucks	Utility
Ribbon boards, bracing, ridge boards (1")	No. 3 Common
Collar beams	No. 3 Common
Furring grounds (1")	No. 3 Common
Subflooring, wall sheathing	No. 3 Common
Roof sheathing (pitched)	No. 3 Common
Roof decking (flat)—1" or 2"	No. 2
Exposed decking—3" or 4"	Dense Standard or Select DT&G Deck
Industrial decking—3" or 4"	Commercial DT&G Deck
Trusses	Consult fabricator
Heavy timber beams, posts, and columns (over 5" thick)[2]	No. 1
Finish	
Moldings	Standard molding
Interior paneling—rustic	No. 2
Interior paneling—appearance	C and Better
Shelving	No. 3
Exterior	
Railings, rail posts	No. 1
Decking (bark side up)	No. 2
Trim, fascia, corner boards	No. 1

[1]For sills within 12" of ground, wood should have high natural durability or be pressure-preservative treated.
[2]Higher structural grades may be required by engineering design or building codes.

moisture contents—when the weight of water in the wood exceeds about 25 percent of the wood's dry weight, dry rot can set in and destroy the wood. Since dry rot occurs through dampness, it is a misleading term. It is caused by a fungus that flourishes in damp, still air between 50°F and 90°F. The dry rot fungus grows threadlike roots that withdraw the wood's lignin and cellulose for use as food, causing collapse and decay. Drying to lower moisture levels increases the stability and strength of lumber. Other qualities —workability, nail holding, and paint adhesion—also improve as lumber dries.

So, how dry does lumber need to be? This depends entirely on how you intend to use it. For nearly all uses you will want it below the 25 percent decay hazard level. But most light boards, not larger than 2″ in least dimension, will quickly air-dry below this level if stacked loosely under cover. Wood adjusts itself to a moisture content determined by the temperature and humidity of the air around it. In most climates, wood will gradually air-dry to a range of 12 to 16 percent. At this level, most shrinking is complete, and wood strength and other properties are good.

You can use "green lumber," lumber that is not dried, for a few purposes. It will dry below the 25 percent level after manufacture and during storage, shipment, and construction. It may be satisfactory for such uses as making crates, pallets, or throwaway concrete forms. But avoid it wherever any change in dimensions or warping will create problems. Timbers of 5″ or more in least dimension are normally sold green, since it is not economical to dry them commercially. If you plan to use large timbers, buy them six months ahead. You can then air-dry

them slowly under cover to lower moisture levels.

Air-dried or kiln-dried lumber can be purchased, from most lumberyards, at 19 or 15 percent maximum moisture content (at time of manufacture). The 19 percent lumber is usually stamped "S-dry" (semidry), while the 15 percent may be marked "MC 15" (moisture content 15 percent) or "KD" (kiln dried). This assures you of partial drying, and you can depend upon dry lumber for accurate framing and maximum stability. The 15 percent level is about as dry as you can maintain lumber under outside job conditions, so it would be wasteful to dry it further at extra cost. However, keep in mind that for inside use it will dry and shrink a little more if it is enclosed in a heated building. If you intend it for inside use, you may want to dry it further in heated storage.

Interior finish lumber such as is used in finish flooring, moldings, paneling, and doors needs special drying. Such items may require levels of 10 to 12 percent moisture content to limit shrinking or warping in place. Once lumber is dried to this level, it is very important that you protect it from moisture in shipment and on the job site. Storage in a heated space before installation is a good practice. In summer, lumber usually absorbs moisture and expands. During the winter heating season—indoors or outdoors in the dry northern prairie states—it will shrink as it loses moisture. Never lay lumber on uneven surfaces or in low areas where water may gather.

Sorting It Out

If you're sorting through a pile of lumber at the lumberyard and you're being very particular about getting wood that won't warp, there's a way to

Lumber

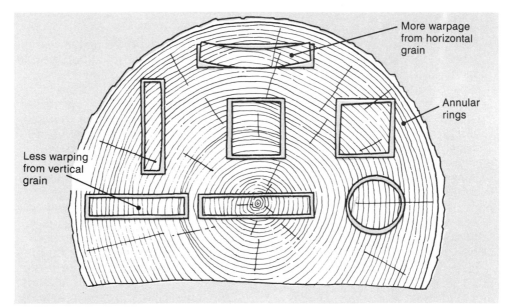

More warpage from horizontal grain

Annular rings

Less warping from vertical grain

Lumber Warping Tendencies

tell how boards will behave as they dry. Simply check the end grain against the illustration above. The illustration provides a key to what happens in the drying process to each different cut of wood. It's all in the grain. Vertical-grained boards shrink best. Flat-grained boards tend to cup as they dry. Because the illustration shows the annular rings, which determine grain, you will now be able to look at the end grain on any piece of construction lumber and match it with one of the indicated cuts.

Wood Defects

When sorting through lumber, eyeball each piece for outrageous defects of the following sort:

Knots. A knot forms when a tree continues to grow around the base of a branch. Loose knots, which may fall out, form when the wood grows around a dead branch. Tight knots may be desirable in such products as knotty pine paneling, and small tight knots

are acceptable in plank flooring. But knots in structural lumber must be

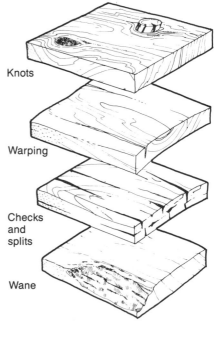

Knots

Warping

Checks and splits

Wane

Wood Defects

limited in number, size, and location. Knots resist nailing and planing. They create finishing problems, since they have to be sealed with shellac or other sealer before painting. Large knots or edge knots can reduce the strength of a plank. Knot-free (clear) material is usually reserved for very high-quality interior finish items like cabinets and moldings. The grading for structural members limits the number of knots by size and location.

Warp. Lumber can twist, bow, and cup during drying. The tendency to warp varies in different types of wood and with the grain or cut of each piece. To avoid cupping, select vertical-grain boards. Slight twists and bows are common in rough carpentry, and part of a carpenter's skill lies in use of nailing tricks to straighten these warps as he works. But serious warps? Forget it.

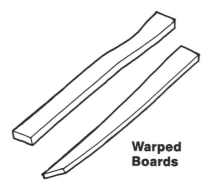

Warped Boards

Checks and splits are separations in the wood along the grain caused by unequal shrinkage during drying. Often they don't matter, but you need to consider what effect they may have on your particular project. Sometimes a nail driven nearby will cause more splitting, although blunting the point of the nail will sometimes prevent this. If it is going to be some time before you are going to use lumber you have

bought, paint or prime the ends to help prevent checking.

Wane is the outside cut of the log, sometimes obvious due to the presence of bark on the edge of a piece. It could weaken structural lumber or compromise a piece's appearance once in place. Be sure that any wane will not impair the planned use.

Wane

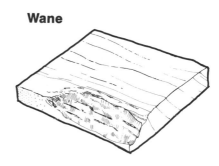

Finally, if you're buying lumber for outdoor use, you may want to purchase **heartwood.** The heartwood of some kinds of wood contains chemicals that resist decay and insect attack. The heartwood of such softwoods as redwood and the cedars is widely used for shingles, siding, fencing, decks, and outdoor furniture. Since there is less of it in each log, it is more expensive than sapwood.

Softwoods

Much of the necessary information on softwoods has been presented in the preceding sections. The types of softwood framing lumbers available in your local lumberyard depend largely on your region of the country, and you usually don't get a wide variety to choose from. But if you do, the table, beginning on page 88, which is a concise reference on the characteristics of common softwood species, will be of help to you.

Lumber

Comparative Characteristics of Some Construction Woods[1]

Woods[3]	Characteristics[2]				
	Dry weight	Hardness	Workability	Nail holding	Paint holding
Douglas-fir-larch	A	A	B	A	C
Hem-fir	B	B	B	B	C
Englemann spruce-lodgepole pine	C	C	B	C	C
Eastern hemlock	B	B	B	B	B
Southern pine	A	A	B	A	C
Idaho white pine	C	C	A	C	A
Spruce/pine/fir (Canada)	C	C	B	C	C
Western cedar	C	C	A	C	A
California redwood	C	B	A	B	A

[1]Letters do not refer to lumber grades. Woods selected are those available in commercial quantities and most commonly used.
A—among the woods relatively *high* in the characteristics listed.
B—among woods *intermediate* in that respect.
C—among woods relatively *low* in that respect.
[2]All woods have adequate strength and stiffness for most uses. Lower strength and stiffness can be compensated for by increasing size or grade or by closer spacing of pieces.
[3]Ratings for wood groups are for the lowest wood in the group.

Characteristics of Common Softwoods

Common names of species	Specific gravity	Static Bending	
		Modulus of rupture	Modulus of elasticity
		Kilo-pascals	Mega-pascals
CEDAR			
Alaska	.42	80,000	11,000
Northern white	.30	42,000	4,300
Western red cedar	.31	54,000	8,200
FIR			
Douglas fir	.45	88,000	13,600
Subalpine	.33	56,000	10,200
Pacific silver	.36	69,000	11,300
Balsam	.34	59,000	9,600

		Characteristics[2]			
Freedom from shrinking	Freedom from warping	Freedom from pitch (resin)	Decay resistance (heartwood)	Bending strength	Stiffness
B	B	B	B	A	A
B	B	A	C	B	B
B	B	A	C	C	C
A	B	A	C	B	B
B	B	C	B	A	A
B	A	A	C	C	C
B	B	A	C	B	B
A	A	A	A	C	C
A	A	A	A	B	B

Compression parallel to grain—maximum crushing strength	Compression perpendicular to grain—fiber stress at proportional limit	Shear parallel to grain—maximum shearing strength
Kilopascals	Kilopascals	Kilopascals
45,800	4,800	9,200
24,800	2,700	6,900
29,600	3,400	5,600
50,000	6,000	9,500
36,400	3,700	6,800
40,900	3,600	7,500
34,300	3,200	6,300

Lumber

Characteristics of Common Softwoods (Concluded)

Common names of species	Specific gravity	Static Bending	
		Modulus of rupture	Modulus of elasticity
		Kilo-pascals	Mega-pascals
HEMLOCK			
Eastern	.40	67,000	9,700
Western	.41	81,000	12,300
Larch, Western	.55	107,000	14,300
PINE			
Eastern white	.36	66,000	9,400
Jack	.42	78,000	10,200
Lodgepole	.40	76,000	10,900
Ponderosa	.44	73,000	9,500
Red	.39	70,000	9,500
Western white	.36	64,100	10,100
SPRUCE			
Black	.41	79,000	10,500
Engelmann	.38	70,000	10,700
Red	.38	71,000	11,000
Sitka	.35	70,000	11,200
White	.35	63,000	10,000
Tamarack	.48	76,000	9,400

NOTE: The values for each species are adjusted from the green condition to 12 percent moisture content using dry to green clear wood property ratios as reported in ASTM D 2555-70. Table courtesy of Alfred E. Oviatt, U.S.D.A. Forest Products Laboratory.

Hardwoods

Hardwoods are bought for beauty and durability. Thus, you'll consider pattern, color, graining, and size when buying. Your selection may be limited by the selection stocked by your local lumberyards. However, in most areas there is a wholesaler who specializes in rare woods, so you can place special orders. Get a quotation first. Rare woods can be surpisingly expensive.

Before you order you will want to consider other characteristics such as workability, nail holding, acceptability to paint, and weight. The table reviewing hardwoods (page 92) tells the characteristics of many commercially available varieties.

Hardwoods graded by the National Hardwood Associations are identified by an asterisk in the table starting on page 94.

Hardwood lumber is graded according to three basic industrial market categories:

Factory lumber reflects the proportion of a piece that can be cut into useful smaller pieces.

Dimension grades are based on the anticipated use of the entire piece.

Finish market products are pieces already finished for end use such as trim molding.

The ease of working hardwood with hand tools generally varies somewhat with the specific gravity of the wood.

Compression parallel to grain—maximum crushing strength	Compression perpendicular to grain— fiber stress at proportional limit	Shear parallel to grain— maximum shearing strength
Kilo-pascals	Kilo-pascals	Kilo-pascals
41,200	4,300	8,700
46,700	4,600	6,500
61,000	7,300	9,200
36,000	3,400	6,100
40,500	5,700	8,200
43,200	3,600	8,500
42,300	5,200	7,000
37,900	5,000	7,500
36,100	3,200	6,300
41,600	4,300	8,600
42,400	3,700	7,600
38,500	3,800	9,200
37,800	4,100	6,800
37,000	3,400	6,800
44,900	6,200	9,000

The lower the specific gravity, the easier it is to cut the wood with a sharp tool. Specific gravity compares the weight of 1 cubic inch of solid material to the weight of 1 cubic inch of water (0.0361 pounds). If you know a wood's specific gravity, you can multiply by 0.0361 to get the actual weight of a cubic inch of that wood.

A wood species that is easy to cut will not necessarily plane to a smooth surface when it is machined. Tests have been made with many United States hardwoods to evaluate them for machining properties. Results of these evaluations are given in the table on page 92. Nailing without splitting depends as much on the moisture content (dry wood splits) and nail sharpness (sharp nails split the wood) as it does on the density and wood structure. The lower the rating for screws and nails, in the table referred to on page 92, the less splitting can be expected.

Three major factors other than density may affect production of smooth surfaces during hardwood machining. These factors are:

(1) interlocked and variable grain; (2) hard mineral deposits; and (3) reaction wood, particularly tension wood.

Interlocked grain is characteristic of the majority of tropical species and presents difficulty in planing quarter-sawed surfaces unless attention is paid to feed rate, cutting angles, and sharpness of knives.

Lumber

Some Machining and Related Properties of Selected Domestic Hardwoods

Kind of Wood[1]	Specific Gravity at 12% MC	Planing	Shaping	Turning	Boring
Alder, red	.41	4	9	2	4
Ash	.49	3	5	3	1
Aspen	.39	8	10	4	3
Basswood	.39	4	10	4	3
Beech	.64	2	8	2	1
Birch	.65	4	5	2	1
Birch, paper	.55	6	8	—	—
Cherry, black	.50	3	3	2	1
Chestnut	.43	3	8	2	1
Cottonwood	.35	8	10	4	4
Elm, soft	.50	7	9	4	1
Hackberry	.53	3	10	3	1
Hickory	.72	3	9	2	1
Magnolia	.48	4	8	3	3
Maple, bigleaf	.48	5	5	3	1
Maple, hard	.54	5	3	2	1
Maple, soft	.47	6	8	3	3
Oak, red	.61	1	8	2	1
Oak, white	.64	2	7	2	1
Pecan	—	2	7	2	1
Sweetgum	.52	5	8	2	1
Sycamore	.49	8	9	2	1
Tanoak	—	3	7	2	1
Tupelo, water	.50	5	5	3	4
Tupelo, black	.50	6	7	3	2
Walnut, black	.55	4	7	1	1
Willow	.39	5	10	5	3
Yellow-poplar	.42	4	9	2	2

Key: Ratings are from 1 (excellent) to 10 (poor)
[1]Commercial lumber nomenclature
 A—Best with resin adhesive.
[2]Softwoods take paint better: Cedar, cypress, redwood rate 1 in paint holding; pine rates 2; fir and spruce rate 3.
Courtesy of Forest Products Laboratory, U.S. Dept. of Agriculture.

Hard deposits, such as calcium carbonate and silica, may have a pronounced dulling effect on all cutting edges. This dulling effect becomes more pronounced as the wood is dried.

Woods that contain tool-dulling minerals include:

Angelique, apitong, kapur, okoume, palosapis, rosewood (Indian), teak.

Mortising	Sanding	Gluing	Nailing	Screwing	Paint Tenacity[2]	
					Require Filling	Rating
5	—	3	—	—		5
5	3	5A	4	3	X	8
5	—	1	—	—		5
5	9	3	6	5		5
1	6	8	6	5		8
1	7	8A	7	6		8
—	—	8	—	—		8
1	—	5A	—	—		8
4	4	1	4	5	X	—
5	9	1	2	3		8
3	4	3A	3	3	X	—
3	—	3	4	4	X	—
1	3	8A	7	4	X	8
7	7	3A	3	3		—
3	—	5A	—	—		8
1	7	8	8	5		8
7	7	5A	5	4		8
1	2	5A	4	3	X	8
1	2	5	4	3	X	8
1	—	5	6	4		—
5	8	3	4	4		—
1	8	5A	3	3		8
1	—	—	—	—		—
7	7	5A	4	4		—
8	8	5	4	4		—
1	—	5	6	5	X	8
8	8	1	2	4		—
4	9	1	3	4		—

Reaction (tension) wood may cause fibrous and fuzzy surfaces. It can be very troublesome in species of lower density. Reaction wood may also be responsible for the pinching effect on saws, due to stress relief. The pinching may result in burning and dulling of the sawteeth.

The following are reaction (tension) woods:

Andiroba, banak, lupuna, mahogany, nogal, sande, Spanish cedar.

In the United States the most commonly used tension wood is mahogany.

Lumber

Review of Wood Species

Type	Characteristics	Used for
Alder, Red	A pale pinkish brown with faint growth ring. Sometimes has scattered flakes. Available in northwestern states. Specific gravity: G.41 Weight: 28.5 lbs./cu. ft.	Sash, doors, panel stock, and millwork
Andiroba (Carapa)	Light to dark reddish brown. Imported. Is not insect-resistant. Easy to work, paint, glue; it looks like but is superior to mahogany in hardness, shear, and toughness. A reaction wood, it may have excessive longitudinal shrinkage when dried below fiber saturation point. Specific gravity: G.44 Weight: 41 lbs./cu. ft.	Flooring, framing, furniture, cabinetwork, and millwork
Arodise	Cream to pale yellow. Imported. It has a natural luster, gradually darkens to a golden yellow, and has interesting figuring. Specific gravity: G.51 Weight: 34 lbs./cu. ft.	Used chiefly as a decorative plywood veneer
Ash[1] Black Blue Green Oregon White	Strong, heavy, hard, tough, elastic, durable, tight straight grain. Resists shrinkage. Looks like oak; pale tan color. Tends to split easily. Specific gravity: G.60 (white ash) Weight: 41 lbs./cu. ft.	Cabinets, furniture, boxes, millwork, hammer and ax handles, and sports equipment such as tennis racquets and baseball bat
Aspen[1] Bigtooth Quaking Northern	White sapwood, tan and brown streaked heartwood. Easy to work—soft and light in weight. Indoor use only. Has interesting mottled pattern crossing grain. Specific gravity: G.39 (bigtooth) Weight: 27 lbs./cu. ft.	Paneling and furniture

Review of Wood Species (Continued)

Type	Characteristics	Used for
Balsa	This white imported wood is a favorite of model builders, being the lightest of all woods and easy to carve. Soft but longitudinally strong. Specific gravity: G.17 Weight: 12 lbs./cu. ft.	Flotation, model making, and kites
Banak	Pinkish brown and straight-grained. First-class veneer. Ilamba is similar but coarser textured. Both are imports. Specific gravity: G.45 Weight: 31 lbs./cu. ft.	Veneers and utility uses
Basswood, American[1]	Does not twist or warp and cuts, screws, and nails easily. Very uniform but shrinks and is soft, light, weak, brittle, and not durable. Light yellow with a brown tinge and hardly noticeable grain. Specific gravity: G.37 Weight: 26 lbs./cu. ft.	Drawing boards, plywood core stock, interior finish, moldings, woodenware, drawers and shelving, as well as millwork
Beech, American[1]	Heavy, hard, and strong. Works easily and takes a high polish. Close grain with a maple sugar color. Poor exterior durability. Shrinks and checks. Specific gravity: G.64 Weight: 44 lbs./cu. ft.	Interior finish, wood dowels, flooring, furniture, carving, boxes, crates, and tool handles
Birch[1] Paper Sweet Yellow	A reddish-brown heartwood and white sapwood. Similar properties to beech—hard, strong. Not suitable for outdoor exposure. Works easily and is a good base for white enamel. Specific gravity: G.65 Sweet Weight: 46 lbs./cu. ft.	Cabinetwork, imitation mahogany, good-quality furniture doors, trim, plywood, dowels, and toothpicks
Boxwood	A yellow hardwood with indistinct grain pattern. Imported. Specific gravity: G.38 Weight: 26 lbs./cu. ft.	Rulers and inlay

Lumber

Review of Wood Species (Continued)

Type	Characteristics	Used for
Cherry, Black[1]	A scarce wood, which is unfortunate, as it has the best machining properties (planing, shaping, turning, boring, and mortising) of the commercially available hardwoods; although ash, birch, hickory, maple, and pecan are close. Moderately heavy, hard, and strong, cherry can be sanded to a fine finish. A red-brown with multilayered grain-patterned heartwood. Specific gravity: G.50 Weight: 36 lbs./cu. ft.	Fine furniture, spindles, chair legs and backs
Chestnut, American[1]	Due to a blight in the eastern United States this is presently available only in a wormy grade. It has a durable, coarse-textured, reddish-brown heartwood with large pores and broad, bold annular rings. Easy to work, moderately hard. Specific gravity: G.43 Weight: 45 lbs./cu. ft.	Used for stairs, doors, rectory tables and benches, door frames, or wherever the aged appearance of the worm holes adds attraction. Also used for paneling, trim, and picture frames
Cottonwood[1] Eastern and swamp Carolina poplar Whitewood Swamp and river cottonwood Swamp poplar Black and balsam cottonwood	Gradual shift from gray-white or light brown heartwood to whitish sapwood. Straight grain, uniform texture, odorless. Soft and limber, with low bending and compressive strength. Large shrinkage. Hard to work as tension-wood causes fuzzy surfaces. Warps, shrinks, and rots but is available in wide boards and holds nails well. Low cost. Specific gravity: G.31 to .41 Weight: 26 lbs./cu. ft.	Boxes, lumber veneer, cheap furniture, and temporary buildings

Review of Wood Species (Continued)

Type	Characteristics	Used for
Elm[1] American ⎱ **Soft** Slippery ⎰ Rock ⎱ Winged ⎱ **Hard** Cedar ⎰ September ⎰	Dutch elm disease and a blight (phloem necrosis) have decimated these beautiful trees. The sapwood is white, the heartwood light brown. Hard elms have Hard elms have excellent bending properties and are heavier than soft elms. Soft elms have high shock resistance. Elm is slippery, heavy, hard, tough, and durable. G.46-.50, Rock G.57-.63, slippery G.48-.53 Weight: 32 to 44 lbs./cu. ft.	Used for barrel staves and bent tool handles. As a veneer for furniture and boxes. Each type is known by other names: American as white, water, or gray elm; rock as cork or hickory elm; winged as wahoo. Slippery, cedar, and September are also called red elm
Hickory[1] True Shagbark Pigment Shellbark Mockernut	Hickory is exceptionally tough, heavy, hard, and strong but shrinks considerably in drying. It check-splits easily and is difficult to shape. It is subject to decay and insect attack. Sapwood is white, heartwood is reddish. Excellent for boring, mortising, turning, planing, and sanding. Specific gravity: G.69 to .75 Weight: 48 to 49 lbs./cu. ft.	Has high shock resistance, making knot-free lumber ideal for tool handles. Also used for ladder rungs, dowels, poles, balance bars. Hickory chips are popular for flavoring meat by smoking
Holly, American	Both heartwood and sapwood are white. Takes dyes exceptionally well. Specific gravity: G.63 Weight: 44 lbs./cu. ft.	Furniture inlays and marquetry
Inboya and Koa	Similar to walnut. Hard and heavy. Dark brown. Specific gravity: B.44 Weight: 41 lbs./cu. ft.	Wood carvings, cabinets, musical instruments, paneling, and quality furniture
Lacewood	Beautiful figuring, yellow swirling curlicue grain on tan background. Best if quarter-sawn. Specific gravity: G.44 Weight: 31 lbs./cu. ft.	Overlays, tabletops, and wall paneling

Lumber

Review of Wood Species (Continued)

Type	Characteristics	Used for
Ligrum Vitae	Imported. One of the hardest, densest, heaviest, and oiliest woods. Green in color. So hard it requires carbide-tip tools. Is self-lubricating, having a resin content about one-fourth of the air-dry weight of the heartwood. Overharvested and now scarce. Specific gravity: G.1.09 Weight: 72 lbs./cu. ft.	Block sheaves, pulleys, mallet heads, and shaft bearings exposed to water
Magnolia[1]	Also known as sweet bay, bull bay, cucumber tree, and laurel bay. Sapwood is yellow-white while heartwood is yellow tinged brown. All of its properties can be described as moderate. Resembles yellow poplar. Specific gravity: G.48 Weight: 33.5 lbs./cu. ft.	Used for doors, window sashes and frames, furniture, veneer, and millwork
Mahoganies	Different types from different sources have unique properties, as described below. Requires filling but takes a beautiful finish.	One of the most popular woods for furniture, cabinets, paneling, decks, trim, and carvings
Honduras Mahogany	Turns and carves particularly well. Handsome, even mocha color.	Turned salad bowls and tabletops
African Mahogany[1]	Coarser texture, but has a swirling grain pattern improved by quarter cutting.	Furniture
Philippine Mahogany[1]	The poor man's mahogany, having a more variable coloring and coarse, open grain. Specific gravity: G.46 Weight: 32 lbs./cu. ft.	Furniture, trim, and plywood core stock
Maple[1] Sugar } **Hard** Black {	The sapwood, often 3″ to 5″ wide, is white with a slight reddish-brown tinge. Heartwood may be reddish-brown or darker. Hard maple	Used for flooring, furniture, bowling alleys, tool handles, boxes, woodenware, and countertops

Review of Wood Species (Continued)

Type	Characteristics	Used for
Maple (continued) Big Leaf—**Oregon**	has a fine uniform texture but is hard to work with hand tools; it machines easily. Is heavy, strong, stiff, hard, and resistant to shock. Has large shrinkage. Good grades of soft maple can be used in place of hard maple. Sometimes available with curly birdseye or fiddleback grain. Not too durable. Specific gravity: G.48-.63 Weight: 44 lbs./cu. ft.	
Silver } **Soft** Red }		
Oak[1]—White Chestnut oak Overcup oak Swamp chestnut oak Swamp white oak Bur oak Chinkapin oak Live oak	Sapwood is nearly white, the heartwood a grayish brown and filled with tyloses—a membranous growth that makes oaks impenetrable by liquids (except for chestnut oak), which is why oak was chosen for building ships and cooperage. The heartwood is moderately decay-resistant. White oak is heavy, hard, and strong. Hard to work with hand tools but easy with power tools. Specific gravity: G.64-.72 (Live oak, G.88) Weight: 47 lbs./cu. ft.	Furniture, carvings, lumber, high-quality planks and millwork, doors, interior finish, boat trim, barrels, and as fuel lumber
Oak[1]—Red Northern red Scarlet Shumard Pin Nuttall Black Southern red Cherry bark Water Laurel Willow English	Sapwood is nearly white, the heartwood brown with a tinge of red. Can be distinguished from white oak because it lacks tyloses. Very tough, hard wood difficult to work with hand tools. Large shrinkage in drying. Specific gravity: G.61-.69 Weight: 45 lbs./cu. ft.	Lumber, flooring, furniture, trim, picture frames, tabletops, trays, millwork, wood ware, handles, crates, boxes, and pallets. Veneer, fence posts, railroad ties, and as a fuel wood. Develops an interesting flake pattern when quarter-sawn

Lumber

Review of Wood Species (Continued)

Type	Characteristics	Used for
Pearwood	A fine-textured yellowish wood with vague grain pattern and occasional mottling. Specific gravity: G.40 Weight: 28 lbs./cu. ft.	Fine furniture, rulers, and marquetry
Poplar, Yellow[1]	Olive-brown heartwood with grayish-white sapwood. Soft, light in weight, even textured. Resists warping and works well with hand or machine tools. Holds nails well. Specific gravity: G.40-.46 Weight: 34 lbs./cu. ft.	Toys, trunks, interior finishing, shelves, drawers, and boxes. Core stock for plywood
Rosewood Brazilian	Overharvested, it is now scarce. So heavy it will hardly float. Russet brown to black with black grain. Specific gravity: G.75 Weight: 52 lbs./cu. ft.	Musical instruments, billiard cue butts, and other turned items. Veneer for plywood
Indian	Purplish brown. Contains calcareous deposits that dull tools. Hard to work. Specific gravity: G.76 Weight: 53 lbs./cu. ft.	Decorative veneer
Sweet Gum[1]	Heartwood is a dark reddish brown, while the sapwood is a light color. Moderately heavy, hard, strong, and stiff and fairly high in shock resistance. Stains well. Machines well but needs careful drying, as it has a tendency to warp. Specific gravity: G.52 Weight: 36 lbs./cu. ft.	TV, radio, and phonograph cabinets; interior trim; millwork; cabinets; furniture; and paneling
Sycamore[1]	Reddish-brown heartwood with lighter sapwood. Fine texture with interlocking faint grain. All characteristics are moderate—hardness, weight, stiffness, strength—but has good resistance to shock. Specific gravity: G.49 Weight: 34 lbs./cu. ft.	Used for veneers, fences, furniture, flooring, and chopping blocks. Also decorative panels, door skins, and as a fuel

Review of Wood Species (Continued)

Type	Characteristics	Used for
Tan Oak	A light reddish-brown wood that gets darker with age. Glues and stains easily. Heavy and hard. Specific gravity: G.58 Weight: 41 lbs./cu. ft.	Baseball bats, flooring, high-quality furniture, and veneers
Teak	Imported. The heartwood varies from yellow-brown to chocolate. Coarse texture, straight grain, oily feel. Naturally durable and dimensionally stable. Contains silica, which dulls tools. Does not cause rust in contact with metal. Scarce and one of the most expensive of all woods. Specific gravity: G.63 Weight: 44 lbs./cu. ft.	Decking and trim on expensive boats, furniture, flooring, carvings, and veneer
Tupelo	Has a dozen different names (and four species) such as black gum, swamp tupelo, black tupelo, sour gum, oggeechee tupelo, and gopher plum. Heartwood is brownish-gray and merges with a slightly lighter and wide sapwood. Weight varies by location on trunk—the lower part that grows in swamps is lighter than the top part of the tree. Specific gravity: G.50 Weight: 34-36 lbs./cu. ft.	Cut for lumber, veneer, furniture, boxes, and crates
Walnut, Black[1]	Sapwood is nearly white, but heartwood varies from a light to a very dark brown. Straight-grained walnut is easy to work with all tools. It is heavy, hard, strong, stiff, and resists shock. Well suited for natural finishes and accepts steam bending. Generally expensive and scarce. Specific gravity: G.59 Weight: 38 lbs./cu. ft.	Architectural woodwork, gun stocks, musical instruments, quality furniture, plywood veneer, cabinets, doors, mantlepieces, and paneling

Lumber

Review of Wood Species (Concluded)

Type	Characteristics	Used for
Willow, Black	Sapwood is creamy yellow, while the heartwood is gray to reddish brown. Light in weight with uniform texture, it has very low beam strength, is soft, and is easily dented, although it has good shock resistance. Tends to fuzz when machine planed. Specific gravity: G.36-.39 Weight: 27 lbs./cu. ft.	Used for subflooring, roof and wall sheathing and studding. Often used as a veneer in furniture and toys. Used as a core stock in plywood.

[1]Woods that are graded by the National Hardwood Association.

NOTES:

Specific gravity based on oven-dry weight and volume at 12% MC (moisture content).

Weight per cubic foot based on weight and volume at 12% MC.

Specific gravity is used for determining allowable loads for nails and staples and is reflected in specifications for size and spacing.

All numbers given are comparative approximations that will vary by piece and, depending on the moisture content, in use. In a dry house, lumber kiln dried to 12% may balance out at 6%.

Toxic Woods

Some woods are known to cause allergic, toxic, infectious, or respiratory reactions. Although researchers point out that not everyone is equally sensitive to these woods, they warn that woodworkers should be particularly cautious when sanding or milling them. In the table the category "respiratory ailments" includes bronchial disorders, asthma, rhinitis, and mucosal irritations; "skin and eye allergies" includes contact dermatitis, conjunctivitis, itching, and rashes.

Toxic Reactions to Certain Woods

Respiratory Ailments	Skin and Eye Allergies	
✔		Arbor vitae (Thuja standishii)
✔	✔	Boxwood, Knysan (Gonioma kamassi)
✔	✔	Cedar, western red (Thuja plicata)
✔	✔	Ebony (Diospyros)
✔	✔	Iroko (Chlorophora excelsa)
✔	✔	Mahogany, African (Khaya ivorensis)
	✔	Mahogany, American (Swietenia macrophylla)
	✔	Rosewood, Brazilian (Dalbergia nigra)
	✔	Rosewood, East Indian (Dalbergia latifolia)
✔		Sequoia Redwood (Sequoia sempervirens)
	✔	Teak (Tectona grandis)

"Toxic Woods" by Brian Woods and C. D. Calnan (British Journal of Dermatology, Vol. 95, Supplement 13, 1976) is an excellent source on skin reactions to woods, with case histories and an inclusive list of toxic species.

Plywood

Plywood is now the product of choice for jobs such as subflooring, roof decking, and sheathing. Its use extends to countertops, siding, and many other applications. Its popularity is due to its low price and high strength.

Plywood is made of thin veneers of wood glued together in a sandwich. The grain of one layer runs perpendicular to the grain of its neighbors, which is what gives plywood its strength and resistance to warp. Common thicknesses run from 1/4″ to 3/4″. The near-universal size of a sheet is 4′ × 8′, although some mills make lengths of 9′ and 10′ for special sheathing needs.

When you buy plywood, you'll be asked to specify which grade of quality you want. Grades are N, A, B, C, and D (see table below), N and A being finishes you could stain and show off in your living room, and D being something you'll cover with roofing shingles. A nice feature of plywood is that, often as not, the board you buy will have two letters; one grading the front, the other grading the back. And after all, if you'll be showing only one side, why pay extra for an A-A board?

For many people, the foregoing is all they need or want to know about plywood. But if you do need to know more, the American Plywood Association has made your job incredibly easy. Its labeling program can tell you everything about the board you're buying. Typical trademark with callouts explaining what each number and description means is shown on page 108. The trademark will appear on the least finished side of the

Veneer Grades

N	Smooth surface "natural finish" veneer. Select, all heartwood or all sapwood. Free of open defects. Allows not more than 6 repairs, wood only, per 4 × 8 panel, made parallel to grain and well matched for grain and color.
A	Smooth, paintable. Not more than 18 neatly made repairs, boat, sled, or router type, and parallel to grain, permitted. May be used for natural finish in less demanding applications.
B	Solid surface. Shims, circular repair plugs and tight knots to 1″ across grain permitted. Some minor splits permitted.
C— Plugged	Improved C veneer with splits limited to $\frac{1}{8}$″ width and knotholes and borer holes limited to $\frac{1}{4}$″ × $\frac{1}{2}$″. Admits some broken grain. Synthetic repairs permitted.
C	Tight knots to $1\frac{1}{2}$″. Knotholes to 1″ across grain and some to $1\frac{1}{2}$″ if total width of knots and knotholes is within specified limits. Synthetic or wood repairs. Discoloration and sanding defects that do not impair strength permitted. Limited splits allowed. Stitching permitted.
D	Knots and knotholes to $2\frac{1}{2}$″ width across grain and $\frac{1}{2}$″ larger within specified limits. Limited splits are permitted. Stitching permitted. Limited to interior (Exposure 1 or 2) panels.

Lumber

plywood or, if both sides are finished, on the edge.

To help you, here is what each call-out on the APA trademark means.

APA. Signifies that the manufacturer has agreed to comply with the American Plywood Association's program of quality supervision and testing and has agreed to submit to an APA audit.

Panel grade. Panel grades are generally identified in terms of the grade of veneer used for face and back plies (A-B, B-C, etc.), or by a name suggesting the panel's intended end use (APA RATED SHEATHING, APA RATED STURD-I-FLOOR, etc.).

Veneer grades define veneer appearance in terms of natural unrepaired growth characteristics and allowable number and size of repairs that may be made during manufacture. The highest-quality veneer grades are N and A. D-grade veneer is the lowest grade veneer and used only for backs and inner plies of panels intended for interior use or applications protected from exposure to permanent or severe moisture.

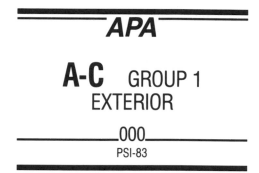

Veneer Graded Trademark

The panel may be graded "303 Siding." "303" is the number of the FHA bulletin covering siding. If no other number follows the 303, it is a top-of-the-line product with no patches permitted. The numbers that follow—such as in 303-6, 303-18, 303-30—indicate that 6, 18, or 30 wood or synthetic patches are permitted per 4' × 8' foot panel. The group number tells the ranking of the lowest of the two face veneers. The seventy species of wood used for plywood veneer are ranked into five groups by strength and stiffness properties (see table titled Group Number Classifications, page 106). The lower the number, the stronger, and stiffer the wood.

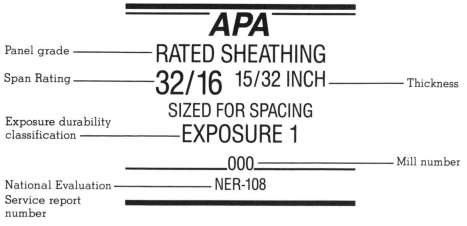

Typical Registered Trademark

APA

303 SIDING 6-S

24 OC GROUP 1

EXTERIOR

———000———

PS 1-74 FHA-UM-64

Span ratings. Products intended for sheathing, flooring, and siding carry ratings appearing as two numbers separated by a slash. The left-hand number is for roof sheathing and denotes the maximum span when the long dimension is installed across at least three supports. The right-hand number denotes the maximum span for flooring.

If the product is designated as Sturd-I-floor, the product can be used for single-layer floor applications under carpet or flexible floor covering. The span ratings will be given as 16," 20," 24," or 48." 303 sidings will have a number, such as 16 or 24, which indicates the largest span between rows of nails over other structural bases or studs. 303 siding can be used horizontally, attached on 16" or 24" spacing, providing the horizontal joint is blocked.

Thickness and dimensions. Unlike other lumber, this is the actual dimension plus or minus 1/32." Panel sizes are normally 4' by 8', but 48" by 95½" sheathing panels are made to always meet over the rafters, studs, or joists. If the panels are the full 96" and a slight space is left between each, on a larger roof the last panels would start overlapping the rafter. On a 95½" panel the stamp will say "sized for spacing."

Exposure durability. There are four exposure classifications: Exterior, Exposure 1, Exposure 2, and Interior.

Exterior panels are made with 100 percent waterproof phenolic glue that can take continuous exposure to the weather without delaminating. While the bond can take the exposure, the plywood veneer facing can still deteriorate due to ultraviolet radiation, water, or pollutants, so the face should be stained, coated, or painted, particularly if left directly exposed. For long-term exterior exposure, pressure-treated plywood would be a better choice.

Exposure 1 panels (called CDX in the trade) use the same bonding but often less rugged facings. They can stand moisture and exposure during building construction but are designed to be covered or secured in protected locations, such as under roof overhangs. If Exposure 1 panels are pressure treated to AWBP (American Wood Preservers Bureau) FDN (foundation) standards, they can be used on the exterior of permanent wood foundations, even though constantly exposed to weather at the top and damp soil below. However, you must use the approved type 304 or 316 stainless 8d nails or 16 gauge 1½" stainless staples. Even above ground with Exterior or Exposure 1 plywood, you should use galvanized or other corrosion-resistant nails to prevent staining and dark streaks.

Exposure 2 panels are designed for interior use or protected construction applications, and only moderate construction exposure is expected. These panels are hot-pressed using phenolic glue, but the facings are more delicate.

Interior panels are manufactured with interior glues and should not be subjected to weather exposure.

Lumber

Group Number Classifications*

Group 1	Group 2	Group 3	Group 4	Group 5
Apitong	Cedar, Port	Adler, Red	Aspen	Basswood
Beech,	Orford	Birch, Paper	Bigtooth	Poplar, Balsam
American	Cypress	Cedar, Alaska	Quaking	
Birch	Douglas Fir	Fir, Subalpine	Cativo	
Sweet	No. 2[1]	Hemlock,	Cedar	
Yellow	Fir	Eastern	Incense	
Douglas Fir	Balsam	Maple, Bigleaf	Western	
No. 1[1]	California	Pine	Red	
Kapur	Red	Jack	Cottonwood	
Keruing	Grand	Lodgepole	Eastern	
Larch, Western	Noble	Ponderosa	Black	
Maple, Sugar	Pacific	Spruce	(Western	
Pine	White	Redwood	Poplar)	
Caribbean	Hemlock,	Spruce	Pine	
Ocote	Western	Engelmann	Eastern	
Pine, South	Lauan	White	White	
Loblolly	Almon		Sugar	
Longleaf	Bagtikan			
Shortleaf	Mayapis			
Slash	Red			
Tan Oak	Tangile			
	White			
	Maple, Black			
	Mengkulang			
	Meranti,			
	Red[2]			
	Mersawa			
	Pine			
	Pond			
	Red			
	Virginia			
	Western			
	White			
	Spruce			
	Black			
	Red			
	Sitka			
	Sweet Gum			
	Tamarack			
	Yellow-Poplar			

[1]Douglas Fir from trees grown in the states of Washington, Oregon, California, Idaho, Montana, Wyoming, and the Canadian Provinces of Alberta and British Columbia shall be classed as Douglas Fir No. 1. Douglas Fir from trees grown in the states of Nevada, Utah, Colorado, Arizona and New Mexico shall be classed as Douglas Fir No. 2.

[2]Red Meranti shall be limited to species having a specific gravity of 0.41 or more based on green volume and oven-dry weight.

*American Plywood Association Species Grades.

These wood species are graded under Product Standard PSI-66 according to stiffness of the face and backplys of plywood. The group is indicated by a group number under the appearance grade on the American Plywood Association grade trademark stamped on the plywood. Group 1 is the stiffest wood, group 5 the most flexible.

Vapor barriers. Exterior and Exposure 1 and 2 plywood panels can be used in lieu of a vapor barrier if joints are sealed with glue or a vapor barrier tape. A common example is the subfloor over an insulated basement floor. The advantage of this is that you can glue-nail the floor, which would be impossible if the joists were covered with polyethylene. **Caution:** Interior grade plywood does not provide a satisfactory vapor barrier.

Mill number. If you find you need more panels than you purchased, it's handy to have the mill number; you'll stand a better chance of getting a match. The mill number is directly below the exposure declaration on the APA stamp. If you have a complaint, the mill number will enable your lumberyard to get in touch with the manufacturer.

Product standards. The bottom line on the APA stamp tells the standard to which the particular product was made. Most plywoods conform to the production, marketing, and specification standard jointly developed by the U.S. Department of Commerce and the plywood industry known as PSI-83. For structural applications, always use a PSI-83 product. For very demanding jobs, Structural 1 rated sheathing should be used.

On this same line, you may find reference to FHA-UM-64, which means the product complies with Specification 64 in the Federal Housing Administration "Use of Materials" bulletins. If building to FHA requirements, you will need to get this bulletin from the Government Printing Office.

APA Performance-rated Panels.

For less demanding jobs and a multitude of projects around the home, you can use performance-rated panels.

Some of these do meet the U.S. Product Standard PSI-83 for construction. Others may be panel constructions, veneer grades, or species not recognized in PSI. This may be due to lower strength, but on nonstructural interior jobs you may want to use them because of the desirable hardwood veneers on decorative panels. These may carry a high price tag if the wood species is rare, or they may be lower-cost particle- or waferboard.

Formaldehyde Out-gassing.

Phenolic adhesives used in plywood have less out-gassing than formaldehyde adhesives used in decorative hardwood paneling. The industry is trying to find suitable nongassing adhesives for bonding hardwood, but most carry a heavy cost penalty. Some mills will supply these, but they are scarce. High heat combined with humidity induces out-gassing. By buying your panels ahead of time and storing them in a shelter outdoors, much of the odor will disappear by the time you use them.

Specialty Panels.

These are designed for special applications. *Plyform®* is designed for concrete forms. *Overlay panels* are designed to take paint for uses such as signage. *Marine,* as its name suggests, is manufactured from Douglas fir or Western larch for boat hulls and other marine uses. *Decorative panels* are designed for interior accent walls, counter facing, paneling, built-ins and, in Exterior grade, for use as siding. *Plyron®* is a non-PSI plywood panel with hardwood on each side. Faces can be tempered, untempered, smooth, or screened for use as counter-tops, cabinet doors, and concentrated-load flooring. Thicknesses vary by type from $11/32''$ to $3/4''$.

Lumber

Pressure-treated Lumber

Pressure-treated lumber is becoming increasingly popular for outside construction projects that must resist rot, decay, and insect and fungus attacks. Wood and plywood is dehydrated under vacuum and then impregnated under pressure with water-borne preservatives that leave the wood fibers toxic as a food source for fungi and insects (termites). One of the common trade names for this process is "Wolmanizing," which imparts a greenish cast to the wood. In this process, a preservative solution is inserted at high pressure into the wood cells of selected species such as Southern pine, Western hemlock, Douglas fir, and Ponderosa pine. The chemicals react with wood sugars, fixing the preservative chemicals in the wood and providing resistance against rot and decay without need for continuous renewal or maintenance. Many manufacturers of pressure-treated lumber guarantee their product against decay for 30 years.

The treated wood can be sawed, drilled, nailed, and chiseled. Clean and odorless, pressure-treated lumber can be stained or painted when dry (allow two months if the lumber has not been redried after treatment) or left unfinished to weather to a driftwood gray color. (This is not true of commercial treatments using creosote or Penta.) Use only wood treated by water-base preservatives such as chromated copper arsenate (CCA), ammoniacal copper arsenate (ACA), acid copper chromate (ACC), and chromated zinc chloride (CZX). CCA is the most common.

Some of the more popular residential projects using pressure-treated lumber are decks, fences, and outdoor furniture. Hot-dipped galvanized or stainless steel nails should be used.

Use 10d nails for 2" dimension lumber, 8d for 1" to 2" boards, and 6d for lesser thicknesses.

A Typical AWPB Quality Mark

ABC LUMBER CO.
CITY, STATE

LEGEND
A Year of treatment
B American Wood Preservers Bureau trademark
C The preservative used for treatment
D The applicable American Wood Preservers Bureau quality standard
E Trademark of the agency supervising treating plant
F Proper exposure conditions
G Treating company and plant location
H Dry or KDAT, if applicable

Pressure-treated Wood Stamps (Ground Contact Shown)

Pressure-treated lumber is also gaining acceptance as the primary ingredient for the "all-weather wood foundation" or "permanent wood foundation" a wood-frame wall system designed for below-grade use as a foundation for light-frame construction.

Pressure-treated lumber and plywood are sold in the same sizes as nontreated lumber and plywood and are available at most lumberyards. Make sure the lumber or plywood carries the AWPB (American Wood Preservers Bureau) seal of third-party inspection and, if used for ground contact, the AWPB-FDN label (see illustration above). The wood will bear

Selection Guide for Pressure-Treated Timber

Application	Preservative Retention (In pounds per cu. ft.)	Typical Uses	Grade
Aboveground use	0.25	Decking, fencing, sills, railings, joists	LP-2 AWPB
Soil or freshwater contact (nonstructural)	0.40	Posts, landscape timbers, grape stakes, retaining walls	AWPB-FDN
Soil or freshwater contact (Structural)	0.60	Wood foundations, building poles	LP-22
Piles—soil or freshwater	0.80	Foundation piles	
Saltwater contact	2.5	Timbers, bulkheads, pilings	

its original grading marks plus the treatment grade LP-2 for aboveground or LP-22 for ground contact.

Caution: Never burn scrap pressure-treated wood. It will produce toxic smoke. Dispose of it with your trash. When pressure treated-lumber is sawed the exposed ends must be treated. The use of these chemicals is subject to regulation by the Environmental Protection Agency. Consult your local wood preserver. It may pay to buy and cut your lumber or timber to size and then have it pressure-treated.

Manufactured Wood Panels

Because they have the strength of plywood at a considerably lower price, manufactured wood products are rapidly becoming the choice of builders and do-it-yourselfers for underlayments, wall and roof sheathing, and other covered areas. The "good-two-side" feature of some panel types lends them to such applications as shelving, interior paneling, and even cabinets.

Panel products are made from softwood scrap edges and trim, which are ground into particles, chips, wafers, and flakes, then bonded with resins under heat and pressure to form a variety of products having unique, practical, and cost-saving advantages.

These panels can be manufactured similar to conventional veneered plywood (as composites with veneer faces bonded to reconstituted wood cores) or as nonveneered panels (such as particleboard, waferboard, or oriented-strand board).

Some panel products are coded by the American Plywood Association and marked APA Rated Sheathing or APA Rated Sturd-I-Floor. These products are designed and manufactured to meet specific performance criteria and carry the APA label, showing the span rating and exposure-durability classification.

Be aware that these and other reconstituted pulp products may create formaldehyde out-gassing. If you are sensitive to this, avoid their use or buy the materials weeks before you need them and air them out. Seal them before installing.

Manufactured panels are supplied as veneered, nonveneered, and composite. Veneered panels are made from a number of cross-laminated layers. The grain of each layer runs perpendicular to its adjacent layers to increase strength and stiffness. The grain on the outer layers normally runs parallel. Each layer may consist of one or more plies, and the inner layers may

Lumber

be thicker than the outer layers. Plywood decorating paneling, and hardboard are examples of veneered panels.

Composite panels are made with a nonveneered core covered on both sides with a veneer. The core can be reconstituted wood or low-density material such as plastic foam or honeycomb paper. The veneer is often plywood, decorative hardwood, or hardboard. Panels using the low-density material are also called "sandwich" panels. Using the reconstituted wood provides a strong, stiff panel at a considerably reduced cost, while the low-density core delivers a strong, lightweight structure.

Hardboard is made from *very fine* softwood pulp that has been forced into sheets under heat and pressure. Its faces may be tempered to provide a harder and more moisture-resistant finish. Hardboard panels may be purchased with one or both sides smooth.

Standard hardboard is usually finished on one side and textured on the other. The finished side is often tempered, and in this form, it is used for cabinets, drawer bottoms, or concealed panels. When perforated with spaced round holes it is known as "pegboard," commonly used for hanging tools or garden implements in workshops. When the smooth surface is prepainted it is called enameled hardboard and is used for wall or bath paneling. Enameled hardboard is often embossed with tile or plank patterns. Plastic laminated hardboard is often used on sliding doors because it is decorative and easy to clean.

Hardboard panels are usually 4' wide and come in standard lengths of 8', 10', 12'. Standard thicknesses are 1/8" and 1/4", although other thicknesses are available. Some dealers will cut to the size you need.

Reconstituted boards have both advantages and liabilities. They are heavier than plywood. They are harder to nail and saw. When wet they swell—more at the edge than in the center—a bad problem when used as roof sheathing. However, they have no voids, will not delaminate, and provide a more consistent nailing base for power nailers. Avoid buying panels labeled "seconds"—they are rejects that may delaminate later. Make sure you allow a space between panels. (Sheathing: 1/8" at end joints and 1/4" at edge joints. Sturdi-floor: 1/8" at ends and edges.) Look for the APA mark to check appropriate spans and exposures.

Particleboard is manufactured from reconstituted wood particles (larger than pulp). Because of the high percentage of bonding resin, it is subject to formaldehyde out-gassing. One solution is to thoroughly seal and paint it for indoor use. Then it can be used as an underlayment or closet shelving. Some specific classes of particleboard qualify as structural panels under APA performance standards. Normal thicknesses are 3/8", 1/2", 5/8", and 3/4". Panels are sold in standard 4' widths and 8', 10', or 12' lengths. Some jobbers sell particleboard in standard shelving widths (8", 10", and 12").

Oriented-strand board (OSB) is manufactured from compressed strandlike wood particles and bonded with phenolic resin. The product is commonly used instead of plywood due to its lower cost. OSB panels are rated by the American Plywood Association for protected residential and light-frame construction applications, including subflooring and wall and roof sheathing. Sometimes OSB is used as the core of composite panels, due to its low cost and high strength. Structural OSB panels are made of three to five perpendicularly arranged layers.

Panels are usually 4′ wide and come in lengths of 8′, 10′, and 12′, although longer lengths are available. The most common thicknesses are $\frac{3}{8}$″, $\frac{7}{16}$″, $\frac{1}{2}$″, $\frac{19}{32}$″, $\frac{5}{8}$″, $\frac{23}{32}$″, and $\frac{3}{4}$″. Either square or tongue-and-groove edges are available, and the edges can be sealed with a waterproof sealer. Surfaces can be sanded smooth during manufacture, although additional underlayment layers are recommended when thin, nontextile, resilient flooring is applied over oriented-strand board.

Waferboard is manufactured from waferlike wood chips or flakes bonded with phenolic resin. The flakes may range in size and thickness and may be either randomly or directionally oriented. In some cases the wafers may also be arranged in layers according to size and thickness. Waferboard is used as subflooring and wall or roof sheathing in residential or light-frame construction. Its "good-two-sides" feature lends to its use as shelving or interior paneling.

Panels are usually 4′ wide and come in lengths from 8′ up to 16′. Shorter lengths are available on special order. Common panel thicknesses are $\frac{7}{16}$″, $\frac{1}{2}$″, $\frac{5}{8}$″, and $\frac{3}{4}$″. Panel edges are either square or tongue-and-groove and can be sealed with water-repellent sealer at the factory. Surfaces can be sanded smooth at the factory.

Decorative paneling is designed for interior walls. Panels come in a diversity of hardwood and softwood facings and finishes. Usually supplied 3-ply and $\frac{1}{4}$″ thick 4′ × 8′ sheets, but thinner and thicker panels are available. The more expensive varieties have a real wood veneer and are often acrylic- or urethane coated. Simulated wood-grain panels are created by printing on a paper or plastic substrate applied to the plywood. These panels are more regular in pattern but cannot match the depth or beauty of true veneers. However, these panels are less costly. Panels with plastic or paper substrate should not be used in areas of high heat or humidity. Simulated wood grain panels cost between $6 and $16 while real veneer plywood can cost between $19 and $34 per 4′ × 8′ panel.

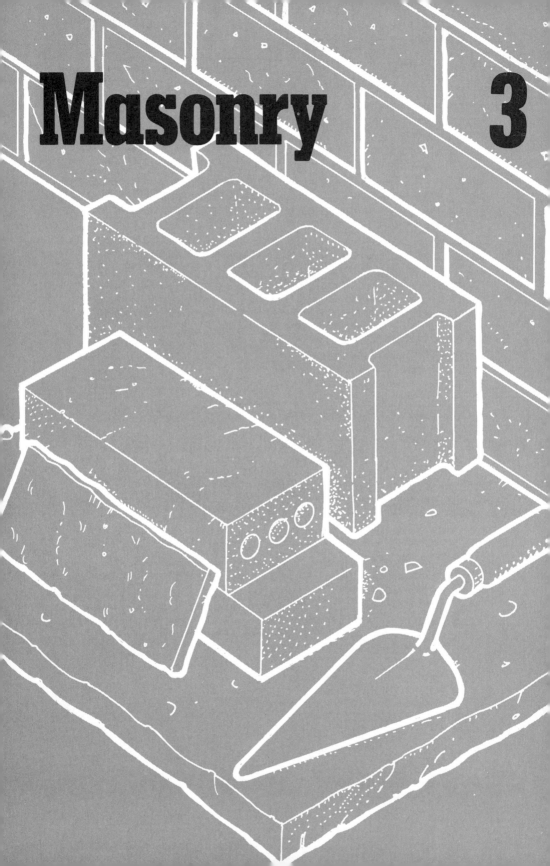

Masonry

3

3. Masonry

Whether you're building a barbecue, pouring a patio, installing a walkway, or laying up a retaining wall, you'll need the information in this chapter. Masonry is the most ancient of building materials; it also requires the most strength and endurance to handle. But most home projects, especially the small ones, are well within the capabilities of the average do-it-yourselfer.

This chapter discusses brick, mortar, stone, concrete, and concrete blocks.

Whatever your project, you will need the tools of the trade. You will also need to know how to buy and mix mortar. These two subjects are covered first.

Tools

Other than a wheelbarrow, the tools used for masonry work are relatively inexpensive. It doesn't matter whether you are using a ready-mix mortar or mixing your own, you'll need a *mortar box*. A steel box, available from your masonry supply house, is a sound investment if you plan on several jobs. Or, for pointing or a small job, a cheap plastic box is available.

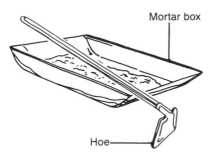
Mortar box

Hoe

You will need a *wheelbarrow* to carry the brick or block and maybe the batch of mortar. The two-wheeled variety (the rugged professional model with pipe frame) with sloping ends is easier to

steel wheelbarrow

move and control than the regular single wheeler unless the ground is wet and you need to run on planks. In fact, for pointing jobs you can use one of these as your mortar box.

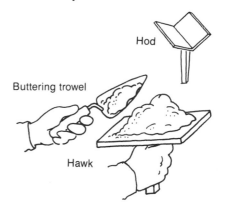
Hod

Buttering trowel

Hawk

To carry your mix at the work site you'll need a *hawk* (not to be confused with a *hod,* which is larger and used to carry brick or block). It should have a surface of at least 10″ × 10″ and a large enough dowel handle (at least 1″ in diameter) so your hand doesn't

Spoteboard

Masonry

get cramped. Your *spoteboard* (mortarboard) should have 2 x 4's underneath to keep it level and be about 3' square. To carry bricks you'll find a hod indispensable.

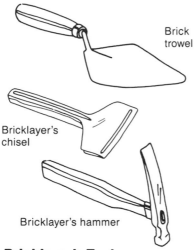

Brick trowel

Bricklayer's chisel

Bricklayer's hammer

Bricklayer's Tools

To cut and shape bricks and stone you'll need a *bricklayer's hammer.* The heavy-duty variety will make the job easier, although the pick variety is more useful for slate or flat rocks. You can trim bricks with the hammer or use a *bricklayer's chisel,* at least 4" wide to cut bricks neatly.

Trowels are the tools you'll use most. You'll need three. The brick trowel should have a blade at least 8" long and 5" across at its widest part. You'll use the handle for tapping the brick into the mortar, so look for a strong wood handle and brass ferrule. The buttering trowel (for spreading mortar) is smaller and rounded, while the pointing trowel is very small. Always clean and dry your trowels at day's end, as you will not want rust staining your work.

Mortar joints can be "pointed" or "repointed" with a ⅜" *cape chisel* and a *brick pointer.*

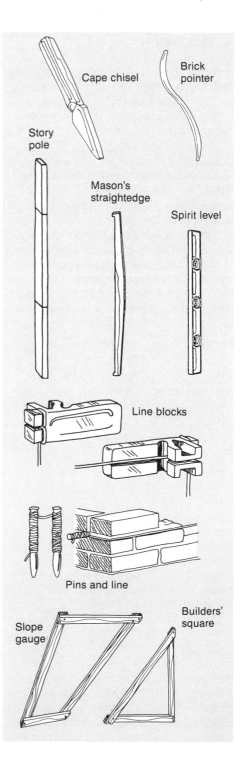

Cape chisel

Brick pointer

Story pole

Mason's straightedge

Spirit level

Line blocks

Pins and line

Slope gauge

Builders' square

114

Cement shovel

Water bucket

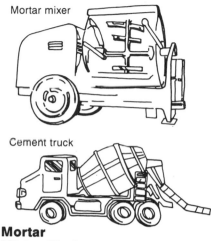

Mortar mixer

Cement truck

Mortar Mixing Tools

You'll also need some items used for other jobs: a *spirit level,* at least 2' long wood with brass or aluminum edges; a *builder's square* and a *story pole.* A *story pole* is a long measuring stick (1" ×2" by the height of the wall) that is marked with the proper height of every horizontal member of the wall as shown on the plans. A matched pair attached to corners can be used with a chalk line to mark horizontal lines for clapboards, shingles or furring strips all around the house. A *paint roller* is handy to moisten bricks. A *mason's straightedge* will help you level longer courses than you can with the level by itself. Other special tools include a pair of *line blocks* to guide you in laying the courses. *Pins, line,* and a *line level* can also be used to level the courses. A *slope gauge* will help in laying stepped walls. And you'll need *two water containers*—one for adding water to your mix, the other for cleaning your tools.

You should have a *cement shovel,* which has a square, flat front and sloped sides. You'll also need a *pointed shovel* for measuring sand and a *hoe* for mixing the batches.

If the job is over 2 cubic yards, you may want to rent a mortar (or cement) mixing machine. If you are in good physical shape, buy ready-mix and mix by hand.

Mortar

Mortar has several functions, and all are important. It bonds units together

and keeps water out of the wall. It attaches metal ties so they act integrally with the wall. It compensates for size variation in the bricks or stone. It contributes to the beauty of the structure by providing shadow lines and contrasting color.

Mortar is a combination of cementitious material (it may be portland cement, masonry cement, lime, or a mixture of these), sand, and water. It may have coloring or other additives to speed setting or increase water retention.

In its plastic state, mortar should smooth easily, bulk without slumping, hold together, bear the weight of brick or stone added on top of it, and extrude from joints yet cling to vertical faces without dripping or smearing.

Upon hardening the mortar must have excellent bond strength, durability, and resistance to freeze-thaw cycles. Compressive strength is improved by higher portland cement ratios in the mix. The higher the wall or heavier the stones, the more essential it is to use a portland cement mortar, but it's harder to work.

Masonry

The gradual appearance of a white or green deposit on brickwork, called *efflorescence,* is a defect caused by salt in the brick or mortar migrating to the surface due to an excess of water. As the water evaporates on the surface it leaves a crusty residue. Until completed, all walls should be covered and kept dry. The best long-term protection is to build a watertight wall. If efflorescence does appear, it can usually be removed. First try brushing or, if that doesn't work, use muriatic acid (1 part acid to 9 parts water). If you do this, wait at least a week after the construction is complete. Your masonry yard sales representatives may be able to advise you which brick types are least likely to effloresce.

Additives

For dirt resistance and resistance to staining you can add (in the dry mix stage) aluminum tristearate, ammonium stearate, or calcium stearate in an amount equalling up to 3 percent of the weight of the portland cement.

These stearates are crystalline acids, so handle with care and use protective clothing and face masks. Stearates are sold in 1-pound packages at masonry yards.

Up to 1 percent by weight of granulated sodium chloride (salt), dissolved in a minimum amount of water, can be added to masonry cement to provide a quicker set. Although this crystalized salt is sold by plumbing outlets for use in water softeners, it stores poorly, so you will save money if you purchase only as much as you need for the job at hand. This salt does *not* act as an antifreeze. If it is used in quantities sufficient to retard freezing, the mortar will not bind, and you will get efflorescence on the wall surface. Never add calcium chloride if you are using metal ties or reinforcements—heat the water instead.

White sand and ground granite, stone, or marble will provide permanent color without weakening the bond. You

Selecting the Type and Quantity of Mortar

Applications	Type	Proportions (in parts or units) Portland Cement
Foundation and exterior walls: concrete block and brick walls below and above grade, reinforced walls, and general use	S *or*	1 ½
Bonding stone, reinforced high exterior load-bearing, and concrete block walls	M *or*	1 1
Exterior brick veneer walls or load-bearing interior walls	N *or*	1
Interior non-load-bearing walls	O	1

can use up to 20 percent by weight of these. Iron, manganese, chromium oxide, carbon black, and ultramarine work successfully, but avoid organic colorings such as zinc chromates, prussian blue, or cadmium lithopane. Use the minimum coloring material necessary to achieve your design. Add no more than 2 to 3 percent carbon black or 10 to 15 percent by weight of the metal oxides.

The correct temperature for masonry work is between 50°F and 80°F. But we all know there are times when an unexpected freeze catches us with the job half done.

Some contractors add ethylene glycol to mortar to prevent freezing. However, experts frown on this practice, since the antifreeze, rather than evaporating or dissolving, will envelop the mortar components and weaken the bond. If later it seeps out, it will leave a void for water to enter the wall. If you add enough salt to prevent freezing, you'll also inhibit bonding and weaken

the wall. ASTM (American Society of Testing Materials) Specification C270 expressly forbids the use of antifreeze or salt in mortar to retard freezing!

In colder weather, below 40°F, it's best to keep the masonry in a heated area until needed and use hot water to warm the mix. The wall you are building should be protected from freezing until the mortar is set. Even in normal temperatures, never mix more batch than you can use in one-and-a-half to two-and-a-half hours. Remember to point holes made by line pins or nails while the mortar is still "green" (unset) or water will enter the wall.

Mixing

How should you buy and mix mortar? The size of the job determines the type and quantity. On jobs over 2 cubic yards you may want to rent a rotary mixer or purchase commercial mix by the cubic yardage or truckload, for which there will be a minimum charge. For less than that use packaged

Masonry Cement	Hydrated Lime	Damp Sand	Water
	½	4½	Always use
1		4½	the maximum amount of water that will produce a workable
1		6	mortar.
	¼	3	
1		3	
	1	6	
	2	9	

Masonry

ready-mix. Let it stand for 10 to 12 minutes after mixing before you use it.

Packaged ready-mix costs the most per pound, but for small jobs it will save you money, as the larger bags of portland or masonry cement may be more than you need, and will deteriorate unless stored in a very dry location. Commercial mix, sold by the cubic yard and delivered in a rotary cement truck, is the next most expensive and is economical only if you have a large job and several people laying the brick. If you have a strong back you can save the most money by mixing your own.

Mortar needs to be aerated, fluffy, and buttery so you can smear a ½" thickness on a vertical surface and have it hold without losing shape, dripping water, or slipping off. Aeration also helps the mortar retain water, stay workable longer, and greatly increases resistance to freeze-thaw cycles. Mix only enough for an hour and a half's work, less in a hot, dry climate. If only a small job, you can do a more thorough job of aerating the mix by hand with a *heavy-duty* (½", ¾ horsepower or larger) electric drill equipped with a rotary paint mixer. (You may be able to rent these from a tool rental shop.)

Stains

Mortar stains can be removed by using 1 part muriatic (hydrochloric) acid to 9 parts of water and scrubbing with a brush. (*Caution:* Wear protective clothing, gloves, and goggles and always add the water to the acid. *Never pour acid into water, as it will react violently and splatter you.*)

Test this acid solution in a small, inconspicuous area of the wall first, as this cleaning method can stain some bricks. Don't attempt to clean the bricks until the completed work is at least a week old. Mortar smears on concrete masonry can never be removed, because the acid will dissolve the masonry. So work carefully.

Types of Mortar

There are four types of mortars that will fill most do-it-yourself needs: portland cement mortar, portland cement lime mortar, masonry cement mortar, and a premixed (ready-mix) mortar. Generally, you should avoid straight lime mortars. They harden too slowly and have poor resistance to freeze-thaw cycles (but they're very important in restoration work, since they were the prevalent bonding agent in masonry construction up through the late nineteenth century).

Components are mixed on the basis of cubic feet. For example, one bag of portland cement weighs 94 pounds and equals 1 cubic foot. One bag of masonry cement weighs 70 pounds and equals 1 cubic foot. One bag of dry hydrated lime weighs 50 pounds and equals 1 cubic foot. Sand can be measured roughly by using a pointed shovel; 6 shovelfuls roughly equal a cubic foot. Ready-mix, which comes in 60-pound and 80-pound bags, is already mixed, so you don't need to figure the proportions.

The standard mortar mix is 3 parts damp sand to 1 part cement. Mix these components dry, then add water slowly while mixing with a hoe until the desired buttery consistency has been achieved.

Portland cement lime mortar will generally be your best choice and can be used above or below ground. The portland cement contributes early strength, consistent hardening rate, and high compressive strength. The lime content makes the batch more workable, water retentive, and elastic. Together they provide good bond strength and durability. The dry cementitious materials are mixed first, then the sand is added, followed by the water. For ingredients and proportions see the table on pages 120 and 121.

Portland cement mortar is used chiefly by professionals for high walls. This 1-to-3 combination of portland cement and sand develops high compressive strength and is very resistant to freeze-thaw cycles, but it hardens quickly and is difficult to work. You may need to use it in building stone walls where the weight of the stones could squeeze out too much of the more plastic mortars. It is recommended for reinforced masonry below ground level and for retaining walls and walkways. However, where codes permit, it is easier to use Type S portland cement-lime mortar.

Masonry cement mortar is sold as dry bagged mortar mixes. You add the right proportions of sand and water. Known as Type N, this too is 3 parts sand to 1 part masonry cement. These mixes usually contain a high proportion of portland cement or natural cement, plus ground limestone or hydrated lime, with an air-entraining additive and gypsum to control set time. The bags should be labeled according to ASTM Specification C91 as Type I or II. Type I is a general-purpose portland cement but Type II generates less heat, stays workable longer, and offers better resistance to sulfate attack. For mortar, Type II is preferable, but is not usually available as ready-mix. Masonry cement comes in 70-pound bags equal to 1 cubic foot.

Ready-mix mortar content varies by manufacturer, but usually it is a Type I masonry cement mortar premixed with sand. The masonry cement included normally contains about 70 percent portland cement and 30 percent lime and is mixed at a ratio of 1 part

masonry cement to 3 parts sand. Using it will certainly save you time, and you'll be assured of a sand content having the right amount of large and fine particles. Add about 5 to 6 quarts of water per 60-pound bag. (It also comes in 80-pound bags.)

Sand

When obtaining sand separately, you can use either manufactured or natural sand, but never use beach sand from the ocean or salt lakes. The salt it may contain can accelerate setting, weaken binding strength, and cause efflorescence. The excess of particles and organic materials will produce a weak mortar. Use a sand with a range of particles from fine to coarse (but never larger than $1/4''$ and less than that on tile work). Make sure your sand has at least 5 percent to 15 percent "fines" or your mortar will be hard to work. The larger particles are essential for the strength of the bond. Sand can be bought in 80-pound bags or in bulk.

Water

The water you add should be drinking (tap) water so that you are sure it is free of acids, alkalines, or organic matter.

In hot weather, evaporation may remove the water too quickly. It is permissible to add water to the mix once, but if it dries again, discard the batch and mix a new one.

Lime

You will usually want to use Type S lime, which is quicklime (CaO)—a calcined or oven-heated limestone—that has been soaked in water for at least two weeks to become calcium hydroxide ($CaOH_2$). Type S lime can be purchased by the bag (40-pound) from some home centers and all masonry yards and can be used as it

Masonry

Calculating and Preparing Mortar Needs

BRICKS, TIES AND MORTAR
(per 100 square feet of surface area)

Wall Thickness (inches)	Joint Thickness (inches)	Bricks[1] (per 100 sq. ft.)	No. of ties[2]	Mortar (cu. ft.)	Portland Cement (bag or cu. ft.)	+	Masonry Cement (bag or cu. ft.)	+	Damp Sand (cu. ft.)	Ready-mix 60-lb. bags	80-lb. bags
					TYPE S MORTAR (3:1)					(Type S)	
4	1/4	658	22	5.19	.43		.86		3.9	11	8.3
	3/8	622	22	6.49	.53		1.06		4.9	10.4	7.8
	1/2	589	22	9.19	.76		1.53		6.9	9	7.4
	5/8	558	22	11.19	.93		1.86		8.4	9.3	7.0
8	1/4	658	22	9.44	.78		1.56		7.1	11	8.3
	3/8	622	22	12.94	1.08		2.16		9.7	10.4	8.0
	1/2	611	22	18.39	1.53		3.06		13.8	10.2	7.7
	5/8	558	22	22.41	1.87		3.74		16.8	9.3	7.0

CONCRETE BLOCK AND MORTAR
(per 100 square feet of surface area)

Wall Thickness	Wall Height (ft.)	Wall Length (ft.)	Joint Thickness (inches)	Blocks (per 100 sq. ft.)	Mortar[3] (cu. ft.)
8	8	12	3/8	150	3.5
8	8	16	3/8	112	3.28
12	8	16	3/8	112	3.28

[1]Based on standard modular brick height 2⅔" × thickness × length 8". In calculating quantities, *deduct* for square footage of windows and doors—40 sq. ft. of windows and doors using 4" brick with ½" joints would be 40 × 5.89 = 235.6 or 236 bricks to deduct from your total count.

[2]One ³⁄₁₆" steel tie for every 4½ sq. ft. of wall surface. Not more than 18" apart vertically or 36" horizontally with ties in alternate courses staggered—see code requirements.

[3]This is the number of cu. ft. or bags you'll need if using ready-mixed mortar.

Adding Water

Batch Size (cubic feet)	Mixing Portland Cement (no. of 94-lb. bag.)	Hydrated Lime (no. of 50-lb. bags)	Sand (cubic feet)	Water gallons to add if sand is: Dry	Damp	Wet
2	1/4	1/2	1¼	1¼	1⅛	1
6	1/2	1	4½	2½	2¼	2
12	1	2	9	5	4½	4
	Using Masonry Cement (no. of 70-lb. bags)					
2	1/2		1½	7/8	3/4	5/8
6	1½		4½	2½	2¼	2
12	3		9	5	4½	4
	Using Ready-Mix (no. of 80-lb. bags)					
2	2			7/8	3/4	5/8
6	6			2½	2¼	2
12	12			5	4½	4

| TYPE M (3:1) | | | TYPE N (3:1) | | TYPE O (3:1) | | |
Portland Cement (bag or cu. ft.) +	Masonry Cement (bag or cu. ft.) +	Damp Sand	Masonry Cement (bag or cu. ft.) +	Damp Sand	Portland Cement (bag or cu. ft.) +	Hydrated Lime (bag) +	Damp Sand (cu. ft.)
.65	.65	3.9	1.3	3.9	.43	.86	3.9
.80	.80	4.8	1.6	4.8	.54	1.08	4.8
1.15	1.15	6.9	2.3	6.9	.76	1.52	6.9
1.40	1.40	8.4	2.8	8.4	.93	1.86	8.4
1.10	1.10	7.0	2.3	6.9	.76	1.52	6.9
1.62	1.62	9.7	3.2	9.6	1.07	2.14	9.7
2.30	2.30	13.8	4.6	13.8	1.53	3.06	13.8
2.81	2.81	16.9	5.6	16.8	1.87	3.74	16.8

| TYPE S (3:1) | | | TYPE M (3:1) | | |
Portland Cement (bag) +	Masonry Cement (bag) +	Damp Sand (cu. ft.)	Portland Cement (bag) +	Masonry Cement (bag) +	Damp Sand
0.27	0.58	2.62	0.44	0.44	2.62
0.27	0.55	2.46	0.41	0.41	2.46
0.27	0.55	2.46	0.41	0.41	2.46

comes from the bag. Don't use quicklime. It is caustic and can burn skin and particularly the mucous surfaces of the mouth, nose, and eyes. Lime putty is damp hydrated lime and comes in 80-pound bags of which 40 pounds is water.

The first-time mason is often in a quandary about how much water to add, so the chart on page 120 may provide a reasonable starting point. Remember, if you start mixing your batch and it rains, you'll have to recalculate based on damp or wet sand. In mixing batches, measure components carefully. A common error is to include too much sand because sand is cheap. Don't! You'll have an unworkably stiff mortar and a weak bond.

Pointing Mortar Joints

A good joint requires compressing the mortar and should be designed to shed water. Here we indicate good and poor pointing styles. You'll note that some of the most popular styles are poor practice. They either let water into the top of the brick or are not compressed. For example, the common

Pointing with Cape Chisel

Masonry

Types of Troweled Joints

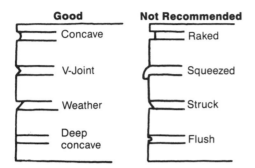

flush joint is rated "poor." It produces an uncompacted joint and develops hairline cracks where the trowel pulls the mortar away from the brick. Professionals advise that the weather joint is the best. It allows the brick surface to drain and shed water. Always work when the temperature is between 50°F to 80°F and when no frost or heat wave is expected.

In repointing old brick walls, chisel out ½" of the old mortar or any that is loose, using a 2½-pound hammer and a cape chisel. Brush out the cracks with a long-handled stiff-bristle brush. (Remember to wear safety goggles.) Mix mortar with a higher than usual amount of hydrated lime—1 cubic foot masonry cement, 2 cubic feet of lime, and 8 cubic feet of damp sand. Use less water than normal and, if using quicklime, allow it to slake (soak) in water (prehydrate) for twenty-four hours before mixing. If coloring is desired, add inorganic pigment after slaking the lime and before mixing with the sand.

If matching the color of old mortar, add enough pigment to make it slightly darker; it will lighten when dry.

Bricks

No other man-made building material has passed the test of time as well as brick. In fact, brick can be as durable as stone. It's better than stone in that it is faster to lay.

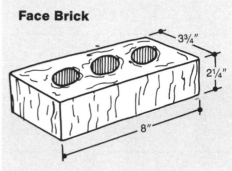

Face Brick

For outdoor use you need to select a hard brick that is low in water absorption and has open pores in the top and sides to provide "tooth" for the mortar to bind.

Bricks are graded

- SW (severe weathering), necessary for climates having multiple freeze-thaw cycles or heavy rain (see map; page 123).
  can be used in all temperate climates
- NW (no weathering), which is chiefly for interior use.

Use only SW bricks below ground or for paving. The map also shows which bricks should be used for each section of the country.

The table on page 120 tells you the number of bricks and other materials you need per 100 square feet of wall that you build. It allows for 20 percent waste on all head and base joints. Deduct square footage for windows and doors.

Face brick comes in a variety of sizes and colors and has sharp edges and square corners. The surface may be rough, smooth, or enameled. Face brick is made only in SW and MW grades. To determine which to choose, see the weather map on page 123.

Choosing Bricks for Vertical Aboveground Applications

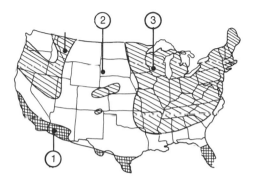

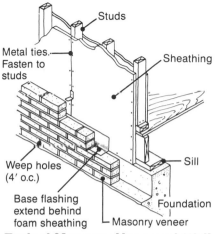

Typical Masonry Veneered Wall

Weathering Index*

1. Less than 100—Use MW brick
2. 100 to 500—Use MW brick
3. 500 or more—Use SW brick

*
NOTE: Weathering index: The product of any winter rainfall in inches and the average annual number of freezing cycle days.

For veneer application of face brick you will also need to purchase wall ties to provide an essential 1″ air space between the exterior wall sheathing and the veneer wall. You'll require one tie for every 2 square feet of wall.

If you prefer used brick, tap one with a hammer to be sure it doesn't crumble. Also be sure that most of the mortar has been removed. When you tap the bricks together they should ring.

At your local brickyard you'll find bricks in a broad variety of colors and textures. Red, pink, yellow, brown, white, and "burned" (blackened) bricks are common. The coloring is influenced by the local clay used.

Plastic flexible "bricks" can be applied directly to stucco or plywood

sheathing and can be used to bend around gentle curves.

There are also special-purpose bricks such as *fire bricks.* These can

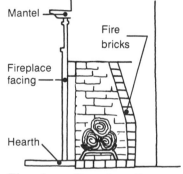

Fireplace Construction

withstand high heat and are used to line the fireboxes (inside surfaces) of fireplaces and barbecues. Because of the high temperatures, they must be bonded with fire clay, not mortar. A specialty item, fire clay is sold in bags by firebrick companies. It is a prepared clay mix ready for slurrying with water. The porous fire bricks are dipped in the soupy material, which clings to the side and bottom surfaces, making them ready for setting. Mixed with less water, this fire clay can be used for patching, pointing, or repointing. Fire clay does not completely harden until exposed to the heat of a fire.

Bricks also make handsome walkways. You'll need SW (severe weathering) bricks for this use. Lay the bricks on a 2″ bed of sand or stone dust, then push more of this material in between the bricks with a broom. Trim the walkway's edges with pressure-treated 2″ × 6″ or 2″ × 8″ lumber to reduce the effect of frost heaves.

Stone

The fieldstone "fences" of New England and brownstone Colonial houses of Pennsylvania are admired for their beauty, as are the polished marble and granite monuments of Washington, D.C. Stone, with its varied textures, color, and patterning can mix with any architectural style or period. Stone is, of course, durable, but it is also heavy, expensive, and difficult to move and install. Whether for a fireplace, room divider, or exterior wall, laying stone provides a challenging and satisfying project for do-it-yourselfers.

Stone generally comes from local quarries, and you can usually choose from a selection including limestone, sandstone, granite, marble, bluestone, and slate. Of course, the farther it's been transported, the higher the cost.

Finishes and Grading

Stone yards sell stone in three or four finishes:
1. *Dressed* stones are trimmed to your dimensions and very expensive.
2. *Semidressed* stones are rough cut on four sides and sorted into common sizes. These need further trimming before use.
3. *Undressed* stone is as it comes from the quarry unsized and uncut.

Common Stone Shapes

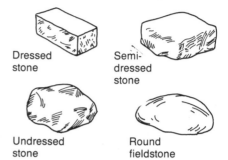

Dressed stone

Semi-dressed stone

Undressed stone

Round fieldstone

4. *Rounded river* stone and *glacier* stone (fieldstone) are native only to certain locations.

Other rocks such as volcanic lava stone, quartz, and pebble-bearing sedimentary stones are usually sold undressed. Artificial stone is made by embedding crushed stone in cement.

Most stones are sorted according to size in the yards. They even have large pieces for use as mantels or arches. However, you may want to select some large (between 12″ and 24″) and medium (8″ to 12″) stones for appearance and construction savings. Small stones and rubble are easier to handle but are not substantial and take longer to lay and bond.

Stones can be bonded with Type M mortar or fitted together without bonding. Unmortared, or "dry-laid," masonry is generally confined to landscaping projects such as building retaining walls or outlining plantings or walkways.

Since most stone for exterior use comes from local sources, check with a local mason to find out which available type has the best weathering characteristics. As a general rule, you'll need at least 4 to 5 cubic feet of mortar per 100 stones. Due to the weight of the stone and lack of porosity, type M mortar should be used—90 percent portland cement and 10 percent lime to 3 times their combined volume in sand.

Stonelaying Patterns for Walls

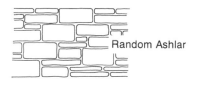

Random Ashlar

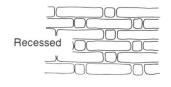

Recessed

Random Rubble

Barn Wall

Fieldstone

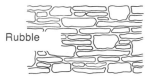

Rubble

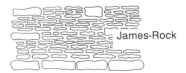

James-Rock

Coursed Ashlar

Veneer stones are much easier to handle and install. Usually 2″ to 3″ thick, the face is naturally shaped stone with the back cut flat. These are installed on steel stud walls faced with expanded metal lath, which is coated with Type M mortar. When laying

Napa Valley Fieldstone

Glazien

Green Driftstone

Flintstone

Palo Verde

Gray Copperfield

Brown Copperfield

Apache

Veneer Stone Patterns

Masonry

veneer stone, wet the back of the stone as well as the wall cavity; then apply mortar to the back of the stone and set in place.

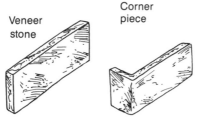

Veneer stone

Corner piece

Typical Veneer Shapes

Mortar stones are made with real rock chips or grindings bonded with portland cement and tinted with mineral oxide colors. These veneer stones are lighter in weight, as durable as genuine rock, and provide an authentic appearance.

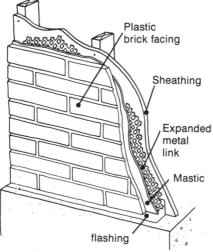

Plastic brick facing

Sheathing

Expanded metal link

Mastic

flashing

Installing Brick Veneer Panels

Plastic panels with actual brick or stone dust embedded in the surface are available in two grades, one for interior, the other for exterior use. Particularly indoors, these have the advantage of light weight and need no special footings. They are quick and easy to install, fastening to standard wood studs or furring, with staples or nails. These panels are approximately 4′×1′ but vary by manufacturer. Unfortunately, they usually look fake and end up giving the home a hint of shabbiness.

Concrete, Glazed, and Glass Blocks

Standard concrete blocks measure $7\frac{5}{8}'' \times 7\frac{5}{8}'' \times 15\frac{5}{8}''$. (When estimating the quantity of these standard blocks needed, remember that each block and mortar joint is equal to 1 square foot of face. See the table on pages

Typical Concrete Block Shapes

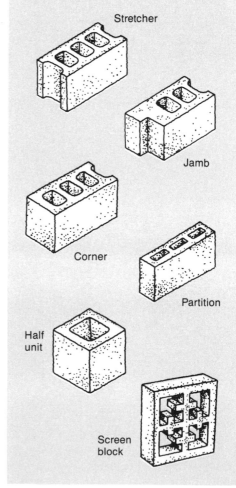

Stretcher

Jamb

Corner

Partition

Half unit

Screen block

120 and 121 for estimated quantities and mortar required.)

Lightweight concrete blocks, weighing 22 to 28 pounds per block, made from cinders, pumice, expanded shale or slag, or scorin tend to be porous and absorbent and are generally unsatisfactory as a base for asphaltic waterproofing. For foundations use 35- to 40-pound blocks which also have higher compressive strength.

Blocks are graded into SI, SII, NI and NII. SI and SII blocks are limited to walls not exposed to the weather and to aboveground walls protected with weather-resistant coatings. NI and NII blocks may be used above or below ground but need waterproofing below ground.

There is an amazing variety of large blocks, decorative blocks for screening and integrally insulated blocks available. Do not let your stock of blocks get wet. Concrete blocks can be painted with masonry type sealants.

Glazed blocks, for swimming pools and washrooms, are available with a modular face size of 15¾″ × 7¾″. Thicknesses vary from: 1¾″ to 11¾″.

Structural clay tile designed for walls 4″, 6″, 8″, 10″, or 12″ thick is available with face sizes of 12″ × 12″, 8″ × 8″, 8″ × 12″, and 5⅓″ × 12″ and 6⅔″ × 12″.

Decorative blocks have recessed faces and are generally used for exterior walls and sunscreens.

Cement and Concrete

One bag (1 cubic foot) of portland cement plus 3 cubic feet of gravel and 2 cubic feet of damp sand mixed with water produces concrete. Most do-it-yourself projects can be handled by buying bags of ready-mixed cement (60 pounds per bag), adding gravel and water, and mixing with a hoe. Add enough water to make it workable, but no more—too much will weaken the concrete.

Five bags of cement are required per cubic yard of concrete. When steel reinforcement is used, six bags per cubic yard are normally specified.

Masonry cement (a mixture of portland cement and lime) and portland cement are used for concrete. Either can be purchased by the sack for on-site mixing with gravel or dry sand. You can buy ready-mixed dry concrete. For small projects—generally those requiring 1 cubic yard or less of concrete—you can mix it yourself. But for larger jobs, ready-to-pour concrete can be delivered by motorized cement mixer trucks. For the quantities required, see the tables on pages 128 through 130.

Concrete ready for pouring weighs 150 pounds per cubic foot. So you need strong forms, even for pouring steps. Use ¾″ plywood or 1″ boards without knotholes. Join them tightly and stake them every 4′ to 5′ to prevent leaks.

Concrete cures by hydration. It does not dry, but chemically reacts and must be kept damp during the initial stages of cure, usually about a week. After initial set, lay on burlap or straw and wet down with a hose whenever it appears dry. Concrete does not gain its full bearing strength for at least twenty-eight days.

All concrete slabs and walls will crack. This is why it is essential to apply basement-wall waterproofing and provide good drainage to ensure a dry basement. Standard "black jack" (often required by codes) is little more than a paint. It loses flexibility below 40°F and will crack with the wall. Normally it is applied in coats too thin to permanently withstand hydrostatic

Masonry

pressure and emulsifies (dissolves) in water, gradually washing away. Hot applied asphaltic coatings, Benonite clays or rubberized membranes are good foundation waterproofing products.

Since concrete slabs will crack even though reinforced, it is wise to cover the ground with a 6 mil polyethylene film before pouring the concrete. If a concrete or concrete tiled slab extends around a corner, it will crack outwardly from that corner. The use of expansion joints extending from each wall, or cutting straight lines with an abrasive saw and then caulking the joint, can prevent these cracks.

Reinforcing Rods, Mesh, and Anchor Bolts

Reinforcing rods are required at intersections of concrete walls. These should be ½" deformed (bent) rods, usually 36" long.

Metal straps are used at intersections of connecting block walls.

Wire mesh (6" × 6" No. 10) should be used to reinforce floor slabs.

Anchor bolts ½" or ⅝" in diameter and 18" long (or 8" minimum in block) are set no more than 4' apart to retain the sill plate in concrete and block walls.

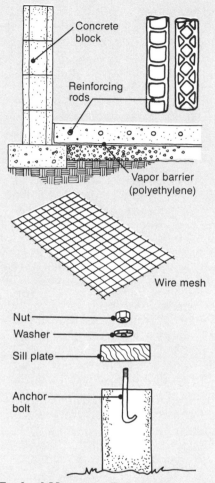

Typical Masonry Reinforcements

Estimating Ready-Mix Concrete

Thickness	Surface Area of Job in Square Feet					
	20	50	100	200	500	
2"	3.3	8.3	16.7	33.3	83.3	**cubic feet**
	(.1)	(.3)	(.6)	(1.2)	(3.1)	**(cubic yards)**
4"	6.7	16.7	33.3	66.7	166.7	**cubic feet**
	(.2)	(.6)	(1.2)	(2.5)	(6.2)	**(cubic yards)**
6"	10.0	25.0	50.0	100.0	250.0	**cubic feet**
	(.4)	(.9)	(1.9)	(3.7)	(9.3)	**(cubic yards)**

Pouring Concrete Slabs

| Thickness | Material | |
	Cubic Feet of Concrete per Square Foot	Square Feet from 1 Cubic Yard
2″	0.167	162
3″	0.25	108
4″	0.333	81
5″	0.417	65
6″	0.50	54

NOTE: Square feet × thickness in feet ÷ 27 gives you the cubic yards of concrete you need.

Concrete Walls

| Wall Thickness | Material Per 100 Square Feet Wall | |
	Cubic Feet Required	Cubic Yards Required
4″	33.3	1.24
6″	50.0	1.85
8″	66.7	2.47
10″	83.3	3.09
12″	100.0	3.70

Fill Capacity Per Cubic Yard of Concrete

This table gives the area in square feet that 1 cubic yard of concrete will fill for each indicated thickness.

CONCRETE ESTIMATING
1 CU. YD. OF CONCRETE WILL FILL

Thickness (in.)	Sq. Ft.	Thickness (in.)	Sq. Ft.	Thickness (in.)	Sq. Ft.
1	324	4¾	68	8½	38
1¼	259	5	65	8¾	37
1½	216	5¼	62	9	36
1¾	185	5½	59	9¼	35
2	162	5¾	56	9½	34
2¼	144	6	54	9¾	33
2½	130	6¼	52	10	32.5
2¾	118	6½	50	10¼	31.5
3	108	6¾	48	10½	31
3¼	100	7	46	10¾	30
3½	93	7¼	45	11	29.5
3¾	86	7½	43	11¼	29
4	81	7¾	42	11½	28
4¼	76	8	40	11¾	27.5
4½	72	8¼	39	12	27

Masonry

Estimating the Material for Footings

Footings	Material		
Size (inches)	Cubic Feet Concrete Per Linear Foot	Cubic Feet Concrete Per 100 Linear Feet	Cubic Yards Concrete Per 100 Linear Feet
6 × 12	0.50	50.00	1.9
8 × 12	0.67	66.67	2.5
8 × 16	0.89	88.89	3.3
8 × 18	1.00	100.00	3.7
10 × 12	0.83	83.33	3.1
10 × 16	1.11	111.11	4.1
10 × 18	1.25	125.00	4.6
12 × 12	1.00	100.00	3.7
12 × 16	1.33	133.33	4.9
12 × 20	1.67	166.67	6.1
12 × 24	2.00	200.00	7.4

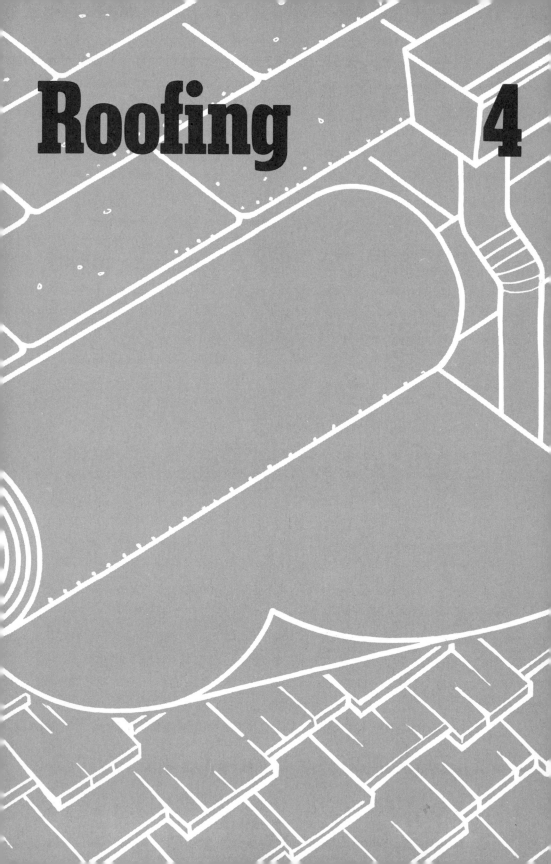

Roofing

4

4. Roofing

When you buy roofing materials, you definitely get what you pay for. Extra dollars translate directly into roofs that are longer-lasting and give a better curbside appearance—important at resale time. So, when shopping, look beyond initial prices. After all, a cheap roof replaced every ten years is always more expensive in the long run than a top-of-the-line roof replaced every thirty years, especially if you hire a contractor to do the work.

Most homes in North America have roofs of asphalt shingles. These shingles are widely available in a variety of colors, textures, weights, and fire-resistance ratings. Because working on a roof is extremely hazardous, particularly if you are inexperienced and don't have the right equipment, shingle manufacturers strongly recommend you use a contractor. If you are experienced and have the right ladders, lifting equipment and tools, a healthy respect for heights, and a not-too-steep roof, there is no law against doing it yourself. Step-by-step roofing instructions are available in books, how-to magazines (especially the spring issues), and contractors' directions from leading roofing manufacturers.

In the 1960s, manufacturers introduced a "new, improved" asphalt shingle, the fiberglass shingle. Earlier asphalt shingles consisted of a felt paper base covered by asphalt and mineral granules. The problem with these was that the cellulose felt absorbed water. The new product substituted fiberglass for the felt, resulting in a shingle with less weight, resistance to water wicking, longer life, and greater fire resistance. The fiberglass-backed asphalt shingle is now the norm.

Besides asphalt shingles, you can still buy wood shingles or shakes, wood-fiber sheets that look like shingles, enameled metal tiles, metal sheets, concrete or clay tiles, slate, built-up roofing, and asphalt roll roofing. All are discussed in detail in this chapter.

No matter what type of roofing material you buy, you'll need to understand a few common terms. First of all, a *square* is a common unit of measurement for roofing. It's simply 100 square feet of roof surface. You may see shingles sold, for example, as "4 bundles per square." Knowing that, you can figure out how many bundles to buy, once you've calculated the square footage of your roof.

A *course* of shingles is one horizontal row. *Exposure* is the amount of shingle or shake that's exposed to the weather, as opposed to the part that is overlapped by the course above it. The exposure, expressed in inches, may vary depending upon the *slope* of your roof. (Steeper slopes allow more exposure.)

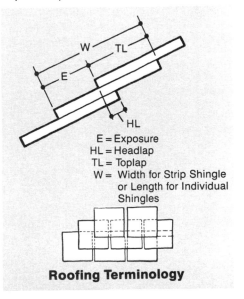

E = Exposure
HL = Headlap
TL = Toplap
W = Width for Strip Shingle
or Length for Individual
Shingles

Roofing Terminology

Roofing

Roofing Installation Parameters

Roofing Product	Attachment or Bonding Material	Underlayment (a)
Asbestos cement shingles	Use asphalt shingle nails	Single layers of No. 15 asphalt-saturated inorganic felt or No. 30 asphalt-saturated felt
Asphalt shingles	Use asphalt shingle nails or staples	Single layers of No. 15 asphalt-saturated felt
Fiberglass shingles	Use asphalt shingle nails or staples	Single layer of No. 15 asphalt-saturated felt
Wood shakes	Only 2 nails per shake	One No. 30 asphalt-saturated felt underlayment starter course at eaves and interlayment between each shake course over entire roof
Wood shingles	New construction 3d for 16" and 18" shingles; 4d for 24" shingles (use 5d or 6d for reroofing)	None required
Roll roofing and asphalt	Plastic asphalt cement for flashing lap; and asphalt cements for overlaps	
Granulated roofing shear	Plastic asphalt cement for flashing; lap cements for overlaps	
Resiply	Under surface remelt bonding	
Slate	Zinc-coated or copper 3d nails for 18" slate; 4d for 20" or longer and 6d for hips and ridges. Cover all nail heads with elastic cement compound.	No. 30 asphalt-saturated felt (b)
Tile	Mission tile is installed over 1½" furring strips nailed to roof sheathing vertically. English tile requires horizontal furring strips.	

(a) 2" toplap at all horizontal joints; 4" side lap at end joints; 6" lap both sides over hips and ridges.
 NOTE: Eave flashing for normal slopes extends up the roof to at least 12" above interior wall line with cemented underlayment extending 24" above interior wall line. Each layer requires 10" overlap. Or use Deck-Dri® self-adhesive flashing, to at least 24" above interior wall line. Use drip edges.
(b) Slates normally require a 3" overlap. Exposure: $\frac{Length - overlap}{2}$. e.g. 18" slate $- 3 = 15 \div 2 = 7\frac{1}{2}$" exposure. Slate lengths are from 10" to 24" in 2" increments normally $\frac{3}{16}$" to $\frac{1}{4}$" thick. Also available in $\frac{3}{8}$", $\frac{1}{2}$", $\frac{3}{4}$", and 1" (the last two are generally used for paving).

Normal Slope (inches)	Minimum Slope (inches)	Special Requirements for Minimum Slope
5 in 12	3 in 12	Double underlayment over entire roof
4 in 12	2 in 12	
		Strip shingles only
4 in 12	2 in 12	Double underlayment or use adhesive tab shingles
4 in 12	3 in 12	Solid sheathing only. Single layer No. 30 underlayment over entire roof and interlayment between each shake course over entire roof.
5 in 12	3 in 12	Reduced weather exposure
3 in 12	Flat	
3 in 12	2 in 12	
Flat or 3 in 12	Flat	
5 in 12	4 in 12	
5 in 12	4 in 12	

Roofing

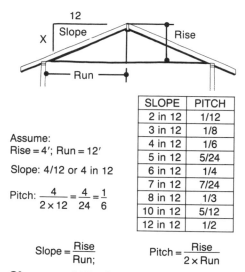

Assume:

Rise = 4'; Run = 12'

Slope: 4/12 or 4 in 12

Pitch: $\dfrac{4}{2 \times 12} = \dfrac{4}{24} = \dfrac{1}{6}$

SLOPE	PITCH
2 in 12	1/12
3 in 12	1/8
4 in 12	1/6
5 in 12	5/24
6 in 12	1/4
7 in 12	7/24
8 in 12	1/3
10 in 12	5/12
12 in 12	1/2

$\text{Slope} = \dfrac{\text{Rise}}{\text{Run}};$ $\text{Pitch} = \dfrac{\text{Rise}}{2 \times \text{Run}}$

Slope and Pitch

Slope is measured by the *rise in inches,* that is, the number of inches the roof rises for each 12" of horizontal run. Thus, a roof with a 4-in-12 slope rises 4" every foot. See the table on roofing installation parameters for the kinds of roofing materials permitted by the slope of your roof.

Finally, roofing materials are rated according to three classes of fire resistance. These three classes are determined by tests developed by Underwriters Laboratories. *Class A* materials can withstand severe exposure to fire, *Class B* materials can withstand moderate exposure, and *Class C* materials can withstand light exposure.

Estimating Materials

The first step in estimating roofing materials is to calculate the total surface area of your roof. A simple method is to determine the total ground area of the structure, including eave and cornice overhangs. Then convert the ground area to roof area by adding a percentage determined by the roof slope as follows:

- Slope 3 in 12—add 3 percent of area
- Slope 4 in 12—add 5½ percent of area
- Slope 5 in 12—add 8½ percent of area
- Slope 6 in 12—add 12 percent of area
- Slope 8 in 12—add 20 percent of area

After the total square feet of roof surface has been estimated, divide it by 100 to find the number of squares to be covered. For example: If the total ground area plus overhang is found to be 1560 and the slope of the roof is 4 in 12, apply the following calculations.

Roof area = 1560 + (1560 × 5½%)
   = 1560 + (1560 × .055)
   = 1560 + 85.80 (or 86)
   = 1646 square feet

Number of squares = 1646 ÷ 100 = 16.46 (or 16½)

Now add additional amounts for waste, hips, valleys, and other extras. For fiberglass or asphalt shingles, up to 10 percent is generally recommended, although plain gable roofs usually

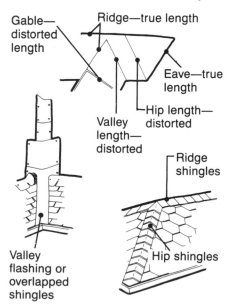

Gable—distorted length

Ridge—true length

Eave—true length

Hip length—distorted

Valley length—distorted

Valley flashing or overlapped shingles

Ridge shingles

Hip shingles

require less and a complicated intersecting roof may require more than 10 percent additional material. Wood or asphalt shingles generally require one additional square for each 100 lineal feet of hips and valleys.

Starter strips, eave flashing, valley flashing, and ridge shingles must be added to obtain the total shingle requirements. All of these are figured with linear measurements. A plan view of the roof will be helpful in determining the linear length of the various roof components. Ridge and eaves are shown in true length and may simply be scaled to find their length. To find the length of hips and valleys, which are *not* pictured in their true length, measure their length on the plan and add a percentage equal to that used when converting ground area to roof area (shown on page 136).

Roofing Materials

Material	Features	Maintenance	Durability
Asphalt Shingles	A cellulose mat saturated in asphalt and coated with colored mineral granules. Can be installed over previous asphalt shingle roof.	Tendency to wick (soak up) water leads to deterioration in damp climate.	May last 15 to 20 years, depending on weight of asphalt used. Damaged shingles should be replaced.
Fiberglass Shingles	Asphalt-saturated fiberglass mat coated with colored mineral granules. Lighter in weight than asphalt shingles and more durable. Can be installed over old asphalt or fiberglass shingled roof.	Durable. Damaged shingles can be replaced.	Available with warranties up to 25 years. Available with UL Class A fire-resistance label and UL wind-resistance label.
Wood Shakes and Shingles	Shakes are hand-hewn from heartwood. Shingles are machine cut and may use less durable sapwood. Can only be used on a 4-in-12 slope or steeper roof. Combustible unless treated.	Tend to warp. Will be stained by rusting nails. Damaged shingles or shakes can be replaced but will be different in color until aged.	Heartwood shakes or shingles are very durable on steep slopes: i.e. up to 60 years for roofs with 8-in-12 pitch or steeper; 40 years if 4-in-12 or steeper. Can be less on low-pitched roofs. Chief concern is combustibility. Damaged shakes must be replaced quickly to avoid further roof damage.

Roofing

Roofing Materials (Continued)

Material	Features	Maintenance	Durability
Asbestos Cement Shingles	Made of asbestos reinforced portland cement, this fire-resistant material costs more than wood.	With the phase out of materials containing asbestos, replacement shingles will be difficult to find.	Up to 50 years, but they may darken with age.
Slate, Clay Tiles	These are heavy, expensive, and fireproof. Tiles are common to the southwest and slate is popular in the east, close to the quarries.	Individual tiles or slates can be replaced—although it's a tricky procedure. Always buy and stock some extra tiles as replacements may be difficult to find.	Slate and tiles never wear out as long as you make repairs when needed.
Roll Roofing	Cheaper than asphalt shingles, this comes in wide strips that are lapped horizontally across the roof's surface. Use only on shallow slopes.	Use only on temporary structures. Will need frequent repair.	From 5 to 15 years. Check if the contractor's warranty covers labor and materials.
Metal Roofing	Terne roofing is a high quality ribbed roof of durable copper-bearing steel that is heat treated and hot dip-coated in a lead-tin alloy and is expensive. Enameled metal tiles in a wide choice of colors are also on the expensive side. Corrugated aluminum and galvanized steel can be used on rural buildings but are unpopular in residential neighborhoods.	Will need occasional painting. Use only aluminum nails when applying aluminum.	Terne, copper and enameled tiles will last 30 years or more.

Roofing Materials (Concluded)

Material	Features	Maintenance	Durability
Built-Up Roofing	Only used on low sloped or flat roofs. A build up of layers of felt and asphalt. Installation with hot asphalt requires use of a contractor with the right equipment to ensure roof is watertight.	Easily damaged and requires annual inspection. Easy to repair.	Manufacturers give estimates of life span which basically depends on number of layers.
Deck-Dri® Membrane	A self-bonding membrane to protect leading edge of roof from ice dams. Seals around shingle nails driven through it into sheathing. Does not prevent ice dams but does seal out melting snow and ice. A strip of adhesive on upper edge ensures watertight laps.	No maintenance required.	New product, so life span not known, but likely to last as long as the shingle protecting it.

Asphalt Shingles

Both the classic asphalt shingle and the now popular fiberglass shingle are three-tab shingles, so called because their exposed area is precut to appear as three distinct shingles, or tabs. The shingle's asphalt provides the necessary waterproofing, and the mineral granules protect the shingles from the sun's rays. The granules provide color and, together with the fiberglass mat, give fire protection. Some shingles are built with several plies to make them thicker and give them a dimensional appearance. These may be two or more shingles bonded together, with only the top layer having granules.

Shingles commonly measure 12″ × 36″, although metric sizes are

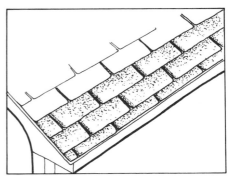

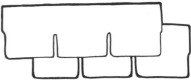

Three-Tab Shingles

Roofing

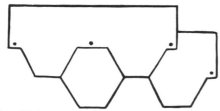

Two-Tab Hexagonal Pattern Shingles

now being introduced which are 39⅜" long. Many are available with self-adhesive spots. These spots are activated by the sun's rays to glue to the overlapping tab above it and prevent the wind from lifting the tabs. Space between each seal helps the roof to breathe.

Shingles are usually laid with a 5" exposure. This is considered double coverage. A 4" exposure gives triple coverage.

You can also buy shingles in a hexagonal pattern. These shingles are available in two- or three-tab strips. Application is similar to that for the strip shingle. The starter course is inverted so that the space between tabs will be the same color as the shingles themselves. The strips are applied so that the lower edges of the tab center cover the top cutouts of the preceding course.

Wood Shingles

Wood provides a durable, rugged, attractive roof. Most wood shingles are of cedar, a wood that naturally resists decay. Left alone, a new cedar roof will

Color Guide for Shingles and Trim

House or Siding Color	Shingle Color Northern Climates	Shingle Color Southern Climates	Trim	Shutters and Doors
Brick	Imperial Black	Aspen Gray	White	White
(Russet or pink)	Colonial Slate	Onyx Black	Gray	Charcoal
	Barnwood	Canyon Red	White	Natural Wood
Natural Wood	Onyx Black	Dark Brown	White	Natural Wood
Siding	Driftwood	Autumn Brown	Light Brown	Dark Brown
	Dark Brown	Desert Tan	White	White
White Siding	Imperial Black	Onyx Black	Light Gray	Charcoal
or Paint	Onyx Black	Aspen Gray	White	White
	Barnwood	Shasta White	White	Gray
Beige Siding	Weathered Wood	Desert Tan	Brown	Brown
or Paint	Dark Brown	Autumn Brown	White	Dark Brown
	Driftwood	Western Sand	Dark Green	Olive Green
Yellow	Weathered Wood	Desert Tan	White	Dark Brown
	Autumn Brown	Autumn Brown	White	Dark Green
	Driftwood	Forest Green	White	White
Gray	Aspen Gray	Shasta White	White	Olive Green
	Onyx Black	Aspen Gray	White	Maroon
	Barnwood	Surf Green	White	Black
Green	Weathered Wood	Surf Green	White	White/Brown
	Surf Green	Mint Green	Light Green	Beige
	Onyx Black	Shasta White	White	Light Green/ Dark Green

NOTE: These are conservative recommendations acceptable in most established neighborhoods. Today in remodeling areas of Victorian homes, combinations of bright colors are used on the shingle siding with brilliant accents of color for doors and shutters. These colors should be selected by a competent architect.

Typical Asphalt Shingles

| Product | Configuration | Per Square | | | Size | | | Underwriters Laboratories Listing |
		Approximate Shipping Weight	No. of Shingles	No. of Bundles	Width	Length	Exposure	
Self-sealing random-tab strip shingle **Multi-thickness** 	Various edge, surface, texture, and application treatments	240# to 360#	64 to 90	3, 4 or 5	11½" to 14"	36" to 40"	4" to 6"	A or C Many wind resistant
Self-sealing random-tab strip shingle **Single-thickness** 	Various edge, surface, texture, and application treatments	240# to 300#	65 to 80	3 or 4	12" to 13¼"	36" to 40"	5" to 5⅝"	A or C Many wind resistant
Self-sealing square-tab strip shingle 	Two-tab or four-tab	215# to 325#	65 to 80	3 or 4	12" to 13¼"	36" to 40"	5" to 5⅝"	A or C All wind resistant
	Three-tab	215# to 300#	65 to 80	3 or 4	12" to 13¼"	36" to 40"	5" to 5⅝"	A or C All wind resistant
Self-sealing square-tab strip shingle **No-cutout** 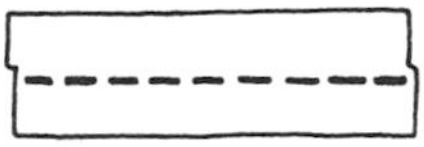	Various edge and surface texture treatments	215# to 290#	65 to 81	3 or 4	12" to 13¼"	36" to 40"	5" to 5⅝"	A or C All wind resistant
Individual interlocking shingle **Basic design** 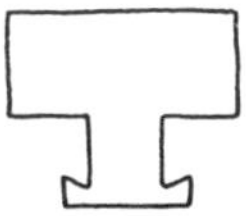	Several design variations	180# to 250#	72 to 120	3 or 4	18" to 22¼"	20" to 22½"	—	A or C Many wind resistant

Roofing

gradually change to a gray color over a few years. You can treat your roof with a bleach to hasten this change or with a semitransparent stain to maintain the tan hues.

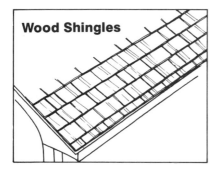

Wood Shingles

The main drawback of a wood roof is its lack of fire resistance: Untreated shingles have no UL grade, and some local codes prohibit their use. However, shingles can be pressure treated with a leach-resistant, fire-retardant compound to achieve a UL Class C rating for use where there is light exposure to fire. These cannot be bleached and will not change to gray.

The use of wood shingles may increase the cost of your house insurance. Another drawback is that if your house is in a shaded site in a humid climate, moss may grow on your roof. The moss should be periodically removed to prevent decay of the shingles. Never let leaves gather on a roof, as they will hold moisture and cause damage.

In estimating how many bundles of shingles to buy for your roof, be sure first to determine your exact roof slope. On roofs with slopes of 4-in-12 or steeper, the exposures are 5″ for 16″-long shingles, 5½″ for 18″-long shingles, and 7½″ for 24″-long

Wood Shingles—Grades and Specifications.

Grade	Length	Thickness (at Butt)	No. of Courses per Bundle
No. 1 **Blue Label**	16″ (Fivex) 18″ (Perfections) 24″ (Royals)	.40″ .45″ .50″	20/20 18/18 13/14
No. 2 **Red Label**	16″ (Fivex) 18″ (Perfections) 24″ (Royals)	.40″ .45″ .50″	20/20 18/18 13/14
No. 3 **Black Label**	16″ (Fivex) 18″ (Perfections) 24″ (Royals)	.40″ .45″ .50″	20/20 18/18 13/14
No 1 or **No. 2** **Rebutted-** **Rejointed**	16″ (Fivex) 18″ (Perfections) 24″ (Royals)	.40″ .45″ .50″	33/33 28/28 13/14
No. 4 **Undercoursing**	16″ (Fivex) 18″ (Perfections)	.40″ .45″	14/14 or 20/20 14/14 or 18/18

shingles. On slopes less than 4-in-12 but no less than 3-in-12, the exposures are 3¾″, 4¼″, and 5¾″, respectively.

It's a lot more complicated than figuring an asphalt shingle roof. For a concise review of wood shingle grades, weights, lengths, and ordering information, see the Wood Shingles—Grades and Specifications table below.

Wood Shakes

Wood shingles are machine-sawn; shakes are hand-split. This gives a shake roof its rough, textured look. Three types of shakes are common: taper-split, hand-split and resawn, and straight-split.

Shakes are manufactured in 18″ and 24″ lengths and a 15″ "starter-finisher course" length. Sometimes 32″ lengths are available. Thicknesses are shown in the table. Random and

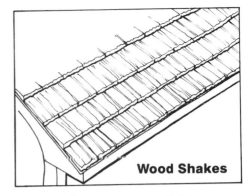

Wood Shakes

"specified" widths are available. Because they are longer and thicker than shingles, they have greater exposure. Typical exposures are 7½″ for 18″ shakes, 10″ for 24″ shakes, and 13″ for 32″ shakes. Pitch must not be less than 4-in-12 to ensure good drainage.

In climates subject to snow loads or high winds, 30-pound felt roofing

Bdls./Cartons per Square	Shipping Weight	Description
4 bdls. 4 bdls. 4 bdls.	144 lbs. 158 lbs. 192 lbs.	The premium grade of shingles for roofs and side-walls. These top-grade shingles are 100% heartwood; 100% clear and 100% edge-grain.
4 bdls. 4 bdls. 4 bdls.	144 lbs. 158 lbs. 192 lbs.	A good grade for all applications. Not less than 10″ clear on 16″ shingles, 11″ clear on 18″ shingles and 15″ clear on 24″ shingles. Flat grain and limited sapwood are permitted in this grade.
4 bdls. 4 bdls. 4 bdls.	144 lbs. 158 lbs. 192 lbs.	A utility grade for economy applications and secondary buildings. Not less than 6″ clear on 16″ and 18″ shingles, 10″ clear on 24″ shingles.
1 carton 1 carton 4 bdls.	60 lbs. 60 lbs. 192 lbs.	Same specifications as above but machine trimmed for exactly parallel edges with butts sawn at precise right angles. Used for sidewall application where tightly fitting joints between singles are desired. Also available with smooth sanded face.
2 bdls. 2 bdls. 2 bdls. 2 bdls.	60 lbs. 72 lbs. 60 lbs. 79 lbs.	A utility grade for undercoursing on double-coursed sidewall applications or for interior accent walls.

(Red Cedar Shingle and Handsplit Shake Bureau)

Roofing

Wood Shakes—Grades and Specifications

Grade	Length and Thickness	20" Pack # Courses per Bdl.	# Bdls. per Sq.
No. 1 **Hand-split and Resawn**	15" Starter-Finish	8/8	5
		10/10	4
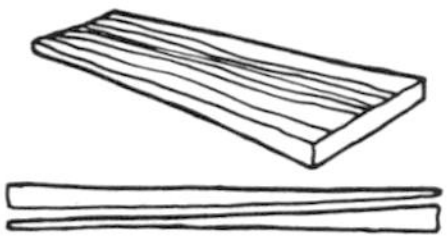	18" × ½" to ¾"	10/10	4
	18" × ¾" to 1¼"	8/8	5
	24" × ⅜"	10/10	4
	24" × ½" to ¾"	10/10	4
	24" × ¾" to 1¼"	8/8	5
	32" × ¾" to 1¼"	6/7	6
No. 1 **Taper-split**	24" × ½" to ⅝"	10/10	4
No. 1 **Straight-split**	18" × ⅜" True-Edge	14 Straight	4
	18" × ⅜"	19 Straight	5
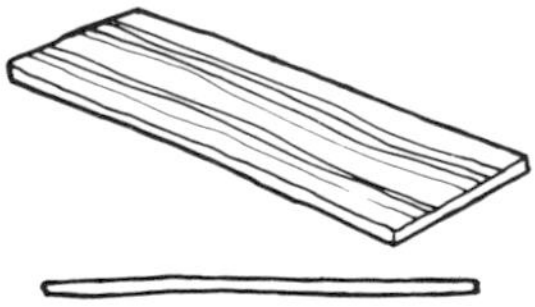	24" × ⅜"	16 Straight	5

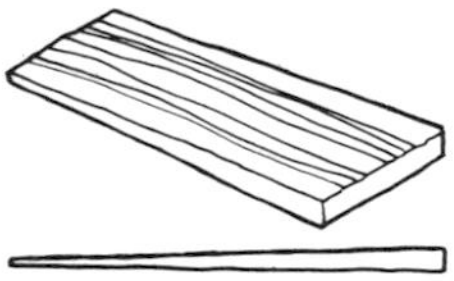

should be used as an underlayment. Open or closed valleys can be used, although open valleys are the most common and practical. Valleys should be underlayed by 30-pound felt and a layer of 26-gauge galvanized iron sheeting. Use only hot-dipped zinc-coated nails with cedar shakes. Ordinary galvanized nails are not sufficiently rust-resistant. Use two nails per shake. Nails should be at least 6d size and long enough to penetrate the sheathing boards.

Wood shingles are sawn from Western red cedar, Northern white cedar, and redwood. Shingles that are all heartwood give the best resistance to decay. Edge-grained shingles give better resistance to warping than flat-grained shingles. Thick butt, narrow shingles are less likely to warp than thin butt, wide shingles.

Shingles are usually packaged four bundles to the square.

Rebutted-rejointed shingles are machine trimmed to ensure parallel edges and precise right angles for sidewall application where tight fitting joints are necessary.

Shingle and Shake Panels

Shingles and shakes are available

18" Pack # Courses per Bdl.	# Bdls. per Sq.	Shipping Weight	Description
9/9	5	225 lbs.	These shakes have split faces and sawn backs. Cedar logs are first cut into desired lengths. Blanks
9/9	5	220 lbs.	or boards of proper thickness are split and then run
9/9	5	250 lbs.	diagonally through a band saw to produce two
9/9	5	225 lbs.	tapered shakes from each blank.
9/9	5	280 lbs.	
9/9	5	350 lbs.	
		450 lbs.	
9/9	5	260 lbs.	Produced largely by hand, using a sharp-bladed steel froe and a wooden mallet. The natural shingle-like taper is achieved by reversing the block, end-for-end, with each split.
		120 lbs.	Produced in the same manner as taper-split shakes
		200 lbs.	except that by splitting from the same end of the
		260 lbs.	block, the shakes acquire the same thickness throughout.

Typical Shake and Shingle Styles

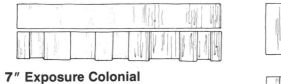

7" Exposure Colonial

7" Exposure Colonial

7" Exposure Colonial

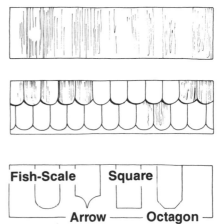

Fish-Scale   Square

Arrow — Octagon

Roofing

in panels to speed up your roofing job. The two 7" courses of shingles are bonded to 12" × ½" sheathing-grade plywood to form 8' panels. The panels are designed for roofs with a 4-in-12 or steeper pitch. Special starter strips are available. These starter strip ends must break on rafter centers. If panels other than starter panels meet between rafters, use plywood clips at the panel joints.

Shingle and shake panels are described in the table giving shingle and shake panel specifications. Use these panels on higher-pitched roof or gable facings, where good drainage is provided.

Slate Roofing

Slate roofs are among the most expensive of all roof coverings. Slate will last indefinitely and is totally fireproof, which may offset its cost. The industry often uses the old federal grading system of A (best) through C, but today for architectural specifications American Society of Testing Materials (ASTM) testing numbers have taken over. But any quarry will know what you want if you ask for the best "A"—clear!

Slate consists of layers of sedimentary clay subjected to high temperatures and pressures that have aligned its granules in parallel fashion to form a flat, hard, durable sandwich of cleavage planes. Premium-quality slate has straight grain running lengthwise. New York and Vermont slate is the most durable. Smooth grain is easier to work with and is as durable as coarse grain. Slate with ribbon streaks of color contains unusually high intrusions of sands and may not be as durable.

Shingle and Shake Panel Specifications

	Exposure	Thickness at Butt	Nominal Height	Exact Length	Coverage Per Bundle (In Square Feet)	Panels Per Bundle	Bundles Per Square	Staggered Butt Line	Even Butt Line
	2 × 7"	⅝"	15" × 96"		37	4	2.7	No	Yes
7" exposure (Colonial)	14"	⅞"	18" × 96"		37	4	2.7	Yes	*
	7"	⅝"	9" × 96"		37	8	2.7	Yes	*
7" exposure (Colonial)	14"	¾"	18" × 96"		37	4	2.7	Yes	*
	7"	⅝"	9" × 96"		37	8	2.7	*	Yes
7" exposure (Colonial)	14"	¾"	18" × 96"		37	4	2.7	Yes	*
	7"	⅝"	9" × 96"		37	8	2.7	*	Yes
	14"	¾"	18" × 96"		37	4	2.7	*	Yes
	7½"	45"	18" × 96"		20	4	5.0	No	Yes

*On special order only.
Individual Fancy Cuts are packaged 96 shingles per carton. Each carton covers from 25 sq. ft. at 7½" exposure to 33⅓" sq. ft. at 10" exposure. Shingles are 4¹⁵⁄₁₆" wide × approximately 18" long.

146

Colors are qualified as "unfading" or, for those subject to color change, "weathering." Sold by the square (100 square feet exposed) slate will cost at least $300 plus freight from the quarry. Most of the quarries are in Vermont, New York, Pennsylvania, and Virginia. The slate, nominally 3/16", can be ordered in sizes 10" × 6" to 24" × 16" with the larger sizes being faster to install. Typical 12" × 8" slates come 400 to the square. Slate is usually ordered in random widths. A graduated slate roof starts at the eaves with large slates up to 1½" thick, getting thinner and smaller with each course. This is probably the most beautiful and expensive roof you can install.

The color of the slate will depend on the quarry. The quarries are all on the eastern side of the Appalachians from Maine to Georgia.

- Gray slate is available year-round from Structural Slate Company, 222 East Main Street, Pen Argyl, PA 18072; (215) 863-4141.
- Black slate is quarried by Buckingham Virginia Slate Corporation, 4110 Fitzhugh Avenue, Richmond, VA 23220; (804) 355-4351.
- Grade A green, grays, or purple are offered by Rising and Nelson Slate Company, West Pawlet, VT 05775; (802) 645-0150. They will also sell you Pennsylvania gray or Virginia blacks.
- Vermont Structural Slate Company, Inc., Box 98, Fair Haven, VT 05763; (802) 265-4933 quarries unfading green, unfading mottled green and purple, unfading purple, and unfading red, and these are all grade A slates.

Green Mountain Mist is a very hard slate most often used for paving and set in mud (cement) but it can also be used for roofing. Consult the quarry for special instructions.

Ice dams with snow and ice accumulation at the eaves can damage a slate roof. In severe climates the section over the eave area of the roof is often covered with metal flashing and the slate section started above this. A new product called "Deck-Dri" Membrane can be used to keep out melting snow and ice, allowing slate to be installed to the roof eave. In addition you may choose to install roof guards and a preformed ridge flashing in severe weather areas.

Tile Cutter

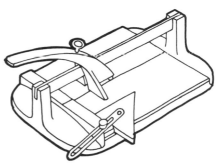

Remember that slate is heavy. Check that your rafters are rated to carry its weight *plus* the local snow load before you commit to a purchase.

Just as you can build with used brick, you can reuse old slate. If you see a slate roof building scheduled for demolition and can buy the slate, you can save a lot of money and still have a beautiful and durable roof. However, as with old brick, you'll need to tap each slate to be sure it "rings" (gives an echo), an indication that it is still firm. Old slate can be cleaned by dipping in oxalic acid.

If you have trouble locating slate roofing tools, they can be purchased from John Stortz and Sons, Inc., a manufacturer located at 210 Vine Street, Philadelphia, PA 19106. You'll need a regular tile cutter, a slater's

Roofing

stake, and a slater's hammer. The stake has a point that can be driven into any convenient framing member and is used as a base for punching, cutting, or smoothing slate. The slater's hammer is used to drive or pull nails, punch holes, or trim the slate.

The quarry will supply slate with two attachment holes prepunched. A drift punch can be used to punch extra nail holes. Slate is usually laid with a 3″ head lap on an underlayment of saturated felt for roofs 6-in-12 or steeper. Otherwise it requires a 4″ lap. Copper or "slater's" nails are used for fastening. Slate may also be installed over 4″ by 2″ lath.

Roofing Tiles

Clay, concrete, and enameled metal are the three main materials used to make tile roofs.

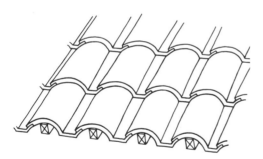

Among the styles available today are French, Spanish, mission, English, and shingle tile.

Clay tile has been in use for a long time, and a number of styles have been developed. They are made with a mixture of shale and clay, placed in molds, and then fired. The common half-cylinder mission tile shape came from the original method of making them. Women would sit and shape rectangles of "slip" over their thighs.

Making Tiles

Available Roofing Tiles

French tile

English tile

Shingle tile

Mission tile

Spanish tile

Concrete tile is a more recent product, and its shapes for the most part resemble more traditional clay tile shapes. The two most common are the French and English styles.

Enameled steel tiles are also available, but they are most often used on commercial structures.

Metal Roofing

The most common metal roofing is the terne metal roof. This roofing is made of copper-bearing steel that is heat-treated, then hot dip-coated with terne metal, an alloy of 80 percent lead and 20 percent tin. The high weather resistance, for which this type of roofing is notable, is due primarily to the lead; tin is included because the resulting alloy makes a better bond with steel.

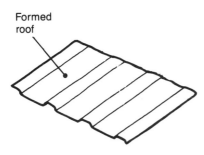

Formed roof

Terne metal is graded in terms of the total weight of the coating on a given area. This area, by old trade custom, is the total area contained in a box of 112 sheets that are 20" × 28" in size and amounts to 436 square feet. The best grade of terne coating is 40-pound, and it provides a roof surface that will last for many years.

A wide variety of sheet sizes are available, as well as 50' seamless rolls in various widths. These permit its use for many different types of roofs and methods of applications. Metal roofing

is also used extensively for flashing around both roof and wall openings.

For best appearance and longest wear, terne metal roofs must be painted. A linseed oil-based iron oxide primer is recommended for a base coat, over which nearly any exterior paint and color can be used.

Another kind of sheet metal roofing is the corrugated galvanized sheet. Sheets that are heavily coated with zinc (2.0 ounces per square foot) should be used on permanent construction. Lighter-coated sheets can be used for temporary buildings or for permanent buildings if the sheets are protected by paint. Galvanized sheets can be used on slopes as low as 3-in-12 ($\frac{1}{8}$ pitch) with end laps of 8". Roofs with pitches of $\frac{1}{4}$ or greater can use 4" end laps. Sheets should have side laps of $1\frac{1}{2}$". Corrugated sheets are supplied in 26 and 28 gauge.

Aluminum alloy sheets available for roofing are supplied with corrugation spacing of $1\frac{1}{4}$" or $2\frac{1}{2}$" and should be side-lapped like galvanized sheets. Aluminum alloy nails, with nonmetallic washers between the nail heads and roofing, should be used for attachment. Saturated felt should be used under the sheets and over the sheathing. Aluminum sheets should not be in contact with any type of wood or attached to other metals that will cause them to corrode.

Aluminum roofing also is available in shingle form. Most aluminum shingles are made to interlock. A bake-on vinyl-plastic coating is applied to some brands to provide a permanent, colorfast finish. Saturated felt is normally used as an underlayment. When applied in a diagonal pattern, the first course is applied as a half shingle. Each shingle is affixed with one nail in the upper corner.

Roofing

Built-Up Roofing

Because of the equipment and skills required to lay a satisfactory built-up roof, a well-qualified roofing contractor should be hired to do the work. This is the one roofing job a do-it-yourselfer should not attempt.

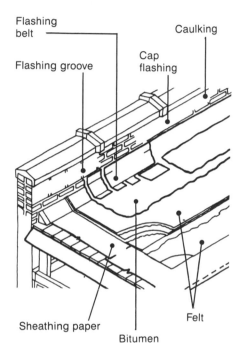

Built-up Roofing

Built-up roofing is generally used on decks with a pitch of 2″ or less. It consists of several layers of roofing felts laid between coatings of hot tar or asphalt. The top is surfaced with gravel slag or crushed rock. For residential construction, the gravel or rock is applied in a ratio of 300 pounds to 100 square feet.

On wood decks, a base layer of roofing felt is securely nailed with a 4″ overlap. This is followed with applications of hot tar or hot asphalt between layers of 40-pound felt. The crushed rock or gravel is embedded in the final coating of tar or asphalt. A gravel stop is used to retain the coating.

Roll Roofing

Roll roofing is generally used on temporary buildings or when price is a dominant factor. It consists of asphalt-impregnated felt made in varying widths and lengths and surfaced with mineral granules in a wide variety of colors. The edges may be straight or patterned.

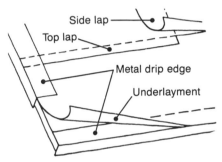

Double-Coverage Roll Roofing

Roll roofing may be applied with either exposed or concealed nailing. The concealed method makes for greater durability, however. Nails used must be 11- or 12-gauge, hot-dipped galvanized and with ⅜″ heads. Shanks should be at least ⅞″ long. The lap cement should be stored in a warm place until ready for use. When using the concealed-nail method, apply the edge strips (metal strips along the

Roll Roofing

150

Typical Asphalt Rolls

Product	Per Roll	Per Square	Squares Per Package	Length	Width	Selvage	Exposure	Underwriters Laboratories Listing*
	Approximate Shipping Weight							
Mineral surface roll	75# to 90#	75# to 90#	1	36′ to 38′	36″	2″ to 4″	32″ to 34″	C
Mineral surface roll (double coverage)	55# to 70#	110# to 140#	½	36′	36″	19″	17″	C
Smooth surface roll	50# to 86#	40# to 65#	1 to 2	36′ to 72′	36″	2″	34″	None

*UL rating at time of publication. Reference should be made to individual manufacturer's product at time of purchase.

eaves and rakes) with a ¼″ to ⅜″ overhang.

Double-coverage roll roofing, also called 19″ selvage roofing, provides double coverage over the entire roof area. It has the same effect as a built-up roof. Roofs with a rise of only 1″ per foot may be covered this way. The material comes in 36″ widths and is applied with a 19″ lap and 17″ exposure. Because specifications differ among manufacturers, their directions for application should be followed carefully.

Underlayment

An underlayment is an asphalt roll placed over the roof's wood decking before the finish roofing is applied.

The most common underlayment is building paper. Building papers are asphalt-saturated felts sold by the roll and according to the number of pounds of asphalt per roll. Use only vapor-porous (perforated) felts on roofs, because coated felts, tar-saturated felts or laminated waterproof papers are vapor barriers and will allow moisture to condense or even freeze

Roofing

Underlayment Specifications

Product	Approximate Shipping Weight Per Roll	Per Sq.	Sqs. Per Package	Length	Width	Side or End Lap	Top Lap	Exposure	Underwriters Listing
Saturated Felt	45#	11#	4	144'	36"				
	60#	15#	4	144'	36"	4"	2"	34"	None
	60#	20#	3	108'	36"	to			
	60#	30#	2	72'	36"	6"			

on the underside. That could cause the sheathing to warp or even rot. Underlayment is installed with staples.

The underlayment has four purposes:

- It protects the sheathing (often interior plywood) from moisture absorption until the shingles can be applied. (Never apply felt over wet sheathing.)
- It acts as a fail-safe barrier to driving rain that may get through the shingles or tile.
- It provides a barrier to stop any resin extracted from wood sheathing from reacting unfavorably with the shingles.
- It provides a good marking surface to make snapped chalk lines clearly visible.

In calculating quantity required, remember that you will need a double layer at the eaves (in cold climates) and will be laying the felt with overlaps of 19" and 17" exposed.

Deck-Dri® Membrane

Deck-Dri Membrane is a new product recently introduced by Owens-Corning Fiberglas to prevent the water occasioned by melting ice and snow, which forms a roof dam, from penetrating the roof. This Fiberglas-reinforced membrane is self-adhesive and comes with a release paper applied during manufacture to permit rolling and easier application. Applied along the bottom edge of sheathing to 24" beyond the interior wall, this flexible modified asphalt seals around the shingle nails and keeps water out. An adhesive top edge helps provide a watertight 6" lap. Deck-Dri Membrane is sold in 76' rolls, 36" wide, weighing 83 pounds and covering 200 square feet.

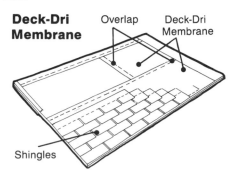

Deck-Dri Membrane — Overlap — Deck-Dri Membrane — Shingles

Flashing

A roof is especially prone to leaks at its edges and where it is penetrated by chimneys or vent pipes. At these weak points, pieces of metal called flashing are used to provide durable waterproof seals.

Flashings are attached with cement and nails or staples. Use nails or staples only where their heads will be covered by roofing or cement.

Drip edges are preformed with the bottom edge bent out so that water drips do not contact the fascia. These are used at eaves and over doors and windows. They are normally nailed with galvanized roofing nails.

For the average 1700-square-foot home, you will need between 200' and 360' of flashing, depending on construction. Flashing is usually

Flashing Designs

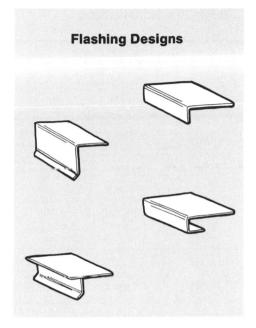

Flashing Needs

Location	Description	Purpose
Chimney	Cap flashing is built into chimney and soldered to shingle flashing.	To make the junction between chimney and roof watertight.
Eaves	From roof sheathing over fascia and into gutter. Recommended where the temperature goes below 0°F or where there is a potential for ice dams. A new 36" wide asphaltic roll product with an adhesive backing, "Deck-Dri Membrane," has been developed to stop melting ice and snow from penetrating the roof. Laid in one or two courses so it extends to 24" above the wall junction, it provides a waterproof barrier under any ice dam. NOTE: Ice dams are usually caused by insufficient attic insulation, allowing escaping heat to melt snow on the roof peak while snow over the eaves is still frozen. Ice dams may also form on roofs with wide overhangs where cold winds blowing up under the soffits freeze the roof run-off melted by the sun.	To protect fascia and prevent dammed water from backing up and leaking through the roof.

Roofing

Flashing Needs (Concluded)

Location	Description	Purpose
Roof	Used for ridge flashing, valley flashing, and at intersections with walls or other roofs. Also at intersection between wall and flat roof.	To protect wood sheathing and direct rain into gutters.
Vent	Vent flashing for stack vents is available prefabricated in the form of a collar or a boot. All joints should be caulked with roofing mastic. For soil stacks you will need to make a collar from 50-lb. roll roofing and adhere with asphalt plastic cement.	To prevent leaks at joints. Due to frequent temperature changes, such as caused by emptying hot bathwater in frigid weather, stacks expand and contract, moving up and down through the roof. The junction needs to be caulked with a flexible caulk and checked every year or so for cracks or delamination.

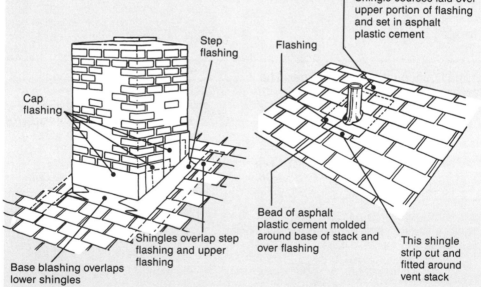

Flashing A Chimney

Step flashing

Cap flashing

Shingles overlap step flashing and upper flashing

Base blashing overlaps lower shingles

Flashing A Vent Stack

Shingle courses laid over upper portion of flashing and set in asphalt plastic cement

Flashing

Bead of asphalt plastic cement molded around base of stack and over flashing

This shingle strip cut and fitted around vent stack

purchased in rolls by width from 6" to 20" and is made from stainless steel, tinplate, lead-clad iron, lead, copper, or aluminum. Aluminum should not be used in contact with asphalt or shingles that will cause it to corrode. Aluminum is also difficult to solder. Copper should not be used with red cedar shakes, as it will darken the wood. Eighteen-gauge galvanized steel can be used, but it needs paint and maintenance. Galvanized flashings are sometimes coated with primers and roof coatings.

Cements

Roof cements are used as sealants and adhesives in roofing work. All of the cements and coatings are asphalt-based and are flammable. They should never be heated over an open fire or placed in direct contact with a hot surface. If they must be softened before application, place the unopened containers in hot water or store them in a warm place until ready for use.

Apply asphalt cements and coatings to clean, dry surfaces. Trowel or brush them vigorously onto the surface to eliminate air bubbles and to force the material into all cracks and openings.

The different types of cements and coatings include:

Asphalt plastic cement (also known as flashing cement). This is generally applied to flashings where the roof meets a wall, chimney, vent pipe, or other vertical surface. It is formulated so it will not melt and run off at the high surface temperatures normally encountered in summer. The cement remains pliable at low temperatures.

Lap cement. Generally not as viscous as asphalt plastic cement, lap cement is used to provide a watertight bond between lapped plies of roll roofing. Exposed nails used in conjunction with lap cement should pass through the cement so that the shank of the nail is sealed where it penetrates the deck.

Quick-setting asphalt cement. This may be applied by brush, trowel, or gun, depending on its consistency. It is manufactured with a solvent that evaporates quickly on exposure, permitting the cement to set quickly. The cement is used to bond free tabs of strip shingles and roll roofing laps applied by the concealed-nail method.

Follow the manufacturer's recommendations for using any of the asphalt cements described above. Avoid application of excessive quantities, which can lead to blistering.

Masonry primer. This is an asphalt primer used to prepare masonry surfaces for bonding with other asphalt products such as built-up roofing components, asphalt plastic cements, or roof coatings. On application, the primer must penetrate the masonry surface pores. Masonry primers are very fluid and are applied by brushing or spraying.

Roofing tapes. These tapes are made from asphalt-saturated cotton or glass fiber. They are used in conjunction with asphalt cements and coatings for flashings and for patching seams, breaks, and holes in metal and asphalt roofs. The tapes are available in rolls up to 50 yards long and 4″ to 36″ wide.

Gutters and Downspouts

Gutters or eaves troughs collect rainwater from the roof edge and carry it through downspouts, to run-offs which direct the water away from the foundation. The term *gutter* refers to a separate unit that is attached to the eaves fascia, while the term *eaves trough* applies to a waterway built into the roof surface over the cornice. Because eaves troughs require careful design and installation, gutters are normally found in most residential construction.

Gutters are available fabricated from steel, aluminum, vinyl, copper or wood. They come in standard 10′ lengths. The table outlines the good and bad features of each material. You will also need downspouts for every 35′ and run-offs (concrete or roll-up plastic) for

Roofing

each downspout to drain rainwater well away from the foundation. Failure to provide these is one of the most common causes of leaky basements.

Most of the gutter systems used in residential construction today are prefinished vinyl and aluminum. They consist of a series of modular pieces that are assembled to fit each different situation.

Parts slip together easily and are held with either pop-rivets or sheet metal screws. New vinyl gutters with snap-on joints make installation much easier.

Gutters and downspouts are sized to correspond to the roof areas from which they receive water.

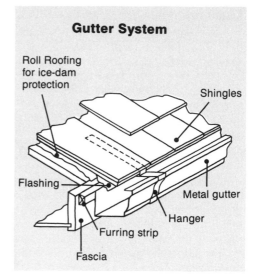

Gutter System

Roll Roofing for ice-dam protection

Shingles

Flashing

Metal gutter

Hanger

Furring strip

Fascia

Gutter Materials Selection Guide

Material	Features	Special Considerations	Maintenance/ Durability/Cost
Steel	Galvanized guttering in 4″, 5″ and 6″ box sizes. Generally unpainted but enameled steel is available. Heavy material. All standard accessories available.	Must be painted for protection. Do not attach with aluminum spikes.	Tendency to rust so must be wire brushed and repainted or will not last many years. Inexpensive.
Copper	In 4″ and 5″ sizes. A specialty item of interest to remodelers. Requires all joints to be soldered.	Will develop an attractive patina.	Joints may require resoldering. Are seen on many fifty-year-old houses. Durable and very expensive.
Wood	Flow area equivalent to 4″ and 5″ gutters. Thick, heavy, and subject to rot and decay. Only use for artistic effect or in authentic remodeling of historic homes. Few accessories available.	Must be painted.	Must be cleaned and treated inside and painted outside every year. Have been known to warp. Lifetime depends on maintenance. Moderately expensive.

Gutter Materials Selection Guide (Concluded)

Material	Features	Special Considerations	Maintenance/Durability/Cost
Vinyl	Standard 4″ and 5″ gutters. Available in white, brown and gray with color-matched components. Snap together units require a silicone lubricant, other type is solvent welded. Most attach with special molded fittings to accommodate expansion and contraction of as much as ¼″ in 10′. Cannot be directly nailed.	For draining large roof areas request new high velocity drop outlet fittings—this is less expensive than going to a large size gutter. New spillover outlet sluices leaves, keeping downspout clear and reducing maintenance. Can be painted but this is not necessary.	Available with 20-year warranties—very durable with little maintenance other than cleaning out shingle gravel and leaves. Can withstand hail. Relatively expensive.
Aluminum	Available in 4″, 5″ and 6″ gutter sizes. Variety of white and colored plastic-coated and enamel finishes. A wide variety of prefinished accessories is available. Parts are joined with blind rivets and downspouts are secured with straps and, on brick or masonry walls, nylon pin anchors.	Lighter weight than galvanized. Because of expansion and contraction it is better to attach with aluminum spikes through slots instead of holes or use straps.	Easily damaged by ladders and branches. Should last 10–20 years but may need repainting. Moderately expensive. If cheap they may be made with too light a gauge aluminum and be subject to twisting.

Gutter and Downspout Sizing

Roof Area	Gutter Size	Downspout Size
Up to 750 sq. ft.	4″	3″
750 to 1400 sq. ft.	5″	4″
Over 1400 sq. ft.	6″	4″

If you are replacing parts of an existing system, don't mix metals. Copper, steel, and aluminum aren't compatible with each other. Also, some materials, such as vinyl, are especially sensitive to expansion and contraction. Be sure to follow the manufacturer's joining instructions carefully.

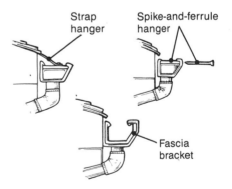

Strap hanger · Spike-and-ferrule hanger · Fascia bracket

Gutters are attached to the fascia by one of three methods. *Strap hangers* work only with flexible roof materials

Roofing

such as asphalt shingles. If your roof has rigid wood shingles or slate, use *fascia brackets* or *spike-and-ferrule hangers. Spikes* are the easiest of all to install, but they're more likely to sag under loads of heavy ice and snow.

Ventilation

Attic and soffit ventilation play an important role in maintaining a roof. The fresh air keeps rafters and decking dry, thus preventing dry rot. Louvered vents, cupolas, ventilated ridge vents, and exhaust fans can be used together with soffit vents to provide the necessary ventilation. FHA regulations require 1 square foot of ventilating area per 150 square feet of ceiling. If the ceiling has a vapor barrier, the ratio drops to 1 per 300 square feet. Ridge, roof, or gable vents must be at least 3′ above eaves vents.

Since the requirements are for unobstructed area, the following adjustments to ventilated area must be made for screens and louvers:

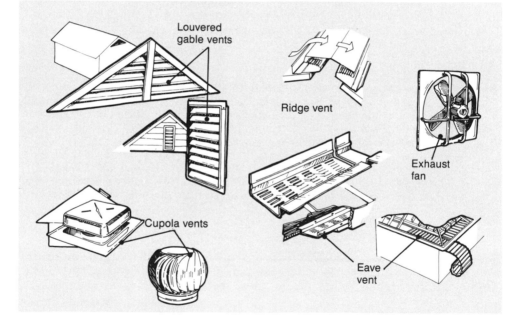

Louvered gable vents

Ridge vent

Exhaust fan

Cupola vents

Eave vent

Ventilator Adjustment Factors

Covering	Adjustment Factor
¼″ hardware cloth	1 × recommendations
¼″ hardware cloth with rain louvers	2 × recommendations
⅛″ mesh screen	1.25 × recommendations
⅛″ mesh screen with rain louvers	2.25 × recommendations
¹⁄₁₆″ mesh screen	2 × recommendations
¹⁄₁₆″ mesh screen and rain louvers	3 × recommendations

NOTE: If there are no eaves vents there must be 1 square foot of ridge, roof, or gable vents for each 300 square feet of ceiling, with half in each end of the gable, if there is a vapor barrier between the attic and the living space. If there is no vapor barrier, you need 1 square foot of vent for each 150 square feet of ceiling.

The Right Tools

Ladders and scaffolding. You will need an extension ladder to reach the roof. If your roof is steep, you may want a ladder with an over-the-ridge hook at one end (sometimes called a "chicken ladder"), allowing the ladder to lie flat and secure. Steep roofs also require roofing brackets or scaffolds to hold your roofing material.

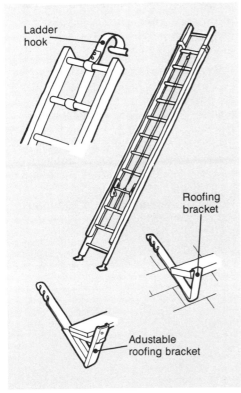

Ladder hook

Roofing bracket

Adustable roofing bracket

Folding and tape rules. Used for measuring shingle overlaps and layouts.

Chalk reel. This is for snapping chalk lines that will be used to align the materials over the roof surface.

Roofing knife. For cutting, shaping, and fitting the various materials.

Hammer or roofer's hatchet. For all nailing. The hatchet may also be used for aligning shingles.

Putty knife, pointed trowel, or brush. These are used for applying asphalt cements.

Caulking gun. For caulking around vents and filling voids before flashing or shingling.

Flat shovel. For removing existing shingles in reroofing applications.

Nails. These should be made of steel or aluminum. Steel roofing nails should be zinc-coated for corrosion protection. Nails should have barbed or deformed shanks. They should be 11 or 12 gauge and have large heads of $\frac{3}{8}''$ to $\frac{7}{16}''$ diameter. The nails should be long enough for the shank to penetrate through the roofing material and at least $\frac{3}{4}''$ into the deck lumber or through a plywood deck.

Staples. A quicker alternative to nails. Staples should be zinc-coated and 16-gauge minimum. They should have a minimum crown width of $\frac{15}{16}''$

Recommended Fastener Lengths

Application	Fastener Length
Roll roofing on new deck	$1''$
Strip or individual shingles on new deck	$1\frac{1}{4}''$
Reroofing over old asphalt roofing	$1\frac{1}{2}''$ to $2''$
Reroofing over old wood shingles	$2''$

Roofing

and, as with nails, the shank should be of sufficient length to penetrate ¾" into deck lumber or through plywood decks.

Pneumatic stapler. Used to drive staples. This is a power tool, attached to a long hose linking it with an air compressor. Do-it-yourselfers can rent this tool, and this is usually worthwhile, since the stapler is fast, easy, and lets you fasten shingles with one hand instead of two. Shop around for the best daily rental rate.

Patio Roofing

In hot climates a standard roof with fiberglass or asphalt shingles may be used for shading. In moderate climates a translucent roof may be preferred to provide more light and an out-of-doors feeling. Two products available for patio roofing are fiberglass-reinforced panels (flat or corrugated) and polycarbonate structured (fluted) sheet (PCSS).

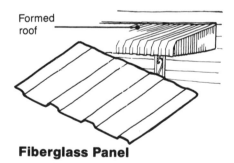

Formed roof

Fiberglass Panel

Fiberglass Panels

Lightweight, strong, and easy to install, these translucent, shatterproof panels are used for their color and light transmission. Installed on rafters 2' on center, these 26"-wide panels have 2½" corrugations or 4" × ⅝" ribs. Standard lengths are 8', 10', or 12'. (Flat panels are rarely used, since rafter spacing has to be close to meet

building codes.) They are installed on corrugated redwood filler strips using special aluminum nails, waterproof sealant, and aluminum flashing. Colors include green, blue, yellow, and clear. Those made with a modified acrylic containing a UV (ultraviolet) inhibitor will outlast cheaper polyester panels. To prevent fiber blooming, these should be scrubbed well and recoated when they lose their gloss. Fibers that become exposed after UV radiation (from sunlight) and rain dissolve and wash off the resin surface are called blooming fibers.

Polycarbonate Sheets

These are lightweight, transparent (or translucent), strong, fluted panels (with two flat sheets separated by ¼" ribs every ⅜"). They can be installed on rafters spaced 2' on centers. They feature gasketed joints. Standard lengths are 8', 10', and 12'; standard widths are 24", 36", and 48". Polycarbonate sheets are attached with aluminum nails.

Exterior
Sidings

5

5. Exterior Sidings

The choice of sidings for your home has never been greater. All the traditional sidings are still available: wood, brick, stone, and stucco. But in the last forty years, other man-made materials have been invented. They are generally less expensive than the traditional materials and have come to dominate the market.

Today the look of painted wood clapboards (bevel siding) on a new house is rarely the real thing. Instead, it may be aluminum, steel, vinyl, plywood, or hardboard (a product made of wood fibers processed into the shape of boards). Both vinyl and aluminum siding are available with imitation wood grain patterns. These new sidings also imitate the shapes of other traditional wood sidings, such as shingles or tongue-and-groove boards.

Increasingly, however, plywood sheet sidings have defined their own style. These 4'-wide sheets have faces of boardlike shapes separated by vertical grooves. The surface veneer of wood may be redwood, cedar, fir, or pine; it may be smooth or rough-sawn in texture; it can be bought unfinished, prestained, or prepainted. Whatever the final appearance, plywood sidings seem most at home with contemporary architecture.

Honest-to-goodness wood boards have not faded from the siding scene, but they are now typically a custom-home product and are less often painted. Instead, they are stained to preserve their natural hues, or left to weather to a gray if the setting is woods or seashore. If the home's style is contemporary, the boards may be tongue-and-groove and laid diagonally. The wood used is generally a top

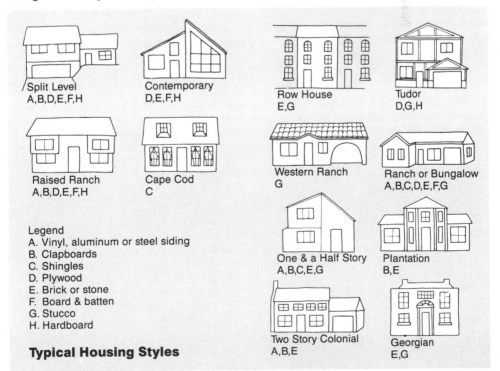

Split Level
A,B,D,E,F,H

Contemporary
D,E,F,H

Row House
E,G

Tudor
D,G,H

Raised Ranch
A,B,D,E,F,H

Cape Cod
C

Western Ranch
G

Ranch or Bungalow
A,B,C,D,E,F,G

One & a Half Story
A,B,C,E,G

Plantation
B,E

Two Story Colonial
A,B,E

Georgian
E,G

Legend
A. Vinyl, aluminum or steel siding
B. Clapboards
C. Shingles
D. Plywood
E. Brick or stone
F. Board & batten
G. Stucco
H. Hardboard

Typical Housing Styles

Exterior Sidings

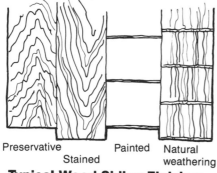

Preservative   Painted   Natural
    Stained   weathering

Typical Wood Siding Finishes

grade of redwood or cedar but pine is not uncommon.

Whether you're choosing siding for a new home or residing your old home, your choice will depend largely on the depth of your pockets, the style of your home, and its location. If you're residing, you may be able to apply the new directly over the old, especially if what's there is wood siding that provides a flat, level, sound nailing surface. If not, you may need to nail furring strips atop the old siding or tear off the old altogether.

If you are residing, now's the time to consider increasing the insulating power of your walls. If your walls aren't already insulated and you are not removing the old siding, consider having insulation blown into the wall cavities. If you are removing the old siding and sheathing, fiberglass batts will be easy to install. And if you live in a cold climate, add polyisocyanurate rigid insulation as sheathing before installing the new siding. This added thickness will require longer fasteners and adjustments at door and window casings.

One important point: Order your siding or plywood ahead of time. The reason for requesting early delivery is to give the lumber or plywood a chance to adjust to ambient moisture levels. Hardboard, particularly, must be on

the site at least five days prior to use. Store on a flat dry surface and keep it clean. Give the bundles adequate support to prevent warping. Cover your siding with a waterproof cover, but don't seal tightly, because the cover could shrink and bind the lumber, cutting off essential air circulation.

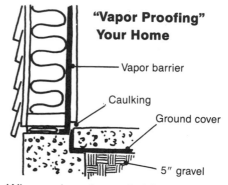

"Vapor Proofing" Your Home

Vapor barrier

Caulking

Ground cover

5″ gravel

When using plywood siding, pay attention to the American Plywood Association (APA) trademark, which gives you allowable stud spans. Use aluminum, stainless steel, or hot-dipped galvanized nails to prevent rust streaks from staining the wood. To allow for expansion leave a ⅛″ space between adjoining plywood panels at all ends and edges. Leave a 3/16″ gap around openings. Caulk all butt joints with silicone or polyurethane; ship-lapped joints need no caulking.

Painting

Your choice of finishes includes solid-color stains, which are good for textured lumber, semitransparent oil stains, which bring out the grain appearance (but should be tested on scrap first), lightly pigmented natural finishes, and acrylic latex paints. Two coats of paint is the most formal finish, but also the finish that requires the most maintenance. The best woods to hold paint are redwood and cedar. The best grain is edge-grained bevel siding. If you plan to paint, avoid Southern yellow pine and Douglas fir having late wood or summer growth. These do not hold paint well due to a tendency to stretch and shrink.

One way to avoid later blistering of paint on your siding is to provide a very tightly sealed and caulked vapor barrier on the inside of the home. When using clapboard over foil-faced foam sheathings, it is wise to use furring strips to avoid condensation getting trapped between the foil and the wood.

If you install cedar shingles and want to let them weather, you may want to apply bleach to get a more even appearance—the weathering process takes several years. Your other option is to use the lightly pigmented natural finishes which will give you a gray color right away.

Repainting

In repainting aged siding that has been oil painted, it is important not to build up a thick coating. You can repaint over a single coat, after washing down with a detergent. Bare areas should be sanded and coated with a zinc-free oil-based primer. Over other painted surfaces, chalk should be scrubbed off with detergent and water and the siding painted with a good-quality exterior gloss vinyl or acrylic latex. You may need to apply two coats.

In re-staining it is vital to get the surface perfectly clean and, unless you want to darken the color, to use a transparent sealer.

Wood Siding

Bevel or taper siding is still the most popular style for horizontal wood siding. The adjoining illustrations show the common styles. One side of bevel siding is usually smooth, while the other is rough-sawn. If you have

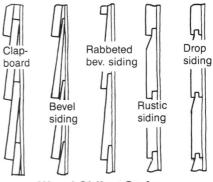

Clapboard   Rabbeted bev. siding   Drop siding

Bevel siding   Rustic siding

Wood Siding Styles

Flat-grained siding does not hold paint well

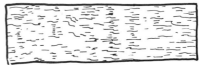

Edge-grained siding—use smooth face for painting

Wood Siding "Paintability"

decided on a stained finish you'll probably want the rough side out, but for a painted surface you'll have an easier job with edge-grained bevel siding if the smooth side is exposed. Avoid flat-grained siding, as it shrinks and swells and will not hold paint well.

In selecting the height of siding, (when installed horizontally) you'll have two concerns. First you'll want the lap or shadow line flush with the bottom of your windowsill. Second, bear in mind that if the house is a ranch type or modest in size, narrow boards will make the house appear larger and wide boards will make the house seem smaller. Horizontal installation will make the house look longer and lower, while vertical

Exterior Sidings

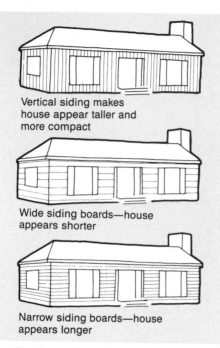

Vertical siding makes house appear taller and more compact

Wide siding boards—house appears shorter

Narrow siding boards—house appears longer

application will make it look taller and more compact.

The trend in wood siding is to new and brighter colors and shades of staining; it doesn't have to be brown. Vivid paints are also in style. But do you really want to use paint? If you are paying to use real wood, you don't want it confused with cheaper metal or plastic siding. Wood has more depth and variation in color and texture, isn't as likely to get dented by hailstones or baseballs, doesn't add to the noise in a rainstorm and, when properly protected and maintained, will last as long as the house. In fact, it may well help you sell your house faster and for more money.

The cost of wood siding is so variable that you'll have to shop around to get the best deal. It's always sold in random lengths.

Estimating Amount of Siding

In figuring the quantity of siding required for a structure, it is necessary to increase the footage by an amount sufficient to compensate for the difference between nominal and finished sizes. Additional amounts must also be added for the machining of joints and the overlap in beveled siding. The table below provides approximate percentages that should be added to the net square footage of the wall surface to be covered.

Example:
  1 x 8 Bevel siding—$1\frac{1}{8}$ lap
  Wall height = 8 ft.
  Wall perimeter = 180 ft.
  Door and window area = 220 sq. ft.

Total area to be covered
  = (8 × 180) − 220
  = 1440 − 220
  = 1220 sq. ft.

Siding Estimate*
  = 1220 + (1220 × 33%)
  = 1220 + 403 (402.6)
  = 1623 board feet
*For eave area add an extra 10 percent (163)

Area for gable ends can be calculated by multiplying the height above the eaves by the width and dividing by two. Considerable waste occurs in covering triangular areas and at least 10 percent should be added to this calculation. When the structure includes an excessive number of corners due to projections and recesses in the wall line, an additional allowance of at least 5 percent should be added to the percentages shown.

The table here lists sizes of horizontal siding. Use the nominal sizes to compute the board footage of lumber you'll need. These sizes are based upon the sizes of boards cut from the logs. Rough, green boards shrink as they dry, and their size is later reduced by machining to pattern. You will need to add a percentage in calculating board footage needed.

Dimensions of Wood Siding

Siding	Nominal Size Width (inches)	Dressed Dimensions	
		Standard Thickness (inches)	Standard Face Width (inches)
Bevel	4	**$7/16$ by $3/16$	$3\frac{1}{2}$
	5	$10/16$ by $3/16$	$4\frac{1}{2}$
	6	. . . .	$5\frac{1}{2}$
Wide Beveled	8	**$7/16$ by $3/16$	$7\frac{1}{4}$
	10	$9/16$ hy $3/10$	$9\frac{1}{4}$
	12	$11/16$ by $3/16$	$11\frac{1}{4}$
Rustic and Drop	4	$9/16$	$3\frac{1}{8}$
(Ship-lapped)	5	$3/4$	$4\frac{1}{8}$
	6	. . . .	$5\frac{1}{16}$
	8	. . . .	$6\frac{7}{8}$
Rustic and Drop	4	$9/16$	$3\frac{1}{4}$
(Dressed and Matched)	5	$3/4$	$4\frac{1}{4}$
	6	. . . .	$5\frac{3}{16}$
	8	. . . .	7

In patterned siding, $11/16''$, $3/4''$, $1''$, $1\frac{1}{4}''$, and $1\frac{1}{2}''$ thick, board measure, the tongue shall be $1/4''$ wide in tongue-and-groove lumber, and the lap $3/8''$ wide in ship-lapped lumber, with the overall widths $1/4''$ and $3/8''$ wider, respectively, than the face widths shown above.   **Minimum thickness

Calculating Added Quantities to Compensate for Joints and Overlaps

Siding	Nominal Size (inches)	Lap	Add +	Standard Face Width (inches)
Bevel	1 x 4	$3/4$	45%	$3\frac{1}{2}$
	1 x 5	$7/8$	38%	$4\frac{1}{2}$
	1 x 6	1	33%	$5\frac{1}{2}$
Wide Beveled	1 x 8	$1\frac{1}{4}$	33%	$7\frac{1}{4}$
	1 x 10	$1\frac{1}{2}$	29%	$9\frac{1}{4}$
	1 x 12	$1\frac{1}{2}$	23%	$11\frac{1}{4}$
Rustic and Drop	1 x 4		28%	$3\frac{1}{8}$
(Ship-lapped)	1 x 5*		21%	$4\frac{1}{8}$
	1 x 6		19%	$5\frac{1}{16}$
	1 x 8		16%	$6\frac{7}{8}$
Rustic and Drop	1 x 4		23%	$3\frac{1}{4}$
(Dressed and Matched)	1 x 5*		18%	$4\frac{1}{4}$
	1 x 6		16%	$5\frac{3}{16}$
	1 x 8		14%	7

*Unusual sizes
+ Percentage to add to net wall surface when estimating quantities of horizontal wood siding. In calculating for triangular eaves or excessive number of corners add an additional 10%.

Exterior Sidings

Lumber Siding Patterns—
Vertical, Diagonal or Horizontal (Random lengths)

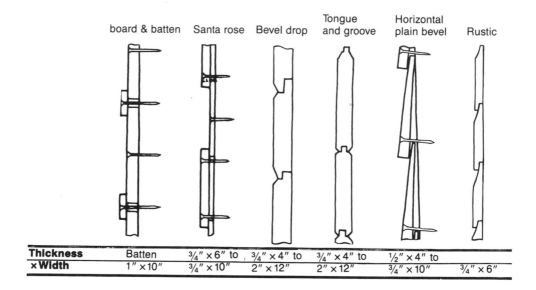

board & batten   Santa rose   Bevel drop   Tongue and groove   Horizontal plain bevel   Rustic

| Thickness x Width | Batten 1″ × 10″ | ³⁄₄″ × 6″ to ³⁄₄″ × 10″ | ³⁄₄″ × 4″ to 2″ × 12″ | ³⁄₄″ × 4″ to 2″ × 12″ | ¹⁄₂″ × 4″ to ³⁄₄″ × 10″ | ³⁄₄″ × 6″ |

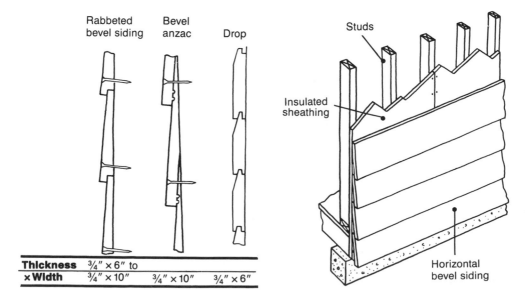

Rabbeted bevel siding   Bevel anzac   Drop

| Thickness x Width | ³⁄₄″ × 6″ to ³⁄₄″ × 10″ | ³⁄₄″ × 10″ | ³⁄₄″ × 6″ |

Horizontal Siding Installation

Studs

Insulated sheathing

Horizontal bevel siding

Plywood Siding

Plywood siding is economical, easy to install, and a good way to achieve the appearance of wood at a lesser price, particularly if you happen to select a rarer species of wood. It's also APA graded, so you know what you are buying.

Typical Frame Construction Using Plywood Panel Siding

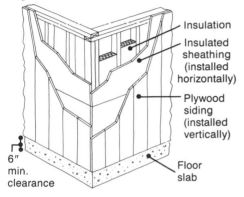

Insulation

Insulated sheathing (installed horizontally)

Plywood siding (installed vertically)

6" min. clearance

Floor slab

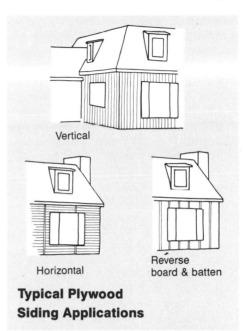

Vertical

Horizontal

Reverse board & batten

Typical Plywood Siding Applications

In selecting plywood siding, appearance is naturally going to be your first consideration so you'll want to select the style, and the species of wood must also be selected. Siding is usually made with facings of Douglas fir, redwood, cedar, or Southern pine, although other species are available. APA 303 siding (manufactured to industry specification 303) offers thirteen different face grades (smooth, overlaid, rough-sawn, and other textures) and a variety of groove patterns. You'll need to choose the

Plywood Species and Strength Ratings

Group	Species	Group	Species
1	Western larch Loblolly pine Douglas fir from the Northwest	4	Aspen Paper birch Western red cedar Eastern hemlock Sugar pine
2	Western hemlock Douglas fir from the Southwest		Englemann spruce
3	Alaska cedar Red alder Lodgepole pine Spruce (red, white, and black)	5	Balsam fir Basswood

NOTE: Other species are used in each group.

Exterior Sidings

stain or paint and color finish you plan to apply when selecting the facing. However, after these four decisions are made there are other important criteria that may narrow your original choice. Are you applying the siding directly to the studs? If so, you'll need a panel rated for either 16″ or 24″ stud spacing. That will depend on your use of horizontal or vertical application of the panel and the plywood thickness. While you can use any thickness over plywood or oriented-strand board sheathing, you may want to avoid the thinnest panels, as they can produce a degree of waviness that is visible when the sun shines down the side of the house, and this can be very disturbing. The effect will be even more pronounced when thin panels are installed on studs without sheathing.

The grade depends on the number and type of patches. There are four basic appearance grades: Special Series 303, 303-6, 303-18, and 303-30. Special Series 303 allows only natural defects and no patches. These are the top-of-the-line panels: 303-OC (clear), 303-OL (overlaid), 303-NR (natural rustic), and 303-SR (synthetic rustic). If you are going to use stain, the investment in this top grade may be worthwhile. Should you be planning to use paint, go for a cheaper grade. A number following the 303 tells how many patches are allowed in that grade per 4′ × 8′ panel: 303-6 allows six patches; 303-6W means they will be wood patches and 303-6S means they may be synthetic patches, while the use of S/W means either or both may be used.

Plywood species are grouped according to strength from No. 1, the strongest, down to No. 5. The table on page 169 lists the more common species used.

The standard plywood panels are 4′ × 8′. Other lengths can be ordered. Nominal thicknesses are $^{11}/_{32}″$, $^{3}/_{8}″$, $^{1}/_{2}″$, and $^{15}/_{32}″$, although you can get additional thicknesses up to $^{3}/_{4}″$ on special order. When installing, always leave a $^{1}/_{8}″$ joint spacing along ends and edges. Nail 6″ on center at edges and 12″ on center at intermediate supports. For $^{1}/_{2}″$ plywood, or less, use 6d nonstaining box, casing, or

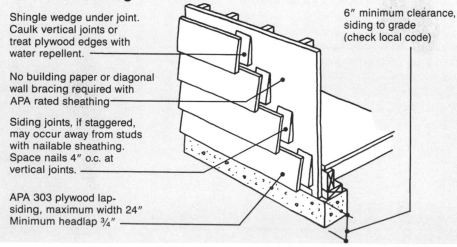

APA 303 Plywood Lap Siding Over Nailable Panel or Lumber Sheathing

Shingle wedge under joint. Caulk vertical joints or treat plywood edges with water repellent.

No building paper or diagonal wall bracing required with APA rated sheathing

Siding joints, if staggered, may occur away from studs with nailable sheathing. Space nails 4″ o.c. at vertical joints.

APA 303 plywood lap-siding, maximum width 24″ Minimum headlap ¾″

6″ minimum clearance, siding to grade (check local code)

303 Siding Surface Patterns

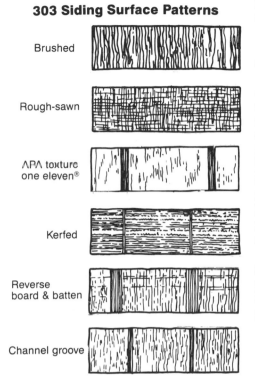

Brushed

Rough-sawn

APA texture
one eleven®

Kerfed

Reverse
board & batten

Channel groove

Typical surface patterns are illustrated. Actual dimensions of groove spacing, width, and depth may vary with the manufacturer. Where the characteristics of a particular wood species are desired, specify by grade and species preference.

siding nails or 8d nails for thicker panels. Corner bracing may be eliminated if you use plywood siding; check local codes.

If you are in a fire hazard area, you may be required to install the plywood over ½" gypsum sheathing to achieve a one-hour fire rating.

Some plywood today is imported. Most foreign manufacturers have adopted U.S. Department of Commerce standards, but their plywood will not bear the informative APA mark. These imports include some attractive hardwood facings for exterior use, but make sure they are laminated with an exterior adhesive.

Plywood lap siding comes in 6", 8", 12", and 16" widths and in 8', 10', 12', and 16' lengths.

Unlike vinyl, aluminum, steel, and hardboard sidings, plywood siding offers no warranty. This is chiefly because the finish, which provides the weather protection, is applied at the job site and not by the manufacturer. It is not a reflection on the durability of the product. Properly protected and maintained plywood siding will last as long as the house. However, it will require more maintenance than vinyl or metal sidings.

There are four ways to finish plywood siding. You can use water-repellent preservatives, semitransparent stains, opaque (solid-color) stains, or house paints.

Siding Panel Textures

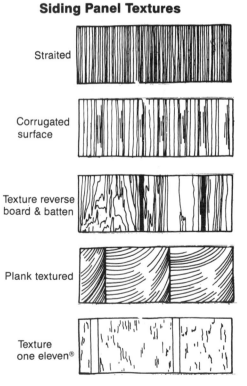

Straited

Corrugated
surface

Texture reverse
board & batten

Plank textured

Texture
one eleven®

Exterior Sidings

If you choose to use a water-repellent preservative to retain the natural finish, use only penetrating finishes that do not leave a film on the surface. These usually contain a fungicide, a small amount of wax to act as a water repellent, a drying oil or resin, and an aromatic solvent. Never use shellac or varnish on a plywood exterior; they tend to stay on the surface and crack or peel due to sunlight and trapped moisture.

Semitransparent penetrating stains are popular for rustic effect. They will provide hue and color but will tend to emphasize knotholes or patches. Two coats of oil-based semitransparent stain will provide adequate weathering protection. Apply the second coat before the first coat has dried or it will not be able to penetrate. These stains cannot be used over solid-color stain or old paint. Never use wire brushes or steel wool to clean off old paint,

because wire particles left in the surface will rust and stain. Never use semitransparent stain on 303-OL (overlaid) plywood siding, and only risk it on knotty 303-18 or 303-30 when the color is similar to that of the wood.

Solid-color stains will conceal the grain and natural color but will still permit the texture to show. Use acrylic latex, solvent-based solid-color stains, or oil-based stains. On brushed or overlaid plywood, water-based latex works better.

If you wish to use paint, top-quality acrylic latex is recommended. You'll need a primer and a top coat (apply second coat within two weeks or film will prevent adhesion). Do not use oil or oil-alkyd paints except over MDO (overlaid) panels, because these paints will flake.

Paint applied over edge-grained facings will perform better than on flat-grained boards.

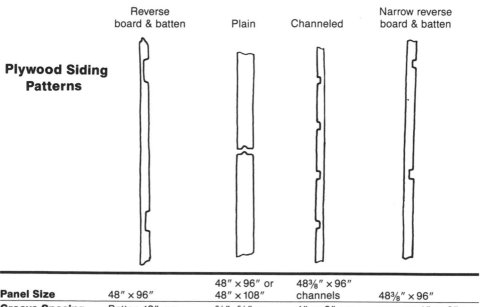

Plywood Siding Patterns

	Reverse board & batten	Plain	Channeled	Narrow reverse board & batten
Panel Size	48″ × 96″	48″ × 96″ or 48″ × 108″	48⅜″ × 96″ channels	48⅜″ × 96″
Groove Spacing	Batten 12″ o.c.	⅜″, ⅝″ or	4″ or 8″ o.c.	grooves 4″ or 8″ o.c.
Thickness	⅜″ or 19/32″ thick	19/32″ thick	⅜″ thick	⅝″ or 19/32″ thick

Hardboard Siding

Hardboard is not plywood and does not bear the APA stamp. Its chief selling feature is its impact resistance. Hardboard comes in three grades: Tempered (for improved moisture resistance), Standard, and Service Quality, where high strength is not critical. The lower-density Service Quality is less likely to stretch and shrink. The hardboard used for siding is usually medium density and is supplied with a factory-applied finish—one surface and edges are primed or given one or more coats of paint or a baked-on tempering compound. Colors offered include a choice of white, gold, gray, beige, yellow, brown, ivory, and blue. Higher-priced variations are prefinished with two or three coats. Manufacturers often supply attachment systems that can be concealed. If made by the wet slurry process, the back may have a belt pattern. Made by a dry heat and pressure process, back and front will be sanded smooth (identified as S-2-S). Both types have the same properties. Hardboard siding is also available with wood grain embossing.

Available ⅜″ or ⁷⁄₁₆″ thick in 4′ × 8′ or 4′ × 9′ panels, or as planks in 12″ courses 8′ or 16′ long, hardboard is durable and easy to maintain but doesn't have the variety of tones and shadings provided by plywood or lumber siding. It is designed to simulate clapboard, shingles, shakes, and other patterns. There's even a stucco finish often used between beams in low-cost, imitation Tudor-style homes. It is a poor substitute for real stucco. Don't confuse hardboard, a hot-pressed resin-bonded ground-up wood felt material, with hardwood, which is natural wood from deciduous trees. Hardboard is manufactured with both sides smooth (S-2-S) or one side smooth and the other textured (S-1-S).

Use only 6d, 8d, or 12d galvanized box nails, when applying hardboard siding.

Hardboard Plywood Patterns

	Reverse board & batten	Lap-raised grain	V-groove	Channeled rough-sawn or smooth	Stucco	Beaded hardboard
Panel Size	48⅜″ × 96″	12″ × 96″	48⅜″ × 96″	48⅜″ × 96″	48″ × 96″	8″ × 192″
Groove Spacing	12″	12″	5⅓″ o.c.	8″ o.c.	or 108″	8″
Thickness	⁷⁄₁₆″	⁷⁄₁₆″	⁷⁄₁₆″	⁷⁄₁₆″	⅞″	⁷⁄₁₆″

Exterior Sidings

Estimating Panel Coverage

It is relatively easy to estimate your needs for coverage using square edge panels. Simply figure the area to be covered in square feet. For each 1000 square feet, you will need thirty-two panels measuring 4' × 8' or twenty-eight panels measuring 4' × 9'. (Thirty-two panels measuring 4' × 8' cover 1024 sq. ft.; twenty-eight panels measuring 4' × 9' cover 1008 sq. ft.) It would be wise to add 5 percent for waste allowance.

Hardboard is particularly moisture sensitive and must be stored inside or carefully covered outside on a flat dry surface. Adequate ventilation is needed. It should never be installed to the 4" side of studs (except at corners) and must not be installed contacting wet studs, wet sheathing, or damp or uncured concrete or stucco.

Maximum stud spacing is 16", but it is much better to install hardboard over sheathing. Do not overdrive nails. Applying 7/16" hardboard siding to 24" on center studs (where local codes permit), some waviness may develop. The use of aluminum "H" expansion moldings is necessary to accommodate

Aluminum "H" Expansion Molding

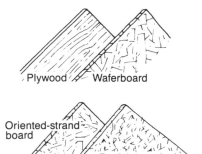

its inevitable expansion and contraction.

Composite Siding

Exterior particleboard, flakeboard, and composite wood fiber panels are also used for siding. Made in the same patterns as hardboard siding,

Plywood   Waferboard

Oriented-strand board

Particleboard

Types of Composite Siding

Lap Siding Coverage
(Includes 5% for waste)

Siding Width (inches)	Exposure (inches)	Square-Foot Quantity to Cover 1000 sq. ft. (includes 5 percent for waste)
12	11	1150
12	10½	1200
12	9⅝	1305
11½	11	1150
8	6	1200
8	5	1400
6	5	1260

they are generally ¼″ to ⅜″ thick and made with phenolic resin to resist weathering. These products vary greatly, depending on the manufacturer, so no generalization can be made regarding their properties —see the manufacturers' literature. The best weather protection for particleboards is provided by paint or solid-color stains. Some are supplied factory primed.

Wood Shingles and Shakes

A shake is made by splitting lumber along the grain into blanks that are band-sawn diagonally so each piece is tapered. These shakes are called "hand-split-and-resawn." There are also "straight-split" shakes, which have no taper, and "taper-split" shakes, which are made by hand using a mallet and steel froe (blade), angling the cut and reversing the block after each cut. Shakes that are all heartwood will give greatest resistance to decay. Edge-grain shakes are less likely to warp than flat-grain shakes. Also, the thicker the butt (bottom edge) and the narrower the shake, the less it will warp.

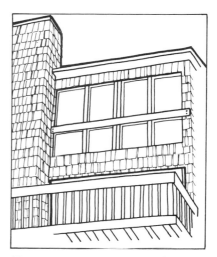

Shingle Application as Siding

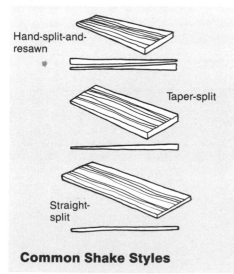

Common Shake Styles

For grades, labeling, and specifications see the chart in the Roofing chapter.

Shingles and shakes are measured by the number of shingles and total butt thickness in inches. For example, 4/2 means four shingles, stacked together, add up to 2 inches of butt thickness; 5/2¼ indicates five shingles yield 2¼″ of butt thickness, etc. A designation of 16″ × 5/2 would mean 16″ long shingles with five shingles to each 2″ of butt thickness.

The chart gives you the coverage of one square (that means four bundles) of shingles based on inches of weather exposure. The coverage is approximate and allows for starter and finisher courses. If you are using a 16″ × 5/2 shingle and leaving 8″ exposed, four bundles will cover 14½ square feet. After you have deducted for doors and windows, add 8 percent for the double starting course, breakage, and waste. While the 24″ shingles are available, they are thick, expensive, rarely used, and require special ordering.

Exterior Sidings

The idea originally was that a square of shingles would cover 100 square feet of roof area using standard exposure *for roofs.* For single coursing on a wall, the exposure must not be more than half the shingle length less ½". Try to plan an exposed area that will allow butts to be even with top and bottom lines of the windows.

Shingles and shakes are sawn from Western red cedar, Northern white cedar, and redwood. Red cedar and redwood come in grades No. 1 (best), No. 2 (very good), and No. 3 (medium good). White cedar is graded Extra (best), Clear, No. 2 Clear, Clear Wall, and Utility.

Approximate Sq. Ft. Coverage per Square of Shingles by Length and Weather Exposure

Approximate coverage of one square (4 bundles) of shingles** based on following weather exposures					
LENGTH AND THICKNESS	**3½"**	**4"**	**4½"**	**5"**	**5½"**
16" x 5/2"	70	80	90	100	110
	10"	**10½"**	**11"**	**11½"**	**12"**
	200	210	220	230	240 +
LENGTH AND THICKNESS	**3½"**	**4"**	**4½"**	**5"**	**5½"**
18" x 5/2¼"	. . . .	72½	81½	90½	100*
	10"	**10½"**	**11"**	**11½"**	**12"**
	181½	191	200	209	218
LENGTH AND THICKNESS	**3½"**	**4"**	**4½"**	**5"**	**5½"**
24" x 4/2"	. . . .	. . . .	. . . .	. . . .	. . . .
	10"	**10½"**	**11"**	**11½"**	**12"**
	133	140	146½	153±	160

NOTES: *Maximum exposure recommended for roofs.
± Maximum exposure recommended for single-coursing on sidewalls.
+ Maximum exposure recommended for double-coursing on sidewalls.
**Includes starter and finisher course.

Coverage of Shakes at Varying Weather Exposures

Length and Thickness	No. of Bundles	Weather Exposures			
		5½"	**6½"**	**7"**	**7½"**
Hand-split-and-resawn		Approximate Coverage (sq. ft.)			
18" x ½" to ¾"	4	55	65	70	75
18" x ¾" to 1¼"	5	55	65	70	75
24" x ⅜"	4	—	65	70	75
24" x ½" to ¾"	4	—	65	70	75
24" x ¾" to 1¼"	5	—	65	70	75
32" x ¾" to 1¼"	6	—	—	—	—

When applying double-coursed walls you can use low-cost shakes for the undercourse, but be careful not to mix them up with your face-course shakes.

Shingles and shakes can be applied over other materials by installing nailing strips. On new or recovering work, only two nails should be used per shingle—6d or larger nails may be needed. The nails should be hot-dipped, zinc-coated, and driven flush but not into the surface.

Caution: As attractive as wood shingles and shakes appear, they do have one drawback. They are combustible, particularly as they get old and dry out. You may want to buy UL (Underwriters Laboratory) Class B

Approximate coverage of one square (4 bundles) of shingles** based on following weather exposures

6″	6½″	7″	7½″	8″	8½″	9″	9½″
120	130	140	150±	160	170	180	190
12½″	**13″**	**13½″**	**14″**	**14½″**	**15″**	**15½″**	**16″**
. . . .	. . . .	. . . .	. . . .	. . . .	. . . .	. . . .	. . . .
6″	**6½″**	**7″**	**7½″**	**8″**	**8½″**	**9″**	**9½″**
109	118	127	136	145½	154½±	163½	172½
12½″	**13″**	**13½″**	**14″**	**14½″**	**15″**	**15½″**	**16″**
227	236	245½	254½	. . . .	. . . .	. . . .	. . . .
6″	**6½″**	**7″**	**7½″**	**8″**	**8½″**	**9″**	**9½″**
80	86½	93	100*	106½	113	120	126½
12½″	**13″**	**13½″**	**14″**	**14½″**	**15″**	**15½″**	**16″**
166½	173	180	186½	193	200	206½	213+

						Weather Exposures	
8″	**8½″**	**10″**	**11½″**	**13″**	**14″**	**15″**	**16″**
Approximate Coverage (sq. ft.)							
80	85*	—	—	—	—	—	—
80	85*	—	—	—	—	—	—
80	85	100	115*	—	—	—	—
80	85	100	115*	—	—	—	—
80	85	100	115*	—	—	—	—
—	—	100	115	130	140	150*	—

Exterior Sidings

Coverage of Shakes at Varying Weather Exposures (Concluded)

Length and Thickness	No. of Bundles	Weather Exposures			
		5½"	6½"	7"	7½"
Taper-split		Approximate Coverage (sq. ft.)			
24" × ½" to ⅝"	4	—	65	70	75
Straight-split					
18" × ⅜" (True-Edge)	4	—	—	—	—
18" × ⅜"	5	65	75	80	90
24" × ⅜"	5	—	65	70	75

*Recommended maximum weather exposure for single-coursed sidewalls.
**Recommended maximum weather exposure for double-coursed sidewalls.

Wooden Shake Siding

or Class C pressure-treated shingles or shakes for fire resistance, through a local wood preserving company. The chemical treatment will make the shingle a shade darker; treated shingles or shakes will not turn gray.

Aluminum Siding

The baked-on finishes of aluminum siding come in many styles, textures, (wood grain, pebbled, etc.) and colors. Other than the hazard from hailstones and baseballs, which can dent the panels, the material is durable. Some new varieties have a DuPont Tedlar® or other fluorocarbon surface coating

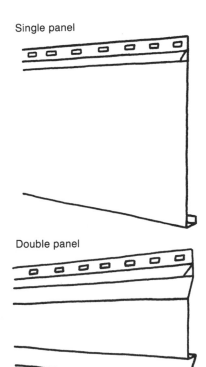

Single panel

Double panel

Aluminum Siding Types

8"	8½"	10"	11½"	13"	14"	Weather Exposures 15"	16"
			Approximate Coverage (sq. ft.)				
80	85	100	115*	—	—	—	—
—	—	—	—	—	100	106	112**
95	100*	—	—	—	—	—	—
80	85	100	115*	—	—	—	—

to shed dirt and retain their color. They reduce maintenance but are not truly maintenance-free. They should be washed once a year; after many years they may need touch-up paint or an entirely new coat.

Aluminum is electrically conductive, so properly ground the siding.

Aluminum may be used over old surfaces, although uneven walls will need to be furred out. A power saw fitted with an aluminum cutting blade (always cut away from you) and simple tools such as tin snips, hacksaw, file, and hammer are needed for installation.

Some siding is offered with insulation attached. The supplier may tell you the "R" value of the insulation (the higher the "R" the greater the insulation value), but fail to point out that the gaps between the insulation strips greatly reduce any insulating value and the aluminum is usually thinner. You are better off using an insulating sheathing that completely covers the wall.

When pricing siding compare the price for the complete package. You may find a material with the lowest siding cost has the highest price for hangers and accessories.

Aluminum siding is available in 8", 10", 12" and double-4" simulated lap siding. Sections are 12' or 12½' long. Thickness is .024". It is sold in squares (each square equals 100 square feet of surface), 2 squares to the carton, weighing about 100 lbs. Some is available with ¼" polyurethane foam backing with 1 square per carton, weighing about 50 pounds. This aluminum is thinner, .019". All color-matched accessories are available. Some have a dirt shedding, weather resistant, Tedlar® fluorocarbon finish, others are PVC (vinyl) coated. Some manufacturers offer as many as 10 colors in wood grain embossed aluminum and one also offers a smooth surface. Warranties are limited to 40 years (5 years for fading).

Steel Siding

Steel siding comes in similar widths to aluminum but shorter lengths (9'4½"). This siding comes 1 square to the carton, but weighs twice as much (100 lbs.), and color selection is similar to aluminum siding. Hot-zinc-dipped material claims high abrasion resistance. Long-term warranties,

Exterior Sidings

similar to vinyl, must be read for clear understanding. Look for 4 mil or thicker PVC (vinyl) coating.

Vinyl Siding

Vinyl siding is more durable than aluminum siding and comes in a great variety of colors and embossed textures. It is extremely easy to wash

Vinyl Siding Application

Vinyl Sidings

Representative Manufacturers & (Sales Territory)	Design/ Appearance (exposures)	Colors and Coatings (Also have color clear through)	Sizes and Packaging (1 square covers 100 sq. ft.)
American vinyl building products (nationwide)	Wood grain embossed. Clapboard design in 8"; double-4" with V-groove for wall or soffit application; triple 4" V-groove for soffit only.	Regal white, royal sandlewood, imperial green, classic cream, premier gray, sovereign blue, almond and monarch yellow.	Length: 12'6" Widths: 8" and 10" Thickness: .042" 2 squares per carton Approximately 100 lbs.
Gold Bond 38 states west to the Rocky Mountains	Wood grain texture. Clapboard design in 8", double-4", double-5" and vertical.	Soft-lustre finish. Vernon white, antique gold, Williamsburg green, mayberry cream, sandy beige, sorrento gray and almond tan.	Lengths: 12'6" and 12'10" Widths: 8" and 10" Thickness: .045" 2 squares per carton Approximately 100 lbs.
Master Shield A division of Danaher Corporation (nationwide)	Wood grain embossed. 8" and double-5" (German style with center cove) no-sag soffit ⅝" panel ridges.	White, almond, adobe tan, cape blue, dove gray, sunshine yellow and driftwood.	Length: 12' Width: 11⅜" Thickness: .045" 2 squares per carton Approximately 110 lbs.
Mastic Corporation Division of Bethlehem Steel (nationwide)	Wood grain embossed and matte finish. 8", double-4", vertical or quad-2½".	White, mist green, silver gray, sunburst yellow, beige, almond, provincial gold, heritage blue. Also musket brown soffit.	Length: 12'6" Width: 8" Thickness: .040" 2 squares per carton Approximately 100 lbs.

clean and less likely than painted metal to lose its gloss. However, it becomes extremely brittle in frigid temperatures and may then shatter if struck by a wind-blown branch or hard ball. Individual panels can be replaced.

Panels are normally 8″ deep by 12′6″ long with slotted holes for center fastening (vinyl tends to expand and contract, so must be free to move). Panels are often offered with a self-aligning lock to make installation easier. This is important because incorrectly installed vinyl siding will buckle when it expands and may have to be taken off and reinstalled. If you are installing vinyl, do it in hot weather; you'll have fewer problems later.

Accessories	Warranty* (Request and read complete manufacturer's warranty)	Product Name
Color-matched trim. Aluminum coil stock for flashing. Soffit and fascia.	60-year limited, non-prorated on labor and material	American Vinyl Siding
Color-matched starter strip, J- and F-channels, outside corner post, window and door trim, white soffit and fascia and aluminum coil stock for flashing.	Lifetime limited, non-prorated, transferable	Gold Bond Vinyl Siding
Color-matched embossed J-channel. F-channel, inside/outside corners. Finish trim and aluminum coil stock for flashing.	50-year limited, non-prorated, transferable	Victorian Vinyl Siding
Color-matched trim, T-channel, frieze runner, corner posts, window casing, soffit and fascia (white), crown molding, door surrounds, mantels, windows and shutters.	Lifetime limited, non-prorated, transferable	T-Cok Vinyl Siding

Exterior Sidings

Vinyl Sidings (Concluded)

Representative Manufacturers & (Sales Territory)	Design/ Appearance (exposures)	Colors and Coatings (Also have color clear through)	Sizes and Packaging (1 square covers 100 sq. ft.)
Vinyl Improvement Products Company (Vipco) (nationwide)	Wood grain embossed. 8", double-4", & double-5".	Cloud white, country beige, gentry gray, clay, green mist, straw yellow, slate blue, almond and ivory.	Lengths: 12' and 12'6" Widths: 8" and 10" Thickness: .042" avg. 2 squares per carton Approximately 100 lbs.
Wolverine Technologies (nationwide)	Low gloss or smooth. Triple-3" square butt. New "Flotrac" channel to hold siding flat.	Snow, almond, pewter and clay.	Length: 12'1" Width: 9" Thickness: .044" 2 squares per carton Approximately 92 lbs.

*Distribution on West Coast is limited. Information subject to change. Actual warranties must be read.

Brick and Stone

Applied as a facade over a wood frame wall, brick and stone can be considered either siding or residing materials. Brick is available in a choice of colors: white, pink, yellow, russet, red, black, and tan. Of course, you can also use used brick—tap it to make sure it isn't brittle; be sure old mortar is chipped off well. The standard building brick measures 3¾" wide by 8" long and is 2¼" high. Specialty bricks in many other sizes are available.

Stone is usually obtained from local quarries, so your selection may be limited. However, in larger cities, market demand justifies ordering of carload quantities and you'll find marble, granite, quartz, slate, bluestone, limestone, and sandstone available. Check with a local mason to find out which, if any, of the last three are durable in your climate. Stone is sold as quarried (undressed), rough-cut (semidressed), or pretrimmed (dressed).

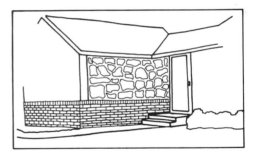

Brick & Stone Siding Application

Stucco

Stucco is applied in three coats over stud walls, but sometimes only two coats are applied over roughened masonry walls. (See table for a choice of formulas.) Limit ranges are given because the aggregates vary by location and trial-and-error testing is needed to attain the desired consistency.

Accessories	Warranty* (Request and read complete manufacturer's warranty)	Product Name
Soffit all colors plus brown. White fascia. PVC coated aluminum coil stock.	Lifetime full warranty	Ambassador Victorian
Color-matched corner post beaded soffit, Springlock starter strip, J-channel, utility trim and aluminum coil stock.	Lifetime, non-prorated, convertible/transferable	Restoration Series Three

Stucco is fire resistant, hard-surfaced (unless it contains perlite), weather resistant, and durable. It does crack, but alkali-resistant glass fibers may be added to help reduce cracking. Stucco helps provide a noise barrier and cannot rot or decay. Mold can attach to stucco but can be scrubbed off. Stucco will last as long as the house. If you want to try applying it yourself, hire an experienced assistant to help and advise you.

Stucco Lath

Expanded Metal	Use only zinc coated or painted copper-bearing steel. Apply with backing paper* and furring fasteners.
Stucco Mesh	For use over solid surfaces, needs backing paper and furring fasteners.
Diamond Mesh (self-furring)	Use only 3.4 weight or heavier.
Flat Rib Lath	In ⅛", ⅜" and ¾" only. Only use 3.4 weight or heavier. Ribbing provides greater stiffness.
Wire Lath	Woven or welded, use only galvanized cold drawn copper-bearing steel wire that has been coated after welding. Available self-furring.
Welded Wire	Use 18 gauge for 1"×1" squares or 16 gauge with 2"×2" openings.
Welded Wire (backed)	Use 18 gauge for 1"×1 squares or 17 gauge for 1"×½" openings.
Woven Wire Fabric	Use 16 gauge for 2"×2" openings and 18 gauge for 1"×1" openings.

*Paper should have a vapor permeance of 5 perms or more to prevent trapping moisture in the wall. Paper facilitates embedment of lath, prevents loss of mix. Do not use absorptive paper on exterior applications.

Exterior Sidings

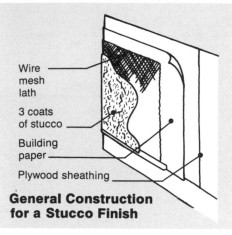

Wire mesh lath

3 coats of stucco

Building paper

Plywood sheathing

General Construction for a Stucco Finish

Asbestos Shingles

Asbestos-cement siding is now called mineral-fiber siding. These shingles are still made from portland cement reinforced with asbestos fibers.

Although it has been proposed, at this time there are no government regulations against their use, but these shingles must never be sanded or treated in any manner that would allow the fibers to escape due to the danger of asbestosis.

Asbestos shingles are inexpensive and easy to install, but they crack or

Stucco Formulas

Coat	Thickness†	Mix
1st (Scratch Coat)	3/8″	A or B
2nd (Brown Coat)	3/8″	A or B or B_1
3rd (Finish Coat)	3/8″	A or B or B_1

†Fasteners should be used to keep self-furring reinforcement ¼″ out from supporting wall.

Tips:
In this table, if you start with mix A for first coat, use A mixes for 2nd and 3rd coat.
If you start with B you can use either B or B_1 for 2nd and 3rd coat.
If you plan to use perlite instead of sand for the finish coat, you must use perlite for 1st and 2nd coats. Don't use perlite on areas subject to impact.
Workability will govern the volume of aggregate within limits shown.
A higher lime content will support a higher aggregate content.
To reduce cracking add 1½″ to 2″ lengths of alkaline glass fibers at a rate of no more than 2 pounds per cubic foot.
Paper backing on lath should be wet before applying scratch coat.
When applying in dry hot weather more water may be added *once*.
Maximum batch life is 2 to 2½ hours—throw out after that.
Don't use ribbed lath on exterior. All lath must be rust and oil free. Use coarse sand devoid of fines and large aggregate.
Keep each coat moist for three to five days before applying next coat.
After top coat, allow at least two weeks before painting and use alkali-resistant paint.

chip easily, requiring that you replace individual shingles as needed. Because they are brittle, they cannot be applied over old clapboard or shingles; you'll have to strip off the old siding and nail directly to the sheathing in those cases. Replacement shingles may become difficult or impossible to obtain.

Asbestos shingles usually are applied with nailheads exposed. For that reason alone, consider the structure's resale value before buying this siding. As a matter of fact, removing exisiting asbestos siding and replacing it with any other product would probably enhance the resale value of your home.

			Parts by Volume			
			Volume per Sum of Cementitious Materials			
Portland Cement	**Lime**	**Masonry Cement**	**Sand**	**or**	**Perlite**	**Water**
1		1–2	2½–4		1½–2	Add and mix
1	0–¾		2¼–4		3–4	noncontaminated
1		1–2	3–5		1½–2	(suitable for
1	0–¾		3–5		3–4	domestic
1	¾–1½		3–5		2–3	consumption)
1		1	3		2	water to desired
1	¾–1½		3		2	application
1	1½–2		3		2½	consistency.

Doors

6

6. Doors

Hanging a door was once a revered part of the carpenter's art. Time and skill were required to place a door on its hinges so it was square and plumb and swung perfectly.

Today that's still true, but if you're buying a new front or back door for your home, it probably will be available prehung in its jamb—the wood frame that surrounds a door. The door itself may be solid wood, but more likely it will be a core of rigid insulation surrounded by a skin of steel or wood. Both are likely to cost about the same, and installing either is a simple do-it-yourself job. The illustration below will familiarize you with the terminology of the pre-hung door.

This chapter deals with entry doors, patio and French doors, storm doors, garage doors and garage door openers, bulkhead doors, attic access doors, fences, and gates.

Wood Doors

Wood doors are graded by the National Woodwork Manufacturers Association (NWMA) according to the quality and appearance of exposed surfaces, limiting the type and extent of defects permitted. Flush door grade regulations cover face veneers only. Stile-and-rail doors are graded according to lumber stock used in stiles and rails and lumber or plywood in panels. Summary of Door Grades on page 188 further explains this grading system. NWMA seals, containing the standard number, are stamped on the top and bottom of each door.

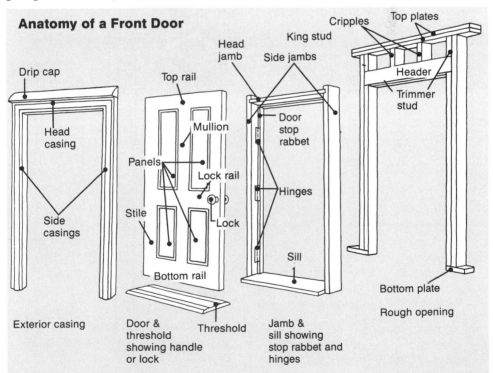

Anatomy of a Front Door

Drip cap

Head casing

Side casings

Exterior casing

Top rail

Mullion

Panels

Lock rail

Stile

Lock

Bottom rail

Door & threshold showing handle or lock

Threshold

Head jamb

Side jambs

Door stop rabbet

Hinges

Sill

Jamb & sill showing stop rabbet and hinges

Cripples

King stud

Top plates

Header

Trimmer stud

Bottom plate

Rough opening

Doors

Wood Door Standards

FLUSH
Hardwood Veneered NWMA IS-1
Ponderosa Pine CS120

PANEL
Ponderosa Pine CS120
Douglas Fir CS73

SASH
Ponderosa Pine CS120
Douglas Fir CS73

STORM & SCREEN
Ponderosa Pine CS120
Douglas Fir CS73

LOUVER
Ponderosa Pine CS120
Douglas Fir CS73

ACCORDION FOLDING
(no industry standard)

Entry Doors

When choosing a front door, choose wisely. You have the opportunity to choose not just a door, but a style of entryway. Standard designs will cost around $300; for $600 or more you can get doors made of exotic woods, manually or "laser" carved with leaded glass panes.

If you're building a new home or remodeling to achieve a major face-lift, you can also determine what exterior decor will surround the door. Consider whether to have decorative molding (such as columns-in-relief) or decorative

Double panel door

Dutch door

Panel door with transom and side lights

Single panel door

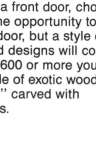

Colonial panel door with carved and columned casing

Choosing an Entry Door Style

glass (called sidelights) on either side of the door. (Codes call for this glass to be tempered safety glass.) Finally, consider whether to have a decorative transom, that is, glass over the door. The common semicircular transom with muntins (the pieces of wood that divide panes of glass) spreading out like sunrays is called a fanlight.

More likely, however, you already have a home and want to replace your front door. Your current door may be too cold or drafty in winter, it may be the weak link in your home security system, it may be falling apart, or it may simply lack pizazz. In any case, you'll be shopping for what's called a replacement door.

One feature of steel replacement doors is that they are prehung in a steel frame. This can be a security advantage: They are more difficult to kick in, because the lock would have to be pushed through a steel jamb rather than just splitting the vertical grain of a wood jamb. They are also easy to install. You remove only the trim and top molding of your old door, then place the new steel jamb over the existing jamb.

Beyond that, shopping for a new door or a replacement door is a matter of shopping for features shared by both. Here's what to look for:

Energy savings. A solid wood door has an insulating value of about R-2. That's not enough to keep out the winter cold or summer heat without an additional storm door. Best are metal- or fiberglass-clad doors filled with rigid insulation. The insulation core with the highest R value—up to R-15—is polyurethane.

A steel door with the best insulation, however, will perform poorly unless it has a good "thermal break." A thermal break runs along the door's edges,

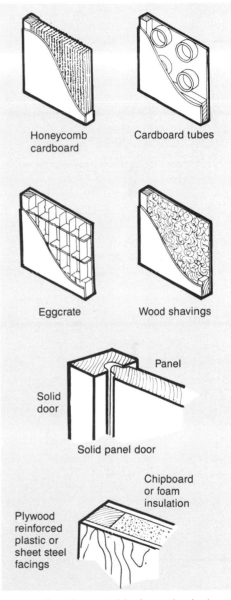

Honeycomb cardboard

Cardboard tubes

Eggcrate

Wood shavings

Solid door

Panel

Solid panel door

Plywood reinforced plastic or sheet steel facings

Chipboard or foam insulation

separating the outside from the indoor side. This break should be more than $1/4''$ wide to reduce conduction effectively. This gap prevents the indoor side from losing heat to the outside and becoming cold, causing chilliness and condensation. (A thermal break is unnecessary on fiberglass-

Doors

clad or wood doors because those materials do not conduct cold as well as steel.) The best thermal breaks clearly separate the metal with wood or vinyl. Metal thresholds should also have thermal breaks.

Hollow-core doors are only for interior use and should not be used between the house and garage or house and unheated basement, as they have R values of less than 1.

Weather stripping. Prehung doors arrive with weather stripping in place. The weather stripping is at least as important as insulation to a door's overall energy conservation. Look for durable, securely fastened, tight-sealing stripping around all four edges. An adjustable threshold and flexible tubular sweep will provide the tightest seal at the bottom.

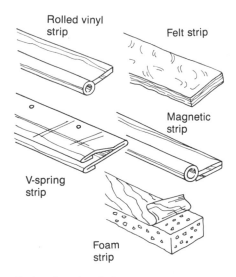

Rolled vinyl strip

Felt strip

Magnetic strip

V-spring strip

Foam strip

Security. Look for peepholes, strike plates that wrap around the jamb, hinges that lock when closed so a door cannot be removed if hinge pins are pulled out, and strong locks. You can order locksets and dead bolts with most doors, or buy your own and install them yourself.

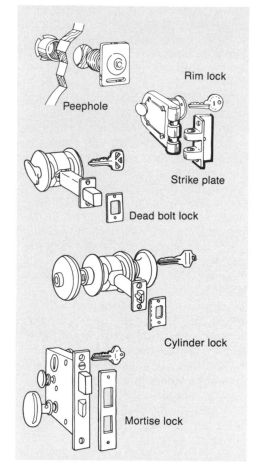

Peephole

Rim lock

Strike plate

Dead bolt lock

Cylinder lock

Mortise lock

Materials. Steel insulated doors normally contain 24-gauge cold rolled steel, but some manufacturers, to be price-competitive, offer 18-gauge or even thinner 14-gauge. Moral: Study the literature. Fiberglass-clad doors are usually look-alikes of wood doors. In fact, some can even be stained! Steel doors can be painted. Sometimes flush steel doors are decorated with wood or foam trim to make them look like paneled doors. This trim may warp or detach, especially if covered by a glazed storm door. When direct sunlight hits the storm door, the space between the doors heats up like a solar collector, and the heat can even melt paint.

Wood doors and wood jambs should have been pretreated at the factory with a preservative to protect against rot and insects.

Flexibility. Are strike plate and threshold adjustable? Are sill and jamb extenders available? Remember, the thickness of your walls has to be covered by the jambs.

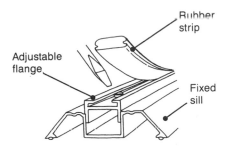

Adjustable Threshold

Sizes. Doors come in standard sizes. Most front doors are 3' wide; many rear doors are 2'8" wide. You can order doors that are wider and higher, the standard height being 6'8".

Hinged Door Sizes

Width × height: 2'0" × 6'8", 2'4" × 6'8", 2'6" × 6'8", 2'8" × 6'8", 3'0" × 6'8", 3'6" × 6'10", 3'0" × 7'0"
Stiles: 5½"
Bottom rail: 9¾"
Mullion: 5⅜"
Top rail: 5½"
Lock rail: 8"
Other rails: 5⅜"
Interior doors: 1⅜" thick
Exterior doors: 1¾" thick

Standard door sizes underlined.
The opening for the door frame should be 3" wider and 2" higher than the door.

Typical Specifications Given by Manufacturers

Single door size: 3'6" × 6'8"
Actual unit size: 3'7⅝" × 6'10"
Rough opening required:
3'8⅜" × 6'10½"
Double door size: 3'0" × 6'8"
Actual double unit size: 6'2⁹⁄₁₆" × 6'10"
Rough opening required: 6'3¼" × 6'10½"

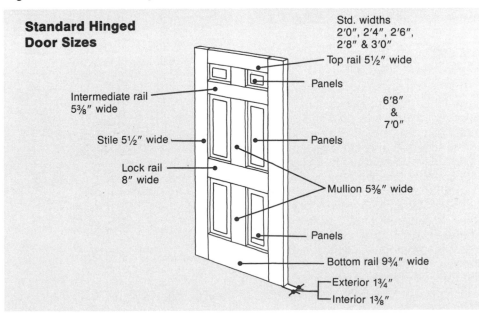

Standard Hinged Door Sizes

Doors

If you're building a new wall with a doorway, you'll need to know the required size of the rough opening—the height of the header and distance between the jack studs of the rough framing. There must be space to fit your door and its jambs. It's safer to make the opening too large rather than too small. Then you can use shims if the space is a little too large or slightly out of plumb. Do not build the rough opening before ordering your door and finding its rough opening dimensions in the product literature. This is especially crucial if you're building a brick or stone wall.

Patio Doors

Patio doors are really door-sized windows that glide in tracks. They first appeared in the American Southwest in the 1950s. Since then they have become an essential ingredient in the trend toward "outdoor living." Patio doors provide wide, easy access between indoors and out. (They are, by now, the standard transition from kitchen to backyard deck.) What's more, they bathe the indoors with light and ventilation, and provide maximum view.

The features that provide these advantages can become disadvantages, however, in a harshly cold and cloudy winter climate. The large areas of glass add to fuel bills and are too cold to sit next to. The doors must be covered with curtains, blocking that lovely view. In addition, the low-cost models display more problems: aluminum frames that could collect frost or drip with condensation on the inside, poor weather stripping, tracks that could leak during rainstorms and collect dirt, and relatively weak locks.

In shopping for a patio door, examine these aspects:

The frame. The best are wood, clad on the exterior with vinyl or aluminum. If they are metal, be sure there is a thermal break—in other words, no aluminum part of the frame should be

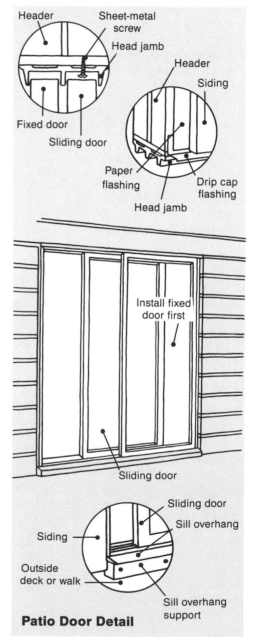

Patio Door Detail

continuous from inside to out. The outside and inside should be separated by a less conductive plastic or rubber spacer.

The glass. Double-pane glass with at least ¼″ air space between loses only two-thirds of the heat of single-pane windows. And a recent worthwhile improvement in double-pane glass is low-E glass (see Chapter 7). If you live in a cold climate, a patio door on the south side will be a passive solar collector in winter; on the north side, an energy drain in winter; on the west side, a source of afternoon heat in summer unless properly shaded. If you live in a warm climate, take care to shade patio doors facing east or west.

On better wood frame units, snap-in grilles provide a divided light, giving the appearance of a French door.

The lock. Ask how many pounds of pull pressure it is able to withstand. A convenient feature is a lock that can secure the door when only a few inches open, allowing ventilation but not burglars.

The sill. Look for a thermal break and effective weather stripping, not the plastic sweep or brush type, which quickly gets sheared off on meeting the threshold. Compare air infiltration ratings, expressed in cfm (cubic feet per minute). Look at the way the door's bottom rail sits on the lower track and whether the connection is loose enough to permit water to leak under the door in a driving rain. Is there a weep hole in the track to allow water to drain outside?

French Doors

French doors have enjoyed a resurgence in popularity in the last decade, partly as an alternative to problems with patio doors but also as a result of renewed interest in classical architectural styles. Instead of a track to collect dirt, there's a standard sill on the side of the door that swings open (the other side is often fixed rather than hinged). The operating door can be fully weather stripped; it can also be equipped with a dead bolt lock.

French Doors

Another major reason for the resurgence is the more elegant, formal look of French doors. The wood frame surrounding the glass is wider and some models have wood muntins (dividers) segmenting the panes of glass.

With quality comes cost. French doors tend to cost more than patio doors.

When comparing models, look at the energy efficiency of the glass, the quality of the wood, and the strength of the locks. Ask for air infiltration rates.

Closet Doors

To save space you will probably want to choose between sliding or bifold doors. These can be purchased together with the components for hanging them.

Doors

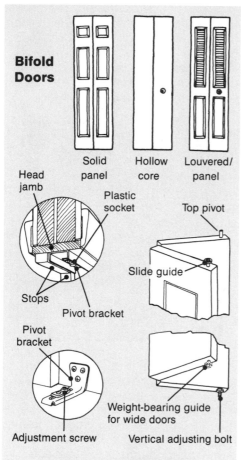

Bifold Doors

Solid panel   Hollow core   Louvered/panel

Head jamb

Plastic socket

Top pivot

Slide guide

Stops

Pivot bracket

Pivot bracket

Adjustment screw

Weight-bearing guide for wide doors

Vertical adjusting bolt

Bifold Door Installation

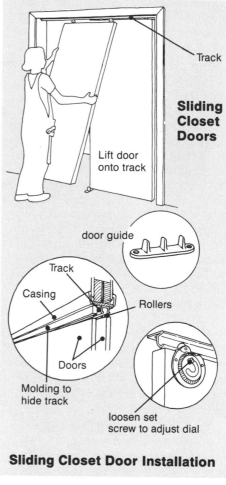

Track

Sliding Closet Doors

Lift door onto track

door guide

Track

Casing

Rollers

Doors

Molding to hide track

loosen set screw to adjust dial

Sliding Closet Door Installation

Storm Doors

Installing a storm door makes sense if you have a solid wood door and want to protect it from the elements and boost your entry's meager R value from 2 to 3 and reduce drafts. A new storm door makes less sense, however, atop today's R-15 steel-clad, factory-weather stripped doors. Its chief virtue in such cases is its summertime screening.

Most storm doors have interchangeable glass and screen panels. Be careful to switch over to the screens fairly early in the spring, and

Storm Door

Removable panels

Optional fixed/removable panel

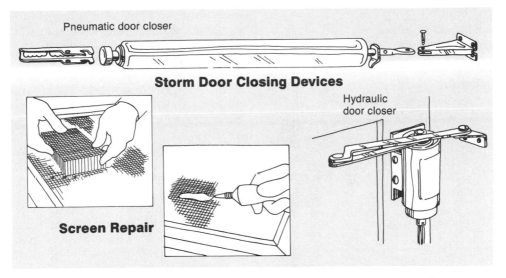

don't put the glass back in until late fall. Under direct sunlight the glass turns the space between it and the door into a solar collector, and temperatures in excess of 160°F can be reached, which may warp the door and certainly melt foam trim and weather stripping. The door should be painted white or a light color; dark colors will increase the temperature.

A storm door should have a strong latch and hinge; a strong wind can whip them open. You'll need to install a pneumatic or hydraulic door closer as well as a spring.

Today's storm door screens are available in aluminum, bronze, plastic, steel, or fiberglass. In replacing screening and maintaining a match with other screens, you will probably select the same material.

Garage Doors

There are three types of garage doors: *roll-up* (doors with hinged sections that roll up on a track), *swing-up* (one-piece doors that arc up), and *hinged* (a pair of doors that open outward). Almost everyone today uses the roll-up doors—usually equipped

with a radio-controlled electric opener and locks.

The roll-up door glides on rollers in a curved track and requires counterbalancing. This can be done with a tension spring and pulley unit, which is safe to install, or a torsion spring. For large or heavy doors, a torsion spring is almost essential. But don't attempt to install one, or even tighten one, unless you've had training and have the right tools. A flaw or corrosion in the spring or the slightest error in controlling the tools will let loose a thousand pounds of kinetic energy with catastrophic results. This shouldn't stop you from buying and installing the door or later attaching the automatic door opener—just get an overhead-door contractor to install, tighten, or replace the spring.

Garage door panels are made of fiberboard, fiberglass, steel, aluminum, or wood. Windows are usually optional. Because many people also use their garages as workshops, the translucent fiberglass doors are available with insulated cores and efficient weather stripping. With an insulated garage, these doors may make it easier to start

Doors

Hinged Section Roll-up Door

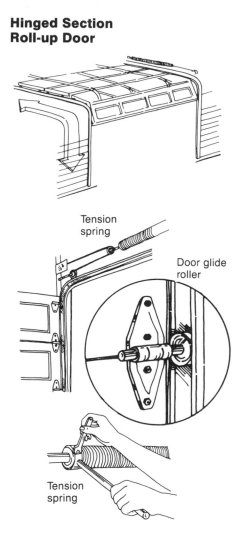

Tension spring

Door glide roller

Tension spring

garage—even if the door is open—except for the few seconds you need to back out your car. The buildup of carbon monoxide can kill you.

Codes dictate the strength and size of the header for each door width. The header can be a steel beam, laminated beam, J beam, a truss, or nailed together 2 x 10's. It is absolutely critical that the jambs are installed plumb, the head is level, and both rails are parallel and level. If the floor slopes or is not level, shop for a door with a large, tubular bottom weather stripping that will create a seal despite unevenness. Otherwise you may have to install and shim a low-profile threshold.

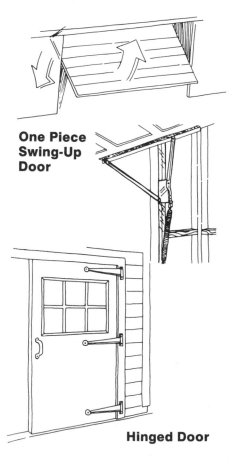

One Piece Swing-Up Door

Hinged Door

your car in winter and will make the garage bright enough to use as a workshop in winter. The problem is to find translucent doors that are made with a fiberglass-reinforced acrylic polyester having a good UV (ultraviolet) retarder, since the cheaper polyester panels can turn yellow and unsightly.

Because today's garage doors shut tight, never run any type of combustion burner or engine in a

Choose the door before you build, if possible, so you will have the manufacturer's specification on allowable rough opening size. This is usually about 3" wider than the door and 1½" higher than the door from the finished floor. The frame is usually included in the millwork order—along with the windows and door panels—to ensure an outside match. You'll also find directions for installing a heavy frame (at least 2" thick and 4" wide) on which the track and hardware are mounted. Whether installed with lag bolts or screws, the heads should be countersunk for safety.

Don't forget to leave adequate headroom inside the garage for the rails, door opener, and hardware. This requires about 18" for most doors, although a compact unit for lightweight single doors taking only 6" is available. If the garage is built and you have no headroom, you will have to install hinged doors. On overhead doors, the tracks, hinges, and bolts should be made of galvanized steel. The track bearing should have ball bearing races. Read the manufacturer's literature for lubricating instructions—graphite or light machine oil should be sprayed on tracks, rollers, hinges, and locks. Using grease will allow sand and dirt to collect. Coat the spring with oil to retard rust.

Single doors are sold in 8', 9', and 10' widths, while double doors are usually 16' or 19' wide. Both are normally 6'6" high, but you can find some 6'8" doors. If you have a van, boat, or travel trailer, a special 8'-high door may answer your need.

For security, most garage doors have twist handles controlling a bar that locks through the side rails. They are unlocked from the exterior with a key and inside with a handle and sliding latch.

The tracks and any cross ties or door opener hangers are installed first. The bearings are installed in the track and attached to each door panel in turn as it is built up from the ground and the hinges attached. If the door rubs the frame, you may have to install the track on brackets.

Overhead Door Openers

There are three kinds of automatic garage door openers: *worm drive* (a spiral thread moves the door), *chain drive,* and *plastic track drive.* The worm drive requires least adjustment. However, if you use your garage as a potting shed or workshop, dust may jam the bearings. Chains tend to stretch slightly with wear. Before you buy a chain unit, inspect to make sure the limit switches are in the controller mechanism. Spring contacts attached

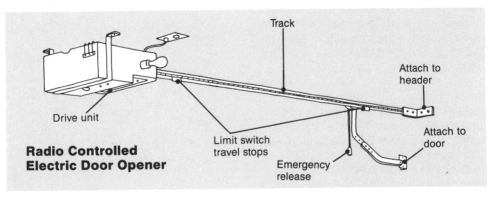

Radio Controlled Electric Door Opener

Track

Attach to header

Drive unit

Limit switch travel stops

Attach to door

Emergency release

Doors

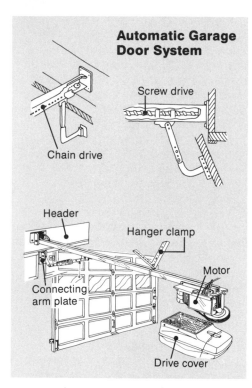

Automatic Garage Door System

Chain drive

Screw drive

Header

Hanger clamp

Motor

Connecting arm plate

Drive cover

return the unit to the store for an alternate channel. The car units are sold separately at the time you buy your transmitter-controller, so you can buy as many as you have cars.

Garage door openers are often used by stores as loss leaders—offered for a limited period at a major reduction in price to get you into the store. You may want to wait for such a sale. In any case you'll want to compare any warranties or guarantees offered, both as to duration and whether the manufacturer or store will make the repair or just replace parts. You can pay for installation of your automatic door opener or save yourself $50 to $100 by installing the equipment yourself. (It takes the better part of a Saturday.) If electrical wiring is already in place and you remember to switch off the current until you are finished, it's relatively easy.

Bulkhead Doors

Bulkhead doors are steel or wood double doors at the top of external access stairs to the basement or cellar. They are sold by commercial steel door fabricators and distributors. Bilco is one of the better known brands.

to the chain tend to break; reordering is by catalog and takes forever.

Whichever type you choose, essentials include an emergency release cord hanging down from the track, so you can open the door during a power failure. There must be a "child safety" stop-and-reverse mechanism. It is essential to install a bottom gasket, not only to provide weather stripping but to prevent the wood of the bottom panel from being in contact with damp or wet concrete, which will warp or rot the door. For the same reason, you'll want to replace this as soon as it shows signs of wear. For frills, you can buy units that have delayed light switches. The bulb on the motor will turn on as the door is activated and automatically turn off about one minute after operating.

If your radio-control opener starts opening another person's garage door,

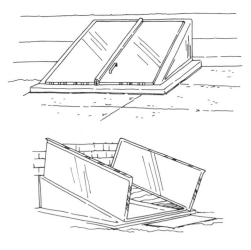

Bulkhead doors were necessary in the days of large furnaces to allow access for large fuel oil tanks and equipment to be moved in and out. In some cases they were used as the entry to coal storage bins. Today's furnaces and oil tanks are designed to fit through standard doors. People once stored garden tools in the basement, but today most find the garage more convenient.

If you still need a bulkhead door, you should probably work with a metal fabrication shop to ensure a secure locking system, a large overhanging edge to avoid leakage, and possibly a counterbalance to help lift the door. You will need to insulate the exterior of your stairway above and below ground. And you should install either an insulated interior door to cover the opening in your basement wall, or lay rigid foam panels horizontally atop the stairwell's sidewalls and cover with gypsum board.

Attic Access Doors

While "disappearing" attic stairs are a great convenience, they leave a big hole in your attic insulation layer that may cost you hundreds of dollars per year in higher energy bills. Now some manufacturers have come to the

Disappearing Stair

rescue with foam plastic insulated hoods that fit over the stairs in the attic. Attached by a pulley to the stairs, the cover lifts up sideways as the stairway is pulled down and returns as the stairway is raised. It pays to tape additional insulation on top of these covers.

Fences and Gates

Before you decide on a fence, check your local building codes and even your neighborhood civic association. There are usually legal restrictions that dictate what type and height of fencing is acceptable. Place your fence 1' in from your lot line to guard against possible title disputes later.

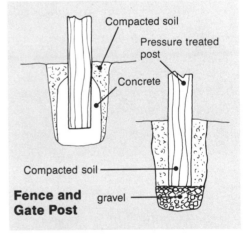

Fence and Gate Post

Contrary to "common knowledge," you should not set untreated wood gateposts in concrete; water will be retained around the wood and cause rot. Posts should be set with one-third of their length in the ground. By using an electric hole digger, available at most tool rental agencies, you will retain the naturally compacted undisturbed soil. All you then need to do is fill the bottom with gravel, compact it, put in the post, and back-fill with soil, tamping every 8". If your soil is sand, it will drain well and you

Doors

can set the post in concrete, but slope the edges so water doesn't stay around the post.

You should use pressure-treated lumber for post materials. Specify "CCA pressure-treated to .40 pounds of chemical per foot." About the only other affordable wood to use is heartwood cedar.

Gates must have diagonal support to prevent racking. This can be accomplished with wooden members or turnbuckle and wire.

The types of fences you can build are shown in the accompanying drawings.

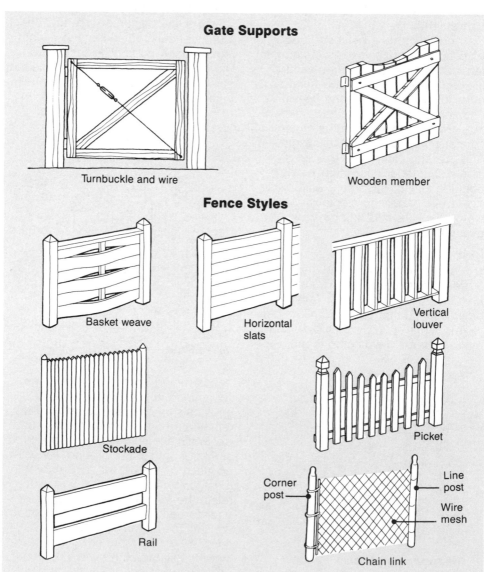

Gate Supports

Turnbuckle and wire

Wooden member

Fence Styles

Basket weave

Horizontal slats

Vertical louver

Stockade

Picket

Rail

Corner post

Line post

Wire mesh

Chain link

7. Windows

Choosing the right windows for your home will add light, provide architectural drama, improve ventilation, enhance your home's value, and lower its energy bills. That's a lot to get, but it is also what you should expect. Windows, after all, are expensive.

In the last few years the world of windows has been alive with innovation, both in terms of style and substance. Odd-shaped windows—ovals, octagons, triangles, trapezoids—have been produced by major window manufacturers to fit with homes of contemporary design. Window walls and skylights have surged in popularity. More recently, as homes have taken a turn again toward traditional forms, the manufacturers have responded with historic window shapes such as half-round transoms.

In the way of substance, windows are getting more energy-efficient. During the 1970s, windows began to be built with better weather stripping and tighter construction to reduce air infiltration. Double-pane units, which boost the insulating value of glass from R-1 to nearly R-2, were promoted, as were triple-pane units for northern climates.

But the advances of the 1980s are proving to be more fundamental and exciting. By now most major window manufacturers are offering some form of "superglass" technology. The most common superglass is called "low-E glass." Low-E glass has a metallic film vacuum-deposited on one side. In a double-pane unit, the film is on the outside of the inner pane.

This superthin, barely visible film prevents the glass from emitting your home's radiant heat to the cold

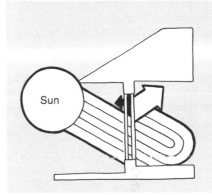

In Cold Weather . . .

Sunlight entering through glass is converted into radiant heat when it strikes walls and floors. This radiant heat escapes through regular glass, but is reflected back into the house by "low-E" glass.

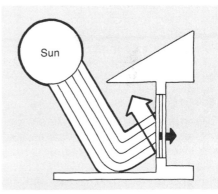

In Hot Weather . . .

Sunlight striking driveways and facing walls is converted into radiant heat that enters the home through ordinary glass but is reflected by "low-E" glass.

outdoors in winter. (The E stands for emissivity.) In doing so, it nearly doubles the R value of the average window from R-2 to about R-3.5. It also raises the roomside temperature of the glass, so you feel warmer when nearby.

In the summer, sunlight striking the pavement, driveways, and facing walls is converted into radiant heat that passes through ordinary windows to increase air-conditioning costs, but

Windows

that same heat is reflected and kept outside by low-E glass.

Low-E glass also inhibits incoming ultraviolet light, a wavelength you can't see, that fades and deteriorates upholstery fabrics, drapes, and carpets.

A variation on low-E technology is called Heat Mirror. The low-E coating is deposited on a clear polyester film, which is then suspended invisibly between two panes of glass. This gives not only a low-E coating, but also the insulating air value of triple-pane glass without the added weight. A window with Heat Mirror has a claimed R value of 4.2, topping out most low-E windows.

Low-E glass is being offered not only in windows, but in patio doors and skylights, too. Expect to pay a price premium of about 10 to 20 percent.

In the next few years, we'll probably see advances such as low-E storm windows and double-pane windows filled with gases like argon instead of air to further boost R values.

Window Types

Casement windows open sideways at the turn of a crank. The advantage is that the whole window can be opened for maximum ventilation. The window can be cracked slightly and still (with crank handle removed) prevent entry by intruders. Casement windows

close tightly, and because the lock draws the sash against the frame, they have the lowest air infiltration of any window style. The glass sash is often hinged for easier cleaning. The screens are on the inside, where they don't get so dirty.

Double-hung windows enhance the traditional look of conventional homes. Their advantages:
- Available in the greatest number of sizes to meet any need
- Rarely need maintenance
- Can accept exterior storm windows and screens

Their disadvantages:
- Do not seal as well as casement or awning windows
- Sliding method of opening wears the weather stripping

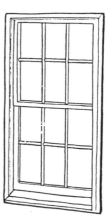

Double-Hung Window

Sliding windows are like patio doors, only smaller. Like casements, they provide a contemporary style. Their primary advantage is that the sash does not protrude outward when open, which might be an obstruction on a first-floor level.

Casement Window

Sliding Window

Transom and circlehead windows go over entry or patio doors or even windows, where ceiling height permits, to admit more light and give an elegant appearance to a home. Rectangular transoms are also available. Most are fixed windows, so they are not true transoms. They are available with single- or double-pane clear glass or with beveled or colored panes, including decorative leaded stained glass. Some are available with grilles that snap out for easier cleaning. Muntins (grilles) make the single piece of glass look like separate panes.

Transom And Circlehead Windows

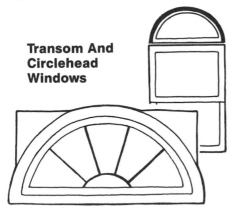

Fixed picture windows can be energy champions with the right glazing. There is no measurable infiltration loss. Double or triple glazed, they may allow you to have a larger

window area to capitalize on a view. There is no need for screens. Their primary disadvantage is that they do not allow for ventilation, although a hopper window can be installed under the picture window. Most codes require operable windows in each room.

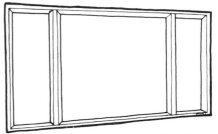

Fixed Picture Window

Awning windows are like casement windows but open upwards instead of sideways. They provide the same advantages as casement windows and may keep out more rain in a downpour. They are better for basement windows because they clear the ground and are an appropriate style for contemporary homes. Among their disadvantages is that they tend to get dirty quickly if left raised.

Awning Window

Hopper windows are commonly used as basement windows and below fixed (nonopening) windows. They are hinged at the bottom and open inward. Side baffles usually limit the amount they can be opened. They may have no locking device, since it's assumed no one can fit though the opening.

Windows

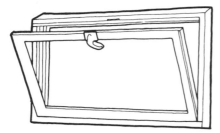

Hopper Window

Jalousie windows are rarely used today. These crank-operated, slatted windows were designed for maximum ventilation in hot climates before air-conditioning. Today, they are still installed on patios. Screens can be attached inside. Plastic sleeves can be attached to the bottom of each pane to reduce infiltration. Their advantages are provision of maximum ventilation without fear of unwanted intrusion and the ability to ward off rain while open. Their primary disadvantage is poor energy performance.

Jalousie Window

High clerestory windows are sometimes used at the top end of a cathedral ceiling. If facing south, these windows are high enough to allow sunlight to bathe the opposite wall. By using a brick or masonry wall, this becomes a solar collector, releasing stored heat as the indoor temperature drops. The windows used are usually awning windows or casement windows installed sideways. A long winding crank has to be made to operate them. They may be preferred over skylights, since they can be shaded by overhangs in summer and skylights usually cannot.

High Clerestory Window

Pivot windows are mounted with a vertical rod in the center. Half the window swings in while the other half swings out. The only way to drape these windows is to attach curtains directly to the sash.

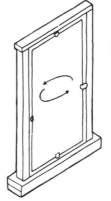

Pivot Window

Basement windows should be purchased before building or pouring the wall to assure correct spacing. If you use awning-type windows that open up, make sure the sash will clear your staked-out grade level. More often these are equipped with hopper windows, which hinge at the bottom and open inward manually. Make sure these windows are equipped with screens and seal tightly. The frame and sash may be steel or wood, but wood needs frequent painting and steel will rust. Someone should develop a nonpeeling, nonrusting basement window.

Bow or bay windows are usually an assembly of three to six windows set in an arc with a built-out floor and roof. Most bows and bays are sold in kit form, complete with fixed central windows, operable side windows, framing, and even roofing for the small projection.

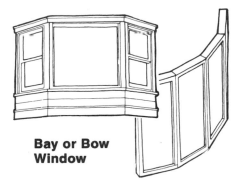

Bay or Bow Window

Greenhouse windows are a recent and very popular innovation. They protrude from the window opening to allow plants to thrive in locations such as the kitchen or den. These windows are attractive but, although available double glazed, cannot be considered energy-efficient.

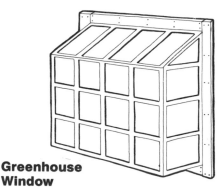

Greenhouse Window

Features to Look For

Energy Savings

As discussed previously, low-E window glass is now being made that loses less heat in winter (and gains less heat in summer). But that's not the only way windows lose energy. Heat is also lost through the sashes and via air infiltration between sash and frame.

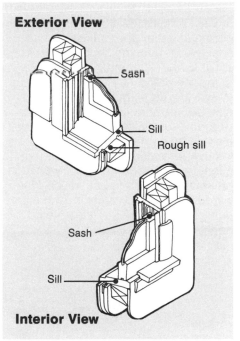

Exterior View

Sash

Sill

Rough sill

Sash

Sill

Interior View

Sashes that lose the least heat include solid wood sashes and insulated vinyl sashes. Aluminum or steel sashes with wide thermal breaks may be acceptable in temperate climates; all-metal sashes (without thermal breaks) lose the most heat. In cold weather all-metal sashes can cause indoor humidity to condense on them, creating puddles on the windowsills.

The amount of air infiltration between sash and frame is tested by major window manufacturers. Don't be afraid to ask for this number, and compare those of several manufacturers. If you cannot obtain a number, look at the quality of weather stripping and the tightness of the sash in its frame.

Windows

Remember that casement windows are tightest, jalousie windows are leakiest, and double-hung windows are prone to leaks as well.

If you have an old house with wood windows, don't be too quick to rip them out and replace them with aluminum or vinyl models. Adding storm windows will be cheaper and may be just as effective in reducing heat loss, because you'll have two frames instead of one to reduce drafts.

By the way, if you live at a high altitude, you should buy drilled windows —double- or triple-glazed windows with a small hole drilled through the panes. Otherwise, a completely sealed unit might implode due to the difference in pressure between the air inside the window and the air outside. The extra energy lost because of the hole is negligible.

Anatomy of a Window

Nothing on a blueprint will scare the novice more than a cross section view of a window. Certainly windows vary by type and manufacturer, but the accompanying sketches should clear up any mystery about the components.

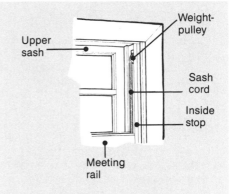

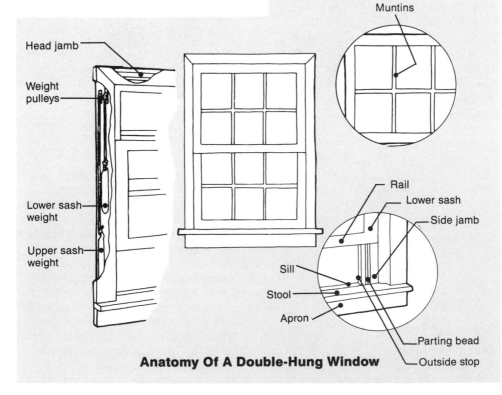

Anatomy Of A Double-Hung Window

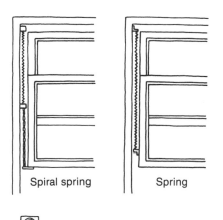

Spiral spring | Spring

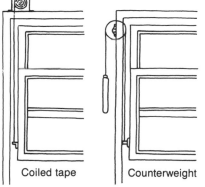

Coiled tape | Counterweight

Balancing Devices Used For Double-Hung Windows

Convenience

Some windows are much easier than others to clean and maintain. Shop for such conveniences as tilt-out sashes so you can clean the window's outside from the inside. If you like the

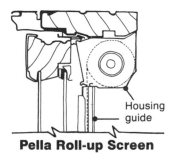

Housing guide

Pella Roll-up Screen

look of muntins, consider the removable grilles that make cleaning easy. Some windows have easily attached interior screens, and Pella windows have a unique built-in roll-up screen.

Many wood windows now have aluminum and vinyl cladding on the exterior of their sashes and frames so you'll never have to paint them. This is an enticing feature. The only drawbacks are that the aluminum and vinyl come in a limited number of colors.

Style

In considering windows, consider the style of your house. Although aluminum and vinyl windows offer low maintenance, their styles are often not appropriate for historic houses or new homes that project traditional elegance. In those cases, wood-sash windows usually offer more complementary styles.

Quality Seals

Quality wood window manufacturers belonging to the National Woodwork Manufacturers Association (NWMA) have their products tested by the NWMA to assure customers that the materials, construction, and tested performance of their products meet established industry standards. When buying windows look for these quality seals.

Window frames and sills treated with a water-repellent preservative are also tested and granted a seal by NWMA.

Because the aluminum window market is large and fabrication can be done by "mom and pop" outfits for low cost instead of performance, it is particularly important to look for a quality seal on these products. The Architectural Aluminum Manufacturers Association (AAMA) administers a random sampling and product evaluation. It grants a red seal to those

Windows

manufacturers who meet American National Standards Institute (ANSI) national standards. This indicates approval for residential use; a blue seal is for commercial applications.

Aluminum storm windows that meet ANSI A134-3 specifications are also given an "AAMA Certified" seal.

A. The National Woodwork Manufacturers Association (NWMA) seal certifies preservative treatment of millwork in accordance with NWMA IS-4.
B. Certification tags such as that of the AWWI indicate the certifying organization, manufacturer, type and class of window, and applicable standard.
C. Red AAMA label for B1 and B2 Residential series aluminum windows. Commercial and monumental series windows are identified by a blue label.
D. AAMA Quality Certified Seal assures conformance with AAMA and ANSI specifications.

Replacement Windows

If you're remodeling an old home, be especially careful about the style of the new windows you choose. Contemporary-looking windows, for instance, look out of place in a remodeling job where the entire house hasn't been given a similar face-lift. Worse yet are instances where only some windows are replaced, creating a mishmash of old and new. Worst of all, perhaps, is changing the opening size when replacing the window. This often results in windows that are obviously out of proportion to the home's overall design. Altering the window size causes extra cost and labor to alter exterior siding, wall framing, and interior finish. And then when you're all done, you may have lowered your home's resale value if you were not careful about the job you did.

When replacing windows, you have an opportunity to increase the conservation of your home. Be guided by the R value—or its opposite, U value—provided by the manufacturer. The higher the R or lower the U, the more the insulating power. R values are easier to work with because they give the insulating value of the whole unit. U values are separate for each surface, space, and material, so have to be totaled. But you can do even better *and* save money, too. Because the spacing between the sealed units on some double-pane windows is too small to provide much resistance, you'll find you can achieve a higher R value by using a less expensive single-pane window and a separate storm window spaced an inch or two away. This also gives you a second seal against infiltration.

Easy-Cleaning Tilt Windows

Wood windows are generally tighter and less conductive and, if covered in PVC or a fluorocarbon, are easy to clean and maintain. A few top-quality aluminum windows with a baked synthetic enamel finish, wide thermal breaks, and good weather stripping match the performance of wood—the price difference may be repaid in energy savings.

Check the weather stripping before you buy a new or replacement window or storm window. Place a dollar bill across the opening and close the window. The bill should be difficult or impossible to pull out.

Guide to Replacement Windows

Material	Finish and Durability	What to Look For
Aluminum A silicon-magnesium-aluminum wrought alloy, 6063 T/5, heat treated, offers better corrosion resistance. Roll-formed alloys are not as durable.	Best: Baked synthetic enamel Very good: Fluorocarbon-coated enamel Good: Anodized or paint finish Fair: Oxidized mill finish (not satisfactory near ocean or areas having abnormal atmosphere)	1/4″ wide wood or plastic thermal break; tight weather stripping; polyvinylchloride or neoprene gaskets; aluminum, plastic, or stainless steel fittings (dissimilar metals will result in galvanic corrosion); sash that tilts for easy cleaning. Look for AAMA red certification seal.
Steel	Needs baked-on synthetic enamel as basemetal conducts heat and is subject to condensation. Needs annual painting for long-term durability. Marble or laminate windowsills recommended to avoid moisture damage.	Complete paint coverage—no scratches. Usually single structure without thermal break—foam plastic coating can help but not very durable. Check seals with dollar bill.

Windows

Guide to Replacement Windows (Concluded)

Material	Finish and Durability	What to Look For
Wood	Look for NWMA water-repellent preservative seal. Vinyl-clad can provide excellent service. If painted will need maintenance, although improved by use of fluorocarbon surface.	Tight seals, hole-free paint coating. Check weather stripping with dollar bill. Ask for R value and compare— the higher the number the better. Give preference to low-E glass and wide spacing (1/4″ or more) between panes. Look for AWWI Quality Approved label.

Window Security

Some double-hung windows have key locks that attach to the top rail of the lower sash. They can be used to keep the window shut or partially open. The locks work by driving a pin into predrilled holes in the jamb.

You can make your own similar security device. With double-hung windows closed, drill a hole in the left and right corners of the upper rail of the bottom sash. Drill into (but not through) the lower rail of the upper sash. Slip a double-head nail into

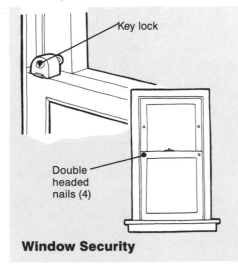

Window Security

each hole. Now the window cannot be jimmied from outside, and the holding device can't be seen from the outside —a mystery to the would-be intruder.

Casement windows and awning windows are rendered inoperable merely by removing the crank handle.

Storm Windows

Combination storm windows and screens offer protection and greatly improved thermal efficiency. The problem is, they almost always have to be factory fabricated. Careful measuring is essential; if you are 1/2″ off, the unit will not fit. Storm windows should be installed using a spirit level and T square, because they will bind if not installed square. If you are attaching them to an old window, make sure it is still level or straight. You will need to remove the casing to measure the opening size. With luck you may find you have a standard size. If so, the unit you buy will be, by design, a fraction smaller than the window opening.

Most aluminum windows come with a nailing flange. To replace a window you may have to cut through the siding around the window with a sabre saw, since the window is installed from the

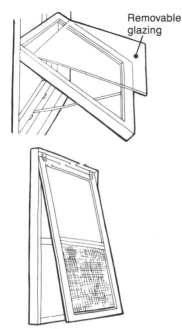

Storm And Screen Windows

outside. You need to cut ¼″ wider than the flange—usually about 1¾″. All edges of the frame should be caulked as it is installed and only aluminum, stainless, or galvanized steel screws should be used on aluminum storm windows, to avoid galvanic corrosion. Use flashing paper between the framing and the aluminum nailing flange. If attaching to a concrete or masonry surface, prime the surface with household aluminum paint. *Never attach aluminum to a damp surface.*

Construction of aluminum screens is simple. Every home center sells the channels and corner fasteners. You can save several hundred dollars on a home by making and installing your own.

Skylights

The advantages of a skylight are usually obvious—it provides dramatic light and view. The disadvantages are usually not obvious at first: a tendency to create heat in summer, lose heat in

winter, leak during storms, and be difficult to clean. If you install one with the romantic idea of being able to look up at the stars, recognize that your room will be bathed in light all night approaching full moon. Shades are a good idea for night and summer use but are hard to find and may mean having a looped operating cord hanging down over the bed or carpet. All these disadvantages can be mitigated or overcome, however, by selecting the right products and locating them wisely.

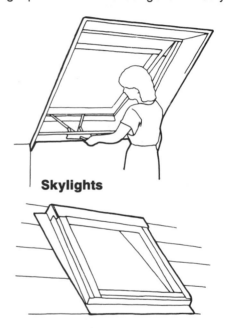

Skylights

My first piece of advice is to buy a skylight that opens and closes, rather than one that is "fixed" (inoperable). A skylight that opens will help vent summertime heat, which naturally rises roofward throughout the house. Open some windows or doors downstairs on the windward side, and you should get a nice "chimney effect" breeze flowing.

To get a skylight's beauty without sacrificing comfort, you'll want to shop for other features, too. Look for a unit with an integrated shading device and

Windows

with screens that don't have to be removed to operate the sash. If cleaning from roofside will be a major problem, buy a pivoting sash so you can clean the glass from within the room. In cold climates, go for at least double glazing and insulated curbing, a tight seal, and a built-in channel that collects condensation.

Try to point your skylights in the right direction. In cold climates, a skylight will make a small net heating contribution only if it faces due south and is pitched steeply to catch the low winter sun. In the Sunbelt, skylights won't ignite your air-conditioning bills if you face them north and shade them.

Skylights installed in a roof above a flat ceiling will require a light well (window chase) to be built in the attic. This will add to your cost and the complexity of the installation. Insulate around the framing of the light well to at least R-28 to prevent excessive heat loss or gain.

To minimize the chances of a leaky skylight, buy a product that sits on a curbing built atop the roofline and comes with its own flashing. Then make sure the flashing is installed correctly.

Interior Moldings

Typical decorative trim for window interiors has to be installed in the specific order given below:

1. The stool at the window base rests on top of and overlaps the sill and generally extends beyond the side casing.
2. Side casing is attached to each side of the window—mitered at 45° to meet the head casing if it is the same shape molding.
3. If installing trimming-paired windows, the vertical mullion casing is installed next between the windows.

The top is cut to fit into the top casing.
4. The head casing, mitered at 45° each end, is fitted into the mitered tops of the side casing.
5. Finally, nail the apron under the stool, closing the gap between sill and wall.
6. Muntins, the wood or plastic grilles that make a single glass look like a set of small panes, are sprung into the holes provided around the frame.

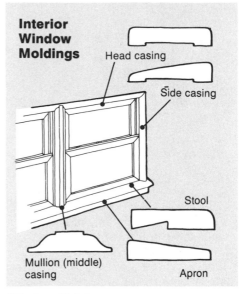

Interior Window Moldings — Head casing, Side casing, Stool, Mullion (middle) casing, Apron

Window Heights

Appearance inside and out will, to a degree, dictate the size of window you buy. To provide symmetry to a house, it has been traditional to frame the top of each window rough opening so the bottom of the header is 6'6" above the *finished* floor. This will normally be the same height as the door. The bottom opening height above the finished floor is likely to vary by room.

Conventionally, a kitchen window will be 3'6" to clear cabinets. A living room window may be 1' but this dimension is changing. Since often all you see out of the bottom foot of the

214

window is the withered leaves of the foundation planting, the cost of that lower window is not warranted. But tall windows do add dignity to a house.

The dining room window rough opening is normally 2'5½". On other rooms, outside appearance is important. Bathroom windows, being generally smaller, can unbalance the house. To help establish window heights around the house you will need to make a "story polo" with dimensions marked for distances above rough and finished floors.

Sizing Charts

Once you have selected the style of window you want and established the heights, look at the manufacturer's literature. You will find a diagram, such as the example shown, that gives all necessary dimensions. Look to the top

left. First it gives you sill-to-floor dimensions (on left) in feet and millimeters for masonry, rough opening, and window frame, while side-to-side dimensions are given above. This information is then repeated in feet and inches adding sash and glass dimensions. Special exceptions—such as "Triple glazing panels not available in these sizes"—are noted, and a different ink color is used to identify egress windows. The order number gives dimensions and type—for example, 2042 WC indicates a 20"-wide by 42"-deep casement window. In the case of casement windows, you must also indicate if you want the hinge on the left (LH) or right (RH) *as viewed from the outside.* TB stands for tempered (safety) glass.

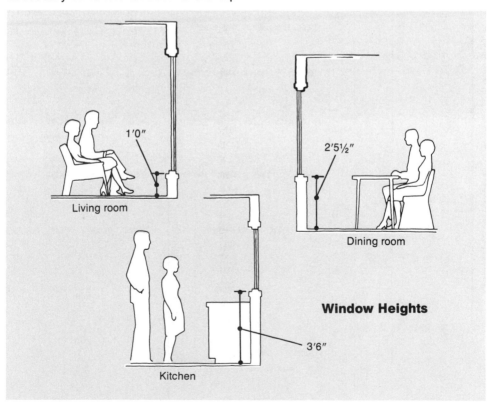

1'0"

Living room

2'5½"

Dining room

Window Heights

3'6"

Kitchen

Windows

Wood Window Opening Dimensions—
To determine rough openings for single units in typical installations, add ½" (13 mm) to frame width and 1⅝" (41 mm) to frame height when Pella subsill is used.

Add 3" (76 mm) to frame width and 2⅝" (67 mm) to frame height to determine masonry openings when Pella subsill and brick mold are used—these are not included in frame dimensions.

To determine openings for multiple window groupings, apply single-unit formulas combined with frame widths and combine frame heights. Dimensions apply only when Pella subsill and brick mold are used.

op WOOD CASEMENT SIZES

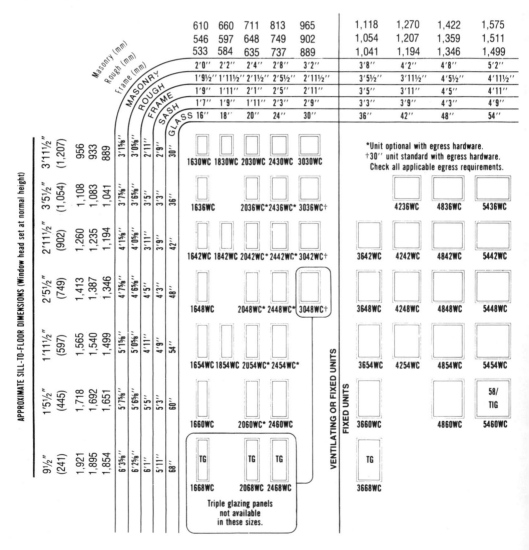

216

Tools Required for Installing Windows and Doors

	Hand Tools		Optional Power Tools
Installing door and lock	Awl	Ladder	Circular or arbor saw
	Brace and bits	Pencil	Drill
	Caulking gun	Plane	Router
	Chisel	Rafter square	Hole saw
	Compass	Screwdriver	
	Gauge	Spirit level	
	Hammer	Steel rule	
Installing window	Awl	Ladder	Drill
	Caulking gun	Screwdriver	
	Chisel	Steel rule	
	Drill	Spirit level	
	Gauge		
	Hammer		
Installing or replacing windowpane	Chisel	Putty knife	
	Glass	Rafter square	
	Glass cutter	Sandpaper	
	Glazier's point	Soldering iron	
	Hammer	Straightedge	
Replacing sash cord	Chain or cord		
	Chisel		
	Hammer		
	Knife		
	Screwdrivers		
	Screws		
	String		
	Weight		
Loosening binding, window or door	Chisel	Sander	
	File	Petroleum Wax or Silicone	
	Hammer		
	Plane		
	Pry bar		
	Putty knife		
	Screwdriver		

Thick Glass and Safety Glass

The window glass you select has to meet local codes designed to minimize (but not prevent) glass breakage. Various service conditions justify special considerations. You should get the advice of your local building inspector or telephone a local glass or window dealer familiar with local codes.

Basically, the thickness will be dictated by size and wind load. Normal residential windows or storm windows are made with single-strength ($\frac{1}{16}$") or double-strength ($\frac{1}{8}$") annealed float glass. The frame of a storm window will be sized for one or the other, so you have to replace broken panes with the same thickness of glass. The rabbeting in a wood sash or frame may allow you to switch from one to the other. The expectation of high wind damage is greatest in coastal regions, exposed

Windows

hilly terrain, and among tall buildings. In these locations one should always use double-strength glass or thicker. Windows whose greatest dimension exceeds 72" should be glazed with ⅛" glass, and where the largest dimension exceeds 96", the use of 3⁄16" or ¼" glass is recommended.

Single-strength glass is available up to 48" × 84". Double-strength 3⁄16" and ¼" glass is available up to 60" × 84".

The majority of window glass is made by the float process (molten glass is poured onto a flat bed of molten tin) and is called annealed or float glass. It is easy to score and break to size. However, most windows today are double or triple glazed for energy savings, and it's quite possible the glass you are replacing may be tinted or coated. Your builder can advise you which manufacturer made the window so you can contact the local window dealer if you need to replace a sash. If it is a sealed double-pane unit, it may take six to eight weeks to get a replacement. Dealers for the better brands generally keep a stock of the common sizes. Single-pane float glass is available from most home centers and hardware stores and can be cut to size.

Federal law prescribes that safety glazing must be used in locations such as sliding patio doors, storm doors, interior and exterior doors, tub and shower doors and enclosures, mirror doors, and glass panels near doors. It is illegal for your dealer to sell you—or for you to install—anything but safety glass or plastic glazing in these locations. Safety glass includes tempered, heat-treated glass; laminated glass; and acrylic or polycarbonate glazing. For your own safety you may also want to consider use of safety or wired glass, fiberglass-reinforced plastic panels, or polycarbonate panels

for overhead greenhouse glass, sloped glass, skylights, or anywhere accidental contact and breakage could cause injury. (Safety glass should also be used for overhead lighting panels or aquariums.)

Safety glass is much more expensive than float glass. Thin acrylic sheet may cost less than float glass. However, this is easily scratched (although some is available with a coating to harden the surface), and it can be blown or pushed out of a window sash. Acrylic panels may do to fill the window while you wait for your replacement order, but generally they do not have the surface hardness for long-term use. Tempered glass meets the requirements, but it cannot be cut, drilled, or edged after it has been tempered. This means you have to order it from a factory and wait two to three weeks for it to be cut to size, then tempered and delivered.

Laminated glass, which generally has a sheet of polyvinyl butyral plastic sandwiched between two sheets of glass, is at least twice the price of float glass and usually more costly than tempered glass. A major advantage besides safety is that it can be cut. (You have to score both sides, crack over a straight edge and then use a knife to cut the plastic.) It will not fall out of the frame if broken and will keep providing weather protection until you can order and receive a new panel. Laminated glass allows less noise transmission and, where thicker plastic is interleaved, is burglar- and bulletproof after heat treating.

Polycarbonate is the most expensive safety glazing for large areas (you have to use thicker panels to attain the rigidity), but may cost less than laminated glass for smaller windows. It is easy to cut with a saber, skill, or band saw. It comes both as flat stock and in the form of structured sheet (having vertical rectangular $\frac{1}{4}''$-thick air channels) suitable for sidelights and patio roofs. Since polycarbonate has a coefficient of expansion eight times that of glass, it needs to be set in a metal frame that grips the sides but leaves adequate space for expansion on all sides. Never use caulking on plastic panes over 24'' in either dimension.

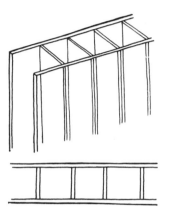

Structural Polycarbonate Glass

All types of safety glazing are available in tints and with coatings to absorb ultraviolet light. This reduces "sun rot" and fading of fabrics and carpets. Acrylics and polycarbonates are available with surface-hardening coatings but cannot offer the hardness or scratch resistance of glass. Tinted or heat-absorbing glass is made by adding various colorants, usually bronze, gray, or green, to reduce solar transmittance of the glass. This has little effect upon solar reflectance, hence increasing the heat (solar) absorption within the glass. This is why tinted glass has to be strengthened or tempered. Color density increases with thickness.

Glasses and plastic panes may also be given textured surfaces to diffuse light or provide privacy. Obscuring glass is translucent and is made by a rolling process that imprints a figure or pattern. Wire is also encased in rolled glass for use as safety glass, but it cannot be tempered and is difficult to cut. Frosting (sandblasting) of glass weakens it, making it subject to easier breakage.

Picture glass can usually be single-strength $\frac{1}{16}''$ float glass. Nonglare glass is also available from home center stores and framing shops.

Glass Blocks

Glass block has enjoyed a small revival in the 1980s. Its advantages include artistic effect, noise reduction, diffused light, energy savings, and security.

Blocks are available in 4'' × 8'' and 6'' × 8'' nominal sizes or in 6'', 8'', and 12'' nominal squares, $3\frac{7}{8}''$ or $3\frac{1}{8}''$ thick. They are also available in curved blocks for corners. They become structural members of the house.

Solid glass blocks, $7\frac{5}{8}''$ square and 3'' thick, are resistant to sound transmission, admit 80 percent of

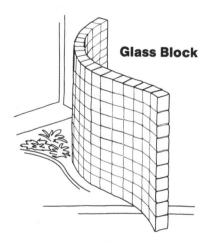

Glass Block

Windows

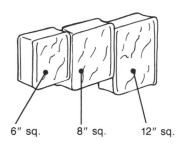

6" sq.   8" sq.   12" sq.

**Glass Block
Window Treatment**

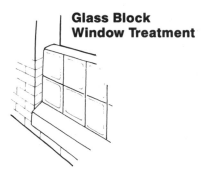

incoming light, and are virtually indestructible. They can be used as covers for floor-recessed lighting. The thermal resistance of these blocks is R-1.15. Slightly thicker, thin-line blocks (3⅛") are available with R values from 1.67 to 1.79. The standard hollow blocks have an R value of 1.79 to 1.89, while those with fibrous glass inserts have R values of 2.06 to 2.27. The latter are made to order.

The surface patterns on blocks include linear (one side horizontal and the other side vertical to diffuse light), rounded flutes (which throw beams of light and provide 80 to 95 percent light transmission), and translucent solar reflective (which reduce light transmission 25 to 50 percent).

Glass blocks are assembled with a masonry cement or mortar containing a metallic stearate waterproofer. Silicone is used as the sealant.

Mirrors

Reflective glass is generally annealed glass, because tempering would destroy the film applied by the normal wet deposition method. Where safety glass mirrors are required, the more expensive vacuum or pyrolitic coating systems have to be used.

Local codes may have restrictions on the use of reflective glass as window glass in some locations where it can reflect solar heat through other peoples' windows, raising their cooling costs. Transparent or two-way mirror glass is designed to allow vision through one direction while presenting a mirror appearance from the other side. It requires five to ten times more light on the object side. It is not recommended for use in residential exterior walls. If you want to see out but prevent outsiders from seeing in, consider solar screens.

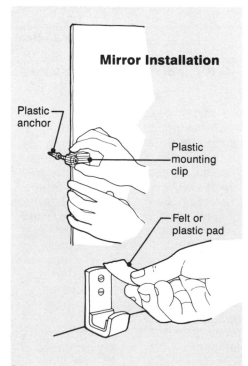

Mirror Installation

Plastic anchor

Plastic mounting clip

Felt or plastic pad

Before you buy your wall mirrors, consider how you plan to hang them. Mirrors should not be mounted flat against a surface, because condensation can react with the reflective chemicals. Always leave vertical space or mount on framing. You may choose to support the bottom with channel metal or plastic clips or baseboard. Using a channel can cause later problems, as someone may use a window cleaner with ammonia to clean the mirrors instead of plain soap and lots of water. The ammonia may get under the frame and destroy the reflective coating. *Do not use window cleaners on mirrors.*

Even if you are mounting the mirror with mastic or double-faced tape (which must have an adhesive capacity of 2 pounds for every square inch), you may want to use clips near the top, at least temporarily for safety reasons. Mastics and tape must be compatible with the mirror backing. Read the manufacturer's recommendations. All metal clips should contain a felt or plastic pad. The mirror must be mounted flat or it will give a distorted reflection.

Mirrors up to 10 square feet are generally mounted using rosettes or screws through a hole in each corner. If more than 10 square feet, holes should be spaced on a minimum of 36" centers.

All holes should be at least 4" from the edge. Holes should be at least $\frac{1}{8}$" larger than the shank of the screw. This is a very difficult hanging method, as any surface irregularity of the wall can cause the mirror to crack when you tighten the screws.

Classifications of Float Glass (in order of descending quality by class)

Class 1—Transparent	Class 2—Heat-Absorbing & Light-Reducing	Class 3—Light-Reducing, Tinted
q1—Mirror Select	q3—Glazing Select	q3—Glazing Select
q2—Mirror	q4—Glazing A	q4—Glazing A
q3—Glazing Select	q5—Glazing B	q5—Glazing B
q4—Glazing A		
q5—Glazing B		
q6—Greenhouse		

NOTE: Style A—Higher light transmission
Style B—Lower light transmission

Standard Sizes of Glazing for Sliding Patio Doors

Tempered $\frac{3}{16}$" Single Pane	Tempered $\frac{3}{16}$" Sealed Insulating Double Pane with $\frac{5}{8}$" Thickness ($\frac{1}{4}$" air space)	
46" × 76"	28" × 76"	42" × 76"
34" × 76"	33" × 74$\frac{7}{8}$"	45" × 74$\frac{7}{8}$"
	33" × 76$\frac{3}{4}$"	45" × 76$\frac{3}{4}$"
	34" × 76"	46" × 76"

Other window sizes vary by manufacturer.

Windows

Glass Thicknesses Available

Nominal Decimal Inch	Traditional Designation	Generally Available in the Following Qualities (The higher the number the better the quality)
0.04	Micro/slide	q4, q5
0.06	Photo	q4, q5
0.08	Picture	q4, q5
	Window Glazing	
0.09	Single $\frac{1}{16}''$	q1, q2, q4, q5
0.11	Lami	q4, q5
0.12	Double $\frac{1}{8}''$	q1, q2, q3, q4, q5, q6
0.16	$\frac{5}{32}''$	q3, q4, q5
0.19	$\frac{3}{16}''$	q1, q2, q3, q4, q5
0.21	$\frac{7}{32}''$	q3, q4, q5
0.23	$\frac{1}{4}''$	q1, q2, q3
0.32	$\frac{5}{16}''$	q3
0.39	$\frac{3}{8}''$	q3
0.49	$\frac{1}{2}''$	q3
0.63	$\frac{5}{8}''$	q3
0.75	$\frac{3}{4}''$	q3
0.87	$\frac{7}{8}''$	q3
1.00	$1''$	q3
1.23	$1\frac{1}{4}''$	q3

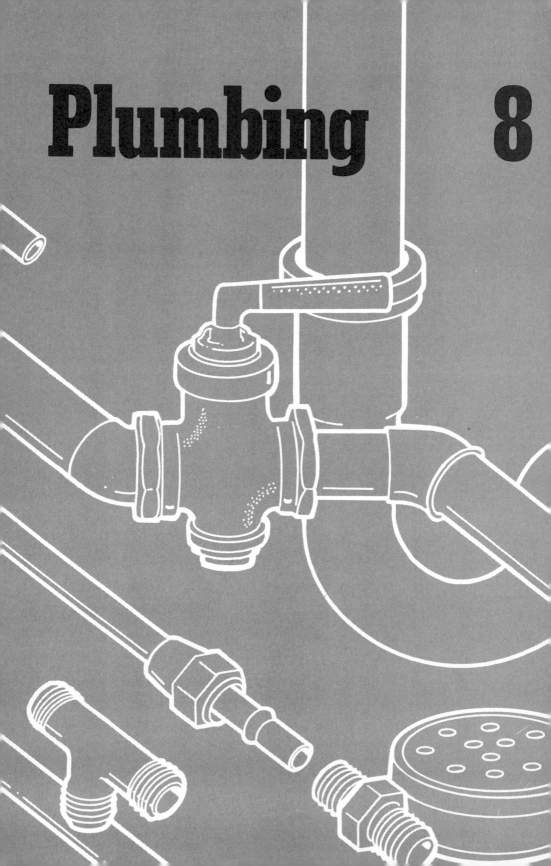

Plumbing

8

8. Plumbing

Plumbing can be complicated. No question. If you own an old home, your plumbing system may be composed of four different kinds of pipe: galvanized steel, cast iron, copper, and finally some plastic, installed when a bathroom was recently remodeled. A turn-of-the-century home may even have lead pipe inside the wall. Each kind of pipe is joined together differently: Steel has threads, copper is soldered, plastic takes a chemical solvent. And then, for all the twists, turns, connections with fixtures, and reductions in diameter, there are an almost infinite number of fittings.

hour provides a powerful incentive, of course. Also, the availability of plastic plumbing allows you to run piping without having to learn the art of sweat-soldering. In fact, the major obstacle to your using plastic is not skill but law—a few local building codes still prohibit its use.

Local codes prescribe a set way to do every major plumbing task. If you're tackling a major job, it's best to consult a plumbing inspector during the planning stage and before you purchase materials.

A home plumbing system is schematically simple: Water enters the home through a black steel or galvanized steel pipe. Municipal water systems normally connect to a water meter mounted between two valves. A

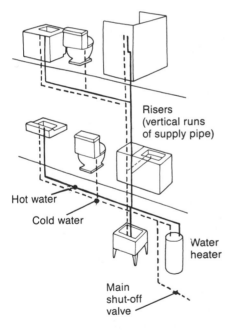

Risers (vertical runs of supply pipe)

Hot water

Cold water

Water heater

Main shut-off valve

Water Supply Lines

Despite the complications, more homeowners are attempting a wider variety of plumbing jobs. The fact that master plumbers charge over $50 an

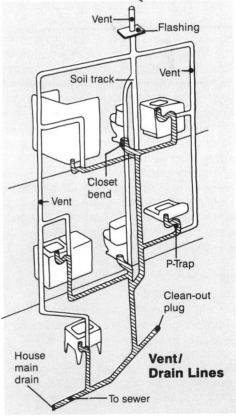

Vent

Flashing

Soil track

Vent

Vent

Closet bend

P-Trap

Clean-out plug

House main drain

Vent/ Drain Lines

To sewer

Plumbing

branch of the supply line from the meter is connected to the water heater. The outlet line from the water heater runs parallel with the cold water supply line to serve the various fixtures and appliances throughout the home. These supply lines are usually under 50 to 60 psi (pounds per square inch) pressure and are made of either copper or chlorinated polyvinyl chloride (CPVC) plastic pipe.

The drain-waste-vent (DWV) pipe system is separate from the supply lines. It carries away water and waste to a city sewer or septic system and vents potentially harmful gases to the outside. Plastic ABS or PVC pipe is in common use in these systems today, while cast iron pipe is often found in older construction.

Soil pipe is used in drainage or septic systems outside the building perimeter. Soil pipe is made of vitreous clay, bituminous fiber, plastic, drainage type copper (DWV), or cast iron. Each has certain advantages, depending upon location, soil types, and price. Copper and cast iron are more expensive but serve better where rigidity is a must or where tree roots are massive enough to crush fiber or enter clay joints.

Gas lines are usually made of black steel pipe, although some building codes permit flexible brass pipe to be used when connecting appliances to the gas line.

Types of Pipe

Cast Iron Pipe

Cast iron pipe, though seldom used in indoor plumbing these days, is still available in diameters from 2" to 4" and lengths of 5' to 10'. It is used only in the DWV system and underground near tree roots or beneath driveways. It comes in two grades: Service and Extra Heavy.

Old cast iron drainage pipes had wide ends called "hubs" and were sealed together with molten lead and

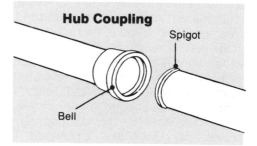

Hub Coupling

Spigot

Bell

No-Hub Coupling Installation

1. Slide neoprene gasket over end of one pipe; clamp band on other pipe.

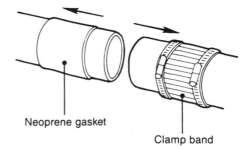

Neoprene gasket

Clamp band

2. Insert pipe into gasket.

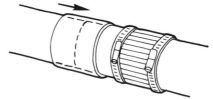

3. Slide clamp band over gasket and tighten clamps.

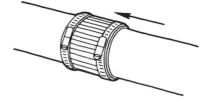

oakum. Today's iron pipe is "hubless" and is joined together with metal-clamped neoprene gaskets.

Galvanized Steel Pipe

Galvanized steel pipe is used as a main water supply line and in steam and hot water heating systems. It is sold in sizes from ⅛" (inside diameter) to 12". Each end of a steel pipe is threaded, and lengths are joined by threaded fittings. All threads are made to IPT (international pipe thread) standards. If you're working with galvanized steel pipe, you can ask the plumbing supply shop that sells you the pipe to cut the pipe to length and cut threads in the ends, rather than having to cut the threads yourself.

Copper Pipe

Copper is common, both in supply and DWV lines. Type M, the thinnest type (see chart, page 228) is the most frequently used as a supply line, usually in ½" diameter. Type M is rigid only, but types K and L come in both hard and soft versions. The soft type is so flexible it can be wound in coils. It permits longer runs without joints and is therefore easier to install.

Though soft copper tubing is easier to bend, you should not bend it without the aid of a springlike tube bender. Tube benders are available in the same sizes as copper pipe; be sure to get the correct size.

Typical Steel Pipe Sizes*

Nominal Pipe Size (In.)	Shipper Wts		Diameter			Weight per Foot Pounds		Threads Per Inch
			External	Internal	Thickness	Beveled or Plain Ends	Threaded and Coupled	
⅛	630 ft.	154	0.405	0.269	0.068	0.244	0.245	27
¼	504 ft.	216	0.540	0.364	0.088	0.424	0.425	18
⅜	378 ft.	216	0.675	0.493	0.091	0.567	0.568	18
½	252 ft.	216	0.840	0.622	0.109	0.850	0.852	14
¾	147 ft.	168	1.050	0.824	0.113	1.130	1.134	14
1	105 ft.	175	1.315	1.049	0.133	1.678	1.684	11½
1¼	63 ft.	144	1.660	1.380	0.140	2.272	2.281	11½
1½	63 ft.	172	1.900	1.610	0.145	2.717	2.731	11½
2	21 ft.	77	2.375	2.067	0.154	3.652	3.678	11½
2½	21 ft.	122	2.875	2.469	0.203	5.793	5.819	8
3	21 ft.	160	3.500	3.068	0.216	7.575	7.616	8
3½			4.000	3.548	0.226	9.109	9.202	8
4	21 ft.	229	4.500	4.026	0.237	10.790	10.889	8
5			5.563	5.047	0.258	14.617	14.810	8
6	21 ft.	403	6.625	6.065	0.280	18.974	19.185	8
8			8.625	8.071	0.277	24.696	25.000	8
8	21 ft.	525	8.625	7.981	0.322	28.554	28.809	8
10			10.750	10.192	0.279	31.201	32.000	8
10			10.750	10.136	0.307	34.240	35.000	8
10			10.750	10.020	0.365	40.483	41.132	8
12			12.750	12.090	0.330	43.773	45.000	8
12			12.750	12.000	0.375	49.562	50.706	8

*Unthreaded pipe shipped in 21′ lengths. Threaded pipe shipped in 10′ lengths with protecting caps at both ends.

Plumbing

Copper Pipe Types

Type	Use	Commonly Stocked Sizes	Comments
K	Municipal, commercial, residential construction	20' rigid (hard) 60', 100', & 200' coils (soft)	Heaviest of copper pipe Sized by inside diameter
L	Residential water lines	20' rigid (hard) 60', 100' & 200' coils (soft)	Sized by inside diameter
M	Light domestic water lines	20' rigid & under	Some plumbing codes prohibit use Sized by inside diameter
DWV	Drainage, waste, and vent lines	20' rigid	Sized by inside diameter
Refrigeration	All refrigeration lines and sometimes used in heater connections	20' rigid 50' coils	Moisture removed and ends sealed Sized by outside diameter

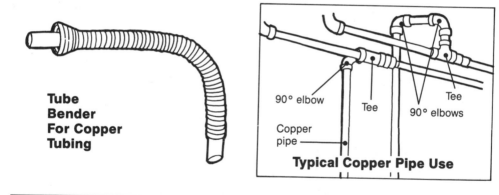

Tube Bender For Copper Tubing

90° elbow

Copper pipe

Tee

90° elbows

Tee

Typical Copper Pipe Use

Types K, L, and M Copper Tubing Sizes

Nominal Size (inches)	Outside Diameter (inches) Types K-L-M	Inside Diameter (inches)		
		Type K	Type L	Type M
3/8	.500	.402	.430	.450
1/2	.625	.527	.545	.569
3/4	.875	.745	.785	.811
1	1.125	.995	1.025	1.055
1 1/4	1.375	1.245	1.265	1.291
1 1/2	1.625	1.481	1.505	1.527

Plastic Pipe

There are a variety of plastics used to make plumbing of different uses. But all of them share some common virtues: They are lightweight, inexpensive, durable, and easy to join. The two flexible kinds, polyethylene (PE) and polybutylene (PB), won't burst when water inside them freezes. The other types are rigid.

The rigid CPVC and flexible PB pipes can be used for hot water supply lines, if your local code permits. The CPVC tubing generally comes in ½" and ¾" nominal sizes and 10' lengths. PB comes in ⅜", ½", and ¾", all by 100', and 1" by 25'. It can be cut with a hacksaw. For hot water systems these pipes are rated only to 100 psi at 180°F, so you may have to change your 125-psi-at-210°F water heater relief valve to one with the lower pipe rating.

Schedule 40 PVC and ABS pipes are most often used as waste pipes.

Polyethylene (PE) is most often used in outdoor cold water service—it remains flexible in temperatures as low as minus 50°F. PE is also sold in 100' coils rated for 125 psi for extensive underground sprinkler systems.

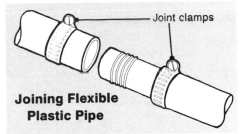
Joint clamps

Joining Flexible Plastic Pipe

Flexible plastic pipe is joined by insert fittings and metal clamps. Rigid plastic pipe is joined by solvent, compression fittings or flared fittings. All plastics may be joined to copper and steel pipe with special adapters called transition fittings. Check with a local plumbing supplier to get the right kind.

Plastic Pipe Characteristics

Type	Characteristic
Polyvinyl chloride (PVC)	Fire resistant (self-extinguishing)
Chlorinated polyvinyl chloride (CPVC)	Requires special solvent cement for joining Nontoxic Excellent fire resistance
Polyethylene (PE)	Good flexibility Good low-temperature performance Comes corrugated and perforated for subsoil drainage systems
Polybutylene (PB)	Good flexibility, flare or compression fittings Not weldable
Acryaonitrile-butadiene-styrene (ABS)	Excellent low-temperature strength
Rubber modified styrene (SR)	Lightweight Brittle at low temperatures
Polypropylene (PP)	Very high chemical resistance Lightweight
Polyacetal (acetal)	Approved for potable water Nontoxic

Plumbing

Plastic Pipe Types

Type	Applications	Types of Joints
Polyvinyl chloride (PVC)	Drain waste, vent applications Lawn sprinkler system	Solvent Threaded Transition
Chlorinated polyvinyl chloride (CPVC)	Hot & cold water supply	Solvent Compression Flared Transition
Polyethylene (PE)	Low-pressure water distribution systems Foundation drainage systems	Insert Transition Compression Flared Heat fusion
Polybutylene (PB)	Only flexible plastic tubing suitable for hot and cold pressure water Not suited for fuel oil or kerosene applications	Insert Transition Compression Flared Heat fusion
Acryaonitrile-butadiene-styrene (ABS)	Mobile home and residential drainage systems Gas service systems Electrical conduit underground	Solvent Threaded Transition
Rubber modified styrene (SR)	Used for underground downspout drains Foundation drains Septic tank absorption fields	Solvent Compression Transition
Polypropylene (PP)	P-J-Traps	Compression Threaded Heat fusion
Polyacetal (acetal)	Water lines Faucet bonnet & valve stems	Transition Threaded

*Plastic pipe is often rated at a specific operating pressure at a maximum operating temperature. As an example, PB pipe is rated at 100 psi at 180°F. In most cases, plastic pipe can be subjected to higher temperatures in low- or non-pressure systems

Characteristics			Maximum Operating Temperatures		
Chemical Resistance	Impact Strength	Crush Strength	Pressure	Non-Pressure	Comments
Excellent	Good	Good	120°F	180°F	Fire resistant (self-extinguishing)
Excellent	Good	Excellent	180°F	180°F & above	Requires special solvent cement for joining Nontoxic Excellent fire resistance
Excellent	Good	Excellent	−65°F to 120°F	200°F	Good flexibility Good low-temperature performance Comes corrugated and perforated for subsoil drainage systems
Excellent	Excellent	Excellent	180°F	280°F	Good flexibility flare or compression fittings Not weldable
Good	Excellent	Excellent	180°F	180°F	Excellent low-temperature strength
Fair	Fair	Good	NA	160°F	Lightweight Brittle at low temperatures
Excellent	Good	Good	190°F	190°F	Very high chemical resistance Lightweight
Good	Good	Good	120°F	160°F	Approved for potable water Nontoxic

Plumbing

The only tools you really need are a fine-tooth saw (a hacksaw will do), a knife, sandpaper, a vise, a rule, a spirit level, an electric drill and bits (to drill holes through studs for ½" or ¾" pipe), an adjustable wrench, a claw hammer, a brush for applying solvent, and a pair of goggles. For flaring fittings you can use a standard flaring tool, but you will need to heat the pipe in hot water before you flare the end.

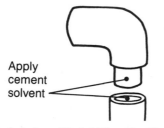

Apply cement solvent

Joining Rigid Plastic Pipe

The best joint solvents contain tetra-hydro-furan (THF) and provide a permanent seal. Before joining and solvent welding the ends of pipes and fittings they must be cleaned with a plastic pipe cleaner to remove any trace of oil. *A quick tip:* Buy all pipe, fittings, and solvents from one manufacturer to ensure a snug fit at joints. Manufacturers do not all use the same tolerances. Do not use resistance cable or hair dryers to thaw frozen plastic pipes—use cloths soaked in hot water. High temperatures can soften and weaken the pipe.

Pipe Fittings

Fittings permit pipes to curve, branch off, and connect with other pipes or fixtures. Each kind of pipe requires its own type of fitting. *Iron* pipe and fittings meet flush and are joined with a neoprene gasket and metal clamp. *Steel* and *brass* pipe fittings are normally threaded. These

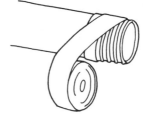

Use Teflon tape on threaded joints

Joining Threaded Pipe

fittings are either *male* or *female*. Male threads are on the outside diameter and female threads are on the inside diameter. In joining all threaded fittings, the use of Teflon tape wrapped around the threads will help make a leakproof joint. The tape will also reduce the chance of corrosion caused when joining two dissimilar metals, particularly copper and galvanized steel.

Copper fittings used to connect two pieces of copper pipe are not threaded; they are joined by *sweat-soldered connections*. Special transitional fittings, which have threads on one end, are available to connect copper pipe to steel, iron, or plastic pipe.

Copper fittings used to connect copper *tubing* are threaded, but a different thread size is used for plumbing and automotive/marine applications.

Copper Joint Is Joined By Sweat-Soldering

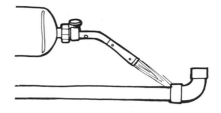

Compression Fitting

Threaded
nut holds composition ring
tight against fitting

Compression ring
provides seal

End of tubing
fits inside
fitting

Flare and *compression* fittings are used mostly for refrigeration and heating systems (liquid petroleum gas). Flare fittings are used with metal tubing, while compression fittings are used with large metal fittings and plastic pipe or tubing. Copper tubing is often threaded, but a different thread size is used for plumbing and automotive/marine applications. (Flare and compression fittings are available for connecting humidifiers.)

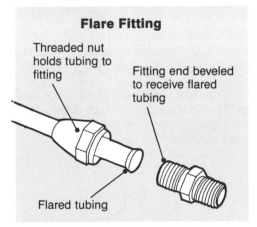

Flare Fitting

Threaded nut
holds tubing to
fitting

Fitting end beveled
to receive flared
tubing

Flared tubing

Plastic fittings are available with threaded, insert, compression, and solvent-weldable connections. Threaded plastic fittings are joined in the same manner as metal fittings.

Insert fittings are inserted into flexible pipe or tubing and sealed with an adjustable clamp around the outside diameter. Solvent-weld fittings have specially formed sockets into which the plastic pipe or tubing is inserted and fused together with a chemical weld using a solvent or cement compatible with the type of plastic being connected.

The typical fittings listed here are illustrated in the pages that follow, with available sizes indicated.

Straight nipples. These extend a line of galvanized steel pipe or provide proper threaded connections at the correct location. Nipples are available in diameters from $\frac{1}{8}''$ to 4" and lengths from *"close"* (short nipples that are threaded from both ends to a point where the threads almost join at the center) to 12". Longer nipples (to 60") are stocked at some jobbers. Lengths of the longer nipples usually increase in 6" increments.

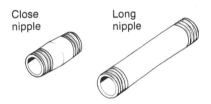

Close
nipple

Long
nipple

Reducing nipples. These reduce pipe size without a reducer, or bushing. These are normally stocked in standard diameters up to 2" but are available in limited lengths. Reducing nipples are used to provide a neater appearance.

Galvanized
Reducing Nipple

Plumbing

Couplings. Used to connect two lengths of pipe or tubing and available in all standard pipe sizes up to 3″. Reducer couplings are also available.

Straight coupling

Reducing coupling

Reducers. Used to reduce pipe size and attached to male pipe threads. Reducers are available to reduce pipe diameter one size or several sizes at one connection.

Bushings. Added inside couplings (female threads) to reduce the pipe size. Using several bushings in series can reduce pipe diameter several sizes at one connection.

Hex bushing

flush bushing

Floor flanges. These connect a pipe to a flat surface such as a floor or wall. Flanges are usually provided with four attachment holes, and are available in standard pipe sizes up to 2″.

Floor flange

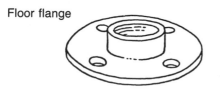

Elbows. Used to change pipe direction. Normally supplied in 45° or 90° bends; female threads are provided on both ends.

90° elbow

45° elbow

Drop ear elbow

Street elbows. Supplied in 45° and 90° bends, with female threads on one end and male threads on the other.

45° street elbow

90° street elbow

Side-outlet elbows. Have three-way outlets spaced 90° to each other. Used for pipe connections on corner construction.

Side-outlet elbow

Tees. Available in standard pipe or tubing sizes. *Straight tees* have three equally sized legs, set 90° to each other, which permits three pipes of the same size to be connected in a T shape. *Reducing tees* are the same shape, but one or two of the legs are reduced one or more pipe sizes.

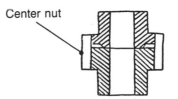

Wye

Reducing Wye

Straight tee
(female threads)

Straight tee—male
(one leg standard
pipe thread—2 legs for
flared tubing)

Unions. Used to connect two pipes simultaneously. Start pipes in each end of union and tighten center nut to tighten two end nuts at the same time.

Center nut

Crosses or four-way tees. These have four legs set 90° to each other in the form of a cross. A straight cross has all legs of the same pipe size. A *side-outlet cross* has an opening in the side for a fifth pipe of the same size.

Caps and plugs. Used to terminate a pipe run from which a valve or similar device has been removed. Caps are applied to male threads and plugs are installed in female threads.

Cap

Square head
plug

Straight cross—female
threads

Hex head
plug

Round
head plug

Y (Wye) bends. Permit attaching three pipes of the same or reduced size in a 45° angle.

235

Plumbing

Solder-Joint Copper Tube Fittings (all dimensions in inches)

Copper to Copper **Coupling (with stop)**	Copper to Copper **Reducing Coupling**	Copper to Copper **Cast Union**	Copper to Female Standard Pipe Sizes (S.P.S.) **Female Adapter**
$\frac{1}{4} \times \frac{1}{4}$	$\frac{1}{2} \times \frac{1}{4}$	$\frac{3}{8}$	$\frac{3}{8} \times \frac{3}{8}$
$\frac{3}{8} \times \frac{3}{8}$	$\frac{1}{2} \times \frac{3}{8}$	$\frac{1}{2}$	$\frac{3}{8} \times \frac{1}{2}$
$\frac{1}{2} \times \frac{1}{2}$	$\frac{3}{4} \times \frac{1}{2}$	$\frac{3}{4}$	$\frac{1}{2} \times \frac{3}{4}$
$\frac{3}{4} \times \frac{3}{4}$	$1 \times \frac{3}{4}$		$\frac{1}{2} \times \frac{1}{2}$
1×1			$\frac{1}{2} \times \frac{3}{8}$
			$\frac{3}{4} \times \frac{3}{4}$
			$\frac{3}{4} \times \frac{1}{2}$
			1×1

No. 604—Copper to Male S.P.S. **Male Adapter**	Copper to Copper **90° Elbow**	Copper to Copper **90° Short-Radius Elbow**	Copper to Copper **45° Elbow**
$\frac{3}{8} \times \frac{1}{2}$	$\frac{1}{2} \times \frac{1}{2}$	$\frac{1}{4} \times \frac{1}{4}$	$\frac{1}{2} \times \frac{1}{2}$
$\frac{3}{8} \times \frac{3}{8}$	$\frac{3}{4} \times \frac{3}{4}$	$\frac{3}{8} \times \frac{3}{8}$	$\frac{3}{4} \times \frac{3}{4}$
$\frac{1}{2} \times \frac{3}{4}$		$\frac{1}{2} \times \frac{1}{2}$	
$\frac{1}{2} \times \frac{1}{2}$		$\frac{3}{4} \times \frac{3}{4}$	
$\frac{1}{2} \times \frac{3}{8}$		1×1	
$\frac{3}{4} \times \frac{3}{4}$			
$\frac{3}{4} \times \frac{1}{2}$			
1×1			

Copper to Male S.P.S. **Cast 90° Elbow**	Copper to Copper to Copper **One-Piece Copper Tee**	Copper to Copper to Female S.P.S. **Cast Tee**	For Tube End **Cap**
$\frac{1}{2} \times \frac{1}{2}$	$\frac{3}{8} \times \frac{3}{8} \times \frac{3}{8}$	$\frac{1}{2} \times \frac{1}{2} \times \frac{1}{2}$	$\frac{3}{8}$
$\frac{3}{4} \times \frac{3}{4}$	$\frac{1}{2} \times \frac{1}{2} \times \frac{1}{2}$		$\frac{1}{2}$
	$\frac{3}{4} \times \frac{3}{4} \times \frac{1}{2}$		$\frac{3}{4}$
	$\frac{3}{4} \times \frac{3}{4} \times \frac{3}{4}$		1
	$1 \times 1 \times 1$		

Solder-Joint Copper Tube Fittings (all dimensions in inches) (Concluded)

(Short-Radius) Fitting to Copper	Fitting to Copper	Copper to Female S.P.S.	Copper to Female S.P.S.
90° Street Elbow	**45° Street Elbow**	**Cast Drop-Ear Elbow**	**Cast 90° Elbow**
½ × ½ ¾ × ¾	½ × ½ ¾ × ¾	½ × ½	½ × ½ ¾ × ¾

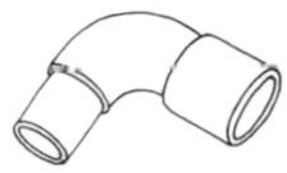

No. 618—Fitting to Copper	Fitting to Copper No. 600-2	Copper to Male S.P.S.
Flush Fitting Reducer	**Fitting Reducer**	**Union**
½ × ⅜ ¾ × ½ 1 × ¾	¾ × ½	¾

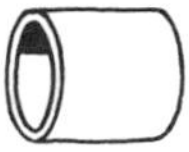

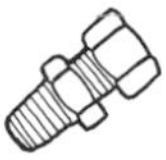

NOTE: All fittings of wrought copper unless otherwise labeled.

Compression Fittings for Copper and Plastic Tubing

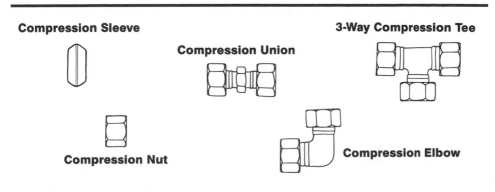

Compression Sleeve

Compression Union

3-Way Compression Tee

Compression Nut

Compression Elbow

These fittings available in ⅛″, ³⁄₁₆″, ¼″, ⁵⁄₁₆″, ⅜″, ½″, and ⅝″ tubing sizes.

Plumbing

Compression Fittings for Copper and Plastic Tubing (Concluded)

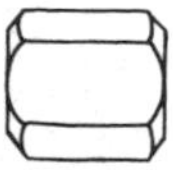 Space Heater Fitting Cap O.D. Tubing × IPT*	 Female Coupling	 Elbow	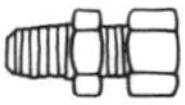 Connector	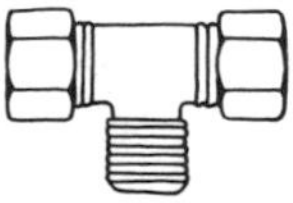 2-Way Compression Tee
⅛ × ⅛		X	X	
³⁄₁₆ × ⅛	X	X	X	
³⁄₁₆ × ¼		X	X	
¼ × ⅛	X	X	X	X
¼ × ¼	X	X	X	
⁵⁄₁₆ × ⅛		X	X	
⁵⁄₁₆ × ¼	X	X	X	
⅜ × ⅛		X	X	
⅜ × ¼	X	X	X	X
⅜ × ⅜	X	X	X	
⅜ × ½	X	X	X	
½ × ⅜	X	X	X	
½ × ½	X	X	X	X
⅝ × ½	X	X	X	X

*Outside diameter × International Pipe Threads (IPT)

Flared Fittings

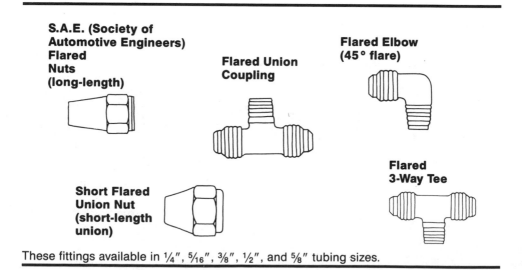

S.A.E. (Society of Automotive Engineers) Flared Nuts (long-length)

Flared Union Coupling

Flared Elbow (45° flare)

Short Flared Union Nut (short-length union)

Flared 3-Way Tee

These fittings available in ¼", ⁵⁄₁₆", ⅜", ½", and ⅝" tubing sizes.

Flared Reducing Fittings

Brass Reducing Flare Nut	Brass Reducing Union (flare to flare)	Flared 3-End Reducing
$3/8'' \times 1/4''$	$3/8'' \times 1/4''$	$3/8'' \times 3/8'' \times 1/2''$
$1/2'' \times 3/8''$	$1/2'' \times 3/8''$	$1/2'' \times 1/2'' \times 3/8''$
$5/8'' \times 1/2''$	$5/8'' \times 3/8''$	$5/8'' \times 5/8'' \times 3/8''$
	$5/8'' \times 1/2''$	$5/8'' \times 5/8'' \times 1/2''$

Flared Fittings to Pipe Thread

Tubing O.D. × IPT*	Flared Tee	Flared Female Coupling	Flared Half Union	Flared Female Elbow	Flared Male Elbow
$1/4 \times 1/8$			X		X
$1/4 \times 1/4$		X	X		
$1/4 \times 3/8$			X		
$5/16 \times 1/8$					
$3/8 \times 1/4$		X	X		X
$3/8 \times 3/8$	X	X	X	X	X
$3/8 \times 1/2$	X	X	X	X	X
$3/8 \times 3/4$		X	X	X	X
$1/2 \times 3/8$	X	X	X		X
$1/2 \times 1/2$	X	X	X	X	X
$1/2 \times 3/4$		X	X		X
$5/8 \times 3/8$			X		
$5/8 \times 1/2$	X	X	X	X	X
$5/8 \times 3/4$		X	X	X	X

*Outside diameter × International Pipe Threads

Plumbing

Plugs, Caps, and Miscellaneous Fittings

Hex-Head Brass Male Flare Plug
¼", ⅜", ½" and ⅝"

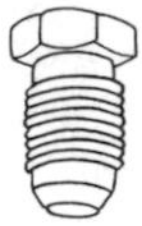

Square-Head Plug
(male pipe thread)
⅛", ¼", and ⅜"

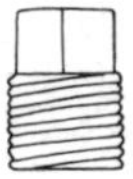

Hex-Head Brass Pipe Plug
(male pipe thread)
⅛" and ¼"

Brass Pipe Bushing
¼" × ⅛" and ⅜" × ¼"
(outside diameter × inside diameter)

Brass Pipe Coupling
⅛" × ⅛" and ¼" × ¼"

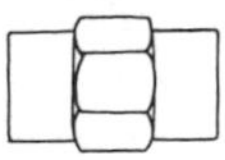

Flare Seal Cap
⅜", ½", and ⅝"

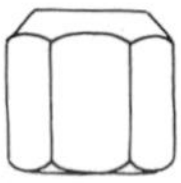

Shut-Off Cock
Compression ¼", ⁵⁄₁₆", and ⅜"
Also available in:
  Compression to IPT
  Flared to IPT
  Flare union couplings
  Flare S.A.E. couplings
  Male to female pipe thread
    (threaded)
  Double female pipe thread
    (threaded)

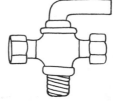

Saddle Valve
Easily installed on ½" or ¾" pipe by drilling ³⁄₁₆" hole, inserting pilot tube, and tightening. For use with ¼" (outside diameter) tubing. Also available without clamp assembly.

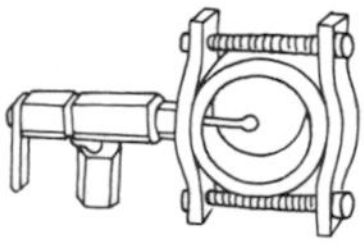

Drain Cock
(spring tension, lever handle)
⅛ and ¼ International Pipe Thread (IPT)

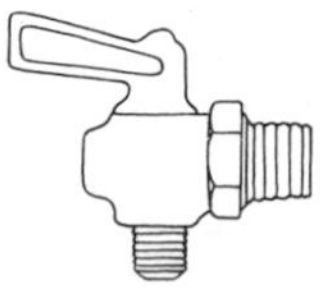

Galvanized Steel Fittings for Plastic Pipe

Coupling
Available in ¾″, 1″, 1¼″, 1½″, and 2″

Male Threaded Adapter
Available in ½″, ¾″, 1″, 1¼″, 1½″, and 2″

Sleeve and Insert for Plastic Tubing
Compression tube fitting for polyethylene tubing. Assemblies consist of plastic delrin sleeves with brass inserts ¼″, ⁵⁄₁₆″, ⅜″, and ½″.

Drain-Waste-Vent Fittings (DWV)

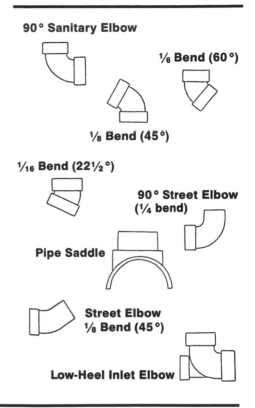

90° Sanitary Elbow

⅙ Bend (60°)

⅛ Bend (45°)

¹⁄₁₆ Bend (22½°)

90° Street Elbow (¼ bend)

Pipe Saddle

Street Elbow ⅛ Bend (45°)

Low-Heel Inlet Elbow

Plastic Insert Fittings

Insert fittings join lengths of flexible pipe in a coupling, tee, or elbow arrangement by inserting the fitting into each length to be joined. Steel clamps are utilized to draw the pipe down onto serrations and provide a permanent, leakproof connection. Insert adapters connect flexible pipe to any standard female pipe thread. They can be nylon or polypropylene.

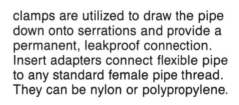

Coupling

Tee

Elbow

Male Adapter

Available in ½″, ¾″, 1″, 1¼″, 1½″, and 2″ pipe sizes.

Plumbing

Twist Lok Clean-out Plug

Twist Lok clean-out plugs require no soldering, threading, or solvent welding for installation and removal. A twist of the wrist installs the plug and provides a gas- and watertight seal for the life of the system.

Closet Flange

The closet flange can also be used as a street closet flange with Schedule 40 fittings. Size 3" × 4".

Adapters—Vinyl Pipe to Iron Pipe

Female Adapter
Sizes: 1½", 2", and 3"
Also available: 1½" vinyl to 1¼" iron

Male Adapter
1¼" inside pipe diameter (IPD) × 1½"
Vinyl sizes: 1½", 2", and 3"

Trap Adapter
(Male)   (Female)
Size: 1½" × 1¼"

Male   Female

No-Hub Coupling*
Clamp-type couplings are quickly applied. Worm drive clamps tighten with a screwdriver or wrench. They are used to couple DWV vinyl pipe to cast iron soil pipe, etc.

*Schedule 30 only

Available Fittings for Sewer and Drain Pipe

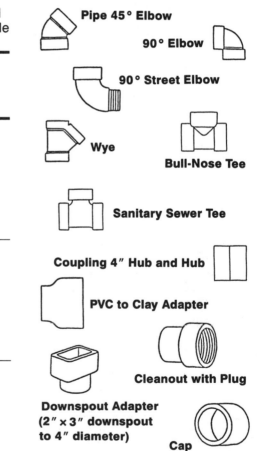

Pipe 45° Elbow

90° Elbow

90° Street Elbow

Wye

Bull-Nose Tee

Sanitary Sewer Tee

Coupling 4" Hub and Hub

PVC to Clay Adapter

Cleanout with Plug

Downspout Adapter
(2" × 3" downspout
to 4" diameter)

Cap

Reducing Fittings

Sizes	Reducing Coupling	Reducing Bushing	Reducing Wye	Reducing Sanitary Tee	Adapter Coupling
2″ × 1½″	X	X		X	
3″ × 1½″	X	X	X	X	
3″ × 2″	X	X	X		
4″ × 3″	X	X	X		
4″ × 2″				X	X

Welding Vinyl (PVC) Pipe
(Cleaner and Cement)
1. Cut pipe to length with fine tooth handsaw.
2. Remove all burrs on pipe using sandpaper.
3. Using a clean rag or brush, wipe the outside of the pipe and inside of the fitting socket with cleaner (such as Novaclean by Genova) to remove any grease or dirt.
4. Liberally brush on vinyl (solvent) cement on pipe and lightly on socket.
5. Push pipe into fitting socket with a slight twisting motion as far as it will go.
6. Using a twisting motion, immediately adjust fitting direction before cement begins to set.

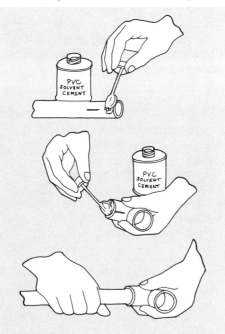

Tubular Goods
Since the advent of garbage disposers, dishwashers, and special kitchen sinks, tubular goods have become popular. Basic hardware stocks consist of P traps, S traps, J bends, repair traps (with slip-joint nuts on both ends), continuous wastes for sinks with double compartments, tailpieces that connect sink strainers to continuous wastes, branch tailpieces that connect dishwasher drains to sink wastes, extensions to slip (straight tube lengths with slip-joint nut), and extensions to solder (straight tube with bell end for a sweat extension). These are primarily used in adding disposers to existing sinks. Threaded tailpieces measuring 1¼″ are used for extending

Plumbing

lavatory wastes the correct distance for trap connection.

Continuous Waste Lines for Two-Compartment Sinks
Usually 1½" diameter, 16" to 21" long.

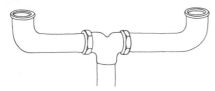

Continuous Waste
Close coupled with short tee tailpiece. Tee and waste bend available separately.

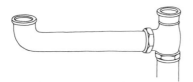

Tailpieces for Sink Strainers
Flanged 22-gauge, satin finish (to connect with 1½" sink strainers).

Threaded one or both ends.

For soldered connections

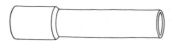

For Slip-Joint Connections

Flexible Drain Tailpiece with reducer washers. Works with hi-line or slip connections and allows for offsets. Use with 1½" × 1¼" plastic or brass.

A corrugated flexible drain is particularly useful when installing new sinks or vanities to older drain systems. Many times the drain of a new installation will not line up with the old drainpipe. Corrugated plastic drainpipe allows matching misalignments up to several inches.

Fittings for tubular brass consist almost entirely of 45° ells, 90° ells, couplings and tees in 1¼" and 1½" sizes—all with slip-joint nuts and washers. Strap wrenches are recommended for most work with chrome-plated brass, and extra slip-joint washers and nuts are a must because corrosion brings on occasional breakage.

90° Elbow
Chrome plated.

Repair Coupling

Straight slip-joint connections, chrome plated.

Short J Bend

Traps

Plumbing fixtures are now equipped with either a P-shaped or S-shaped trap, frequently fitted with a clean-out plug on the bottom. The trap bend holds water, which prevents sewer gases from backing up into the home.

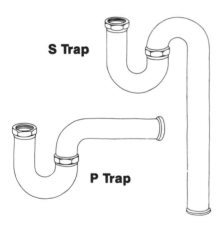

S Trap

P Trap

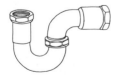

Repair-type P Trap

The clean-out plug enables you to recover small heavy objects such as a ring accidentally dropped in the drain.

In most areas 1¼″ chrome-plated brass traps are used in lavatory drains, and satin-finished or nickel-plated brass 1½″ traps are standard equipment on residential kitchen sinks. (Satin finish is chrome-plated tubular material in an unpolished state).

Because these traps are usually manufactured in gauges ranging from light 22 gauge to heavier 17 gauge in extruded tubing and cast brass, you should check local building codes to be sure you are using the proper gauge. Given the choice, choose the heavier gauge, as detergents and cleaners are corrosive and may quickly eat away the bottom of a light-gauge trap.

Adjustable Sink Trap

20-gauge tubular bend with cast brass swivel elbow, iron pipe thread outlet, slip-joint inlet; satin finish, nickel plated.

Sink Trap

Bath Trap

Plastic P and J traps are increasing in popularity. Plastic traps can be used in retrofit as well as new plumbing work, with adapters and transitional couplings available to connect plastic to other materials.

245

Plumbing

Steel Traps
1½″ or 2″ pipe

Cast Bell Trap
6″ × 6″, 2″ slip outlet; or 5″ × 9″, 3″ slip outlet

Floor-Guard
Floor-Guard operates like a check valve to seal off water backup caused by overloaded sewers. Water flows normally through the drain until the sewer begins to back up. Then the floor-guard float rises to seal off the drain opening until the water recedes.

Valves
Valves and faucets control the residential water supply. Valves and sill cocks are used on pipelines; faucets are installed on fixtures. Metal valves are made of cast bronze or brass and galvanized or black iron.

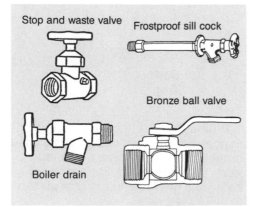

Stop and waste valve
Frostproof sill cock
Bronze ball valve
Boiler drain

Plastic valves are molded from acetyl, CPVC, or PVC plastic. Normally acetyl plastic valves have threaded connections for use in metal piping systems, and CPVC or PVC plastic valves have solvent-weld connections for use only in plastic pipe systems. However, PVC gate valves and ball valves can be purchased with threaded connections.

Acetyl plastic valves are available in globe, stop and waste, boiler drain, sill cock, and sink faucet types and can be used with hot and cold fluid systems throughout a temperature range of −20°F to 180°F and pressures up to 150 psi. CPVC valves are available in globe and boiler drains. PVC valves are available in globe, gate, ball and boiler drains.

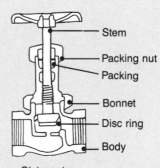

Stem
Packing nut
Packing
Bonnet
Disc ring
Body

Globe valve

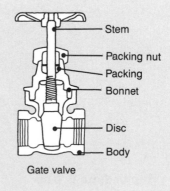

Stem
Packing nut
Packing
Bonnet
Disc
Body

Gate valve

Valves

Type	Description and Operation	Use
Gate valve	A threaded spindle (stem) moves a sliding wedge across the waterway. Valve has either a rising or nonrising stem (shorter bonnet).	Shuts off fluid flow completely. Does not control volume of flow.
Globe valve	Valve body has two chambers with a partition between them that partially restricts fluid flow as it travels through the valve. Spindle controls amount of fluid flowing through valve.	Use valve to control volume of water flow.
Angle valve	Similar to globe valve but with ports at right angles to change fluid flow 90°. Less flow restriction with this valve.	Install where change in flow direction is required and use of an elbow and globe valve is undesirable.
Plug-and-key valves (also called straight stops)	This type valve has a tapered, ground plug, which is seated in a tapered, ground seat in the valve body. The plug is threaded to hold a hex nut and friction ring combination. This is mounted over a spring inside the body that keeps the plug tight. The upper end of plug has either a flat head, square head, or socket head.	Used in gas supply lines as gas stops.
Drainable valves (also called stop and waste valves)	Similar to a globe or gate valve but with a small opening on the non-pressure side to allow drainage of the line when the valve is in the cutoff position.	Used where it is necessary to drain the non-pressure side of the valve when in the "off" position, such as unheated areas during the winter season.
Check valves	These valves operate automatically to restrict flow in one direction. The closing device (disc, ball, or clapper) falls shut by gravity in vertically installed valves.	Use where it is necessary to prevent flow in one direction when pressure is removed from the system. Example: Prevent water pumped to a overhead tank from flowing back when the pump is stopped.

Plumbing

Valves (Concluded)

Type	Description and Operation	Use
Swing check valve	Valve uses a small swing-type gate located in the center of the body. Fluid passing through the "flow" side of the valve opens the gate; closes when fluid attempts to reverse direction.	Use to prevent fluid pumped through the valve from flowing through the valve when system pressure is removed.

When replacing a metal valve with a plastic valve, it is advisable to use a transitional connector to prevent leaks caused by the differing expansion/contraction characteristics of the dissimilar materials.

Pressure-Reducing Valves

Water hammer, the loud bang you hear when you suddenly close a faucet or the washing machine solenoid valve closes, is often caused by system water pressure that's too high. To solve the problem, install a pressure-reducing valve on the houseside of the main shut-off valve next to the water meter. An adjusting screw on the valve regulates water pressure.

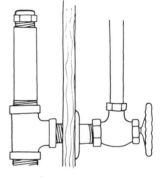

Air Chamber

Installing an air chamber will prevent "water hammer" when the valve is closed. The water will rise in the air chamber when the valve is closed.

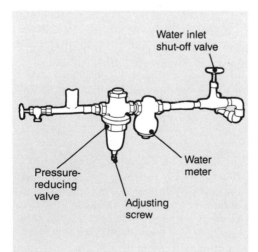

Water inlet shut-off valve

Pressure-reducing valve

Adjusting screw

Water meter

Water Heaters

Copper-, stone-, and glass-lined water heaters perform better than unlined aluminum or galvanized steel heaters. However, a stainless steel alloy called HWT is designed to resist corrosion as well as the lined models.

Unlined galvanized steel tanks perform least effectively but are the least expensive and may prove satisfactory in localities where the water supply does not have adverse effects on equipment.

Internal corrosion can be inhibited by a magnesium-coated metal rod that is hung inside the tank to within 3" or 4" of the bottom. Water heater warranties normally run ten years or longer.

Water heaters account for the highest energy use in your home, after furnaces and air-conditioners. Energy-efficient models have insulated feet and extra insulation. Insulated jackets can also be added. These are available at home center stores and are easy to install.

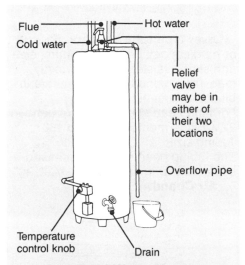

Gas-Fired Water Heater

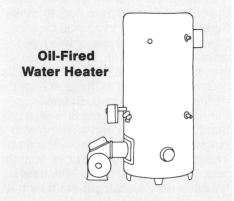

Oil-Fired Water Heater

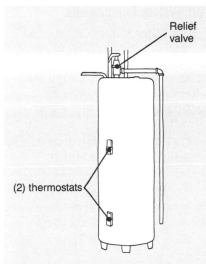

Electric Powered Water Heater

If you are insulating your hot water pipes, also run insulation on the last 3' of the cold water pipe, as expansion sometimes backs up heated water into these last few feet.

Tankless Heaters

These items are small heating units without reservoirs that heat water on an "as needed" basis, as it moves through the unit. Gas-fired or electrically heated units are available. Tankless heaters are more expensive than tank-type heaters but provide the convenience of instant hot water. Electric units draw large amounts of current and usually require a separate 220 volt circuit. If your electric rates are based on peak energy use, these units will escalate your electricity bills. The gas versions operate more efficiently but are very expensive to install. Tankless heaters also have a capacity problem, since they cannot satisfy hot water demands from several places at the same time. Recommended use is to supplement existing tank-type heaters.

Plumbing

Fuel Oil System Components

Oil Tank Filter Valves To be used on any tank or drum without extra nipples, valves, or tubing adapters. Equipped with oil-proof packing and brass-to-brass seat. Available for standard ⅜ O.D. tubing and either ½ or ¾ IPS threads.

Fuel Oil Filters Installed in oil supply line between burner and tank to

increase the burning efficiency of fuel oil systems and remove solids and moisture from No. 1, 2, and 3 fuel oils. Adaptable to gravity or pressure-type burners with cartridge replacement. Standard ⅜" pipe openings.

The Right Tools

Aside from standard hand tools such as screwdrivers and hammers, a number of special tools have been produced to facilitate removal and installation of plumbing systems and their components. Some of these tools are listed below, with a brief description of their use and availability.

Strap wrench. The nylon strap is wrapped around pipe to prevent marking the outside pipe surface.

Tubing cutter. Used to cut off lengths of copper or plastic pipe.

Tubing-type tube bender. An essential for bending tubing evenly so that no crimp develops to obstruct flow through it.

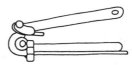

Lever-type tube benders. For soft or hard copper, brass, aluminum, steel, and stainless steel tube. Correctly measured, bends will be accurate to blueprint dimensions within $\frac{1}{32}$". Forming head shows angle of bend in 22½° increments from 1° to 180°. Tubing size: ⅓" O.D. radius to $\frac{9}{16}$". The tubing head can be purchased separately or in sets for ¼", $\frac{5}{16}$", ⅜", $\frac{7}{16}$", ½", and ⅝".

Flaring tool. Flaring tools are used in conjunction with flare nuts to make flared joints in soft-tempered copper tubing. These tools are of two types: drive-in and clamp-in. A drive-in flarer is simply a cone-shaped device that is driven into the end of the pipe until the desired flare is created. Clamp-in flaring tools have two parts: a vise bar that holds the pipe and a clamp with a cone-shaped die that makes the flare. The farther the pipe protrudes from the vise, the bigger the flare. Whichever type you use, always put the flare nut on the pipe before shaping.

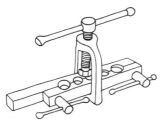

Seat dresser. Used to remove calcium buildup on valve seats so that valve stem stops water flow when valve is shut off. Not usable on Delta-type valves that use 0 rings instead of washers as seals.

Faucet spanner. Another fixture tool, used for installing or removing faucets. You usually get one with a new-faucet installation kit.

Basin wrench. You'll need a basin wrench for working in tight quarters underneath and behind fixtures. It has a long arm that can reach behind a lavatory to loosen or tighten fixture nuts on the water-supply tubes.

Adjustable sput or trap wrench. For use on large nuts such as those on sink strainers, traps, and toilets.

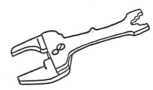

Plumber's force cut. Used to dislodge debris from drains and toilets by creating higher pressure in the area of the obstruction to force the clog through the drain line.

Toilet/closet auger. Uses a short auger to dislodge obstructions from within the toilet drain passages.

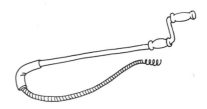

Drain/trap auger. Used to remove obstructions in drain lines throughout the house. The auger is threaded into the line through the drain opening or by removing a clean-out plug. The obstruction is loosened by turning the handle, then flushed out by water pressure.

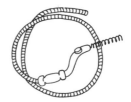

Electrical Equipment 9

9. Electrical Equipment

Most homeowners shy away from electrical work. And it's good to have a healthy respect for your wiring's potential dangers. But even better is a working knowledge of the subject. Then you'll recognize any flaws in your current wiring, and you'll be thinking of ways to improve its safety as well as its service.

Many basic home wiring projects are well within the capabilities of the do-it-yourselfer; you'll find detailed instructions for such projects in countless books and magazine articles. Since the how-to's of home wiring are beyond the scope of this book, I urge you to study several guides before embarking on a project.

This chapter lists all the various pieces of a home's electrical system in alphabetical order. When selecting any of these pieces to repair or improve your system, never compromise on quality or safety of materials. Not ever! Look for an Underwriters Laboratories® (UL®) label on components, and check with your local code, the National Electrical Code (NEC®), or your local building inspector to be sure you're installing the correct equipment in the correct manner. Electrical equipment may at first seem a confusing mass of numbers, colors, and jargon, but at least they are standardized numbers, colors, and jargon. These standards—how many amps a 12-gauge wire can handle, the color of hot wires, etc.—exist to make electricity safe. And as such standards imply, there's always a prescribed way to do a job. If you don't know it, find out.

Before doing any electrical work around your home, your first task is to make a map of your circuitry. As you know, electricity enters your house in two or three large wires. These wires terminate at the main service panel—either a fuse box or a circuit breaker panel, depending on whether your wiring is old or new. The service panel doles out the incoming amperage to the various branch circuits (see illustrations).

Branch Circuits

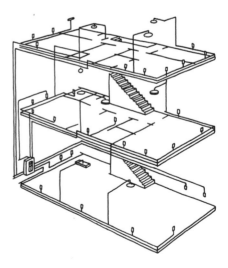

By engaging or disengaging individual circuit breakers or fuses, you can find out which lights, switches, and receptacles are on each circuit.

Markel Products Company		LISTED (UL®) 547G
JOHNSON CITY, TN	MADE IN U.S.A.	AIR HEATER
MODEL NO.	VOLTS AC HZ	WATTS
198TE	120 60	1500

(1)National Electrical Code® and NEC® are registered trademarks of the National Fire Protection Association, Inc., Quincy, MA. Underwriters Laboratories Inc® and UL® are registered trade names of Underwriters Laboratories Inc. UL does not approve products but is a testing service that provides periodic inspection of production of listed equipment or materials. Such listing indicates the equipment or material meets nationally recognized standards or has been tested and found suitable for use in a specified manner.

Electrical Equipment

Moving a radio from outlet to outlet is a big help in doing this. Then label them accordingly on a floor plan of your house. The map will prove invaluable anytime you have electrical work to do.

Next, check the load on each of your circuits. Most household circuits are rated for no more than 15 or 20 amps—the number is marked clearly on each fuse or breaker switch. Then tally the appliances on each circuit, taking their maximum wattages (see chart) and dividing by 120 to obtain their combined amperage. This will tell you something as minor as why your toaster oven keeps blowing a fuse and where you should plug it so it won't. But it will also tell you if you can add new switches and receptacles to an existing circuit, rather than running wires all the way back to the main service panel.

Circuit Breaker Panel

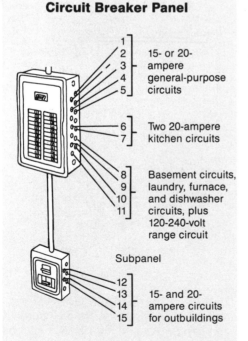

1 2 3 4 5	15- or 20-ampere general-purpose circuits
6 7	Two 20-ampere kitchen circuits
8 9 10 11	Basement circuits, laundry, furnace, and dishwasher circuits, plus 120-240-volt range circuit

Subpanel

| 12
13
14
15 | 15- and 20-ampere circuits for outbuildings |

Typical Wattage Ratings for Home Appliances

Item	Watts
Airconditioners (room)	
½ ton	800–900
¾ ton	1000–1200
1 ton	1350–1550
Blanket	175–200
Blender	275–1000
Bottle warmer	450
Broiler	1000–1500
Can opener	75
Carpet steam cleaner	1600
Casserole	500
Clock	1–2
Coffee grinder	85–130
Coffee maker	1200
Corn popper	440–600
Crock pot	100–1500
Dehumidifier	185–200
Dishwasher	1000–1500
Fans	
Attic	300–350
Floor circulator	100–120
Kitchen exhaust	75–175
Portable	50–100
Floor polisher	450–475
Food mixer	130–200
Food warmer	250–300
Frying pan	1085–1500
Garbage disposal	300–850
Hair dryer	415–1200
Heat lamp	250–300
Heater	up to 1650
Heating equipment	
Baseboard	1600
Humidifier	150–190
Oil burner	200–240
Warm air furnace fan	320–350
Heating pad	60–80
Home computer	
Keyboard	
Diskette drive	
Electronic module	
Total Circuit:	200
Display center	114
Printer	100–450
Hot plate	750–1500
Iron, steam	1100–1320
Power tools	up to 1000

Typical Wattage Ratings for Home Appliances

Item	Watts
Projector	up to 1000
Radio	30–100
Record player	50
Recorder	70–90
Refrigerator	900–1200
Roaster	1320–1500
Sandwich grill	900
Sewing machine	75–100
Shaver	10
Sun lamp	275–300
Tea kettle	500
Television, color	250–300
Toaster	800–1500
Trash compactor	1200–1500
Trivet	50
Vacuum cleaners	
Bag type	300–350
Canister type	500–725
Tank type	600
Vaporizer	250–380
Waffle baker	900–1200
Washer, clothes	500–1000

Circuit Breaker

A circuit breaker connects a branch circuit to its power source, the two "hot bus bars" in the circuit breaker box. The circuit breaker's function is to reduce the high amperage entering the house to a level that can be handled safely by branch circuit wiring. If too much power is being drawn somewhere on the branch circuit, the breaker's switch automatically trips from "on" to "off."

Circuit breakers are now used instead of fuses because fuses have to be replaced after each overload. Circuit breakers can simply be switched back to the "on" position.

Breakers may be push-button or toggle-type. Some breakers have three positions: "off," "on," and "reset."

Typical Circuit Breakers

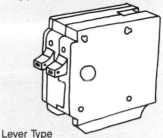

Lever Type
120-volt, two circuit breaker

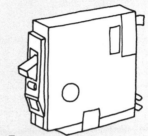

Lever Type
Single-pole circuit breaker

Half Size circuit breaker

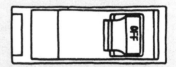

Single circuit breaker

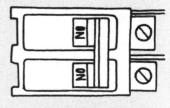

Double circuit breaker

These require moving the switch from "reset" to "off" to "on" before power can be restored.

Standard circuit breakers for

Electrical Equipment

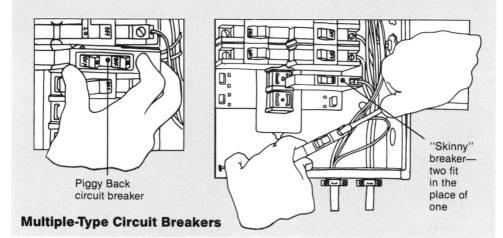

Piggy Back circuit breaker

"Skinny" breaker—two fit in the place of one

Multiple-Type Circuit Breakers

residential use are available with amperage ratings of 15, 20, 30, 40, 50, 60, and 100. These amperage ratings are labeled on the face of the breaker. The 15-amp breakers are used on older, 14-gauge house wiring. Newer 12-gauge wiring takes a 20-amp breaker.

Both the 15-amp and 20-amp breakers are single-pole switches, drawing only 120 volts. They may be doubled up as two independently operating dual breakers, providing two 120-volt circuits in the space of one. Double-pole switches—two linked toggles—control a single 240-volt circuit.

Breakers are mounted on the hot bus bars according to the type of breaker box in use. Some breakers are bolted, some plug into place, some clip into place. When buying additional circuit breakers for your home, be sure to get a type that fits your breaker box. It also pays to buy a spare to have on hand in case of a nighttime or weekend failure.

Circuit Breaker Box

The breaker box, also known as the distribution panel, is the hub of your home's branch circuits. Breaker boxes for residences can carry from two to

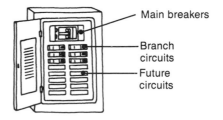

Main breakers

Branch circuits

Future circuits

Typical Circuit Breaker Type Distribution Panel

forty-two circuits. The circuit breakers are normally arranged in two rows. Normally, boxes and circuit breakers are purchased separately.

If your home's wiring was done with any foresight, there will be empty spaces at the bottom of the two rows of breakers. This is where you can expand your electrical capacity by adding new circuits and breakers. If you're buying a breaker box for a new home, be sure to buy a box with greater circuit capacity than you plan to install initially.

Breaker boxes are clearly marked for the total amperage they can supply. If you want to add circuitry but all breaker spaces are taken up, you may be able to add a subpanel, as long as the circuits you're adding won't overload the main box's capacity. If they will, then you'll need to install a new main panel, a job that calls for a professional electrician.

Breaker boxes are available flush-mounted or surface-mounted.

Conduit

Conduit is pipe used to protect wiring. Conduit is made of thin-wall galvanized steel (for use indoors) and rigid steel or PVC plastic (for use outdoors and underground). Common diameters are $\frac{1}{2}$″, $\frac{3}{4}$″, 1″, $1\frac{1}{4}$″, and larger sizes, and it is generally sold in 10′ lengths.

Around the home, conduit is often used to run wiring underground to an outbuilding or outdoor lighting. It's also used to shield wiring that can't be run behind wallboard—for instance, wiring that runs along a concrete basement wall.

When installing metal conduit in anything but a straight-line path, you'll find a conduit bender to be essential. This curved-shoe device can create 90° bends without putting a crimp in the conduit.

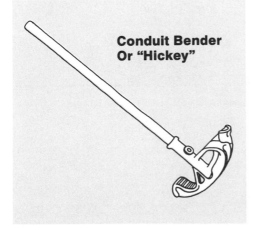

Conduit Bender Or "Hickey"

Electrical Boxes

In residential construction, wiring for switches, receptacles, or fixtures should be joined in permanently mounted electrical boxes. These boxes are made of metal or plastic and are supplied in a wide variety of shapes and sizes.

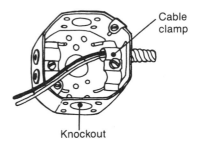

Cable clamp

Knockout

Typical Electric Box

When selecting a box for a particular location, consider the number of wires to be joined, the kind of mounting available, and whether the box must provide a mounting for a switch, receptacle, fixture, or just wires.

Boxes are supplied in three basic shapes: *octagonal,* used in ceilings to mount fixtures; *square,* used to mount switches, receptacles, or combinations of switches and receptacles; and *rectangular,* mounted in walls to contain switches or receptacles. Some rectangular wall boxes can be "ganged" together to provide mountings for two or more switches or receptacles at one location. These are made in a variety of depths from $\frac{3}{4}$″ to 3″.

Knockout plugs are provided in the sides and bottom surface of electrical boxes to provide access for the wires. Some boxes are supplied with internal cable clamps to secure the wires as they enter through the knockout opening. Other boxes require externally mounted connectors, which secure nonmetallic (Romex) sheathed cable,

Electrical Equipment

"armored" cable, or rigid conduit to the box.

"Old work" switch boxes can be mounted in existing drywall, paneling, metal lath, or lath-and-plaster walls. Special expansion brackets are located on the sides of metal old work boxes. When installed in the cutout, "adjustable ears" prevent the box from falling into the hole, and tightening the screws expands the brackets, preventing the box from falling out of the hole.

Plastic electrical boxes often have mounting brackets with captive mounting nails. These boxes are mounted by simply holding the box in position against a stud and driving the nails "home."

Typical Electric Box Capacities

Box Type	Material	Typical Size (inches)	Minimum Cu. In. Capacity
Octagonal or Round	Metal	$4 \times 1\frac{1}{4}$	12.5
	Metal	$4 \times 1\frac{1}{2}$	12.5
	Metal	$4 \times 2\frac{1}{8}$	12.5
Square (junction)	Metal	$4 \times 1\frac{1}{4}$	18.0
	Metal	$4 \times 1\frac{1}{2}$	21.0
	Metal	$4 \times 2\frac{1}{8}$	30.0
	Metal	$4\frac{11}{16} \times 1\frac{1}{4}$	25.5
	Metal	$4\frac{11}{16} \times 1\frac{1}{2}$	29.5
	Metal	$4\frac{11}{16} \times 2\frac{1}{8}$	42.0
	Plastic[1]	$4 \times 2\frac{23}{32}$	
	Plastic[1]	$4\frac{1}{4} \times 1\frac{1}{2}$	
Rectangular (switch box)	Metal	$3 \times 2 \times 1\frac{1}{2}$	7.5
	Metal	$3 \times 2 \times 2$	10.0
	Metal	$3 \times 2 \times 2\frac{1}{4}$	10.5
	Metal	$3 \times 2 \times 2\frac{1}{2}$	12.5
	Metal	$3 \times 2 \times 2\frac{3}{4}$	14.0
	Metal	$3 \times 2 \times 3\frac{1}{2}$	18.0
	Metal	$4 \times 2\frac{1}{8} \times 1\frac{1}{2}$	10.3
	Metal	$4 \times 2\frac{1}{8} \times 1\frac{7}{8}$	13.0
	Metal	$4 \times 2\frac{1}{8} \times 2\frac{1}{8}$	14.5
	Plastic[1]	$3\frac{19}{32} \times 2\frac{1}{4} \times 2\frac{19}{32}$	
	Plastic[1]	$3\frac{3}{4} \times 2\frac{1}{4} \times 2\frac{23}{32}$	
	Three gang—plastic[1]	$4 \times 5\frac{25}{32} \times 2\frac{23}{32}$	

[1]Sizes, capacity and maximum number of wires calculated not stated in *NEC*.
For nonmetallic boxes the *National Electrical Code* [Sec. 370-6] dictates that each wire must have a specific number of cubic inches:
    No. 14—2 cubic inches
    No. 12—2.25 cubic inches
    No. 10—2.5 cubic inches
    No. 8—3 cubic inches
    No. 6—5 cubic inches
NOTE: Wires from a fixture to wires in the box are not counted. Count each hickey, fixture stud, grounding clamp, receptacle, and switch as one conductor. Count each wire entering and leaving box without a splice as one conductor. Do not count pigtails. See Nat. El. Code 1984, Table 3706(a) for full requirements and masonry box/gang and single cover gang requirements.
[2]Also permits use of 6 No. 6 wires for termination only.
Reprinted with permission from NFPA 70-1984, National Electrical Code, Copyright © 1984, National Fire Protection Association, Quincy, MA 02269. This reprinted material is not the complete and official position of the NFPA on the referenced subject which is represented only by the standard in its entirety.

Extension rings and expansion boxes are available to extend the depth (capacity) of boxes, compensate for additional thicknesses of drywall, or provide a mount for special fixtures.

When a tight vapor barrier is specified for the house, you can use Series 4000 plastic boxes with broad rims to which the vapor barrier can be adhered. Then caulk the wire entry.

CAUTION:

Never attempt to work on the electrical power hookup entering the house between the utility wires and the service panel. These wires carry high voltage and are dangerous. Notify your local utility company if they are damaged. Never work on any circuit that cannot be de-energized by shutting off the main power at the service panel.

Maximum Number of Wires			
No. 14	No. 12	No. 10	No. 8
6	5	5	4
7	6	6	5
10	9	8	7
9	8	7	6
10	9	8	7
15	13	12	10
12	11	10	8
14	13	11	9[2]
21	18	16	14
21	19	17	14
13	12	10	9
3	3	3	2
5	4	4	3
5	4	4	3
6	5	5	4
7	6	5	4
9	8	7	6
5	4	4	3
6	5	5	4
7	6	5	4
10	9	8	7
11	10	9	8
31	28	25	21

Electrical Equipment

Electrical Boxes

Box Type	Uses	Mounting
Octagonal/Round Outlet Boxes	Mounts ceiling fixtures on ceiling-mounted junction box. Can be used with special covers to mount switches and/or receptacles. Boxes available in metal or plastic. Pancake box (thin) available for limited space areas, but will accommodate only 5 wires. Do *not* use flange-mounted plastic boxes to hang heavy light fixtures or ceiling fans.	Boxes with flanges or self-contained nails mount directly to joists or studs. Nonflanged boxes are mounted on angle brackets or hanger bars, which position box between the joists and support the load. Some hanger bars telescope to fit joist spacing and permit easy installation through hole for outlet box.
Square Junction Box	Used as a connection point for wire and cable junctions. Plain cover used when box contains only wire splices. Switches and receptacles can be mounted on "plaster rings" or raised box covers. Available in metal or plastic. Extender ring mounts to box face to increase capacity of box.	Can be nailed to joists or studs through nail holes in box or can be supported solely by conduit. Some boxes available with nailing flanges (both front and side mount).
Rectangular Switch Box	Used to mount switches and receptacles in walls. Single metal box holds one single switch or one duplex receptacle. Some metal boxes have removable sides and can be "ganged" together to hold more than one device. Electrical device is attached to box, rather than the cover. Available in metal and plastic. Plastic gang box holds two or more devices.	Can be nailed to joists or studs using nailing flanges or self-contained nails. Some boxes provide adjustable ears for attaching to paneling or lath-and-plaster walls.

Electrical Boxes

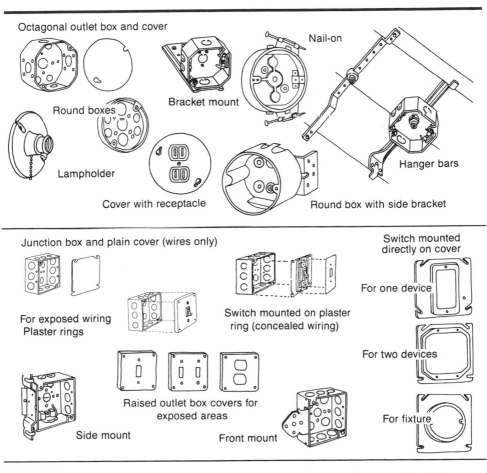

Octagonal outlet box and cover

Round boxes

Lampholder

Bracket mount

Cover with receptacle

Nail-on

Hanger bars

Round box with side bracket

Junction box and plain cover (wires only)

For exposed wiring
Plaster rings

Switch mounted on plaster
ring (concealed wiring)

Raised outlet box covers for
exposed areas

Side mount

Front mount

Switch mounted
directly on cover

For one device

For two devices

For fixture

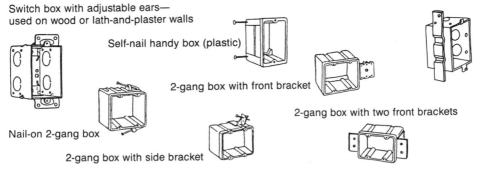

Flange-mounted metal switch box

Switch box with adjustable ears—
used on wood or lath-and-plaster walls

Self-nail handy box (plastic)

2-gang box with front bracket

2-gang box with two front brackets

Nail-on 2-gang box

2-gang box with side bracket

Electrical Equipment

Electrical Boxes (Concluded)

Box Type	Uses	Mounting
Expanding a Switch Box		
Weatherproof Boxes	Weatherproof boxes have one conduit inlet and gasketed cover. Spring-loaded covers often cover receptacles when not in use.	Weatherproof or utility boxes are usually attached by clamps around conduit, which attaches to the box.
"Old Work" Boxes (Cut-In Boxes)	"Old work" boxes are used to install new switches or receptacles in existing construction. These are available in metal or plastic.	"Old work" boxes have side clamps, separate bracket, or spring-metal ears that hold the boxes in place in the wall cutout.

Enclosures

Enclosures provide mechanical protection for equipment and shock protection for you. NEMA Type 1 and 3R enclosures are normally supplied for residential use. These are classified "general" or "light-duty" devices.

NEMA® Type 1 enclosures are suitable for most indoor applications where a measure of protection from accidental contact with enclosed equipment is required.

NEMA Type 3R enclosures are primarily intended for outdoor applications where falling rain, sleet,

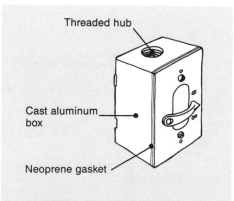

NEMA Type/Enclosure

Electrical Boxes (Concluded)

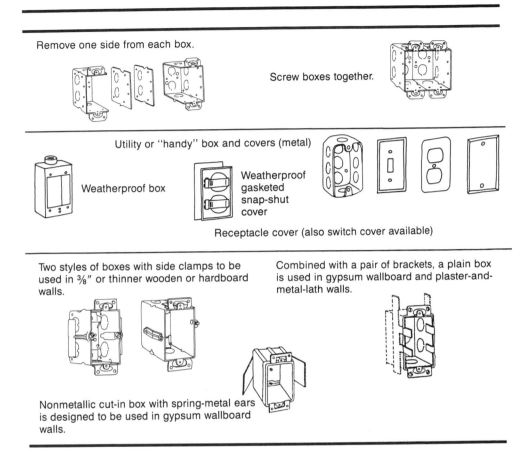

Remove one side from each box.

Screw boxes together.

Utility or "handy" box and covers (metal)

Weatherproof box

Weatherproof gasketed snap-shut cover

Receptacle cover (also switch cover available)

Two styles of boxes with side clamps to be used in ⅜″ or thinner wooden or hardboard walls.

Combined with a pair of brackets, a plain box is used in gypsum wallboard and plaster-and-metal-lath walls.

Nonmetallic cut-in box with spring-metal ears is designed to be used in gypsum wallboard walls.

or ice formation are present. Each features a gasketed snap-shut cover designed to meet tests for rain, rod entry, external icing, and rust resistance.

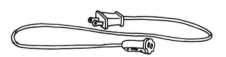

Extension Cord

Standard-duty extension cords normally have only two small-gauge (16/18) wires encased in plastic and are for use with one appliance or light. Some cords may have sockets that will accommodate up to three appliances.

Heavy-duty extension cords, for use with electric power tools or outdoor appliances, have a third (grounding) wire, normally attached to the grounding prong of a three-pronged plug. The extension cord socket also incorporates a female grounding point to accommodate the grounding plug on the power tool. Heavy-duty cords have larger-gauge wire and better

Electrical Equipment

insulation, normally water resistant.

As the extension cord increases in length, the wire diameter should also increase to avoid excessive current drop due to line loss. The accompanying table provides recommended wire sizes for current load and cord length.

Extension Cord Lengths

Length	7 amp.	7-10 amp.	10-15 amp.
To 25'	No. 18	No. 16	No. 14
To 50'	No. 16	No. 14	No. 12
To 100'	No. 14	No. 12	No. 10

Heavy-duty extension cords are brightly colored to make them visible and are normally available in lengths of 10', 15', 25', 50', and 100'. Standard-duty extension cords are white, tan, black, gray, or brown; they are normally available in lengths of 6', 9', 12', 15', and 20'.

Special extra-heavy-duty extension cords are available for specific applications—range and dryer cords, airconditioner extension cords, and heater cords. These cords are normally 2' to 6' in length and use heavy gauge wires (No. 6 or 8) to carry large amounts of current and withstand higher voltages.

Typical Uses for Heavy-Duty Extension Cords

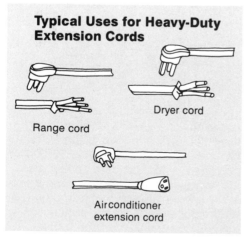

Range cord

Dryer cord

Airconditioner extension cord

Fluorescent Lights

Fluorescent lights provide bright, even illumination at a lower operating cost than incandescent lights. The greater length of the illuminator reduces shadows. In addition to providing more light per watt of power used, fluorescent bulbs last four or five times longer than incandescent bulbs. A major factor in determining the life-span is the frequency that the lights are turned on and off. Since fluorescents use little power, it is better to leave them on than to turn them on and off for short time periods. Their one drawback is the higher initial cost of the fixtures and lamps.

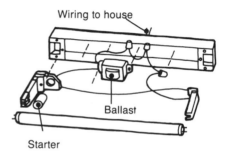

Wiring to house

Ballast

Starter

Wiring Arrangement for Fluorescent Fixture

The main operating component (other than the lamp) is the *ballast,* a special transformer that produces the high-voltage surge necessary to start current flow within the tube. The ballast also limits current flow through the tube. Some types of fluorescent fixtures use a *starter,* a small metal cylinder that mounts in a socket near one of the lamp holders. The starter acts as a switch to turn the filaments on and off, apply the high-voltage surge, and switch in the ballast to limit current flow. When power drops, a fluorescent tube will go out while an incandescent bulb will continue to provide light at a lower output.

Types of Fluorescent Lights

Rapid-start. This is currently the most widely used type of fixture. It lights almost immediately when switched on. Rapid-start fixtures also have the advantage of being readily adapted for use with fluorescent dimmer switches. Lamps for rapid-start fixtures have two pin-type connectors at each end.

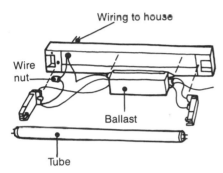

Wiring Arrangement for Rapid-Start Fluorescent Tube

Instant-start. This type of fluorescent fixture lights a second or two after it is switched on. It requires a higher initial voltage surge than other types. Lamps for instant-start fixtures may have one or two pin-type connectors at each end. On this type of fixture, the lamp holder contains a built-in switch that allows high voltage to be applied only when the fixture contains a lamp.

Starter type. This type of fixture has a separate starter. It uses lamps that have two pin-type connectors at each end. The starter, like the lamps, has a limited life but is replaceable. Some have a reset button located in a socket near one of the lamp holders. For replacement, power to the fixture is turned off and the lamp is removed. Then the starter is twisted and pulled out of its socket. Replacement starters must match the wattage of the lamp.

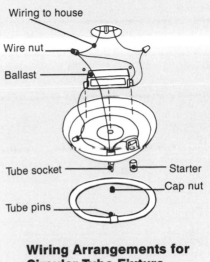

Wiring Arrangements for Circular Tube Fixture With Starter

Screw-in. Circular fluorescent bulbs are now available to screw into standard bulb holders. This provides an opportunity to reduce energy consumption without having to add new fixtures.

Circular Screw-In Type Fluorescent Bulb

Starters

Designation	Watts
FS-2	14, 15, & 20
FS-4	13, 30, & 40
FS-12	32
FS-25	22, 25
FS-40/400	40
FS-85	90, 100

Fuses

A fuse, like a circuit breaker, is a safety device designed to halt an overflow of electricity. The most common type, the *plug fuse,* has a

Electrical Equipment

Fluorescent Lamp Comparison Chart

Designation	Diameter	Length Available (in.)	Starter Required
T-5	⅝″	6, 9 & 12	Yes
T-8	1″	18 & 36	Yes
T-12	1½″	18 & 24 28 & 33	Yes
T-17	2⅛″	24, 36 & 48	Yes
T-12	1½″	24, 36 & 48	No
T-12	1½″	48, 72 & 96	No
High-output	NA	48, 72 & 96	No
1500 MA	NA	96	No
T-9 & T-10	1⅛″ or 1¼″	8 & 12 Circle	No

metal strip under the glass melts under excess current, stopping the current.

Fuses are rated at the amperage of the circuit they protect. The problem with using common plug fuses is that some people replace them with higher-amp fuses when they blow. This may reduce the need to replace fuses, but it also defeats the purpose of the safety protection! Today codes require the installation of Type S fuse adapters. These threaded adapters are screwed into the fuse box first, preventing any but the correct amp fuse from being placed in that circuit.

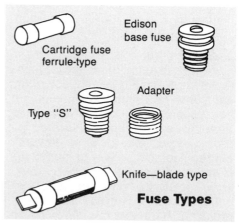

Cartridge fuse ferrule-type

Edison base fuse

Type "S"

Adapter

Knife—blade type

Fuse Types

Fluorescent Lamp Comparison Chart

Base	Lamp Descriptions Available	Approximate Hours of Life	Watts
Miniature Bi-Pin	Cool white	4000 to 6000	4, 6, & 8
Medium Bi-Pin	Cool white Daylight Plant light	7500	15 & 30
Medium Bi-Pin	Cool white Daylight Soft white Blue Plant light	7500 9000	14, 15, 20, & 25
Mogul Bi-Pin	Cool white Daylight	9000	90
Medium Bi-Pin	Cool white Soft white Warm light Daylight Lite white	7500 to 20000	30, 25, & 40
Single Pin	Cool white Daylight	9000 to 18000	40, 50, 55, 60, & 75
Recessed Oblong Contact	Cool white Lite white	12000	60, 85, & 110
Recessed Oblong Contact	Cool white Daylight	9000 to 12000	215
4-Pin	Cool white Soft white	12000	22, 32, & 40

Even if you have a circuit breaker box in your home, you may also have *cartridge fuses* in your electrical system. Cartridge fuses usually protect 240-volt circuits for individual appliances, such as electric clothes dryers. The fuses may be located in their own separate metal box. A blown cartridge fuse may show no visible sign of damage, so you'll need to test it with a continuity tester or replace it with a good fuse to find out.

Ferrule-type cartridge fuses carry ratings of 10 to 60 amps. Knife-blade types are designed for more than 60 amps.

GFCI's

A ground-fault circuit interrupter (GFCI) shuts off the flow of electricity anytime an accident or tool malfunction causes current to flow through you on its way to the ground. That can happen, for example, while wielding hedge clippers that have frayed wires inside or while sitting in a bathtub and accidentally knocking an electric appliance into the water with you. The

Electrical Equipment

GFCI shuts off the electricity in $\frac{1}{50}$ of a second. You will get a shock, but it won't be fatal.

GFCI's are now mandatory in bathroom, garage, and outdoor sockets. But if your home was built before the early 1970s, you probably don't have them. The solution is to install them. You can protect just one outlet by replacing your current plugs with a receptacle-type GFCI, or you can protect an entire branch circuit by installing a circuit breaker GFCI at the circuit breaker box.

When a GFCI trips and shuts off power, power is returned simply by pressing the reset button on the face of the receptacle or circuit breaker.

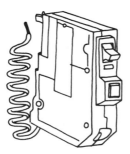

Circuit Breaker GFCI

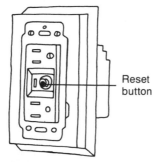

Reset button

Receptacle GFCI

Grounding Electrode Conductor

The *National Electrical Code* requires every 120-volt electric system to have a system of grounding. The electrode conductor connects the

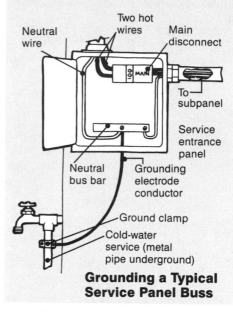

Grounding a Typical Service Panel Buss

ground wires from all house circuits to a buried $\frac{3}{4}''$ steel rod or to the street side of the cold water main through a $\frac{1}{2}''$ galvanized iron pipe.

High Intensity Discharge (HID) Lighting

Relatively new, these efficient lamps combine features of both fluorescent and incandescent lighting. They are named according to the vapor in the bulb—mercury, metal halide, or sodium vapor. The light given off is directional and powerful. They can be aimed at an entry or flood a whole parking lot. They last much longer than incandescent lights but care must be taken not to handle the glass if a bulb should get broken. The coating is poisonous. Wear gloves, use a dustpan and brush and dispose of broken pieces in a tough plastic bag with a tie. These lamps are usually used with timers—it takes three to fifteen minutes for them to warm up before going on.

Mercury. These come in 50- to 1500-watt sizes. They provide twice the light per watt compared to incandescent lights. Fifty- to 75-watt lamps will be sufficient for most driveway or yard applications. Use 175-watt eave lights where security is a concern.

Metal halide. Available in wattages from 175 to 1000. They provide a strong green-white light and provide four times as much light as incandescent lights of the same wattage. Fifty- to 75-watt metal halide lights are enough to floodlight a yard. They can be used with an automatic light sensor to go on at night, off at dawn.

Sodium vapor. Available in 250-, 400-, and 1000-watt sizes. They emit an orange-yellow hue and are about six times as efficient as incandescent bulbs. This suits them for use where large areas need light.

Incandescent Bulbs

The least efficient lighting. These bulbs create too much heat, shortening filament life and providing less light per watt.

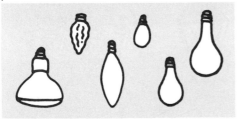

Clear bulb. This simple bulb provides a harsh and uneven light and is rarely used.

Frosted bulb. Available etched or with silica coating. The silica coating provides better light diffusion but at a 2 percent cost in light output.

Growth-enhancing (plant) lamps. These are specially designed to facilitate photosynthesis and help plants grow indoors.

Fiberglass-wrapped. Designed for long-duration outdoor use. Some come with a ten-year warranty.

Floodlights. For bright, broad lighting of a wall. Available for either indoor or outdoor use. Rated at 300 watts and above.

Spotlights. Often used in recessed fixtures to light art objects on tables below or wall-hung objects.

Orange bulbs. Designed for patio use. Orange light does not attract moths and insects.

Nightlights. Low-wattage bulbs that plug directly into wall receptacles.

Lighting Systems

Residential lighting systems can be divided into three groups: general, task, and accent.

General lighting usually consists of ceiling or wall fixtures supplemented with table or floor lamps. Living and sleeping areas usually require 1 watt per square foot (1.5 watts if recessed fixtures are used). Kitchens, baths, and laundries need as much as 4 watts per square foot (1.5 watts if fluorescent lamps are used).

Task lighting illuminates specific areas of a room, such as counter tops, workbenches, or your favorite reading spot. Most tasks require 150 watts of incandescent light or 40 watts of fluorescent light. However, prolonged reading may require 200 to 300 watts (60 to 80 watts fluorescent). In the kitchen, provide 120 watts incandescent (20 watts fluorescent) for each 3 running feet of counter-top surface.

Accent lighting can be used to supplement general lighting or task lighting. Cornice, valance, or cove lighting can provide subdued general lighting. Strategically placed track

Electrical Equipment

lights can provide a reading lamp or highlight a fireplace or favorite art piece. Accent lighting should be separately switched, possibly even with dimmer switches, to vary the mood of each location.

Your lighting options include:

Ceiling—surface-mounted. Distributes even, shadowless general lighting. Must be shielded to minimize glare. Normally uses several smaller incandescent bulbs rather than one large bulb. If under an attic, the fixture may require penetrating the ceiling vapor barrier—not advisable in climates over 5000 heating degree-days.*

Ceiling—recess-mounted. Often used in baths and kitchens, in combination with heaters or fans, to provide general lighting and ventilation or auxiliary heat. Recessed spotlights provide accent lighting. *Warning:* Note special instructions provided with unit regarding leaving insulation gap around recessed fixture to prevent fires and

---

*The number of heating degree-days in a calendar day is the average of the high and low temperatures of the day subtracted from 65. For example, if the high for the day is 60°F and the low is 30°F, there are 20 degree-days in the day: 65 − [(60 + 30)/2] = 20. Performing this calculation for each day of the calendar year provides the heating-degree climate for your specific region. Refer to the climate map in chapter 10, Insulation.

the likelihood of premature lamp failure due to overheating. Some recessed fixtures are now rated for coverage by attic insulation. Shop for them, if possible.

Ceiling—suspended. Chandeliers provide general lighting for dining rooms or breakfast areas. They are also used in entry areas or large halls. Swag-mounted lights are popularly used in bathrooms or dressing areas. Lights mounted from ceiling-hung paddle fans are also popular.

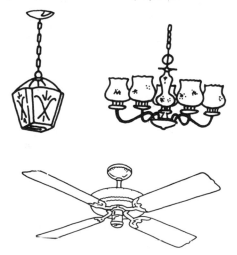

Wall-mounted. Wall-mounted fixtures are used for general lighting in bathrooms and as accent or task lighting in other areas. Fluorescent lamps are used for cornice, cove, and valance lighting installations. Wall-mounted lights are frequently used for outside entrance lighting.

Electrical Equipment

Cornice lighting. Cornice lights mount at the intersection of a wall and ceiling, bathing the wall with soft, downward light to dramatize draperies or other wall treatments. You can build a cornice treatment with 1×2 and 1×6 lumber. Mount the tube so its center is 6″ from the wall.

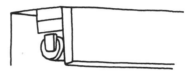

Track lighting. Offers great versatility by permitting you to add or subtract fixtures at will, aim them in any direction, and select from a broad choice of fixture types. These fixtures can be mounted on ceiling or wall.

Cove lighting. Cove lighting dramatizes a ceiling. You can buy commercial metal or plastic fixtures or make your own with wood and angle brackets, as illustrated. Mount the light about a foot below ceiling level, and paint the inside white to maximize reflection.

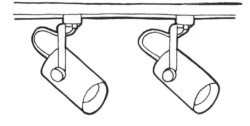

Under-cabinet and shelf fluorescents. These provide task lighting for kitchen counter tops and workbenches by installing fluorescent fixtures under overhead cabinets or wall shelves.

Valance lighting. Valances resemble cornices, but they're installed lower on the wall, often over draperies, providing both up-and-down light. To build one, you'll need 1″ ×2″ and 1″ ×6″ material and angle brackets, as shown. Top off the unit with a strip of plastic and you can also use it as a display shelf.

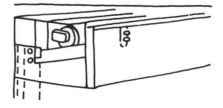

Electrical Equipment

Low-Voltage Circuits

You probably have several circuits in your home that are operated on less than 120 volts. In your doorbell circuit there is a transformer that steps the voltage down to anywhere from 6 to 24 volts. The thermostat is similarly equipped. You may have a step-down transformer in your burglar alarm system. Your telephone current is supplied by the telephone company, usually a 2-volt direct current line. Telephone hand or desk sets with memory systems, recording, or message-relaying components may operate off batteries or be plugged into your main electric circuit, again with a built-in transformer to reduce voltage. Don't connect the low-voltage wires of these circuits—those with thin 18- or 16-gauge conductors—to any 120-volt electrical outlet. All live parts of electrical equipment operating at 50 volts or more must be guarded against accidental contact.

Doorbell System

By using a transformer to step down house current to 6 or 12 volts, you can use low-voltage lighting to dramatize your yard. Simply run lightweight cable to outdoor patio locations or to light the driveway. You can even run the cable a few inches underground. You can change your layout at will, and there is little chance of severe electric shock. However, you will be limited to 25- and 50-watt bulbs. Use this system to dramatize a patio for a party or to light up various flower beds as they reach their prime.

Outdoor Wiring

Outdoor mounted receptacles and switches must be waterproof and their circuit protected by a ground-fault circuit interrupter (GFCI). The opening around the switch box must be caulked to make a weatherproof joint between the box faceplate and wall surface. Outdoor receptacles have a spring-loaded or screw-type cover that protects the outlet when not in use. Timers or a photoelectric eye can be used to turn lights on or off automatically. Wiring must be "approved" plastic-coated or routed through conduit.

NOTE:
To retain integrity of vapor barrier, route conduits through cross bracing— then caulk around conduit.

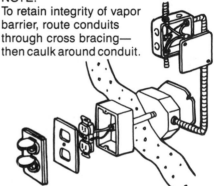

Installing an Outdoor Receptacle

Receptacles

Although single receptacles are available, most receptacles used in residential construction are of the "duplex" type, made up of two receptacles attached to the same mounting strap. Connections are made by screws or push-in type terminals. "Break-off links" permit converting many receptacles to split circuits. Normally both receptacles are wired to the same circuit. Most receptacles will accept No. 10, 12, and 14 wire. Residential receptacles are two-pole, three-wire, rated for 125 volts and amperages of 15 or 20 amps. Triple and quad receptacles are also available.

Duplex Receptacle

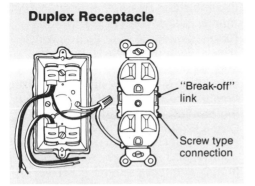

"Break-off" link

Screw type connection

A **clock hanger outlet** is a special receptacle with a large, deep well to conceal the electrical cord. It can also be used for illuminated picture cords.

Clock Hanger Outlet

Heavy-duty receptacles are used on three- and four-wire, dual 120/240-volt circuits. They have three terminals with staggered lug positions, which are determined by the amperage rating of the receptacle. The following chart provides a listing of these lug positions.

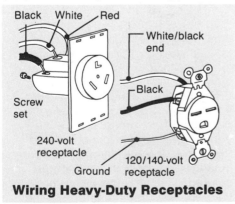

Black   White   Red

White/black end

Black

Screw set

240-volt receptacle

120/140-volt receptacle

Ground

Wiring Heavy-Duty Receptacles

Lug Positions on Heavy-Duty Receptacles

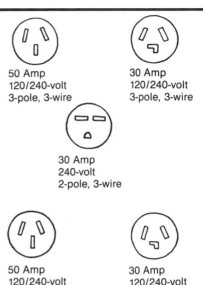

50 Amp
120/240-volt
3-pole, 3-wire

30 Amp
120/240-volt
3-pole, 3-wire

30 Amp
240-volt
2-pole, 3-wire

50 Amp
120/240-volt
3-pole, 4-wire

30 Amp
120/240-volt
3-pole, 4-wire

20 Amp
240-volt
2-pole, 3-wire

50 Amp
240-volt
2-pole, 3-wire

240-volt receptacles and plugs use two hot wires and an equipment ground. The rectangular terminals are the "hot" wires; center terminal is ground.

Safety receptacles have spring-loaded covers to prevent small children from poking metal objects into the slots of the electrical receptacle. To insert a

Safety Receptacle

Electrical Equipment

plug into this type receptacle, you must twist the cover, by hand or with the plug prongs, until the cover slots are aligned with the receptacle slots.

Locking receptacles are normally used in heavy-duty electrical circuits to prevent accidentally unplugging the electrical cord. These receptacles are designed so the plug must be twisted as it is inserted or removed from the receptacle. The receptacle slots and connector prongs are curved to permit twisting, which locks the plug in position during insertion.

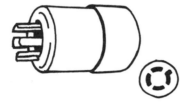

Surface Wiring

There is a way to add a switch, outlet, or fixture without going through the bother of running new wires behind your walls. You run the wiring *on* your walls, in channels called raceways.

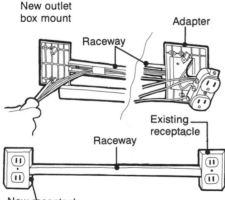

New outlet box mount

Adapter

Raceway

Existing receptacle

Raceway

New receptacle

The components for surface wiring are now sold in home centers, with packaging that contains clear instructions for do-it-yourselfers. Some

channels can be painted or stained to match your decor. The hardware required consists of adapters, which alter existing outlet boxes to permit you to pick up power from them; vinyl raceways, which carry the wires; and new outlet boxes. Inside and outside elbows and special fixture boxes are also available. Components are normally secured with pan-head screws, and raceways can be cut to length with fine-bladed hacksaws.

Switches

Switches break the flow of electricity when open and conduct current when closed. Three standard types of switches are used in residential construction:

Single-pole, single-throw (SPST). This type switch acts like an old-fashioned knife switch to complete or interrupt the hot wire of an electrical circuit. The switch has two brass-colored terminals and has "on" and "off" marked switch positions.

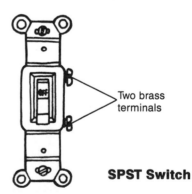

Two brass terminals

SPST Switch

Single-pole, double-throw (SPDT). This switch is used in circuits that permit lights or receptacles to be controlled from two locations. The switch has three terminals: one copper colored (common) and two brass colored. Throwing the toggle connects the common terminal to one of the

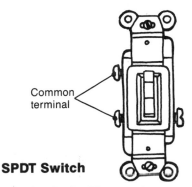

Common terminal

SPDT Switch

other two terminals. The toggle positions are not marked. This type of switch is often called a "three-way" switch.

Four-way switch (DPDT). This type switch has four terminals of the same color, and the toggle positions are not marked. This switch can control lights or receptacles in three or more locations. Current can flow through the switch in both toggle positions. The difference is that one position provides straight-through connections and the other position provides crossover connections.

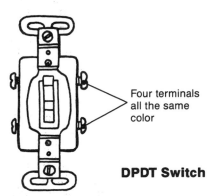

Four terminals all the same color

DPDT Switch

Specialty Switches

Quiet switch. This switch is mechanically designed to move from one position to the other with almost no noise. Although an SPST switch is shown, this sort of switch is available in all electrical types. A quiet switch is

slightly more expensive than a snap-action switch.

Locking switch. This switch is designed so that the toggle can be locked in either the "on" or "off" position to prevent unauthorized use of tools or receptacles.

Locking toggle

Time-delay switch. This switch contains a short-term timer (35 to 60 seconds). When the switch is turned off, the timer is started, and the light or receptacle the switch controls will remain energized for the timed duration. This permits you to leave an area while it is still lighted, then have the light shut off automatically behind you.

Electrical Equipment

Time-clock switch. This switch provides the same control as a plug-in timer, but it can be mounted in wall switch boxes. It can be used to control lights, air conditioners, or other devices over a twenty-four-hour period.

Silent (mercury) switch. This type of switch breaks electrical contact by tilting a sealed container of mercury. When the mercury flows to one end of the container, it breaks the circuit between two contacts. When the container is tilted so it is flat, the mercury connects both the contacts. This action is completely silent and almost wear-free, but it is more expensive. This switch must be installed with the right end up—it is labeled "top."

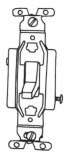

Switch-receptacle combination. This device combines a standard SPST switch and one wall outlet in a single package. It provides an easy way to add a receptacle at any middle-of-run or end-of-run switch location.

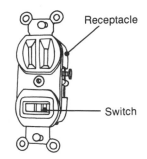

Receptacle

Switch

Loop switches. These contain no neutral wire conductor, and therefore a receptacle cannot be installed at that location. The outlet can be wired independently of or controlled by the switch. Some models have a pilot light to indicate when the switch is on.

Dimmer switch (or rheostat). Dimmer switches control the on-off switch function and the brightness of lights in a circuit. Although slightly larger than a standard switch, this type switch can be mounted in a standard switch box. Two different types control either incandescent or fluorescent lighting. The switch itself can be round (as illustrated) or toggle-shaped. Tabletop dimmers are also available to permit control of lamp intensity while seated next to the switch.

Duplex switch. Two switches encased in the same housing are independent of each other on the same circuit. Available with two single-pole switches or one single-pole and one double-pole switch. Standard snap or quiet switches are available.

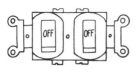

Pilot-light switch. Two types of pilot-light switches are available. One type has a toggle that glows, the other has a separate light that works in conjunction with the switch. The pilot light can be wired to come on in either the "on" or "off" switch position or to operate independently of switch position.

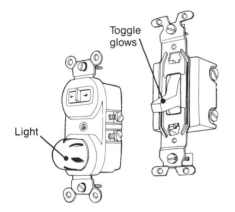

Tip switch. The whole face panel is mounted on a center swivel. Push the top half to turn it on and vice versa.

Sound-activated light switch. You can set this to operate at any sound level and duration. It serves two main purposes: It acts as a burglar deterrent, since any attempt to open a window will turn on the lights. When people leave the room—more specifically, when all noise activity ceases—it will, after a set delay time, turn off the lights to save energy. This switch contains a photoelectric cell so it will not turn

lights on during daylight. It also has a manual override and a built-in dimmer. It is available for incandescent lighting or fluorescent lighting up to 300 watts.

Wiring

Local electrical codes specify the wire to use for a specific project. Your electrical supplier knows local codes and can advise you accordingly.

The accompanying tables provide information on the most common electrical wire, including the current carrying capabilities of various wire sizes. Before you buy, check with your local building department and electrical supplier for the type of wire or cable required for your particular situation.

Wire sizes are rated by number—the smaller the number, the larger the wire diameter. Wires size 7 or smaller—the higher the number, the smaller the wire—are normally solid; No. 6 and larger are stranded. No. 14 wire is the smallest permitted in residential construction for 120 volts; No. 12 is recommended for general use.

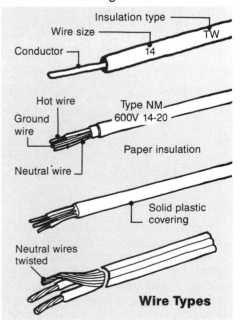

Wire Types

Electrical Equipment

Selecting the Right Wire for the Location

Insulating— Sleeve Material	Identification on Insulated Wire
Moisture and heat-resistant rubber	RHW (RFH-1, RFH-2)[2]
Thermoplastic	T (TF)[2]
Moisture-resistant thermoplastic	TW
Heat-resistant thermoplastic	THHN (No. 14, 12, 10, 8, and larger)
Moisture- and heat-resistant thermoplastic	THW, THWN
Moisture- and heat-resistant	XHHW (No. 14, 12, 10)[2]
cross-linked thermosetting	XHHW (No. 8 and larger)[2]
polyethylene	XHHW (all sizes)[2]
Plastic-sheathed	NM (often called Romex)[1][2]
Plastic-sheathed	NMC or UF
Metal-sheathed (Containing rubber-covered wires) (Containing plastic-insulated wires)	 AC ACT (often known as Bx)[1]

[1] Romex and Bx are trade names of particular manufacturers.
[2] Numbers and codes in brackets are alternate insulations for the same service.
Reprinted with permission from NFPA 70-1984, National Electrical Code, Copyright © 1984, National Fire Protection Association, Quincy, MA 02269. This reprinted material is not the complete and official position of the NFPA on the referenced subject which is represented only by the standard in its entirety.
1983 NEC

Comparative Wire Sizes

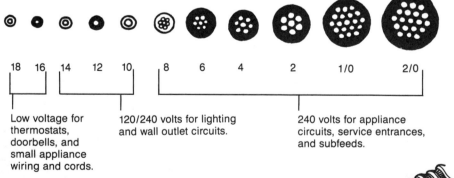

| 18 | 16 | 14 | 12 | 10 | 8 | 6 | 4 | 2 | 1/0 | 2/0 |

Low voltage for thermostats, doorbells, and small appliance wiring and cords.

120/240 volts for lighting and wall outlet circuits.

240 volts for appliance circuits, service entrances, and subfeeds.

Wire with an armored-cable sheath has its type, size, and the number of conductor wires printed inside the sheathing. Plastic-sheathed cable, usually called Romex, has its type and size number marked on the sheathing. Romex is less expensive than metal-

Fiber bushing
Spiral metal
Paper wrapping
Ground strip
Armored-Cable

Selecting the Right Wire for the Location

Maximum Operating Temperature	Application Restrictions
167°F	Can be used in wet or dry locations
140°F	Dry locations only
140°F	Wet or dry locations
194°F	Dry locations
167°F	Wet or dry locations
167°F	Dry locations
194°F	Dry locations
167°F	Wet locations
	Indoor dry locations
	Indoor damp locations and outdoors aboveground (UF may be used underground but not NMC)
167°F	Indoors in permanently dry locations only
140°F	Indoors in permanently dry locations only

clad cable and has been the most common form of household wiring since the 1960s. Armored cable is found in older homes. It may be required by some local codes and is a better option in locations where wiring could be pierced by future nailing or construction.

When estimating your needs for a purchase, add 8″ for every electrical box and 20 percent to the total to allow for twists and turns your tape measure doesn't have to take.

Aluminum wire was installed in some homes from the late 1960s until the mid-1970s. It is no longer recommended for use. Where the wiring's insulation is stripped off to make connections, the bare aluminum can oxidize, causing corrosion and increased resistance. Also, aluminum wire connected to brass

terminal screws creates corrosion as a result of the joining of two dissimilar metals. Either way, the increased resistance generates heat. Lower resistance wire, while more expensive initially, will save money by reducing power loss, blown fuses, and by increasing safety.

CAUTION:
Aluminum wire must never be used with push-in type connectors unless it is copper clad aluminum. Never add aluminum wire to a copper wire system.

If your home has aluminum wiring, be sure that all switches and receptacles are labeled CO/ALR for 15- and 20-amp circuits and CU-AL for higher-amp circuits. These have terminals that can handle either copper or aluminum wire. Also, be sure that all terminal screws

Electrical Equipment

are tight—aluminum wires expand and contract with temperature changes and can work loose. Finally, be alert for warm cover plates on switches or receptacles and for oddly inoperative circuits.

Wire Nut

This is a plastic cap containing a threaded core and is used to insulate twisted wire splices. Commonly used to make splices in household circuits, they are sold by the wire sizes being spliced. Never use on flexible cords. Only use inside of electric boxes or insulated housings.

Wire nuts are color coded by wire size (amperage). They will not hold if you use the wrong size.

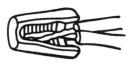

The Right Tools

Continuity tester. Use only after turning power off. This tool contains a miniature neon light bulb or a buzzer, batteries, a lead wire with an alligator clip, and a probe. When the clip is

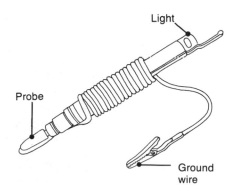

attached to a hot wire and the probe is touched to a ground wire (or neutral bus bar), creating a circuit, the buzzer will sound or the bulb will light.

The continuity tester is used to track down a malfunction such as a broken switch, loose wire, or short circuit. It and the voltage tester (see below) are the two chief diagnostic tools of the home electrician. Both are inexpensive.

Voltage tester. This inexpensive tool has a small neon tube that lights when the tester leads, held by the insulated handles, are touched to both hot and neutral wires of a live (hot) circuit. It is an essential safety device to make sure any wires you're about to handle contain no current.

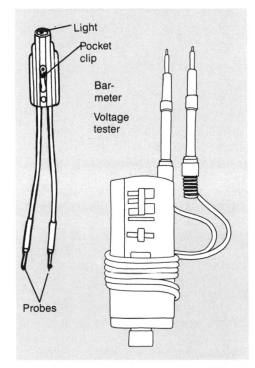

Fuse puller. If there are cartridge fuses on your service panel, you will need a fuse puller for their safe

280

removal. Make certain the puller you buy is the right size for your use.

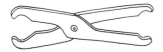

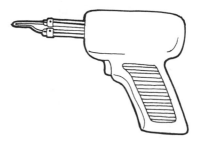

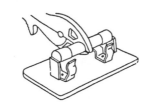

Fish tape. This is a flexible tape available in various lengths. It is used to "fish" wire through walls and floors when installing new wiring. The tape has a hook at the end to which the wire can be attached after the tape is worked through the opening. The tape is then withdrawn, pulling the wire through.

Trouble lights. Used in areas where normal house lighting doesn't provide enough illumination and holding a flashlight is inconvenient. These lights have an incandescent or fluorescent bulb protected by a metal or vinyl housing with a handle and a hook. Normal lengths are 15', 25', and 50'.

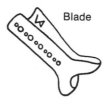

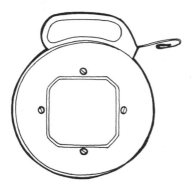

Cable ripper. A simple, low-cost U-shaped spring-steel device with a small triangular blade that slits the plastic coating on cables and plastic-coated conductors.

Blade

Soldering gun. If your work involves wire splicing, it is desirable to solder the splice to ensure good electrical contact. A high-heat electric iron, "gun", or a pencil-flame propane torch will heat the joint quickly and assure a good job.

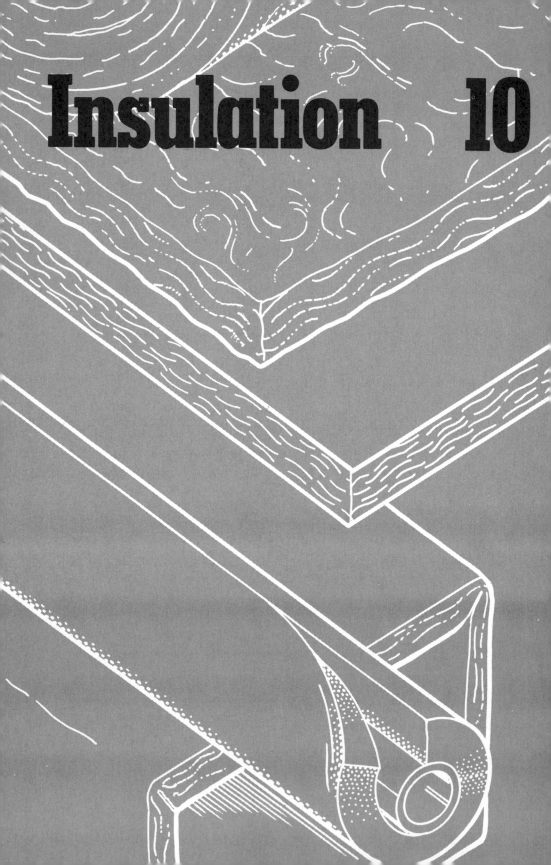

Insulation 10

10. Insulation

Insulation is the one building material that doubles as a money-maker. After you pay for it, it begins paying you in the form of reduced fuel bills. The time it takes to pay for itself may be as short as a couple of years, depending on what insulation you buy, installation cost, where you put it, the cost of your fuel and the severity of your climate. But whether you have a huge oil bill in Portland, Maine, or a huge air-conditioning bill in Phoenix, Arizona, insulation will trim it.

Most people have already put some insulation in their houses during the last ten years. The big question is, How much more should you add? And where should you add it? Those questions are partially answered by the accompanying table and map. Use the map to determine your climate zone, then use the table to see how much insulation should be present in the various parts of your house.

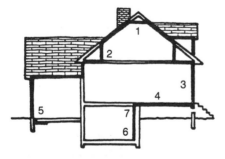

Where to Insulate a Home

1. Ceilings with cold or hot spaces above
2. Rafters and "knee" walls of a finished attic and cathedral ceilings
3. Exterior walls or walls between heated and unheated spaces
4. Floors over unheated or outside spaces or crawl space walls
5. Perimeter of a concrete floor slab close to grade level or under whole slab
6. Walls of finished or heated basement
7. Top of foundation or basement wall

Understanding R Value of Insulation

The term "R value" refers to the resistance to conductive heat flow through a material and is expressed in metric units as (m^2k/w) and imperial units (hr-ft^{2}F/btu). The basic concept to remember is:

The higher the R value, the lower the conductive heat gain or loss will be. Theoretically, doubling the R value of a wall or roof by adding insulation will reduce the conductive heat loss by 50 percent.

Remember, this is heat gain or loss and does not include heat gains due to air leaks or radiation through windows or skylights. This, and because you may only be insulating one area of the building envelope, means that doubling the insulation will not reduce your energy bill by half. However, over a period of time, it will pay for itself, and will make your home more comfortable.

There are many maps and tables giving recommended R values that are all out-of-date by the time they are published. Here we show the "minimum property standards" of the U.S. Department of Housing and Urban Development. Those standards were developed in 1979. Most fuel prices have risen dramatically since then, so adding insulation at appropriately higher levels may be more economical in your circumstances. The numbers in parentheses are fairly recent updated 1984 standards issued by the National Association of Heating and Cooling Engineers. Also, your local building code specifies areas where insulation is needed. Put together, all these areas add up to the "building envelope" of your house. Ideally, that envelope is a gap-free thermal barrier between the mechanically heated or cooled air

Insulation

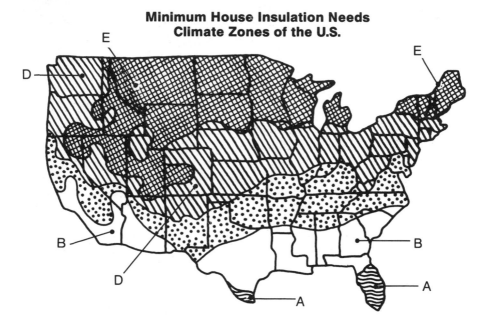

**Minimum House Insulation Needs
Climate Zones of the U.S.**

For Homes Heated with Oil, Gas, or Heat Pumps[1]

Feature	Zone A	Zone B	Zone C	Zone D	Zone E
Ceiling insulation	R-19 (R-19)[3]	R-19 (R-22)	R-26 (R-30)	R-30 (R-38)	R-38 (R-38)
Wall insulation[2]	R-11	R-11	R-13	R-13	R-19
Floors over unheated spaces	none (R-11)[3]	none (R-13)	R-11 (R-19)	R-11 (R-19)	R-19 (R-19)
Foundation walls of heated spaces	none	none	R-6	R-11	R-11
Slab foundation perimeter	none	R-2	R-5	R-5	R-7.5

For Homes Heated with Electric Resistance Heat[1]

Feature	Zone A	Zone B	Zone C	Zone D	Zone E
Ceiling insulation	R-19	R-22	R-30	R-30	R-38
Wall insulation[2]	R-11	R-13	R-19	R-19	R-19
Floors over unheated spaces	none	R-11	R-19	R-19	R-19
Foundation walls of heated spaces	none	none	R-6	R-11	R-11
Slab foundation perimeter	none	R-5	R-7.5	R-7.5	R-7.5

[1]Based on the May 1979 revisions to the HUD Minimum Property Standards as shown in "The Energy Wise Home Buyer," HUD-PDR-412(20).

[2]Does not apply to masonry walls, which should comply with local standards.

[3]R-values in brackets are the new ANSI-ASHRAE-IES Standard 90A-1980 Addenda 1984 standards for all types of heating in residential occupancies.

284

inside and the air temperature outside. If your attic is insulated to R-40 but your basement walls are a measly uninsulated R-1 or so, that's a money-saving opportunity waiting to be tapped.

Standards and Guidelines

Sources of information about required or recommended amounts of insulation are:
- "Minimum Property Standards for One- and Two-Family Dwellings," U.S. Department of Housing and Urban Development
- FmHA Instruction 424.1, "Construction Standards," Farmers Home Administration, U.S. Department of Agriculture
- "All-Weather Comfort Guidelines," Edison Electric Institute
- "NAHB Thermal Performance Guidelines for One- and Two-Family Dwellings," National Association of Home Builders
- Residential Conservation Service Program's "Minimum Insulation Standards," U.S. Department of Energy
- Call your local utility. They are familiar with the local climate, building codes, and utility rate structure and may have up-to-date recommendations.

The effectiveness of insulation is measured by its R value. As you probably know, the higher the R value, the greater the insulating power.

Do not judge insulation's effectiveness strictly by thickness. A fiberglass batt, for instance, has an R value of about 3.4 per inch. Some rigid insulating boards are as high as R-7 per inch. Generally, the insulations with the highest R-per-inch are the most expensive; they are used when space is tight.

Some insulations are more fireproof, odor-proof, vermin-proof or resistant to moisture absorption than other kinds. Insulations that absorb moisture can cause the nails and fasteners on your trusses to corrode. You'll want to take some or all of these important characteristics into consideration. In general, there is no one type of insulation that is right for every circumstance. That's why there are so many different kinds. The qualities of each kind are described below. The accompanying charts give more specifics.

Installation

Insulating is one job you can do yourself and save money. It is not difficult, but you should use goggles, a face mask, a long sleeved shirt or blouse and wear gloves.

To insulate or reinsulate an attic using rolls, batts, or pouring wool, the only tools you'll need are a folding rule and a sharp knife. To insulate open stud walls and add a vapor barrier, you'll also need a stapler to attach the vapor barrier. To install blown insulations in your attic you may want to hire a contractor or, to save money, rent a blowing machine from your local home center and do it yourself. Blowing insulation into existing walls should be left to a professional contractor. Choose a "certified" insulation contractor whose installers have been factory trained. They should have been in business for several years, be able to furnish references from customers and banks, and should belong to the Chamber of Commerce Better Business Bureau.

Blankets and Batts

Blankets and batts are made of fiberglass or mineral wool. They are either 16" or 24" wide, which are the standard widths of cavities between joists, rafters, and studs in modern construction. Best use is in unfinished

Insulation

Insulation Selection Guide—Typical Sizes and Packaging

Insulation	Form	Product Thickness	R-value[15]	Widths and Lengths	Packaging Pcs.	Sq. Ft.
Fiberglass[3] and mineral wool[9]	Attic blanket	8"	R-25	15" × 25'	1	31.25
				23" × 25'	1	47.92
	Batts, flat	12"	R-38	16" × 48"	8	42.67
				24" × 48"	8	64.00
		9½"	R-30	16" × 48"	11	58.67
				24" × 48"	10	80.00
	Rolled[1] batts	6¾"	R-22	15" × 94"	1	48.96
				23" × 94"	1	75.07
		6¼"	R-19[4]	15" × 94"[5]	5	48.96
				15" × 93"[6]	5	48.66
				15¼" × 94"[5]	5	48.96
				23¼" × 94"[5]	5	75.07
				23" × 93"[6]	5	74.27
				23" × 94"[5]	5	75.07
		3⅝"	R-13[7]	15¼" × 94"[5]	8	78.33
				15" × 93"[5]	8	77.50
				23" × 93"[5]	8	118.83
		3½"	R-11	15¼" × 94"[5]	9	88.12
				15" × 94"[5]	9	88.12
				15" × 93"[6]	9	87.19
				23" × 94"[5]	9	135.12
				23" × 93"[6]	9	133.69
		6¼"	R-19[6][8]	15" × 93"[6]	5	48.66
				23" × 93"[6]	5	74.27
		3½"	R-11[8]	15" × 93"[6]	9	87.14
				23" × 93"[6]	9	133.69
Urethane, isocyanurate	Foam[1] board	½"[11]	R-3.6	4' × 8'	41	1312[13]
				4' × 9'	41	1476[13]
		⅝"[11]	R-4.5	4' × 8'	34	1088[13]
				4' × 9'	34	1224[13]
		¾"[11]	R-5.4	4' × 8'	28	896[13]
				4' × 9'	28	1008[13]
		⅞"[12]	R-6.3	4' × 8'	25	800[13]
				4' × 9'	25	900[13]
		1"[10][11]	R-7.2	4' × 8'	22	704[13]
				4' × 9'	22	792[13]
		1¼"[12]	R-9	4' × 8'	18	576[13]
				4' × 9'	18	648[13]
		1½"[11]	R-10.8	4' × 8'	15	480[13]
				4' × 9'	15	540[13]
		1¾"[12]	R-12.6	4' × 8'	13	416[13]
				4' × 9'	13	468[13]
		2"[11]	R-14.4	4' × 8'	11	353[13]
				4' × 9'	11	396[13]

Footnotes on pages 288 & 289

Where to Install

Wood Frame Wall				Masonry Walls Aboveground[1]			Crawl Space/Basement[1][16]			Facings[1][2]
Attic	Interior Face	Exterior Face	Stud Space	Exterior	Interior	Interior or Crawl Space	Under Slab	Basement Floor Between Sleepers	Floors Over Unheated Space	
•			•		•	•		•	•	1
•			•		•	•		•	•	1
•			•		•	•		•	•	1
•			•		•	•		•	•	1
•			•		•	•		•	•	2
•			•		•	•		•	•	2
•			•		•	•		•	•	2
•			•		•	•		•	•	2
•			•		•	•		•	•	3
•			•		•	•		•	•	3
•			•		•	•		•	•	2
•			•		•	•		•	•	2
•			•		•	•		•	•	3
•			•		•	•		•	•	2
•			•		•	•		•	•	2
•			•		•	•		•	•	3
•			•		•	•		•	•	2
•			•		•	•		•	•	2
•			•		•	•		•	•	2
•			•		•	•		•	•	2
•			•		•	•		•	•	4
•			•		•	•		•	•	4
•			•		•	•		•	•	4
•			•		•	•		•	•	4
•			•		•	•		•	•	4
•			•		•	•		•	•	4
•	•	•		•	•	•	• (14)	•		5
•	•	•		•	•	•	• (14)	•		5
•	•	•		•	•	•	• (14)	•		5
•	•	•		•	•	•	• (14)	•		5
•	•	•		•	•	•	• (14)	•		5
•	•	•		•	•	•	• (14)	•		5
•	•	•		•	•	•	• (14)	•		5
•	•	•		•	•	•	• (14)	•		5
•	•	•		•	•	•	• (14)	•		5
•	•	•		•	•	•	• (14)	•		5
•	•	•		•	•	•	• (14)	•		5
•	•	•		•	•	•	• (14)	•		5
•	•	•		•	•	•	• (14)	•		5
•	•	•		•	•	•	• (14)	•		5
•	•	•		•	•	•	• (14)	•		5
•	•	•		•	•	•	• (14)	•		5
•	•	•		•	•	•	• (14)	•		5
•	•	•		•	•	•	• (14)	•		5

Footnotes on pages 288 & 289

Insulation

Insulation Selection Guide—Typical Sizes and Packaging (Concluded)

Insulation	Form	Product Thickness	R value[15]	Widths and Lengths	Packaging Pcs.	Sq. Ft.
Polystyrene, molded or expanded	Foam[1] board	¾″	R-3	2′ × 8′	16	256
				4′ × 8′	16	512
		(Density 1.0 to 1.5 lbs per cu. ft.)		4′ × 9′	16	576
		1″	R-4	2′ × 8′	12	192
				4′ × 8′	12	384
				4′ × 9′	12	432
		1½″	R-6	2′ × 8′	8	128
				4′ × 8′	8	256
				4′ × 9′	8	288
		2′	R-8	2′ × 8′	6	96
				4′ × 8′	6	192
				4′ × 9′	6	216
		3″	R-12	2′ × 8′	4	64
				4′ × 8′	4	128
				4′ × 9′	4	144

FOOTNOTES

[1]Kraft facing, some foil facings, and all foam products are combustible and must not be left exposed in attic, walls, or floors. Foam must be covered with gypsum board providing a one-hour fire rating as soon as it is installed.

[2]Batts 16″ and 24″ wide are of sufficient stiffness and width to hold in place between studs and rafters without fasteners until the interior finish is applied.

[3]Data given is for one manufacturer (Owens-Corning Fiberglas). Other manufacturers generally offer the same R-values and widths, but form and packaging may vary.

[4]R-18 at 5½″ installed thickness

[5]Overwrapped package.

[6]Twin-taped package.

[7]R-12.7 at 3½″ installed thickness on kraft faced.

[8]Flame Spread 25 only available in limited service areas.

[9]Mineral wool or rock wool is available in R-11, R-13, R-19, R-22. It is not available in rolls.

[10]1″ board R-7.2 at 75°F mean (aged R-value)

attic floors, exterior walls that are open during construction or major renovation, around heating ducts, and between floor joists over crawl spaces or unheated basements.

Blankets and batts may be bought with or without a vapor barrier of foil or paper. Install the barrier on the inside of the cavity. When adding to existing ceiling insulation, buy without a vapor barrier and lay perpendicular to joists. Never leave a vapor barrier exposed in occupied space. It may be a fire hazard.

The advantages of blankets and batts are their low cost, ease of installation (but wear face mask, gloves, and long sleeves), and fire-resistance. Their disadvantages are a relatively low R per inch, compared to more expensive plastic foam insulation, and the possibility they may not fit stud spaces of older construction.

Where to Install

| | Wood Frame Wall | | | Masonry Walls | | | | Crawl Space/Basement [16] | | |
Attic	Interior Face	Exterior Face	Stud Space	Exterior	Interior	Interior or Crawl Space	Under Slab	Basement Floor Between Sleepers	Floors Over Unheated Space	Facings [1][2]
	●	●		● (14)		●	● (14)			6
	●	●		● (14)		●	● (14)			6
●	●	●		● (14)		●	● (14)			6
●	●	●		● (14)		●	● (14)			6
●	●	●		● (14)		●	● (14)			6
●	●	●		● (14)		●	● (14)			6
●	●	●		● (14)		●	● (14)			6
●	●	●		● (14)		●	● (14)			6
●	●	●		● (14)		●	● (14)			6
●	●	●		● (14)		●	● (14)			6
●	●	●		● (14)		●	● (14)			6
●	●	●		● (14)		●				6
●	●	●		● (14)		●				6
●	●	●		● (14)		●				6

(11)Standard items
(12)Nonstandard items
(13)Data given for 24"-high package. Also available 48" high with double the number of sheets and square footage.
(14)Consult manufacturer's product data sheet to assure this application is recommended.
(15)R-value at 75°F mean unless another temperature is stated.
(16)Owens-Corning's Warm-N-Dri and poly styrene can be used below ground on basement exterior. Warm-N-Dri provides both drainage and insulation.

FACING LEGEND

Key	Facing
1	Kraft faced and unfaced
2	Kraft faced only
3	Unfaced
4	Foil faced FS-25
5	Foil-kraft foil face each side
6	Available polyfaced both sides.

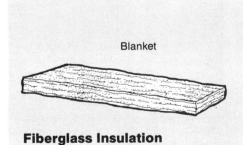

Blanket

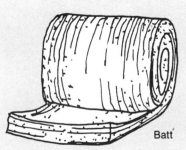

Batt

Fiberglass Insulation

Insulation

Rigid Insulation Board

Rigid Board Insulation

With their high cost and high R value, rigid foam boards are generally used when space is tight. Common applications are: as sheathing on stud walls between the studs and exterior siding, on the inside of the wall before adding drywall, over cathedral ceilings, and on the exterior of masonry foundations. They are also useful for insulating a cold concrete wall or floor, but they must be covered with gypsum board (for a one-hour fire rating) or, on the floor, before laying the plywood. One-hour fire protection is required over any foam insulation used on home interiors.

Expanded polystyrene, also known as "beadboard," is lowest in cost and R value. Its R-4 value can be compromised by water, so it is not recommended for insulating foundations below ground.

Extruded polystyrene is about R-5 and is water-resistant. Thus it can be used for insulating foundations. It will be damaged by ultraviolet light, so must be covered above grade. Typical sizes are 2′ × 8′, 4′ × 8′, and 4′ × 9′ sheets; common thicknesses are ¾″, 1″, and 2″.

Polyurethane and **polyisocyanurate** foam boards have initial R values up to 8, but as gases escape with time, the R-value drops to between R-6.2 and R-7 per inch. This is called "aged" R value. They are commonly sold in 4′ × 8′ sheets and some 4′ × 9′ for sheathing over exterior wall studs.

Phenolic foam boards are a new product in the United States. They have high R values and give off less smoke during a fire than other foam boards. But they—like *all* plastic foam boards—are flammable and, according to fire codes, must be covered with at least ½″ of fireproof material, such as gypsum board, when installed indoors. Be careful when handling them; they are brittle. Care must be taken in nailing. An unwrapped stack outdoors may quickly blow away in the wind—a 2 × 4 isn't heavy enough to hold the boards down.

Semirigid Fiberglass Insulation

Semirigid fiberglass board insulations are used to insulate slabs, provide drainage and insulation for basement walls, and for built-up roofs. These boards are sold in 4′ × 8′ sheets.

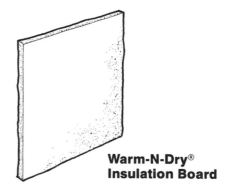

**Warm-N-Dry®
Insulation Board**

An insulation product new to the United States but available in Canada for several years is a sheathing-like board made of fairly dense fiberglass. The vertical fibers allow water to drain freely down the surface of the insulation. When used to insulate foundations below grade, the board acts both to insulate and drain, by giving subsurface water a path of least resistance to drainage tiles at the foundation's footings. Used in conjunction with a good waterproofing it can assure a dry basement. Available in 4′ × 8′ sheets, 1″ and 2″ thick.

Loose Fill Insulation

This insulation is sold in bags. You may buy the bags yourself and pour the insulation in places like an open

Loose Fill Insulation In Bags

ThermaCube® Loose Fill Insulation

The manufacturer recommends these maximum coverages at these minimum thicknesses to provide the levels of installed insulation resistance R values shown below:

R Value*	Minimum Thickness	Minimum Weight per sq. ft.	Minimum Bags per 1000 sq. ft.	Maximum Net Coverage per bag
To obtain an insulation resistance R of:	Installed insulation should not be less than:	The weight per sq. ft. of installed insulation should not be less than:	Number of bags per 1000 sq. ft. of net area shall not be less than:	Contents of this bag should not cover more than:
R-38	17¾ in. thick	0.867 lbs. per sq. ft.	24.8	40 sq. ft.
R-30	14 in. thick	0.684 lbs. per sq. ft.	19.5	51 sq. ft.
R-26	12¼ in. thick	0.593 lbs. per sq. ft.	16.9	59 sq. ft.
R-22	10¼ in. thick	0.502 lbs. per sq. ft.	14.3	70 sq. ft.
R-19	8¾ in. thick	0.433 lbs. per sq. ft.	12.4	81 sq. ft.
R-11	5¼ in. thick	0.251 lbs. per sq. ft.	7.2	140 sq. ft.

- Minimum net weight of the insulation 31.5 lbs.
- This product conforms to the property requirements of Federal Specifications HH-I-1030B Type 1 and ASTM C-764 Type 1.
- The coverage and thermal values as indicated are invalid if this product is combined with other materials.
- *R-values are determined in accordance with ASTM C-518.
- *R means resistance to heat flow. The higher the R-value, the greater the insulating power.
- To get the marked R-value, it is essential that this insulation be installed properly. If you do it yourself, get instructions and follow them carefully. Instructions do not come with this package.
- This material meets the quality standards of the State of California.
- This product conforms to D.O.E. material standards.

Thermal performance (R-value) with blown insulation is attained by a combination of thickness and density. To achieve the desired R-value, thickness and bags per 1000 sq. ft. must not be less than the minimum and coverage must not exceed the maximum, stated in the above table. Failure by the applicator to provide both proper thickness and density will result in reduced insulation value.

CAUTION:

Light fixtures and similar electrical devices, when covered with insulation or other similar materials, can overheat. To avoid this occurance, insulation as well as other materials must be kept at least 3″ away from such devices.

Insulation may cause temporary irritation. Wear longsleeved, loose fitting clothing, glove and eye protection when handling and applying material. Wash with soap and warm water after handling. Wash work clothes separately and rinse washer. A disposable mask designed for nuisance-type dusts is advisable where high dust levels are encountered.

BUILDER STATEMENT

This insulation has been installed in conformance with the above recommendations to provide a value of R _____ using _____ bags of this insulation to cover _____ square feet of area.

| DATE | COMPANY NAME | BUILDER'S SIGNATURE |
| DATE | COMPANY NAME | APPLICATOR SIGNATURE |

® A product of Owens-Corning Fiberglas, Fiberglas Tower, Toledo, Ohio 43659

Typical Loose Fill Bag Label

Insulation

attic, or you may hire a contractor to blow this insulation into closed cavities such as side walls or crawl space attic of an existing house.

This form of insulation usually requires a separate vapor barrier before initial installation in attics.

Fiberglass in loose fill form has an R value of about 2.2 when poured out of the bag and up to about 3.3 when blown into a wall cavity. A new cubed pouring and blowing wool gives more coverage per bag and is dust free.

Cellulose is commonly chopped-up newspaper; it must be pretreated with chemicals to make it fire-resistant. It varies by brand but provides about R-3.13 to R-3.70 when blown into a wall cavity. It absorbs water easily, and loses R value once it does, so vapor barriers are essential.

Perlite and **vermiculite** are fireproof, have an R value of 2 to 2.5 per inch, and are relatively high in cost. They are useful for filling small voids between blankets or batts in odd-sized

Blown-In Insulation for Attics, Walls, and Attic Floors

Blown Density Requirements to Achieve Desired R Values[1]

Location	Insulation	Form	Approx. Product Thickness[2] Inches	Pounds per Sq. Ft. Installed[1]
Attic	Cellulose, loose fiber	Blown in place	3.7	.94
			5.2	1.31
			6.7	1.69
			8.7	2.25
			11.0	2.75
Walls	Cellulose, loose fiber		3.5	.91
Attic	Rock wool, loose fiber	Blown in place	4.5	.67
			6.6	.99
			11.0	1.65
			13.7	2.05
Walls	Fiberglass, cubed	Blown in place	3.63	
			4	
Attic	Fiberglass, cubed	Blown in place	5.25	0.251
			8.75	0.433
			10.25	0.502
			12.25	0.593
			14.00	0.684
			17.75	0.867
Walls	Fiberglass, loose fiber	Blown in place	3.75	0.310
			6.50	0.535
			7.50	0.620
			8.75	0.732
			10.25	0.845
			12.75	1.070
Floored Attic 16" o.c.	Fiberglass, cubed 2" × 6" 2" × 8" 2" × 10"	Blown in place	5.5 7.25 9.25	.761 1.003 1.280

[1]Density and R-value vary by manufacturer. These are examples—check label on bag for more specific information on the product bag label you are using.
[2]See page 294 for weight limitations set by gypsum manufacturers.

cavities, and as insulation in masonry blocks or between the tile liner and outer masonry of a chimney.

Proper Application of Loose Fiberous Fill

The thermal resistance (R value) of fiber loose fill coverage depends on the proper application of the required quantity of material. The correct values for coverage of each loose fill material is stated by the manufacturer in a bag label chart similar to the one depicted on page 291, enabling you to compare products and costs per thousand square feet at any R value.

One of the most significant criteria for achieving the desired R value is meeting the designated minimum weight per square foot of material. It is also important that at least the minimum thickness be achieved, since this along with the required weight per square foot of material is essential to obtain the desired R value.

Before loose fill insulation is installed, the area to be insulated is measured.

				Where to Install		
R value	Min. Bags[1] Per 1000 Sq. Ft.	Maximum Coverage Per Bag In Sq. Ft.	Packaging Lbs. Per Bag	Attic On ½" Drywall[2] 24" O.C.	16" O.C.	Wood Frame Wall
R-13	62	16.0	Nominal 15 lbs.	●	●	
R-19	86	11.5		●	●	
R-24	110	9.0		●	●	
R-32	154	6.5			●	
R-40	182	5.5				
R-13	61	16.5				●
R-13	variable	variable		●	●	
R-19	variable	variable		●	●	
R-32	variable	variable			●	
R-40	variable	variable			●	
R-12	14.3	70				●
R-13	15.8	63				●
R-11	7.2	140	35	●	●	
R-19	12.4	81	35	●	●	
R-22	14.3	70	35	●	●	
R-26	16.9	59	35	●	●	
R-30	19.5	51	35	●	●	
R-38	24.8	40	35	●	●	
R-11	12	77	25	●	●	●
R-19	22	45	25	●	●	●
R-22	25	40	25	●	●	●
R-26	29	34	25	●	●	●
R-30	34	29	25	●	●	●
R-38	43	23	25	●	●	●
R-18	21.7	46	35			
R-24	28.6	35	35			
R-30	36.6	27	35			

Insulation

Framing adjustments may be permissible in determining the net (insulatable) area. From these calculations the required number of bags or pounds of insulation is determined from the bag label chart for the desired R value.

It is important that the correct number of pounds or bags of loose fill be installed in order to ensure that the desired R value is achieved. This holds true for poured or pneumatic applications, and open or closed blown installations.

Attics—Weight Limitations

The maximum R value of insulation installed in attics is limited by the bearing load on the ceiling caused by the insulation weight. Attics may be insulated with batts, blankets, rolls, or blown fiber insulation to R values that don't exceed the support limits of the ceiling. As an example, the weight of overlaid unsupported insulation installed above a new gypsum panel ceiling should not exceed 1.3 psf for ½"-thick panels with frame spacing 24" o.c.; and 2.2 psf for ½" panels on 16" o.c. framing or ⅝" panels on 24"

o.c. framing. The table below provides maximum R values obtainable for several types of insulations installed over a gypsum panel ceiling. Before adding any insulation to an *existing* ceiling, check the weight limitations.

Sprayed-in-Place Foams

The most commonly known foam, *urea formaldehyde,* was injected into the wall cavities of thousands of homes in the 1970s. But largely because of improper installation, the insulation often shrank and gave off toxic formaldehyde fumes. The product was finally banned in both the United States and Canada, but later a court order allowed the product back on the market in the United States.

But not all foamed-in-place insulations have presented such problems. *Urethane* foam that expands when it is applied (not later) can be sprayed into cavities by trained professionals. It does emit cyanide gas when burned, however, so it requires fire protection, and it may be banned in some locales.

Maximum R Values For Selected Gypsum Ceilings

Insulation Form	Max R ½" Gypsum 24" o.c.	Allowable R Values Max R ½" Gypsum 16" o.c.	Max R ⅝" Gypsum 24" o.c.
Blown or poured:			
Cellulose[1] (2.5 pcf per R-3.5)	R-22	R-37	R-37
Rock wool[1] (1.8 pcf per R-2.9)	R-25	R-43	R-43
Glass fiber (standard)	R-51	R-87	R-87
Glass fiber (cubed)	R-56	R-95	R-95
Batts, rolls, or blankets:			
Glass fiber (friction fitting) batts	R-95 +	R-95 +	R-95 +
Rock wool batts (2.0 pcf per R-3.23)	R-25	R-42	R-42

[1]Cellulose and rock wool insulations vary widely in density (pcf) and R value. Although the above values are representative, check the actual weight and performance for the particular material being considered.

High Temperature Insulation

Where a hot flue penetrates through the insulated ceiling level, the chase around it needs to be insulated with a high temperature insulation. One such product is an asbestos-free, rigid calcium silicate block or pipe insulation. Suitable for temperatures up to 1200°F, 1" has a thermal resistance (given at 200°F per ASTM C177 as an industrial product) of R-2.4. Available only through industrial distributors and contractors (look under "Insulation Contractors—Heat and Cold" in the Yellow Pages), it is available in thicknesses of 1" to 4" and 6", 12", or 18" wide by 36" long, or preformed as pipe insulation, compared to residential insulations it is expensive.

Pipe Insulation

There are four reasons for insulating water pipes: (1) to reduce likelihood of freezing, (2) to prevent "sweating" of cold water pipes, (3) to contain the heat in heated water and save on water heating bills, (4) to keep air-conditioning and freezer lines chilled.

If you use hot water only in the morning and evening, the savings on hot water will be minimal because there is little chance of the water staying warm in the pipe for eight hours. However, insulated piping will deliver the water at a hotter temperature to

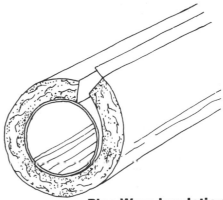

Pipe Wrap Insulation

distant points in the house. That means you will need and use less hot water from the water heater to achieve your desired temperature, or you can turn down the temperature setting of your hot water tank. Either way you save energy.

Both the BOCA and ICBO building ordinances have specific requirements for insulating materials used in plenums. Pipe insulation and facings must exhibit a flame spread of 25 or less and smoke developed of 50 or less. For these applications foam rubber pipe insulation with a smoke-developed rating of 100 is not acceptable.

There are three basic pipe insulations (foam rubber, foam polyethylene and fiberglass) and a couple of pipe wraps.

Minimum Residential Pipe Insulation Thicknesses

(in inches)

		Pipe Sizes		
Pipe System	Fluid Temperature Range, °F	1" & less	1¼" to 2"	2½" to 6"
Low-pressure/temp	251–250	1.5	1.5	2.0
Low temperature	120–200	1.0	1.0	1.5
Chilled water	40–55	0.5	0.75	1.0
Refrigerant or brine	below 40	1.0	1.5	1.5

ASHRAE Standard 90A-1980

Insulation

Selection Guide—Flexible Insulation at a Glance

	Fiberglass Batts, Blankets, 2 Rolls
Used for:	
Attics	●
Sloping roofs	●
Walls (new const.)	●
Walls (existing)	
Floors over unheated spaces	●
R-Value/Inch	3.1
Cost range[1]	Low
Widths and lengths	15 or 23 × 94 16 or 24 × 48 Rolls: 25′ R-25 39′ R-19 70.5′ R-11
Facings and standard R-values available (For approximate thickness divide R value by R value per inch given above) Consult manufacturer's data for exact products and thicknesses.	Unfaced, FS-25, foil & kraft 11, 13, 19, 22, 25, 30, 38. For R-values to 60 and above, use multiple layers.
Fire-resistance	Will not burn
Settling	None
Moisture absorption	Negligible
Corrosion	None
Fungal-bacterial growth	Does not promote growth
Other features	Compression packaging means fewer packages to handle and transport. Easy to cut and 16″ and 24″ widths self-supporting in stud space.

[1]Cost Range High = 6¢ to 10¢/sq. ft./R
      Medium = 3¢ to 6¢/sq. ft./R
      Low = 1.3¢ to 3¢/sq. ft./R
      (Cost data based on D.I.Y. for blankets and batts & contractor-installed price of blown materials, 1984)
Data on properties based on the Residential Energy Audit Manual, U.S. Dept. of Energy.

Fiberglass Cubed and Loose Blowing Wool	Rock or Slag Wool Batts and Blanket	Rock Wool, Loose Blowing Wool
●	●	●
	●	
	●	
●		●
	●	
Attic 2.2–3.0 Walls 3.4–4.0	3.16	Attic 2.6–2.8 Walls 3.75
Low (attic) Medium (walls)	Low	Low (attic) Medium (walls)
NA	15 or 23 × 48 or 94	NA
NA Blown to any R-value desired. See data on packaging to find minimum number of inches, number of lbs. per square foot, and min. number of bags per 1000 sq. ft. necessary to achieve R-value.	FS-25, foil & kraft 11, 13, 19, 22, 30 (sold through contractors not readily available for D.I.Y. use.)	NA Blown to R-value desired. If exceeding 1.3 psf on 24″ o.c. joists, gypsum manufacturers recommend thicker than ½″ gypsum board be used for ceiling to prevent sagging due to weight.
Will not burn	Will not burn	Will not burn
When installed to recommended density, none	None	Installed to recommended density, none.
Negligible None Does not promote growth	Negligible None Does not support growth	Negligible None Does not support growth
Compression packaging provides greater coverage per bag.	Easy to cut and install	Heavier, less likely to hang up in wall cavities

Insulation

Board Insulations

	Polyisocyanurate Polyurethane (Foil Faced)
Used for:	
Frame: ext. wall sheathing	●
Ext. basement/crawl space insul.	(2)
Ext. masonry wall above ground	●
Int. masonry wall	● (1)
Int. frame wall	● (1)
Cathedral ceiling	● (1)
Attic floor	(1)(2)
Basement floor	●
R value/inch	7.1–7.7
Cost range	High
High = 6¢ to 10¢/sq. ft./R	
Med. = 3¢ to 6¢/sq. ft./R	
Low = 1.3¢ to 3¢/sq. ft./R	
(Based on average regular consumer purchase price 1984)	
Standard R-values available	3.6, 4.5, 5.4, 6.3, 7.2,
(For approximate thickness divide R value by R value per inch as given above).	9.0, 10.8, 12.6, & 14.4
Widths and lengths	4′ × 8′, 4′ × 9′
Facings	Foil-kraft foil both sides; Foil-kraft foil one side, foil other
Shrinkage	Some
Moisture absorption	Limited information available
Corrosion	Foil protects
Fungal-bacterial growth	Does not support growth
UV degradation	Foil protects
Other features	Easy to cut and install
Availability	Generally available

(1)Must not be left exposed—must be covered with fire-resistant gypsum board or weather and abuse resistant covering on exterior applications.
(2)Usable but other insulations more commonly used.

Polystyrene Extruded	Glass Fiberboard	Polystyrene Molded or Expanded	Phenolic Foamboard
●		(2)	
●	●	(1)(2)	
●	●	●	●
● (1)	●	● (1)	●
● (1)	●	● (1)	
● (1)	●	● (1)	
(2)	(2)	(1)(2)	
●	●		
5.0	3.85–4.76	3.85–4.35	7.5–8.8
High	High	Medium	High
5.0, 7.5, 10.0	4.0, 8.7, 12.0	3.0, 4.0, 6.0, 8.0, & 12.0	(3)
4′×8′, 4′×9′	2′×4′, 4′×8′, 4′×9′	2′×8′, 4′×8′, 4′×9′	(3)
Foil, foil-kraft foil, and film facings	Unfaced	Film facings, Foil, Foil-kraft foil, film or unfaced	(3)
None	None	Some	(3)
None(4)	None	Some	(3)
None	None	None	(3)
Does not support growth	Does not promote growth	Does not support growth	(3)
Yes	None	Yes	(3)
Easy to cut and install	Easy to cut and install	Easy to cut and install	Tends to crumble—screw installation rather than nailing advised
Generally available	Generally available	Generally available	In test marketing

(3)Information not available at this time—new product.
(4)Underground applications absorb some water.

Insulation

How to Achieve Selected R-Values in Basement/Crawl Space Walls[4]

R-Value Desired	Construction Options	Description	Insulation[6]
R-25 to 30	Poured concrete or concrete block	Interior 2" × 4" × 24" o.c. wall offset 2⅝" *plus* any one of these alternatives:	Glass fiber or rock wool batt or blanket[3] a) Polyisocyanurate foamboard on studs, faced with gypsum board. b) Glass fiberboard on exterior protected to grade or on interior faced with gypsum board. [2] c) Polystyrene foamboard on exterior, protected to grade or on interior faced with gypsum board.[8][9]
	All-weather wood foundation[1]	2" × 8" pressure-treated frame foundation	Fiberglass or rock wool batt or blanket faced with gypsum board
		2" × 12" pressure-treated frame foundation	Fiberglass or rock wool batt or blanket faced with gypsum board
R-20 to 21	All-weather wood foundation[1]	2" × 8" pressure-treated wood foundation	Fiberglass or rock wool batt or blanket faced with gypsum board
		2" × 12" pressure-treated wood foundation	Fiberglass or rock wool batt or blanket faced with gypsum board
	Poured concrete or concrete block	Interior 2" × 4" × 24" o.c. wall offset 2⅝"	Fiberglass or rock wool batt or blanket faced with gypsum board
R-12 to 15	All-weather wood foundation[1]	2" × 8" or 2" × 12" pressure-treated wood foundation	Fiberglass or rock wool batt or blanket faced with gypsum board
	Poured concrete or concrete block	Interior 2" × 4" × 24" o.c. wall	Fiberglass or rock wool batt or blanket faced with gypsum board. Polyisocyanurate foamboard, gypsum faced

[1]Now called Permanent wood foundation.
[2]Insulation board adhered to wall retained with vapor barrier and cross bracing secured with masonry nails.
[3]To get R-value given on right, R-19 blanket insulation plus option a, b, or c must be used.
[4]Any possibility of water damage to the interior insulation and covering gypsum board should be avoided. The exterior of the basement wall to the footing should be positively drained and the exterior basement wall be given a flexible waterproofing coating.

Insulation Layers	Thickness Each (inches)	R-Value[7] Each	R-Value Compression Loss	R-Value Achieved[5]
1 layer	6¼	19 (plus a, b or c)		
1 layer	1½	10.8 (plus a, b or c)		29.8
1 layer	1½	6.5 (plus a, b or c)		29.8
1 layer	1	4.3 (plus a, b or c)		
1 layer	2	8 (plus a, b or c)		27
1 layer	9½	30	−4.3	25.7
1 layer	9½	30		30
1 layer	6¼	19		19
1 layer	6¼	19		19
1 layer	6¼	19		19
1 layer	3½	11		11
1 layer	3⅝	13		13
1 layer	3½	11		11
1 layer	3⅝	13		13
1 layer	1½	10.8		10.8

[5]For 10" concrete wall add R-0.80.
For 12" concrete wall add R-0.96.
For 8" concrete block add R-1.72.
For 12" concrete block add R-1.89.
[6]All interior insulation to be faced with 4 to 6 mil polyethylene vapor barrier.
[7]R-values of 75°F mean.
[8]½ in. gypsum wallboard may be used or ½ in. Type X where required by code.
[9]2 in. extruded polystyrene will provide R-10.

Insulation

How to Achieve Selected R Values in Frame Construction
(Least costly method given first for each construction and R value)

WALL R-Value Desired	Construction Options	Description	Insulation
R-40	Double wall	2 walls of 2″ × 4″ studs on 16″ or 24″ centers, spaced 3½″ apart	Fiberglass or rock wool batts, blankets, or rolls
			Fiberglass or rock wool batts, blankets, or rolls and polyisocyanurate foamboard sheathing
R-30	Double wall	2 walls of 2″ × 4″ studs on 16″ or 24″ centers spaced 2½″ apart	Fiberglass or rock wool batts, blankets, or rolls
	Single wall	2″ × 6″ × 24″ o.c. wall with horizontal 2″ × 4″ strapping 24″ o.c.	Fiberglass or rock wool
		2″ × 6″ × 24″ o.c. wall	Fiberglass or rock wool and polyisocyanurate foamboard sheathing
R-26	Single wall	2″ × 6″ × 24″ o.c. wall	Fiberglass or rock wool and polyisocyanurate foamboard sheathing

How to Achieve Selected R Values in Floors

R Value Desired	Construction Options	Description	Thickness (inches)	R Value Achieved
R-11	On concrete floor of dry waterproofed basement	Install pressure treated 2″ × 4″ sleepers 24″ o.c. Lay R-11 fiberglass floor insulation batts between sleepers, apply vapor barrier and min. ⅝″ plywood flooring	3½	11.8
R-12–14		As above, installing 3 1″ layers fiberglass perimeter insulation or 1¾″ polyisocyanurate,[1] vapor barrier and ⅝″ plywood	3 1¾	12.7 13.4
		As above installing 2″ polyisocyanurate[1] foam board, vapor barrier and ⅝″ plywood	2	14.4

Insulation Layers	Thickness Each (inches)	R Value Each	Compression Loss	R Value Achieved
3 layers (2 vertical, 1 horizontal)	3⅝	13	NA	39
2 layers Exterior	3⅝	13		36.4
Interior	6¼	19	−1	
1 layer sheathing	¾	5.4		
1 layer	6¼	19	NA	30
1 layer	3½	11	NA	
1 layer	6¼	19	−1	29
1 layer (between strapping)	3½	11		
1 layer	6¼	19	−1	28.8
1 layer sheathing	1½	10.8		
1 layer	6¼	19	−1	23.4
1 layer sheathing	¾	5.4		

How to Achieve Selected R Values in Floors (Concluded)

R Value Desired	Construction Options	Description	Thickness (inches)	R Value Achieved
R-30 R-19 R-13	Floors over unheated crawl space or basement floors over unheated basements	Install glass fiber or rock wool batts, vapor barrier side up, and retain with "tiger teeth" (stiff wire rods pointed at each end ½" longer than joist spacing)	9½ 6½ 3⅝	30.0 19.0 13.0
Slab Perimeter R-8–10	Around exterior perimeter monolithic slab	Double layer 1" glass fiber perimeter insulation, hard-faced and top flashed	2	8.6
	Install 20"-wide insulation flat on fill inside perimeter of slab with 4" vertical at slab edge	Glass fiber perimeter insulation 2 layers or Extruded polystyrene foam insulation	2 2 2	8.6 8.0 10.0

(1)Isocyanurate may only be used here if covered with gypsum under the plywood or if the floor is tiled.

Insulation

They must have a sealed vapor barrier facing if they are being used to stop the sweating of cold water or refrigerant pipes.

The simplicity of the strip-and-seal butt strips on fiberglass pipe covering makes that much quicker and easier for the do-it-yourselfer to install than foam rubber piping that has to be slit, snapped over pipe, and carefully buttered with adhesive along both sides.

Foam polyethylene pipe insulation can be used over the temperature range of $-90°F$ up to $212°F$. It fits all standard diameters from $\frac{3}{8}''$ to $4\frac{1}{2}''$ ID and is available in four wall thicknesses: $\frac{3}{8}''$, $\frac{1}{2}''$, $\frac{3}{4}''$, and $1''$. It comes in 6' lengths slit for ease of application. The R value per inch is R-4. The seams are sealed with adhesive from the same manufacturer to provide a vapor barrier.

Foam rubber pipe insulation can be used over the temperature range of $-60°F$ to $220°F$. It fits all standard pipe diameters from $\frac{3}{8}''$ to $4\frac{1}{2}''$ ID and comes in thicknesses from $\frac{1}{2}''$ to $1''$. It is sold in 6' lengths, not slit. The R value per inch (of the three common brands) is R-3.73. The seams have to be doped with adhesive, held until tacky, and then sealed. Butt joints have to be similarly sealed.

Fiberglass pipe insulation can be used over the temperature range of $-60°F$ to $850°F$ (but self-sealing jacket limited to $-10°F$ to $150°F$). It is used with standard iron pipe sizes from $\frac{1}{2}''$ to $15''$ and copper tubing from $\frac{5}{8}''$ to $6\frac{1}{8}''$. Wall thicknesses range from $\frac{1}{2}''$ to $6''$. Available lengths are 4' and 6', slit for ease of application. For other than the self-sealing type, seams are held with staples and a mastic or tape applied to provide a vapor barrier seal. The flame spread rating is 25, smoke developed 50.

Duct Insulation

Heating and air-conditioning ducts running through unheated basements, duct chases, and attics need insulation to avoid energy waste and to ensure the treated air reaches its destination at the desired temperature. With heat pumps, even ducts in the conditioned spaces should be insulated, because the heat produced by a heat pump is at a relatively low temperature and may not be high enough to heat distant

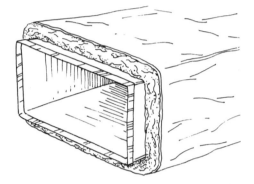

Flexible Duct Wrap Insulation Applied to Duct Exterior

rooms if the duct is not insulated.

Precut, preinsulated air handling systems now available can be used to advantage. Fiberglass pre-faced duct board is available in standard residential sizes—just fold and seal the scored board to provide the duct sound absorption and insulation all in one with its own vapor barrier jacket. Ends are shiplapped to join together and form a tight seal when taped. Flat unscored duct boards are made by three manufacturers and are available through fabricating contractors for nonstandard sizes. Runoffs and returns can be made from the same duct board or by using flexible round ducts.

If you have existing uninsulated metal ducts, fiberglass duct wrap can be used to insulate them. The wrap

Duct Wrap Product Data

Type	Thickness	Unfaced (Standard widths: 24″, 36″, 48″, & 72″)	
		Installed R Value[1]	Out-of-Package R Value
50	1½″	3.6	4.8
	2″	4.8	6.5
	3″	7.3	9.7
75	1″	2.6	3.4
	1½″	3.9	5.2
	2″	5.2	6.9
	3″	7.8	10.3
100	1″	2.8	3.7
	1½″	4.2	5.6
	2″	5.6	7.4
150	1″	3.0	4.0
	1½″	4.5	6.5
		All-Service Faced (Standard width: 48″)	
75	1½″	3.8	5.0
	2″	5.0	6.7
	2½″	6.3	8.3
	3″	7.5	10.0

[1]Based on average installed thickness 75% of nominal thickness.

should not be pulled tight at the corners, and all joints must be securely sealed to prevent condensation. The installed values opposite reflect normal compression at corners.

Rigid Duct System
Standard thicknesses are 1″ and 1½″ NRC .80 (1″). Resistance value for 1″ is R-4.35, and for 1½″ it is R-6.3. It features flame-retardant aluminum foil facing and meets both NFPA 90A requirements for crawl spaces and plenums.

Flexible Duct
Flexible duct is available with all-service reinforced jacket or polyethylene vapor barrier jacket. The thickness ranges are: ½″, 1″ and 2″.
Diameters: 4⅛″ to 10⅛″ in 1″ increments
12⅛″ to 18⅛″ in 2″ increments

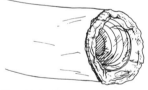

Flexible Duct (Coiled Wire Inside Maintains Shape)

Lengths are 25′ and the R-value per inch is R-4.35. It is compression-packaged to save shipping and storage space.

Duct Liner
Flexible. Standard thicknesses ½″, 1″, 2″. Width 48″.

Rigid. Standard thicknesses:
1″ NRC .80—lengths 48″, 72″; widths 24, 56, 48
1½″ NRC .95
2″ NRC 1.05

Insulation

Infiltration/Vapor Barriers and Ventilation

Although your walls and ceiling may be stuffed with insulation, air can still slip through them. The air can come from the outside, through gaps in the siding, and from the inside through lack of a vapor barrier or holes at electric outlets or pipe penetrations. In winter, when warm inside air enters

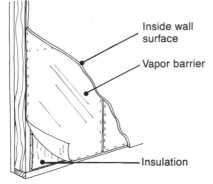

Vapor Barrier Location

your walls, it cools down. And as it cools, its ability to hold water in a gaseous state is reduced, resulting in the condensation of moisture on a cold mass such as a stud or sill plate. If such condensation occurs constantly, it will wet the insulation and decrease the insulation's R value. It can also lead to dry rot of the wood framing. This condensation is particularly liable to build up toward the exterior in freezing weather if there is no insulating sheathing.

A barrier can be placed on either side of the insulation to provide infiltration control. However, a *vapor barrier* must be placed on the warm side (in winter) for moisture control. As the map that follows shows, a vapor barrier is recommended everywhere in the United States.

Polyolefin infiltration "barriers" (used on the exterior) permit vapor transmission and are not true vapor barriers. Rather, they are infiltration retarders and are not vapor barriers.

Having a tight vapor barrier in humid climates reduces the condensation load on your air-conditioning equipment, reducing energy costs. Being able to maintain higher humidity level—about 30–45 percent relative humidity (RH)—in winter provides warmth and comfort at lower thermostat settings, saving energy. However, with a tight vapor barrier one must ventilate a new structure by opening windows and doors for at least a week to allow construction moisture to escape. Fresh

Vapor Barrier Products

Common vapor barriers	Perm rating (the lower the better)
Polyethylene (6 mil)	0.06
Polyethylene (4 mil)	0.08
Rufco 300 and 400 or Tu-Tuf® (3 and 6 mil[1])	less than 0.06
Aluminum foil (0.35 mil)	0.05
Plywood ¼″ thick, exterior grade (joints glued)	0.7
Asphalt-saturated and-coated vapor barrier	0.2–0.3
Vapor barrier paints, two coats	0.3–0.5

[1]Tu-Tuf® manufactured by Sto-Cote Products, Inc. of Richmond, Illinois and Rufco 300 and 400 are molecularly aligned, UV-stabilized, cross-laminated poly sheetings. They are thinner, more puncture-resistant, and more flexible than 6 mil polyethylene with equal or better perm rating.

concrete contains tons of water; water-based paints and plaster add more. Until the humidity level drops below 50 percent RH, ventilation must be maintained using fans if necessary.

There are 7000 "grains" of water to every pound of water. A proper vapor barrier will permit no more than 1 grain of water to pass through 1 square foot of its surface per hour. This quantity is described as 1 perm. For a vapor barrier to perform to its perm rating, all joints must be overlapped and retained between two hard surfaces, and all rips and tears patched with a vapor barrier tape. For very tight (less than 0.5 air changes per hour), superinsulated homes, overlaps are generally bonded with nonskinning acoustical sealant.

Vapor Barriers—Where Required or Recommended

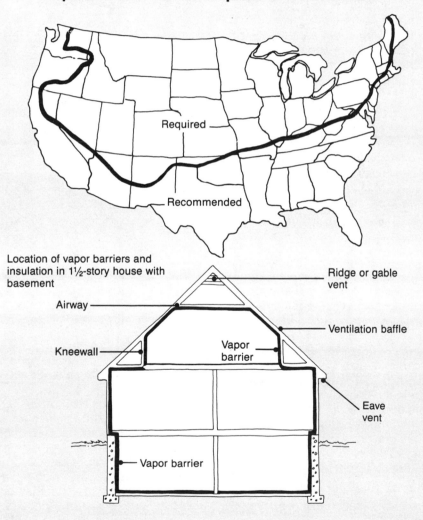

Insulation

While recent research by the Forest Products Laboratory in Wisconsin of various vapor barriers and sheathing materials proved generally inconclusive, it did show that the type of vapor barrier seemed to make little difference in the winter. The addition of an electric outlet in a previously sealed stud space increased vapor transmission 4 to 5 percent in every case. So it seems the sealing of penetrations is more important than the selection of the vapor barrier material.

There was condensation in south-facing walls with fiber board sheathing. In comparison, foam sheathings, foil-faced sheathings, and plywood reduced the likelihood of exterior moisture entering the wall and being driven into the insulation by the sun's heat.

In cooler climates (again, most of the United States and Canada), the specific locations of vapor barriers in the "envelope" components (see illustration), if they are to be effective, are:

- Walls—between the insulation and the wallboard.

- Ceilings—between the insulation and the gypsum board. Currently, many builders are leaving out the ceiling vapor barrier to provide an outlet for the interior water vapor and thus to reduce interior humidity levels. While this may reduce interior humidity somewhat, it also increases air infiltration. This can prove particularly costly in summer by allowing hot humid outdoor air to enter and require removal by the air conditioner. For this reason, a vapor/infiltration barrier at the ceiling must be used for energy-efficient designs.

- Floors—over vented crawl spaces above the insulation either above or below the subfloor.

- Below-grade walls of basements or crawl spaces—with interior insulation; between the insulation and the wallboard; with exterior insulation; between the insulation and the foundation or inside the foundation.

- Slabs (on grade or basement floors) —over the ground before concrete is poured.

- Floor of a crawl space—over the ground.

Attic Ventilation Baffles

When installing attic insulation, it is essential to provide baffles attached to the rafters to allow airflow from the vents in the soffits to the vents in the attic. While these can be made by tacking insect screening or folded cardboard baffles across the rafters, a faster, more efficient method is to use fabricated products.

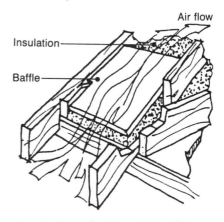

Insulation Baffle at Roof Eave

Proper Vent 1 and 2 are preshaped, expanded polystyrene baffles for 24" on center spans and 11¾" on center for retrofit applications. Both are 4' long. Although formulated to reduce burning, since they are a foam plastic, check local codes to see if they are acceptable in your area. Prices range from approximately $0.16 to $0.20 per square foot. Proper Vent is made by Poly-Foam Inc., 4901 West 77th Street, Minneapolis, Minnesota 55435. Insultray is a moisture-resistant cardboard baffle. It costs about $0.15 per square foot and is made by Insultray, 4985 North Cascade Place, Oak Harbor, Washington.

Attic Vent Recommendations

Attics with a ceiling vapor barrier should be ventilated with 1 square foot of clear vent area for each 300 square feet of ceiling.

Attics without a ceiling vapor barrier should be ventilated with 1 square foot of vent area for each 150 square feet of ceiling.

Attic Ventilation Methods

Attic ventilation can be provided by installing a combination of continuous

Roof Ventilation

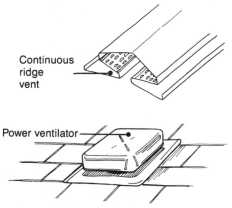

Continuous ridge vent

Power ventilator

soffit vents and any of the following: ridge vent, power attic vent in the roof, screened gable vents, or roof louvers. These are listed in order of efficiency with ridge and soffit vent combinations the most efficient under all wind conditions both in summer and winter.

Crawl Space Vent Recommendations

Moisture can condense in crawl spaces below homes as well as in attics. Vents should be placed opposite each other to get the most effective air circulation. FHA requirements are for a vapor barrier ground cover and 1 square foot of vent for each 1500 square feet of crawl space area. Without a ground cover, 1 square foot is required for each 150 square feet of area. The vent sizes referred to above are for unobstructed vents. See the chart below for screening, louvers, and rain and snow shields.

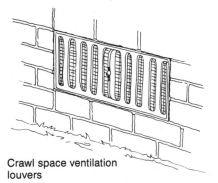

Crawl space ventilation louvers

Adjusting for Vent Covering

Covering	Adjustment Factor
¼″ hardware cloth	1 × recommendations
¼″ hardware cloth with rain louvers	2 × recommendations
⅛″ mesh screen	1¼ × recommendations
⅛″ mesh screen with rain louvers	2¼ × recommendations
1/16″ mesh screen	2 × recommendations
1/16″ mesh screen with rain louvers	3 × recommendations

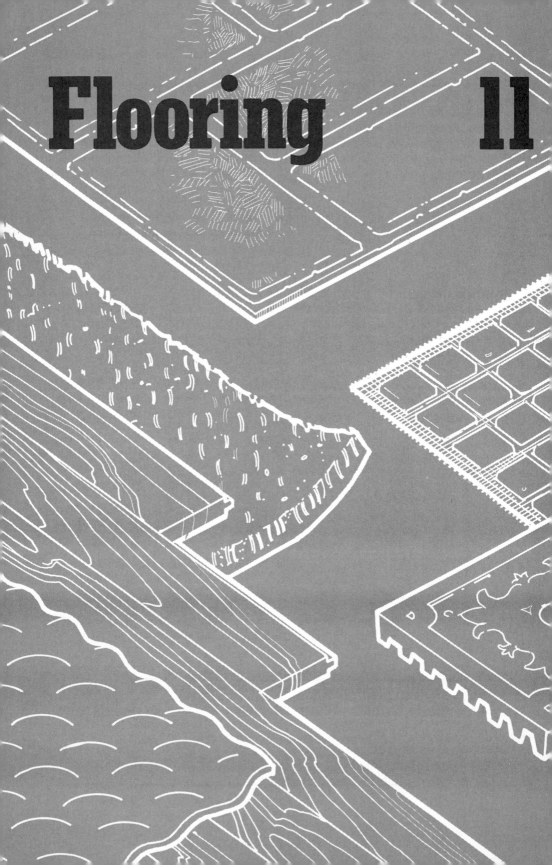

Flooring 11

11. Flooring

Carpet, ceramic tile, brick, slate, sheet vinyl, wood—all these materials can make beautiful floors. But, beyond their appearance are such important characteristics as durability, ease of installation, maintenance and repair, cost, and comfort under foot. Since floor covering represents a considerable investment, selection may be accompanied by some apprehension. For one thing, there is the question of how it's going to look on the floor.

It pays to bring home swatches or samples and place them in the rooms to see if they improve the appearance and match the color scheme. In this way you can avoid using a large pattern that shrinks a small room or a color that is so dark it makes the room depressing. You also want to choose the right kind of flooring for the room in question; then shop carefully to get the most quality for your money.

Sometimes choosing even a general category of flooring isn't easy. Witness, for example, kitchen flooring. Several years ago, the fashion was to install carpeting in kitchens. Carpeting is comfortable to stand on for long periods, but it also shows the stains of spilled foods as well as the wear and tear of heavy traffic. Now, in the 1980s, ceramic tile is a fashionable kitchen flooring. Tile is easy to clean and doesn't show every spill. But it's also a hard surface that bounces noise, breaks dropped glasses and dishes, and can be uncomfortably hard to stand on for long periods. It also raises the floor level, making repair or replacement of your dishwasher an expensive operation, or changing back from tile to a flexible flooring a major project.

Carpet and the resilient sheet floorings are the least durable among your choices; unless you are willing to invest in the better-quality products and care for them, you may need to replace them after five or six years. However, that may be perfectly acceptable to people who like to redecorate every few years.

Carpeting

Carpeting absorbs noise like no other flooring. That can be a blessing. It also absorbs dirt like no other flooring, which is probably its chief liability. Manufacturers recommend once-a-week vacuuming to make it last. Nevertheless, it can make a room feel warm and cozy and look luxurious. It is best suited to low-traffic areas such as bedrooms, dens, and dining rooms. It should be avoided in rooms with direct access to the out-of-doors, because tracked-in sand and dirt can be very destructive.

Should you install wall-to-wall carpeting or a laid carpet? If your floor is plywood, you have less option. If you have hardwood floors and anticipate moving soon, you may want a laid carpet you can take with you.

Wall-to-wall carpet, once available only in wool, now comes in a variety of synthetic fibers. The synthetics may not be as prestigious, but they cost less and are often more resistant to fading, stains, matting, and mildew (see chart). Olefin, the stuff of indoor-outdoor carpet, and nylon seem to provide the longest wear life.

Most carpeting is no longer woven on a loom. Instead it is made of fibers stitched to a backing in a process called tufting. If the fibers form loops, it is called loop-pile carpeting. If the loops are split or cut off, the carpeting is cut pile (see chart).

Woven carpets are made on looms that intertwine the surface yarns into the backing. Sometimes these are

Flooring

Carpet Textures

Type of Pile	Description	Use
Level loop	All loops the same height. Limited selection of textures.	Very durable. Good for high-traffic areas such as hallways.
Multilevel loops	Loops are made in two or three different heights, providing sculptured effect.	Wears well and can be used in den or playroom subject to traffic. Never use on landings or stairs, where loops can catch on heels and trip people.
Cut pile	Basically a level-loop carpet in which each loop is cut into two tufts. The cut ends give this a softer texture called plush. There are two different effects, depending on the twist applied to the yarn: 1. Untwisted or slightly twisted yarn provides a velvet appearance with shadows formed by the direction in which the tufts are pressed. The fibers of one tuft blend in with the next. Tufts need to be close and thick or carpet will mat. 2. Cut twisted yarns keep their individual identity, and tufts are usually longer to provide a deep, dense Saxony plush.	Soft texture makes this ideal for bedrooms or rarely used living rooms not subject to heavy traffic. Reasonable wear resistance—can be used in any room.
Cut-and-loop pile	Provides a multilevel sculptured effect because some loops are cut, exposing soft velvety ends, while other loops have contrasting braided appearance.	More durable and wear-resistant than cut pile. Ideal for dens, living rooms, and dining rooms.
Shag carpeting	Provides an informal, unkempt, shaggy appearance, with long, widely spaced tufts in a variety of lengths, lying in random directions.	For play or casual areas.

made by weaving the yarns through two backings spaced apart so, at the end of the loom, a blade cutting through the yarns separates them into two carpets. Although weaving takes longer and costs more than tufting, a greater variety of patterns can be achieved, including imitations of costly Oriental rugs. Since these are going to have to justify their higher cost, you'll usually find the tufts are closer together and the depth of the pile is greater.

Needle-punched carpets are made by a matting process and provide a hard-wearing carpet with very little pile depth. They are often used for patios or playrooms and, when made with olefin, are used for kitchen or bathroom carpets.

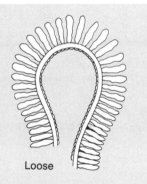

Loose

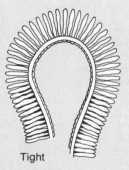

Tight

Weave Tightness Test

When examining carpet for quality, look for:

The tightness of the weave. The more rows per inch, the better the carpet. Bend a section of the carpet back to back to see how closely tufted the fibers are. The closer, the better. A tight weave generally means a durable, crush-resistant carpet.

Before accepting a roll of carpet, rub the surface hard with a paper towel to make sure the dye has set. If color comes off, reject the carpet—the color will track onto your vinyl floors and ruin them.

When buying runners for stairways, always buy sufficient length so you can tuck under a generous tread width behind the first riser. When the tread areas show wear you can then move the whole carpet up the stairway so the worn area is on the riser and the unworn riser sections lay on the treads.

Twist. The more turns per inch, the less bulk and the more durable the carpet. Tightly twisted yarn springs back and is less likely to ravel and fray.

The depth of the pile. The deeper the pile (that is, the longer the fibers), the softer the carpet. However, the pile will not stand up unless the rows are close together. A deep-pile carpet will be harder to clean, and may not be suited to high-traffic areas.

Expect to pay more for tighter weaves and deeper piles.

Weight of yarn. Compare with other carpets made of the same fibers.

Underlayment. Use top-quality rubber padding under carpeting in high-traffic areas.

Jute-backed carpeting should suffice for low-traffic areas.

Sizes available. Wall-to-wall carpet is available in widths of 9′ and 12′. Some usually expensive, commercial

Flooring

carpeting is available in 15' widths. There are even 18" × 18" self-adhesive backed carpet squares that can be switched with those from protected locations as they become worn. A selection of odd widths and lengths of all types of carpet left over from other installations is available in every carpet store. Choose a width wide enough to cover one dimension of the room without seaming. Carpet is sold by the square yard; expect waste material. You can install wall-to-wall carpet yourself, but it takes time, strength, some skill, and special tools such as a knee-kicker and a power stretcher.

There are several attachment methods. You can fold over the edges of the carpet and use rust-resistant tacks. You'll need at least 4" additional in both width and length if you do this, and there is a danger that tacks will be left in the carpet if you take it up for cleaning.

There are two types of "tackless" strips. One is a galvanized steel strip with die-cut barbs; the other is a wood batten with exposed nails.

The use of Velcro tape instead of tackless strips keeps the carpet edge

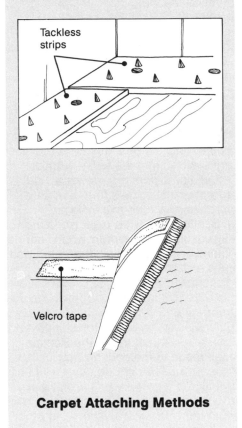

Carpet Attaching Methods

Carpet Selection Guide

Fiber	Relative Cost	Comments	Wear Life	Soil/Stain Resistance
Acrylic	Medium	Has a wool-like finish and appearance, but fine fibered and softer. Higher priced than nylon and olefin, its tendency to ball and form fluff balls has reduced its popularity.	Long	Very good
Nylon	Wide price range	Easy to clean and extremely durable. Is now available with antistatic coating, but if static is annoying, don't blame the carpet—raise the humidity. Static means your house is too dry for health or comfort.	Very long	Good. Hides dirt.

flatter and makes removal for cleaning and replacement much easier. Velcro resists a sideways pull, holding the stretched carpet tightly in position; it readily releases when the carpet is pulled up vertically.

Seams can be joined with "hot" sealing tape. Attached to the flooring under the seam location, the tape's thermoplastic is melted with a heating iron and adjoining sides of the carpet are pressed into the tacky surface.

Most carpet stores will install the carpet you purchase from them, or you can hire your own installer.

Scatter rugs, area rugs, and Oriental rugs usually complement wood flooring. The ever-popular hooked and braided rugs—often made by hand from discarded clothing—add country charm and can last for years but may require frequent and expensive dry cleaning. Oriental rugs are the aristocrats of floor coverings. Traditionally, the Persian rugs made in the country now called Iran have been handed down as family heirlooms. The weaver's art is slowly dying out, and many consider fine rugs from Iran, Turkey, Pakistan, and other exotic lands to be a prime investment. Fine reproductions are available from American and European manufacturers.

Cushion-backed carpeting, which comes with padding attached, is easier to install than conventional carpet. It is either glued to the floor with adhesive, or stuck with double-sided tape. It's inexpensive but often doesn't last as long as regular carpet.

The best form of carpet care is weekly vacuuming, whether the carpet looks dirty or not. Otherwise grit will embed itself in the fibers, damaging the carpet as it's being walked on. Occasionally, you may want to clean your carpet with one of three methods: steam cleaning, a wet shampoo, or dry cleaning. Steam cleaning is often done by professionals, but you can rent both steam cleaners and shampooers for do-it-yourself jobs. If you give your carpet a wet shampoo, avoid the frequent mistake of adding too much detergent, which can remain in the carpet and attract dirt. When using either method, do not get the carpet too wet; you'll risk shrinking the jute backing or staining the surface. With

Fade Resistance	Static Buildup*	Moisture Absorbency	Crush Resistance	Mildew	Synthetic Fiber Brand Name
Colorfast if made from colored fibers; average if dyed	Minimal	Minimal	Average	Resistant	Acrilan Creslar Orlon
Very good	High, but today most is treated with an anti-static coating	Some	Good	Resistant	Anso IV Antron Enkalure Ultron Zeftron

Flooring

Carpet Selection Guide (Concluded)

Fiber	Cost	Comments	Wear/ Life	Soil/Stain Resistance
Polyester	Medium	Very bright colors. Has good bulk and abrasion resistance. Resists soiling, mildew, and moisture.	Long	Stained by contact with oil-based stains. Excellent soil resistance.
Polypropylene olefin	Wide price range	Very durable, moisture resistant, mildew resistant, nonabsorbent, static and stain resistant. Very tough and durable. A good choice if you have a young family or pets. Some brands can be used outdoors or indoors and are suitable for kitchens, bathrooms, and basements.	Very long	Good
Wool	Expensive	Wool from higher altitudes is the best, one reason wool from New Zealand is prized. Also comes from Australia, Argentina, Pakistan, India, Syria, and Europe. Most carpet wools are blends. Wool is not colorfast, mildews easily, absorbs moisture, and stains. Needs mothballing. But is prestigious.	Long	Poor
Silk & Wool	Very expensive	Handwoven carpets in intricate designs using wool, silk, and felt, sometimes stranded with silver or gold, are museum pieces. Probably the most prized of these carpets still being made are the Persian carpets from Iran and Turkish carpets. They make sound investments and family heirlooms. Machine-made versions of Oriental carpets offer the beauty of the original designs at a more affordable price.	Long	Poor
Cotton	Inexpensive	Used in bath mats, braided rugs, and imitation Eastern and Oriental patterns.	Average	Poor

*Static is also a signal that your house is too dry. Relative humidity (RH) should be above 15 percent and preferably close to 45 percent for health, comfort, and energy savings during the heating season. Because you'll feel warmer with 45 percent RH, you can comfortably lower your thermostat.

Fade Resistance	Static Buildup*	Moisture Absorbency	Crush Resistance	Mildew	Synthetic Fiber Brand Name
Average	Minimal	Minimal	Average	Resistant	Dacron Encron Trevira
Very good	Minimal	None	Fair	Resistant	Herculon Marvess Oasis Marquesa
Good	Varies	High	Average	Not resistant	Not applicable
Excellent	Varies	Some	Good	Not resistant	Not applicable
Poor	Minimal	High	Good	Not resistant	Not applicable

Flooring

Oriental or expensive carpets, leave cleaning to the professionals or dry clean. The do-it-yourself water and steam cleaners leave a residue around the base of the fibers, shortening the life of the carpet. Never use one of these wet-cleaning methods or wet-clean a stain unless you have put polyethylene sheeting between the carpet and the padding. Stain from wet felt padding will stain your carpet, and foam padding is damaged by moisture.

Dry cleaning, by brushing in a cleaning powder and vacuuming, will clean adequately and help your carpet last longer.

Suitable Subfloors

Concrete. Before laying padding and carpet on a concrete floor, you must make sure it stays dry. After a rainstorm, tape some 6″ squares of polyethylene to a variety of locations on the floor. After twenty-four hours check to see if any moisture has condensed on the underside. If it has, the floor is not suitable for carpeting. Or buy 3 percent phenolphthalein solution in grain alcohol at the pharmacy and drip it on the floor. If it turns red in a few minutes, it means there is moisture in the floor. If you still want to carpet the floor, you'll have to use a concrete sealant (such as Dutch Standard or Steel-Treat from Klean-Strip) and let it cure. Also check outside the house to make sure your splash blocks are carrying the water from the downspouts away from the house. Make sure there are no dips in the back-fill and repair any cracks in the foundation. Check that your sump pump is operating and that your drainage tile is not blocked by roots or sediment.

Wood. As long as wood floors (plank or plywood) are level, firm, clean, and free of grease, paint, or raised nail heads, they make a suitable base. All cracks should be filled with a latex patching or leveling compound and sanded.

Resilient flooring must be firmly adhered to the subfloor, with all wax and adhesive removed.

Carpet Padding

Conventional wall-to-wall carpet requires an underlayment of padding. The padding keeps the carpet from wearing more quickly, provides extra cushion, and helps absorb noise.

Rubber foam

Waffle

Foam

Jute

Carpet Padding

The padding is usually sold in rolls 3′, 4½′, 6′, 9′, or 12′ wide and is installed up to, but not over, the perimeter "tackless" strips. All joints should be taped with carpet tape. Install the padding waffle (pattern) side up. Thicknesses are generally ⅜", ½", and 9/16". Thicker pads may be available but will allow the carpet to move and need retensioning, so don't go over 9/16".

Paddings are available in a variety of materials. The best choice over dry sealed concrete floors would be sponge rubber foam (use indoor-outdoor carpet). Don't use felt or jute padding under indoor-outdoor carpet or in moist areas. Use jute, not rubber or plastic foam padding, over radiant-heated floors.

All padding is damaged by moisture, so you should put a polyethylene sheet between the carpet and pad if you are going to steam (or water) clean.

How can you tell quality? Pinch the foam pads. If they allow your fingers to almost meet, the density is too light. They should be thick and spongy enough to keep your fingers ¼" apart.

Polyurethane foam is the most commonly used pad today, being less expensive than the better jute padding yet durable if of sufficient density. Polyurethane comes in better quality "prime" foam and as rebonded (scrap) foam. The latter tends to crumble, particularly if it gets damp. Be aware that polyurethane foams are highly combustible and give off toxic fumes when burning.

Latex "bubble pads" provide the best quality, and some have limited warranties for the life of the building, but they, too, can burn and give off noxious fumes.

Jute, both woven and unwoven, rubberized animal hair, and vinyl foams are all good quality but higher priced.

You can install padding using staples or two-sided adhesive tape.

Wood Flooring

Natural-looking wood flooring adds a warm touch to dens, living rooms, and dining rooms. It can be laid as strip flooring, plank flooring, or parquet. Strip flooring comes in random lengths, plank flooring comes in random widths and lengths, and wood block (parquet)

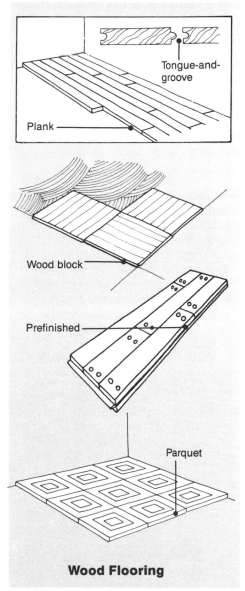

Wood Flooring

319

Flooring

comes in a wide variety of patterns. There are also prefinished laminated plank and parquet floors that save time, labor, and materials.

Hardwood floors are still considered an indication of quality and increase a home's value. Softwoods such as Western hemlock, redwood, Douglas fir, and Southern pine are less expensive than hardwoods but won't stand up as well to heavy traffic. While oak is the most common hardwood chosen, beech, birch, pecan, or maple also are often preferred for their appearance.

Flooring lumber is available as prefinished or unfinished stock. Prefinished laminated floors offer easier installation and greater variety but, other than oak, require special ordering. One manufacturer ships these in standard 8′ lengths. These tongue-and-groove planks come in standard 6½″ and 7¾″ widths or random 3″, 5″, and 7″ widths and are glued and fitted together over an ⅛″ foam underlayment and any sound, flat substrate. Prefinished flooring with planks preattached to 4′ lengths comes with walnut plugs in place and a durable acrylic polyurethane finish. Standard lengths commonly available for prefinished lumber are shown in the NOFMA/OFI chart that follows.

Tips on Installing Wood Flooring

The chief hazard in installing flooring is high humidity or water. Don't bring the flooring lumber into the house until the house is closed-in and the wet jobs such as plastering and painting have been completed. Humidity must be controlled between 30 and 55 percent RH and temperature should be within 15°F of the normal anticipated house temperature. Never open the packages of flooring until you are ready to install them. Subfloors for hardwood flooring are usually ¾″ × 4″ or ¾″ × 6″ square edged kiln dried boards (No. 1 or No. 2

grade) laid at 45° angles, spaced ¼″ apart, and secured with 10d common or coated nails twice at every bearing. However, plywood (½″ actual thickness or heavier) in 4′ × 8′ panels with surface

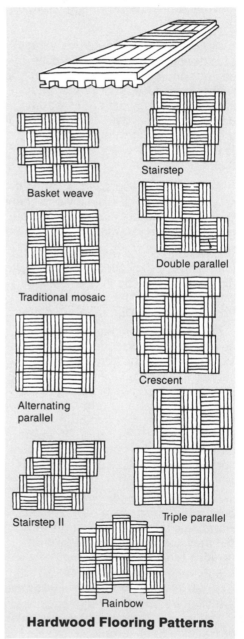

Basket weave

Stairstep

Traditional mosaic

Double parallel

Alternating parallel

Crescent

Stairstep II

Triple parallel

Rainbow

Hardwood Flooring Patterns

grain at right angles to joists and having exterior glue lines can be used. Leave 1/8" space between panels and stagger end joints 4'. Use 8d or 10d common nails on all bearings, spaced 6-8" apart.

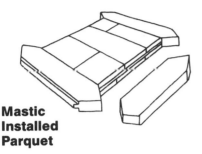

Mastic Installed Parquet

Hardwood floors can be installed over concrete slabs that have been poured on top of a polyethylene ground cover. One method is to lay dry, chemically treated wood screeds or sleepers in mastic and cover with polyethylene before attaching flooring. If there is uncertainty over the base ground cover, the concrete can be covered with 4 mil or thicker polyethylene film lapped 4" at edges and with sleepers fastened to the slab with powder-activated fasteners. Use a latex leveling compound if the floor is not flat. Parquet flooring is glued in place, making it easier for the do-it-yourselfer to install.

Finishing and sanding should not begin less than 1 to 3 weeks after the installation is completed and only if all interior work has been completed.

Hardwood flooring is finished end-matched (EM) and tongue-and-groove (T&G) or as square-edge (SE) strip flooring or parquet flooring suitable for laying in a mastic base. Note that with T&G the installed width will be *less* than the designated plank width.

Hardwood flooring is graded under rules of the Maple Flooring Manufacturers Association (MFMA), the National Oak Flooring Manufacturers Association (NOFMA), and the Oak Flooring Institute (OFI).

NOFMA/OFI Guide to Hardwood Flooring Grades

Appearance alone determines the grades of hardwood flooring since all grades are equally strong and serviceable in any application. Oak, the most popular of the hardwoods, has four basic grades. Flooring that is practically free of defects and made up mostly of heartwood is known as "Clear," though it still may contain minor imperfections. "Select" is almost clear, but this grade contains more of the natural characteristics such as knots and color variations. The "Common" grades have more markings than either of the other two grades and

Standard Sizes

Nominal	Actual
Tongue-and-Groove—End Matched	
3/4" × 2 1/4"	3/4" × 2 1/4"
3/4" × 1 1/2"	3/4" × 1 1/2"
1/2" × 2"†	15/32" × 2"
1/2" × 1 1/2"†	15/32" × 1 1/2"
Limited Production	
3/4" × 3 1/4"	3/4" × 3 1/4"

Plank Sizes
3/4" × 3", 4", 5", 6", 7", 8" Few manufacture
†Chiefly available on West Coast only.

Special Order Sizes

Nominal	Actual
Tongue-and-Groove—End Matched	
3/4" × 2"	3/4" × 2"
3/8" × 2"	11/32" × 2"
3/8" × 1 1/2"	11/32" × 1 1/2"
Square-Edge	
5/16" × 2"	5/16" × 2"
5/16" × 1 1/2"	5/16" × 1 1/2"

Flooring

National Oak Flooring Manufacturers Association Standards

Unfinished Oak Flooring (Red & White Separated)	Unfinished Beech, Birch & Hard Maple
CLEAR **APPEARANCE:** Best grade, most uniform color, limited small character marks. **BUNDLES:** 1¼′ and up. **AVERAGE LENGTH:** 3¾′.	**FIRST GRADE** **APPEARANCE:** Best appearance, natural color variation, limited character marks, unlimited sap. Maple face is all bright sapwood. Red beech and birch face is all red heartwood. **BUNDLES:** 2′ and up. 2′ and 3′ lengths comprise up to 33% of footage.
SELECT **APPEARANCE:** Excellent, limited character marks, unlimited sap, sound **BUNDLES:** 1¼′ and up. **AVERAGE LENGTH:** 3¼′.	**SECOND GRADE** **APPEARANCE:** Variegated, varying sound wood characteristics of species. **BUNDLES:** 2′ and up. 2′ and 3′ lengths comprise up to 45% of footage.
NO. 1 COMMON **APPEARANCE:** Light and dark colors; knots, flags, wormholes and other character marks allowed to provide a variegated appearance after imperfections are filled and finished. **BUNDLES:** 1¼′ and up. **AVERAGE LENGTH:** 2¾′.	**THIRD GRADE** **APPEARANCE:** Rustic; all wood characteristics of species. Serviceable, economical floor after filling. **BUNDLES:** 1¼′ and up. 1¼′ to 3′ lengths comprise up to 65% of footage.
NO. 2 COMMON **APPEARANCE:** Rustic; all wood characteristics of species. A serviceable, economical floor after knotholes, wormholes, checks, and other imperfections are filled and finished. **BUNDLES:** 1¼′ and up. **AVERAGE LENGTH:** 2¼′.	

NOTES:
1. A brief grade description, for comparison only. NOFMA flooring is bundled by averaging the lengths. A bundle may include pieces from 6 inches under to 6 inches over the nominal length of the bundle. No piece shorter than 9 inches admitted. The percentages under 4′ referred to apply on total footage in any one shipment of the time. ¾ inch added to face length when measuring length of each piece.
2. NESTED FLOORING is random length flooring bundled end to end continuously in 8′ long (nominal) bundles. OAK grade requirements apply.

are often specified because of these natural features and the character they bring to the installation. Grades are sometimes combined (i.e., Select and better) and special combinations are made for "shorts" (the short pieces produced in manufacturing in excess of grade requirements).

Special order flooring, usually the best quality or wider planks, must be ordered several weeks ahead of need and will be more expensive. In using wide planks, 6″, 7″, and 8″, sometimes necessary for authentic renovation

Unfinished Pecan Flooring	Prefinished Oak Flooring (Red & White Separated, graded after finishing)
FIRST GRADE **APPEARANCE:** Excellent, natural color variation, limited character marks, unlimited sap. **BUNDLES:** 2' and up. 2' and 3' lengths comprise up to 25% of footage.	**PRIME** **APPEARANCE:** Excellent appearance, natural color variation, limited character marks, unlimited sap. **BUNDLES:** 1¼' and up. **AVERAGE LENGTH:** 3½'.
SECOND GRADE **APPEARANCE:** Variegated, varying sound wood characteristics of species. **BUNDLES:** 1¼' and up. 1¼' to 3' lengths comprise up to 40% of footage.	**STANDARD GRADE** **APPEARANCE:** Variegated, varying sound wood characteristics of species. **BUNDLES:** 1¼' and up. **AVERAGE LENGTH:** 2¾'.
THIRD GRADE **APPEARANCE:** Rustic; all wood characteristics of species. A serviceable, economical floor after filling. **BUNDLES:** 1¼' and up. 1¼' to 3' lengths comprise up to 60% of footage.	**TAVERN GRADE** **APPEARANCE:** Rustic appearance; all wood characteristics of species. A serviceable, economical floor. **BUNDLES:** 1¼' and up. **AVERAGE LENGTH:** 2¼'.

3. Short pieces of unfinished oak flooring (9" to 18" long—averaging 15") can be ordered as 1¼' SHORTS. (Red & white may be mixed) Specify the wood grade desired (NO. 2 COMMON SHORTS).
4. Wood grades can be mixed by special order. For example, ordering unfinished beech flooring as "THIRD AND BETTER GRADE" will provide a combination of FIRST, SECOND, and THIRD grade wood with 1¼' to 3' lengths comprising up to 50% of the footage.
5. Check with your local supplier for grade and species available.

work, one must be aware of the possibility of considerable expansion or contraction with individual planks between dry winter and humid summer conditions. Cracks can, and most likely will, develop during the winter, and conversely a slight cupping during the summer season may occur. Use of standard ¾" × 2¼" or ¾" × 1½" flooring will help avoid these problems associated with wide temperature and humidity changes.

Flooring

Nail Schedule

Tongue-and-groove flooring must be blind nailed.

$3/4'' \times 1\frac{1}{2}''$, $2\frac{1}{4}''$, $3\frac{1}{4}''$	2″ machine driven fasteners, 7d or 8d screw or cut nail.	10″ to 12″ apart*
$3/4'' \times 3''$ to $8''**$ Plank	2″ machine driven fasteners, 7d or 8d screw or cut nail.	8″apart into and between joists

Following flooring must be laid on a subfloor.

$1/2'' \times 1\frac{1}{2}''$ and 2″	1½″ machine driven fastener, 5d screw, cut steel or wire casing nail.	10″ apart
$3/8'' \times 1\frac{1}{2}''$ and 2″	1¼″ machine driven fastener, or 4d bright wire casing nail.	8″ apart

Square-edge flooring face nailed—through top face.

$5/16'' \times 1\frac{1}{2}''$ and 2″	1″, 15 gauge, fully barbed flooring brad.	2 nails every 7 inches.
$5/16'' \times 1\frac{1}{3}''$	1″, 15 gauge, fully barbed flooring brad.	1 nail every 5 inches on alternate sides of strip.
$3/4'' \times 3''$ to $8''**$ Plank	2″ machine driven fasteners, 7d screws, or 8d cut nails.	8″ apart—alternate sides of strip into and between joists

*If subfloor is ½″ plywood (actual thickness), fasten into each joist, with additional fastening between.
**Plank Flooring over 4″ wide must be installed over a subfloor.

Resilient Flooring

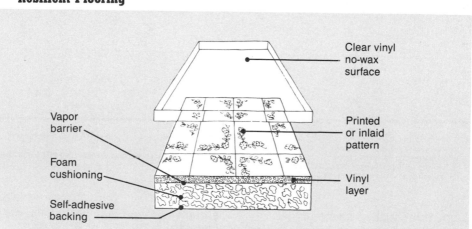

Clear vinyl no-wax surface

Vapor barrier

Foam cushioning

Self-adhesive backing

Printed or inlaid pattern

Vinyl layer

Taped Vinyl Flexible Flooring

Flooring

The term *resilient flooring* is used to describe products like linoleum and asbestos cement tile. Today linoleum is no longer being manufactured in the USA. Virtually all resilient flooring today is made of vinyl, in the form of sheets or tiles. Vinyl flooring is most often installed in kitchens, bathrooms, foyers, and laundry rooms because it's easily kept clean with a warm-water mopping.

Sheet vinyl flooring comes in rolls of 6' and 12' widths. If your room is shorter than 12' in one direction, you can install new flooring in one piece and avoid seams. Floors larger than 12' in both directions will require cutting and bonding two pieces together to form a seam. If done carefully, the seam can be made nearly invisible.

Sheet vinyl is available in a variety of qualities. The lowest-priced floorings are thin and lightweight. Their designs are printed on the surface of the flooring, then covered with a clear vinyl. The best "no-wax" finish can begin to dull after a few years of foot traffic and may require an occasional application of vinyl dressing—a better option than the weekly waxing needed to maintain linoleum.

Low-priced floorings, because of their thinness and flexibility, are easy to install and are usually marketed to do-it-yourselfers. In some cases they are installed by laying directly on the floor, then trimming to fit the space. They are flexible enough to be curved over a cant strip at the wall's edge and extended up the wall a few inches to provide splash molding, if that is desired. They can be "loose-laid"— i.e., simply laid flat and not glued to the subfloor. Their disadvantages, however, are that their thinness leaves them prone to tears or creases, and they may mirror the irregularities of the subfloor; they can be ruined if heavy appliances are moved carelessly across them.

Individual Tiles

Higher-priced sheet vinyl is much thicker and heavier and usually has a thick resilient foam layer. Some varieties have a high gloss "wet look" surface. The designs on these product lines are "inlaid"—i.e., the colors penetrate deeply into the material. These floorings are less flexible. They are glued down, then embedded in the adhesive. To assure good adhesion, professionals use a 150-pound roller.

Creating A Splash Molding With Vinyl Flooring

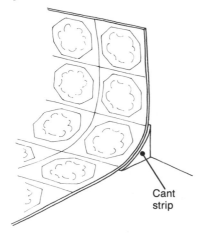

Cant strip

Flooring

Because of installation difficulties, your best bet is to hire a professional installer.

The disadvantage of requiring professional installation may be outweighed by the advantages of higher-priced sheet vinyl—richer colors and patterns (often embossed), a more durable material, and a higher-quality surface coating.

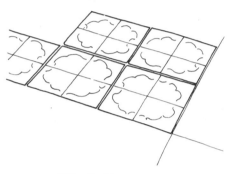

Tile Patterns

Vinyl flooring is also available in tiles, usually 12″ square, which are either set in adhesive or supplied with a self-sticking backing under peel-off paper. While easy to lay, the joints allow spills to penetrate and soften the adhesive, and the tiles tend to stretch and shrink with changes in temperature and humidity. If the room gets cold, the tiles may shrink, opening the joints to catch dirt. On the other hand, if a single tile gets stained, it can be replaced. Suitable for playrooms, dens, and passageways, vinyl tiles would not be the best choice for bathrooms or kitchens.

All vinyl floor covering can be stained with hair dyes, petrochemicals, animal stains, and fruit juices. Never use a rubber doormat on vinyl or track in driveway sealer or carpet dye on your shoes—the stain becomes permanent. However, most spills can be wiped up without staining. Some stains can be sanded off and a vinyl topcoat sponged on to renew the surface.

Vinyl flooring can be applied over old resilient flooring but not over flooring containing a foam layer. Vinyl flooring can be attached to an existing wood floor *if* the surface is clean and sanded. It may be easier to install a new layer of ¼″ plywood over the old flooring before installing the new surface. Ceramic tile does not make a good base.

Finally, do not try to remove old resilient flooring or its backing or lining felt. The old flooring may contain asbestos, and chipping or sanding it will release asbestos fibers into the air. It's much safer to lay the new flooring on top of the old, but a latex leveling compound should be used over worn areas to make the surface smooth and level.

Ceramic Tiles

In the 1980s, homeowners have discovered ceramic tile. Sales have been increasing 25 percent per year.

Ceramic tiles are usually used in damp or high-traffic areas of the home: kitchens, baths, and foyers. They are also used on vertical surfaces around or behind sinks, tubs, and showers. Although ceramic tiles are higher priced than vinyl, they are more elegant, are fire- and heat-proof and far more permanent. While vinyl floors may last five or ten years, tile will last as long as the house, so in the long run it may be more cost-effective. Tiles clean with a wipe, resist stains, and show no signs of aging.

Low-cost tiles are commonly imported from Mexico, where, because of lower natural gas prices, manufacturers can bake them for less.

Italy, England, Holland, Portugal, and France supply tiles with motifs and scenes that are distinctive in design. However, unless these match the dimensions of the area to be covered, they may not work for you. And if you need a replacement tile later, you may have difficulty locating a match.

Consider using the well-known U.S. brands. Besides, American tile manufacturers provide trim with their tile; European tile manufacturers do not. The Americans also supply matching soap dishes, towel hangers, grab bars, and toilet paper holders. These are matched to the tile sizes so they can be put in place without having to cut tiles.

Laying Ceramic Tiles

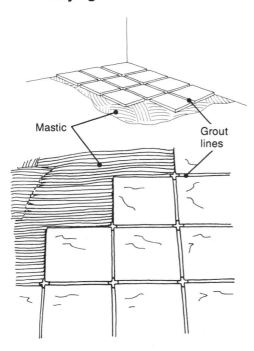

Mastic

Grout lines

The once-standard 4" squares are giving way to new 6", 8", and even 12" squares, which are faster to install and require fewer grout lines. While earth tones are still the favorites, new

applications on walls and counters have led to demand for pastels and brightly painted tiles. New waterproof and stain-resistant colored grouts are now available. Even the standard smooth texture of the tiles has changed. Pebbled and gritty surfaces are now available, which reduce the chance of slipping. Imports are not made to standard sizes and must be laid out in place and matched before grouting to prevent wavy grout lines.

Tiles are either glazed or unglazed. Unglazed tiles are merely fire-hardened clay, called bisque, and have a natural rocky patina. There are four types: terra-cotta, clinker, vitrified, and red stoneware. *Terra-cotta* are thick, brick-colored tiles and come plain or polished. They have been used for kitchen and patio floors for centuries in the southern United States and in countries like Italy and Mexico. *Red stoneware* comes from Italy and is a vitrified tile with resistance to abrasion, chemicals, and frost. *Fully vitrified stoneware,* more often called porcelain or china-tile, is colored by the addition of mineral oxides and either polished or coated with a thin layer of glass. *Clinker tiles* are hardly distinguishable from red stoneware except for the metal oxides used to provide a variety of colors.

Glazed tile is bisque with a glaze applied. Decals, hand paintings, or silk screen designs are applied after initial baking and the glaze is fused over the top in a second pass through the kilns. These double-fired tiles are available in great variety. The most popular is *monocottura,* baked at 2250°F, which can be used indoors or out. *Majolica* is a smooth yellow-pink bisque usually used indoors. *Cottoforte* is a pink-red bisque that takes well to glazing and decoration and is used chiefly indoors. *White-body earthenware,* being a white

Flooring

clay bisque, takes color well and is usually covered with a transparent glaze.

There are four basic categories of ceramic tile:

Quarry tiles are made of clay, not stone, and usually come in an unglazed, red clay color but can be bought with glazed coatings as well. Sizes and thicknesses vary, but large sizes, up to 12″ square, are most common. Styles range from smooth and clean-cut to tiles with rounded edges to uneven surfaces that impart a rugged overall look. They can be coated with a silicone sealer to protect them and the grout from staining.

Pavers are commonly unglazed, rugged tiles, much like quarry tile. Common sizes are 4″ × 4″, 6″ × 6″, and 4″ × 8″.

Imported *patio tiles* are thicker and even less regular in shape than quarry tiles or pavers. They absorb water easily and can shatter if frozen, so should be installed outdoors only in warm climates. American patio stones are made with cement and are not fired in a kiln.

Glazed tiles come in hundreds of different sizes, shapes, and colors. Small glazed tiles less than 2″ × 2″ are called mosaic tiles. Once laid individually, mosaic tiles now are sold mounted and spaced on a backing of mesh, paper, or rubber. Glazed tiles are slippery when wet. If you're planning to install them in a bathroom, choose a textured or matte surface to reduce the chance of accidents.

Glazed tiles are not generally used for floors, as foot traffic can wear through the glaze. Unglazed tiles are the same color all the way through and are a better choice, since they will last for many years.

You can lay tiles over most existing floors—wood, concrete, noncushioned

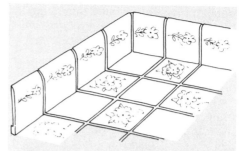

Glazed tile

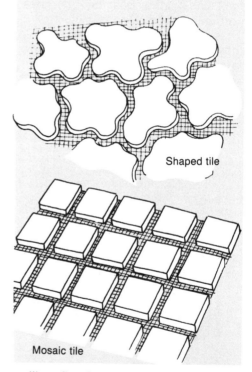

Shaped tile

Mosaic tile

resilient flooring, or old ceramic tile. Just be sure the flooring is strong, dry, level, and clean. You may need to use a latex leveling compound. All baseboard trim, toilets, heating registers, and doors must be removed first; the bottoms of doors may need planing to accommodate the raised floor level.

Tiling a kitchen floor creates a unique problem, as raising the floor level may make it impossible to remove, repair, or replace under-the-counter appliances such as dishwashers and ovens. One solution is to raise the entire cabinet and counter by the thickness of the tile.

The traditional way to lay tile is to set it in an inch-thick bed of cement called "thick-bed" or "mudset." This method is effective when laying tile over an uneven concrete slab or when laying very irregular tiles, but it usually requires the skill of a professional installer. Also, the structure has to be designed to take the added weight.

If you want to install the tiles yourself, there are three basic "thin-bed" or "thin-set" adhesives to use: mastics, epoxies, and cement-based adhesives. Glass-mesh mortar units can also be used as a base, particularly over poor surfaces. Consult your tile supplier for the type of adhesive you should buy and instructions for its use.

The cracks between tiles are filled with grout. Grouts can be cement-based, epoxy-based, or silicone rubber. Cement-based grouts are the most common and can be colored with additives. The grout you choose depends on the type of tile, its location, the size of the gap between tiles, and the type of adhesive. Again, consult your tile supplier.

If installing tile yourself, your tile supplier also is likely to rent (or supply for free) the proper installation tools.

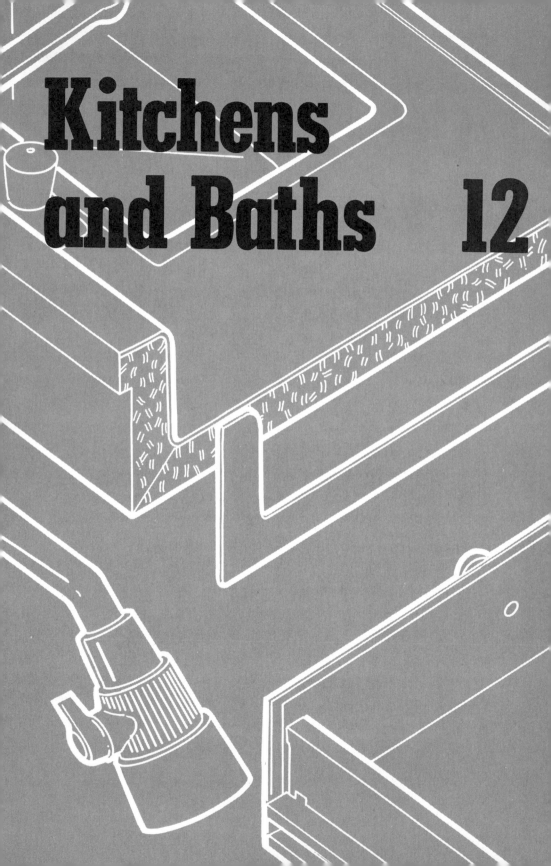

Kitchens and Baths 12

12. Kitchens and Baths

A brand-new kitchen, a brand-new bathroom: two rooms guaranteed to generate excitement, especially now. In the last decade, new products and innovative styles have changed the appearance, the substance, even the role of these rooms. Among the changes: whirlpool baths, European cabinetry, solid laminates for counter tops, sinks in a profusion of shapes and colors, and the expanded use of ceramic tile.

Maybe you're planning a remodeling job to incorporate these changes. If so, plan to spend $1,500 to $2,000 for new bathroom fixtures, $5,000 to $7,000 for a complete revision by a contractor, and $15,000 or more if you want to expand your current 5′ × 8′ cubicle into a "superbath" complete with a large whirlpool tub, stylish tile work, and the best cabinetry. Kitchen remodeling can be just as expensive: New cabinets alone are $2,000 to $4,000, and a complete redo costs from $8,000 to $15,000 or more. The good news is that when you sell your home you'll recover 70 to 100 percent of the cost of adding a new bathroom, 45 to 55 percent of the cost of remodeling a bathroom, and 60 to 100 percent of the cost of a new kitchen (according to a study conducted by *Remodeling World* magazine).

Baths

The typical bathtub is 16″ high, 29″ to 32″ wide, and 5′ long—a length that accounts for the standardized 5′ × 8′ bathroom.

Bathtubs are also made in other shapes and sizes and are available with accessories such as whirlpool pumps, flexible shower hoses, and grab bars. The three most common basic materials are cast iron and stamped steel—both ceramic coated— and glass fiber-reinforced plastic.

The cast iron tub is very heavy, solid and durable, and the most expensive of the three types. The stamped sheet steel tub is about half the weight of the cast iron tub and noticeably more flexible.

Fiberglass Tubs

Fiberglass, or more accurately, fiberglass-reinforced plastic tubs are priced to be competitive with steel tubs. The advantages of the material used are that it is unaffected by water so it cannot rot or rust, is malleable and thus permits soap dishes and shelves to be molded into the matching fiberglass tub surrounds without any edges to leak or gather mold, and is lightweight and thus easy to install. The typical fiberglass tub weighs only 40 to 50 pounds.

There is a big difference between fiberglass tubs made by spraying glass and resin on a mold with a glossy acrylic surface and those that are pressure-molded with a harder polyester, nonslip, softly textured surface. The acrylic fixtures are available in glamorous designs and bright colors, but some are dangerously slippery when wet and require nonslip strips that detract from their appearance, comfort, and cleanability. Look for tubs that have slip-resistant bottoms.

Fiberglass-reinforced plastic pressure molded tubs are made on giant 3,000-ton presses that mold the supporting ribs to form a single, sturdy, rigid unit. The color goes all the way through, so if the tub is nicked before or after installation, it can be invisibly repaired in place. These tubs are available in colors to match most of the standard ceramic bathroom fixtures. Whirlpool bath models are also available. Follow the manufacturer's directions when cleaning, because abrasives will harm the finish.

Fiberglass tubs are also available as four-piece units with a matching tub surround that fits together and is nailed at the edges to form a solid seal without the need for caulking, clips, or glue.

Oval units, with or without whirlpool fixtures, are also available.

Fiberglass units come with ten-year limited warranties; acrylic units are warrantied for lesser periods. It pays to buy from a recognized manufacturer.

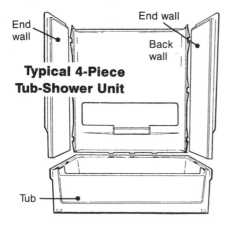

Typical 4-Piece Tub-Shower Unit

End wall
End wall
Back wall
Tub

Steel Tubs

Steel bathtubs sometimes cost less than fiberglass, but they are more difficult and costly to install. The steel has a fairly thin coat of brittle enamel. Although this enamel is commonly cleaned with abrasive cleansers, it should not be—in time, the cleanser will erode the smooth surface. Because steel is also more flexible than iron, the enamel may flake off if a heavy object is dropped on it. Unlike fiberglass tubs, you can't make invisible repairs, and tub removal for recoating may require breaking up the tile surround.

Steel tubs can be noisy when you're taking a bath in them, and will cool bathwater quicker than a fiberglass or cast iron tub. *Tip:* Install fiberglass insulation around and below the tub for sound attenuation and longer-lasting hot water.

Cast Iron Tubs

Cast iron tubs are the most expensive. They are also the most durable. The baked-on enamel finish is thicker than the enamel on steel tubs. Because a cast iron tub weighs three times as much as a steel tub, it is difficult to handle particularly when renovating a bathroom.

Whirlpool Tubs

The new *whirlpool tubs* are generally made of fiberglass or acrylic. What gives them their name, of course, are the multiple jets (from three to eight) that create a strong bubbling or swirling current. Whirlpool tubs may be as small as an average 5' bathtub or large enough to accommodate three or four people. Shapes include square, round, oval, and rectangular. Cost is about $1,000 to $3,000—more, if you select options such as underwater lights and opulent faucets.

Typical Whirlpool Tub

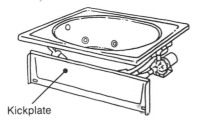

Kickplate

Tub Surrounds

Tub surrounds with acrylic and fiberglass bathtubs sometimes come complete with walls and domes. Some domes are equipped with holes for overhead lighting. Built-in seats, grab bars, and soap dishes are often part of the mold. One-piece tub surrounds are usually suitable only for new construction and, due to their size, must be installed before interior walls are built. For existing homes you can buy four-piece kits.

3-Piece Tub Surround For 4-Piece Tub Shower

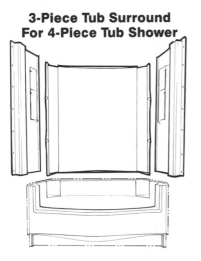

Tile walls add a touch of luxury, but mold growth on the grouting makes them difficult to maintain. However, for an island tub with steps and surrounding walls, tiles are attractive and may justify the extra effort to keep the grout clean and dry. *Tip:* A watercolor paint brush and a transparent penetrating liquid sealer can be applied to the mortar after it has cured for thirty days or more.

Shower Stalls

One-piece, two-piece, and four-piece *shower stalls* run the gamut from inexpensive enameled galvanized steel with a fiberglass base to press-molded fiberglass-reinforced plastic, in 36" and 48" widths. Glass doors—sliding, folding, or swinging—or plastic curtains have to be purchased and installed separately.

Bidets

When shopping for bathroom fixtures you may see an unfamiliar object. The bidet is used primarily for washing one's private parts. Its basin provides both hot and cold water, plus a spray or water jet. Standard equipment around the world from Paris to Tokyo, the utility and sanitary convenience of a bidet is now gaining appreciation and acceptance here in the USA. A bidet is suitable for large bathrooms and comes in colors to match other fixtures. Plumbing is required for hot and cold water lines plus a drain.

Bidet

Kitchens and Baths

Cabinets

With some 6,000 manufacturers of kitchen cabinets in America today, you can count on one thing: variety. There's a wide range of styles, materials, quality, and price to choose from.

Cabinets are either factory-made or custom-made. Factory-made units may come from large, nationally (or internationally) known firms or a local shop. Unless they are custom ordered, they will be made to standard sizes. Standard sizing, such as the height of base cabinets, assures a fit with dishwashers and other standard appliances. The advantage of factory-made cabinets is that you can see what you're getting before you buy it. One sign of durability is the performance seal of the National Kitchen Cabinet Association (NKCA).

The advantage of custom-made cabinets, on the other hand, is that your kitchen may not accommodate standard sizes or *you* may not fit with standard sizes. If you're shorter or taller than average and want counter tops you can work at comfortably, custom cabinetry offers you optional cabinet and counter heights and sizes. Custom cabinetry also offers you the option of using special woods or unique designs. Before you hire a cabinetmaker to do a custom kitchen, be sure to visit his past work.

Traditional wood cabinets are still two-thirds of the cabinetry sold today. Those of the highest quality are called "furniture grade." They will be built with ¾" hardwood, mortise-and-tenon joinery, braced corners, the best hardware, and dovetailed or V-lap joints connecting drawer frames to their fronts. As you go down in price, you'll find the wood to be thinner or replaced with particle board. Interiors will have rougher finishes, shelf and drawer hardware will be plastic instead of metal, and drawer components will be connected with staples and glue.

European cabinets were introduced to the American consumer in the late 1970s. These cabinets are known for their "clean" look of plastic-laminate doors covering the full face of each cabinet. Behind that look is a different construction method: There is no front frame on the cabinet, on which the door is hung with visible hinges. Instead, the door is hung directly on the cabinet with concealed hinges. And drawers have noticeably more space.

Typical Kitchen Using Traditional Wood Cabinets

National Kitchen Cabinet Association Performance Seal

European design has now been taken up by domestic manufacturers, so you don't need to buy imports, which tend to cost more. The better European cabinets have thicker sides, denser particle board beneath the laminate, and seamless edges.

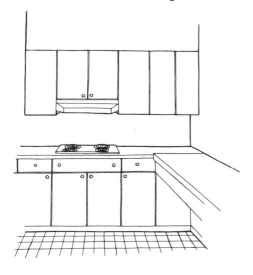

European Design Cabinets
(Notice—Doors Cover Full Cabinet Face)

Counter Tops

Most kitchen and bath counter tops are made of a *plastic laminate* that is glued to a core material such as plywood, oriented-strand board, or particle board. In addition, ceramic tile and "butcher block" counters have become increasingly popular.

Recently, plastic laminates have been introduced that contain the surface color throughout the material. The solid color eliminates the dark line at the counter's edge where two pieces meet at right angles. Another advantage is that surface scratches and nicks are less noticeable. Solid-color laminates can be beveled, routed, and contoured. They can also be stacked and glued; when different colors are stacked together, this can produce a "racing stripe" of different colors at a beveled counter edge.

Another popular counter top product is *synthetic marble*. There are two types: DuPont Corian, a mineral-filled acrylic plastic, is 30″ wide and up to 10′ long. It comes in ¼″, ½″, and ¾″ thicknesses, but only the latter two thicknesses should be used for counter

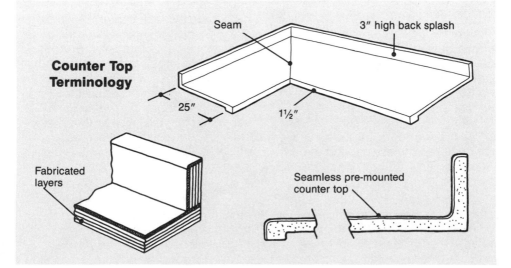

Counter Top Terminology

Seam

3″ high back splash

25″

1½″

Fabricated layers

Seamless pre-mounted counter top

tops. It's attached with a neoprene-based adhesive and can be cut, drilled, and routed with carbide-tip tools. Much heavier than tile, the ¾" material weighs 5½ pounds per square foot and requires strong support. It comes in white, almond, and a swirled pattern of white and soft gray.

Similarly, *synthetic cultured marble* is a counter top material made with marble chips embedded in polyester with a heavy clear polyester coating. It has to be factory cut to your dimensions or purchased in precut standard sizes. Cultured onyx looks and feels like real stone but is very expensive.

An innovation in plastic counter tops goes by the brand names *Color-Core®* and *Solicore®*. These form the counter so do not require a wood base. They attach to the top of the cabinet framing, can be cut out for sinks and edges, and can be decoratively routed to reveal a contrasting color. They resist heat, though not to the high temperatures resisted by tile, and are unaffected by hot dishes or kettles being placed on them. They are easy to clean and can be used as cutting boards. They resist staining except from petrochemicals.

Regular plastic laminates are sold by the square foot. The material for counter tops is ¹⁄₁₆" thick and brittle. Standard widths are 24", 30", 36", 38", and 60" (usually slightly oversized so you can cut two 18" pieces out of a 36" width). Lengths are 60", 72", 84", 96", 120", and 144". They are installed with contact adhesive applied to both the coreboard and the back of the laminate.

Preformed laminate counter tops can be purchased in a variety of widths and in 8', 10', and 12' lengths with preformed end pieces to cover the end cuts. These counter tops can be ordered in one-piece preassembled "L" shapes, but make sure they'll fit through the door. Selection is not as broad as for individual laminates, but you may save precious laminate if you are not experienced in cutting, gluing, and beveling. You can make cutouts for sinks or appliances.

Ceramic tile is attractive, tough, easy to clean, and a timeless favorite. While the standard tile for kitchen counters and bathroom vanities is 4¼" × 4¼", some decorative and imported tiles come in 5", 8", or larger squares. Each 10' row of 4¼" tile will require thirty-nine tiles. You may need a cove base and edging cap for the back of the counter, and bull-nosed edge tile for the front. A variety of these trim tiles are available for corners and other uses. Before adhering tile, lay it out in the proposed pattern to check alignment; tile sizes often vary from their given dimension.

Tile will adhere to moisture-resistant gypsum board, hardboard, or Exterior-grade plywood (*not* particle board). You'll need an organic tile adhesive such as latex mastic, but check with your supplier to make sure the one you have selected is suitable. You'll need grout. Some thirty days after the grout has set, you should paint over it with a penetrating liquid sealer, using a small watercolor brush. This will help prevent the grout from becoming discolored by mildew, mold, or dirt. You can use separate tiles, but choose those with self-spacing tabs to make your job easier, or ask your supplier for plastic spacers.

For tools, you'll need a homemade measuring stick with desired tile spacing marked, a notched-edge trowel, a portable *saber saw* with plenty of *carbide grit* blades, dry cloths, a rubber-faced grouting tool, a sponge, a squeegee, tile nippers, tile cutter. You'll also need a 3′ length of 2″ × 4″ lumber wrapped in carpet and a rubber or wooden mallet for leveling the tiles. If you don't have the tools, you can probably rent them from your tile supplier. If you are using unglazed tile and plan to seal it (wait three days), you'll need a polyurethane sealer and a sponge mop.

Faucets

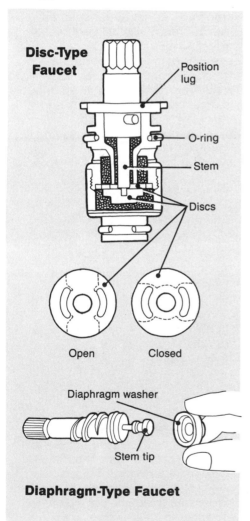

Disc-Type Faucet

Position lug

O-ring

Stem

Discs

Open   Closed

Diaphragm washer

Stem tip

Diaphragm-Type Faucet

Washerless faucets now are the most common type of faucet for the home. Their popularity stems from greatly reduced leakage problems and their relative ease of repair. Washerless faucets use either a rubber diaphragm or two metal discs with holes that allow water flow when holes are aligned and shear off flow when they are separated. The control mechanism is often contained in a cartridge, which can be replaced if necessary.

Repair parts for washerless faucets are available individually or in sets. In this type faucet, the seats normally wear out, usually the hot water side first. Replacement seats, O-rings, diverter valves, handles, balls, and cam assemblies are available. Complete cylinder valve assemblies are also available, if required.

Compression Faucet

Water flow in a compression faucet is regulated by turning a lever or knob attached to a threaded spindle. Turning the spindle clockwise normally presses a washer, attached to the lower end of the spindle, against a ground seat, which surrounds the flow opening, to stop water flow. If the washer and seat

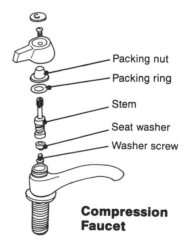

Packing nut

Packing ring

Stem

Seat washer

Washer screw

Compression Faucet

Kitchens and Baths

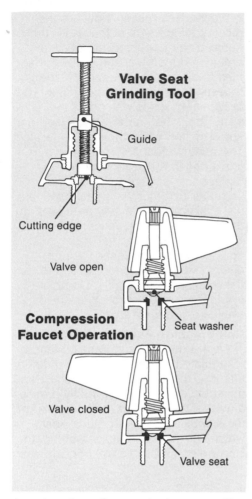

Valve Seat Grinding Tool

Guide

Cutting edge

Valve open

Compression Faucet Operation

Seat washer

Valve closed

Valve seat

and the spout. Rocking the lever positions the ball openings to control the water temperature and flow at the spout. Although the ball can be replaced (replacement parts are available), worn inlet valve gaskets or springs are normally the cause for leaks in this type faucet.

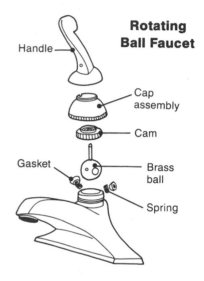

Rotating Ball Faucet

Handle

Cap assembly

Cam

Gasket

Brass ball

Spring

Cartridge-Type Faucet

A cartridge-type faucet has a cylindrical brass plunger or plug that fits snugly into a sleeve bored vertically through the body of the faucet. The plunger, which is rotated by a handle, has holes or a slot bored horizontally through the body of the faucet. Vertical movement of the handle raises or lowers the plunger, controlling water flow. Rotational movement (turning) of the handle controls water temperature.

The plunger or its sleeve may become grooved or worn by sand particles rubbing against the metal and allow water to leak through. The cartridge is normally replaced as an assembly. In this case, an O-ring can be replaced to stop leaks around the valve handle.

do not make a firm contact, water will leak from the faucet spout.

Normally leaks are caused by a worn washer or corroded seat. Most compression faucets have replaceable washers and seats, and replacement seats and washers are readily available. Seats that are not removable can be resurfaced with faucet-seat dressing tools.

Rotating Ball Faucet

Another type of faucet is the rotating ball faucet. This type faucet consists of a ball with openings that can be aligned with hot and cold inlet valves

Cartridge-Type Faucet

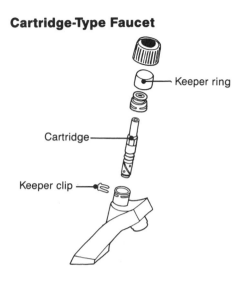

Keeper ring

Cartridge

Keeper clip

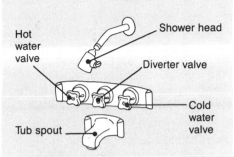

Hot water valve

Shower head

Diverter valve

Tub spout

Cold water valve

Three-Valve Tub And Shower Faucets

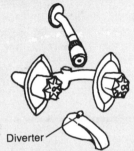

Diverter

Two-Valve Tub And Shower w/Diverter On Tub Spout

Single-Lever Mixing Valve

Faucet Deliver System

Mixing or *single-lever* faucets are produced by a number of manufacturers in the form of swing-spout kitchen faucets, lavatory faucets, and three types of bath faucets. They ordinarily operate by pushing the upright lever straight backward for a 50-50 opening of hot and cold water, back and to the right for cold, and back and to the left for hot water. They have the advantage of being quick opening and closing, and nearly all have complete repair kits. These are mostly ball- or cartridge-type faucets.

Automatic mixing valves maintain water temperature, automatically correcting changes caused by turning on other faucets in the system. Thermostatic safety valves protect against sudden bursts of hot or cold water and are recommended for showers.

Combination faucets mix hot and cold water in a single spout. They are grouped in four categories: tub and shower, lavatory, kitchen deck, and laundry.

Tub and shower faucets are normally sold in sets that include the valve/valves, shower head, and tub spout, with necessary escutcheon flanges. The valves are normally built into the wall above the bathtub. These faucets are available in several patterns.

Three-valve tub and shower faucets use two valves to control water, and a

Kitchens and Baths

third diverts water either through the spout or to the shower head. Two-valve tub and shower faucets have an automatic device on the spout that, when lifted, diverts water to the shower head. The mixing-type tub and shower faucet uses a center control knob or lever with a diverter valve to control water temperature and flow.

Faucet Mounting

Bathroom wash basin faucets are available in several patterns. A ledge-mounted faucet is mounted on either the lavatory or counter top in a horizontal position. The standard faucets are made with 4″ centers, but some faucets are made with alternate center measurements up to 12″.

Another type is called the "shelf-back" and is mounted vertically. Center measurements on these faucets vary with the manufacturer.

Faucet Types

Ledge-mounted dual knob with waste control

Ledge-mounted single-knob mixing faucet with waste control

Ledge-mounted compression faucet without waste control

Normally the control knobs for kitchen sink faucets are located on 8″ centers, with spacing of 6″ and 4″ available on special order. Kitchen deck faucets are available in a variety of patterns. *Concealed faucets* are mounted underneath the sink with only handle flanges and spout visible. *Exposed faucets* are mounted on top of the sink, with or without sprays.

Three-hole concealed faucet without spray

Three-hole faucet without spray

Four-hole exposed faucets with spray

Four-hole concealed faucet with spray

Three-hole concealed faucet

Contemporary Faucets

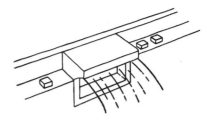

The water rainbow by Jacuzzi has a waterfall spout.

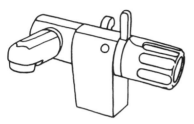

High-tech enamel over brass faucet by Abbaka

High-style European Deco-white faucet by Moen

Single-hole mixer faucet called Harmony in White by Grohe

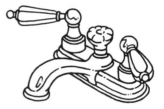

Nostalgia in brass and porcelain for the remodeler by The Broadway Collection

Swing-spout one-hole mixing faucet by Fir

24-karat gold plate with chrome handles and elegant arcing faucet provides touch of elegance. Called the Lexington by American Standard

Kitchens and Baths

Sinks

Bathroom sinks come in all shapes and sizes. Like bathtubs, they are commonly available in fiberglass, steel, or cast iron, but they also may be made of vitreous china (clay that is molded and kiln-fired). Three predominant types are the old-fashioned *wall-hung* style, the old but recently revived *pedestal* style, and the common *vanity-top* sink.

Typical Sink Types

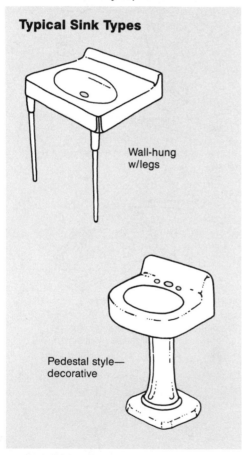

Wall-hung w/legs

Pedestal style—decorative

Vanity-Top Sink Mountings

Recessed vanity

Flush-mounted vanity

Self-rimming vanity

Vanity-top sinks—those that are set into a bathroom counter top—may be mounted in any one of three ways: recessed, flush-mounted, or self-rimming. The latter type, in which the sink rim overlaps the counter surface and rests upon it, is most common and easiest for the do-it-yourselfer to install. It covers any uneven cutting of the rough opening.

You may have seen bathroom sinks that are part of the surrounding counter top. Such sinks are called *one-piece vanity tops.* They are available in three materials: cultured marble, which is actually polyester; cultured onyx, which looks and feels more like stone but costs twice as much as cultured marble; and Corian.® Corian® is a DuPont product that looks very much like marble but can be cut, shaped, sanded, and repaired like wood.

The variety of sizes, shapes, and colors is sufficient to please everyone. You can choose from a large double-basin pedestal to a small triangular basin for that cramped half-bathroom.

Some are intentionally made small with steep sloping sides to encourage water conservation.

Kitchen sink styles have expanded in recent years. Innovative models have three bowls, each of different depth, for various uses such as dishwashing, vegetable cleaning, etc. But they are still made of three basic finishes: stainless steel or enamel over steel or cast iron.

Stainless steel is moderate in price, easy to install, and cannot rust or chip. However, despite its name, it will stain, particularly from fingerprints, and should be wiped clean after each use. It's available in three thicknesses: 18-, 20-, and 22-gauge steel (the lower the number, the thicker the metal).

Enamel may be more expensive, but its appeal is its appearance. New enamel sinks are available in bright colors. Combined with the right surrounding materials, an enamel sink can liven up a kitchen color scheme. But recognize that these sinks can chip if pans or bottles are carelessly dropped in them, and they're difficult to keep clean.

Shower Heads

Standard shower heads can be manually adjusted to vary the intensity and direction of the spray. Many feature self-cleaning rims and swivel ball joints. Quality shower heads are chrome-plated brass, while economy units are plastic.

Water-saving shower heads can save up to 50 to 75 percent of the normal amount of water used in taking a shower. Taking a shower normally uses up to 7 gallons of water per minute. Water-restricting devices can cut this amount down to 2 to 3 gallons per minute. Most units achieve this without sacrificing any comfort.

Massaging shower heads use water pressure forced through a diverting valve to create one or more pulsating water actions that bombard the body. In most cases, the amount of pulsing pressure or force can be varied manually. Massaging shower heads can be hand-held or permanently mounted to the fixture. While all offer massaging action of one or more kinds, they also are easily converted to a conventional shower action.

A *continental shower* is a versatile wall and hand shower combined. Top-quality brands feature on-off flow control built into the handle, a brass push-button diverter valve permitting instant switch from shower head to hand shower, a 6' flexible hose, and a hang-up bracket. It can be attached to existing shower arms.

Toilets

Your choice of a toilet may be predicated on price, color, appearance, water economy, quietness, flushing efficiency, ease of floor cleaning, or a combination of these features.

Most toilets are made of molded or vitreous china heavily glazed in a high temperature oven. Recently some heavily gel-coated fiberglass-reinforced plastic models have been introduced. Each manufacturer has its own color selection with matching seats and covers to coordinate with their line of sinks and tubs.

You have a choice of units with separate wall-hung tanks and floor bowls or wall-hung units, often combining tank and bowl. Some one-piece floor units are also available. The wall-hung units rely on a carrier plate that goes under the floor and up the wall. Their advantage is that they leave the floor unobstructed underneath for easier mopping. Their disadvantage

Kitchens and Baths

Toilet Tank Types

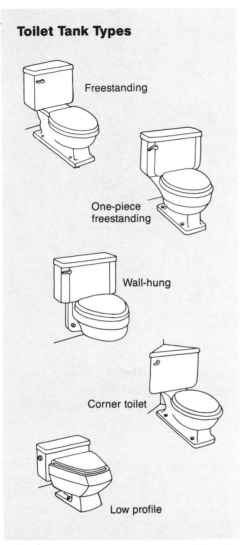

Freestanding

One-piece freestanding

Wall-hung

Corner toilet

Low profile

water tank. It needs a full tank of water to reach the sealing level in the bowl, without which sewer gas can enter the room.

Toilet Flushing Actions

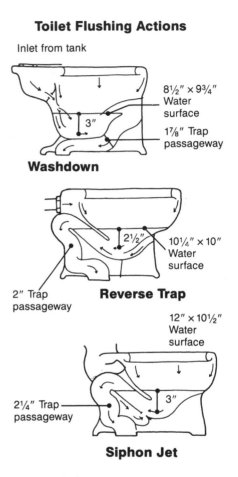

Inlet from tank

$8\frac{1}{2}" \times 9\frac{3}{4}"$ Water surface

3"

$1\frac{7}{8}"$ Trap passageway

Washdown

$2\frac{1}{2}"$

$10\frac{1}{4}" \times 10"$ Water surface

2" Trap passageway

Reverse Trap

$12" \times 10\frac{1}{2}"$ Water surface

$2\frac{1}{4}"$ Trap passageway

3"

Siphon Jet

is that changing seals is more difficult. A corner toilet with a triangular tank is also available.

There are four basic types of flushing action: the inexpensive and inefficient washdown, prohibited by some codes; the quieter reverse trap; the siphon jet and the one-piece siphon vortex. The siphon vortex has larger passages to prevent clogging and is the most efficient but prevents one from saving water by putting a dam, or brick, in the

Water saving toilets make sense, not only because water is scarce in many areas, but because sewer disposal rates are based on water consumption. By saving water you will also reduce your sewage disposal costs. Made by American Standard, Mansfield Plumbing, Villeroy and Boch, and others, these use only 3½ gallons per flush compared to the normal 5 gallons. Flushing the toilet is the single largest daily use of water in the home.

An *up-flush* toilet is available for those who wish to install a toilet in a basement that is below the sewer line. It needs 40 psi water pressure to operate.

Toilet Plumbing

Basically, every flush tank mechanism consists of two control valves. Levers and other parts merely open or close these valves.

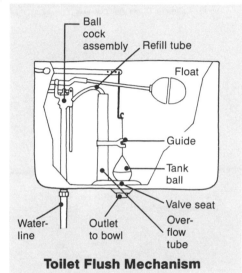

Toilet Flush Mechanism

Flapper
Replaces tank ball

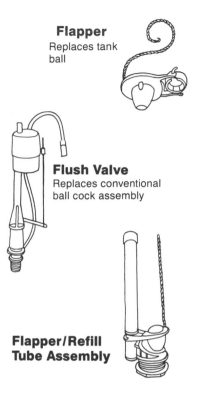

Flush Valve
Replaces conventional ball cock assembly

Flapper/Refill Tube Assembly

When the toilet is flushed, water leaves the tank at the *flush valve.* This is kept closed by a rubber *flush ball, diaphragm,* or *flapper.* When the outside handle on the toilet tank is pressed down, it raises a trip lever that pulls the flushing device off its seat. Water inside the tank pours through the opening to flush the toilet bowl.

The flushing device is held in place by water pressure; however, once the device is lifted by the trip lever, it remains off the seat by floating on top of the water until the tank is empty. As the water level drops, the flush ball or flapper gradually settles back into the opening, sealing it so the tank can refill for the next flush.

Refilling is controlled by a second valve mechanism called the *inlet valve* or *ball cock.* As the water level inside the tank drops, the hollow metal or plastic float ball drops, pulling the float arm down with it. This arm opens the inlet valve inside the ball cock and permits water from the supply line to pour into the tank through the ball cock. As rising water forces the float ball upward, it gradually shuts off the inlet valve until the flow of water is stopped entirely when the tank is full.

A refill tube squirts a small stream of water through the overflow pipe while the bowl is flushing. This refills a trap built into the toilet bowl to keep sewer gases from escaping into the house.

Kitchens and Baths

In some homes and many commercial buildings, a flush valve instead of a tank flushes the water closet bowl.

The most frequent problem involved with flush valves is leaks associated with a vacuum breaker in the valve. It is often difficult to determine just which of several seals and/or diaphragms in the valve are leaking, so it is often best to replace all internal parts. Flush valve repair kits are available, making do-it-yourself repair simple.

Ball cocks are sold in preassembled units; replacement parts are available from the manufacturer, also in prepackaged units. Replacement parts include upper lever, float rod, lower lever, plunger, valve seat, refill tube, nylon seat, eye screw, body, flush tube, regular shank, shank gasket, lock nut, coupling nut washer, riser pipe, and repair shank.

Several other devices perform the same functions as a ball cock. One is a toilet fill valve that can be mounted underwater. It measures water level from its position at the bottom of a toilet tank. As the toilet is flushed and water level falls, its internal diaphragm senses the weight of water above it. As the water level drops, the reduced pressure opens the fill valve and supply water enters.

When incoming water rises to a predetermined point (usually 8" deep), increased pressure on the diaphragm closes the valve. This system is simpler than ball cock valves because it does not need a ball float.

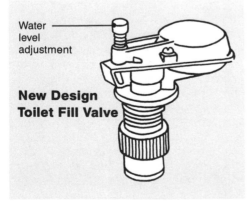

Water level adjustment

New Design Toilet Fill Valve

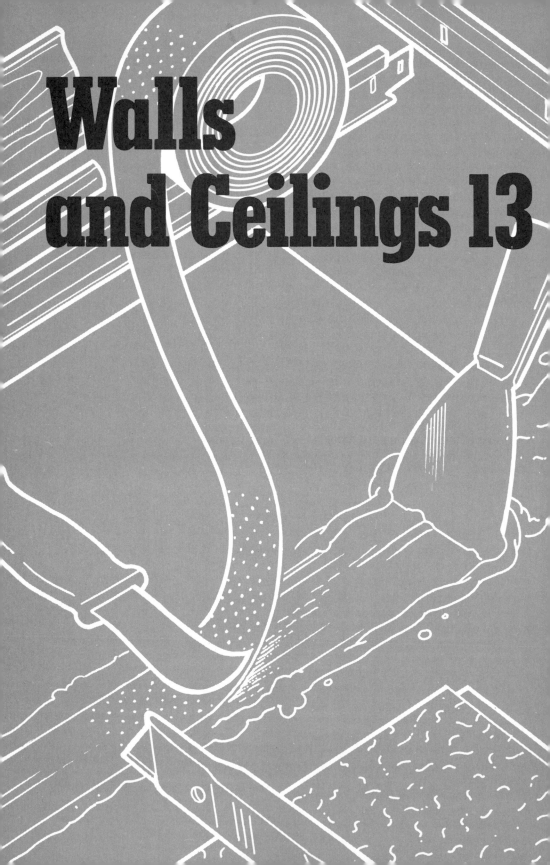

Walls
and Ceilings 13

13. Walls and Ceilings

If the only functions of walls and ceilings were to hide the plumbing and divide a house into rooms, there would be no chapter here. But as it is, entire books have been written about walls and ceilings. That's because the building materials you use to make your walls and ceilings also serve to absorb noise, reflect light, and influence your perception of space. Most of all, they are the backdrop for your decorating tastes. With them, you can change a house from dreary to delightful and make it home.

The various wall and ceiling jobs—putting up drywall, painting, hanging wallpaper, installing paneling and suspended ceilings—are tasks that many homeowners choose to tackle themselves. The easiest of these are painting, paneling, and hanging wallpaper. Putting up drywall and wiring electrical fixtures are more difficult. You may want to hire professionals for these jobs. But hire carefully, check references, and examine their work.

Gypsum Board

You may know Gypsum Board by another name: drywall, sheetrock, wallboard, or plasterboard. Whatever you call it, this is now the standard material for creating ceiling and wall surfaces. It replaced lath-and-plaster after World War II because it is lower in cost and faster to install.

Gypsum Board gets its name from its crumbly core of chalklike gypsum. Gypsum is a common mineral, hydrated calcium sulfate, occurring as crystals known as alabaster, satinspar, and selenite. It is manufactured into drywall, plaster of Paris, water-base paint extenders, and setting retardants for portland cement and mortar. On the backside of most Gypsum Board is kraft paper, although a foil backing is available that can serve as a vapor barrier in mild climates. On the front side is usually a cream-colored paper. Special boards come with blue or green paper; these facings are water-retardant and are used as a tiling surface in bathrooms.

Most do-it-yourselfers deal with 4' x 8' sheets of Gypsum Board that are ½" thick. But boards are available in lengths of 6', 7', 9', 10', 12', 14', and 16', and in thicknesses from ¼" to ⅝". The thinner boards are used for resurfacing damaged walls. The thicker boards are used when nailing to studs 24" apart or when creating a double-layer wall to reduce sound transmission or create a fire wall between two apartments. Double-layer walls and other sound-deadening methods require special construction techniques; these are shown toward the end of this chapter.

The ½" and ⅝" panels are available in "Type X," which has additives to make it more fire-resistant. These panels are used for garages and around fireplaces and furnaces as well as in kitchens and workshops. When applying over concrete or concrete block walls 1" x 3" furring strips are required to attach the Gypsum Board.

Never apply wallpaper to Gypsum Board or plaster until after you have sealed the facing with alkyd paint or commercial wall sizing. Then use a wallpaper paste or strippable wallpaper that will allow you to peel off the wallpaper at a later date. (You can repaper over old wallpaper if it is smooth and firmly adhered.) Remove vinyl wall covering before repapering; it cannot be covered.

Prefinished, decorative-faced Gypsum Board is easy to install and

Walls and Ceilings

an attractive way to cover damaged walls. A broad selection of patterned, textured, and colored facings is available. Unlike regular Gypsum Board, the abutting edges are square and the decorative paper is wrapped around, so there is no need for taping or covering with joint compound. Vinyl filler strips can be factory ordered but are expensive and unnecessary.

Gypsum Board is usually installed with drywall screws or ring-shank nails, sometimes with a cement (resin) coating to help hold them in place. For ⅜″ or ½″ gypsum, you'll need 1⅝″ nails (5¼ pounds per 1000 square feet), and for ⅝″ gypsum you'll need 1⅞″ nails (6¾ pounds per 1000 square feet). You can apply with adhesive and nails or nails alone. However, the adhesive will not provide attachment if you have a polyethylene vapor barrier covering the studs or joists.

"pop," forming an unsightly bump on the wall surface, when the drywall is nailed onto green lumber. The next winter, when the lumber dries out, it shrinks enough to loosen the grip on some nail shanks, allowing the bent fibers to straighten and push the nail back out of the drywall. The resin on "cement"-coated nails tends to bond the fiber in the bent position, but to be sure you don't have this problem, use dried lumber with a moisture content less than 15 percent or use screws.

Types Of Tapered Edges

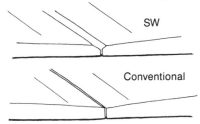

SW

Conventional

Hand tool application

Prefilling Joints. Prefill the V groove between SW Gypsum Panels (diagram above) with joint compound. Apply compound directly over V groove with a flexible 5″ or 6″ joint finishing knife. Wipe off excess compound that is applied beyond the groove. Allow prefill compound to harden. (This step is necessary with SW edge board only.)

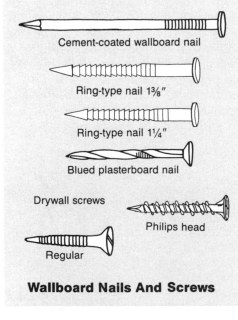

Cement-coated wallboard nail

Ring-type nail 1⅜″

Ring-type nail 1¼″

Blued plasterboard nail

Drywall screws

Philips head

Regular

Wallboard Nails And Screws

In some sections of the country, drywall screws are preferred as a means to reduce nail "popping." Nailheads

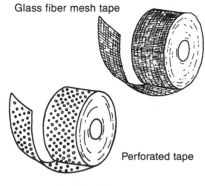

Glass fiber mesh tape

Perforated tape

Joint Tapes

350

The seams between sheets of Gypsum Board are covered with tape and three successive layers of joint compound. You should buy 250′ of tape for every 500 square feet of board. Joint compound is available premixed in 5-gallon containers. You can smooth finish with a wet sponge after leveling with a putty knife.

The dominant tape for drywall joints is paper, but a new tape made of fiberglass mesh has its advantages. With paper tape you have to apply both a layer of compound before and two or three layers after applying the paper. It's easy to get these layers too thick, which means a mess to sand down later. The glass fiber mesh tape is available for staple application or with self-adhesive and takes a layer of compound only after you staple or adhere it to the seam. If you use stapled tape, use ⅜″ staples on staggered 24″ centers. The self-adhesive tape can reduce taping time 50 percent.

Gypsum Board comes with square or tapered edges; the tapered edges make the taping job easier. However, you'll be doing some cutting, so be careful to avoid having a cut edge meet a tapered edge. Ends are always square cut. If the room has any outside corners, you'll also need galvanized steel perforated corner beads.

Since gypsum is heavy, installation requires two people, particularly for ceilings. (One sheet of ½″ thick, 4 x 8 board weighs 58 pounds.) You may even want to rent a gypsum lift.

Professional drywallers use stilts attached to their feet for high and ceiling work, but these require practice and skill to use and are banned in some states. We advise the weekend handyman to use a more secure scaffold to reach the ceiling.

Steps To Covering Drywall Seams

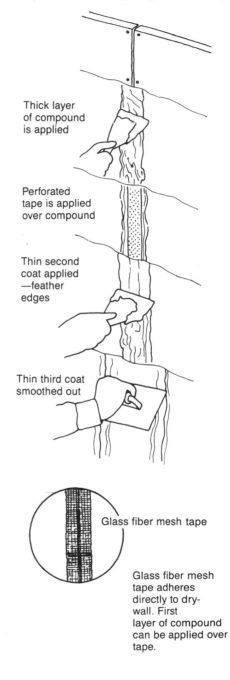

Thick layer of compound is applied

Perforated tape is applied over compound

Thin second coat applied —feather edges

Thin third coat smoothed out

Glass fiber mesh tape

Glass fiber mesh tape adheres directly to drywall. First layer of compound can be applied over tape.

351

Walls and Ceilings

You can cut gypsum by scoring the front surface with a sharp razor knife or utility knife. Then snap one end back so you can straight-cut the back paper. You'll need a keyhole saw to cut out for electric outlets and 4″, 6″, and 10″ finishing knives (actually troweling knives), and a plasterer's hod to carry joint compound.

Because trusses can lift a little if they are not perfectly dry and partitions (walls) tend to shrink as they dry, cracks sometimes appear along the joint line. To avoid this, do not nail either the ceiling or partition drywall close to the joint—leave about 1′ without nails. The reinforced seam can then flex sufficiently to prevent cracking.

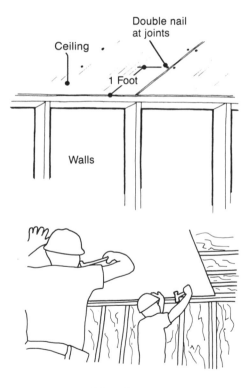

**Nailing Drywall
To Ceiling**

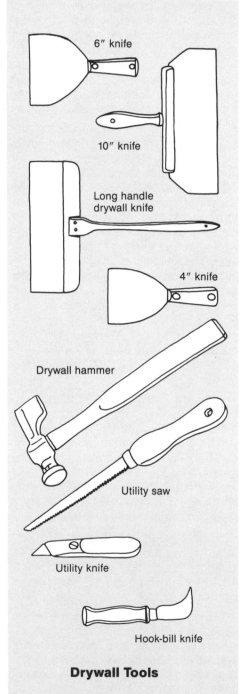

Drywall Tools

Gypsum Board Specifications

Gypsum Board (Plaster board)	Thickness	Sizes*	Use
Regular, paper-faced	$\frac{1}{4}$"	4' × 6' to 14'	Recovering old gypsum walls.
Regular, paper-faced	$\frac{3}{8}$"	4' × 6' to 14'	For double-layer installation.
Regular, paper-faced	$\frac{1}{2}$" & $\frac{5}{8}$"	4' × 6' to 14'	For standard single-ply installation.
Regular, with foil back	$\frac{1}{2}$" & $\frac{5}{8}$"	4' × 6' to 14'	For use as vapor barrier, radiant heat retarder.
Type X, fire retardant	$\frac{1}{2}$" & $\frac{5}{8}$"	4' × 6' to 16'	Use in garages, workshops, and kitchens as well as around furnaces, fireplaces, and chimney walls.
Moisture-resistant	$\frac{1}{2}$" & $\frac{5}{8}$"	4' × 6' to 16'	For tile backing and around kitchens, spas, baths, showers, and laundry rooms.
Decorator panels	$\frac{5}{16}$"	4' × 8'	Any room in the house.
Gypsum lath**, plain or perforated.	$\frac{3}{8}$", $\frac{1}{2}$", $\frac{5}{8}$"	16" × 4' 2' × 8' to 12'	Used as a base for plaster. Use $\frac{3}{8}$" for 16" o.c. stud spacing, $\frac{1}{2}$" or $\frac{5}{8}$" for 24" o.c. stud spacing.

*Available in 1' increments above 6' but 11' lengths not generally available.
**_Gypsum Lath_—is a gypsum core faced with multilayer laminated paper formulated to provide proper absorption, check plaster slide, and resist lath sag. The outer layers of paper are made highly absorbent to draw moisture from the plaster mix so that the plaster obtains anti-slump strength before it can slide from the lath. The inner layers form a barrier against moisture penetration which could soften the gypsum core.

Paneling

Wood paneling can create a warm, cozy mood for a room and is very easy to maintain. It also provides an easy way to hide an old or cracked wall. It can be installed with clips, nails, or adhesives, according to manufacturer's instructions. Look for a real wood veneer; the photo-reproduced facings have a repetitious grain pattern and look artificial.

For a relaxing rustic setting, you can use barn boards or other weathered board. For a formal library, use smooth, tight-grain oak, birch, cherry, walnut, or maple stained dark to provide an appearance of elegance. Bleached pecan or silver ash provides a cheerful look to a sun room in any weather. For traditional farmhouse kitchens and dens use knotty pine, cedar, wormy cypress, or wormy chestnut to capture the nostalgic flavor.

The very best paneling is created with solid wood boards. Such boards are growing in use, not only on walls but on ceilings. More home centers are carrying packaged amounts of boards, including some types that fit together with concealed clips instead of nails. Most, however, have interlocking edges and are nailed either to furring strips or directly through drywall to underlying studs. Sold by the board foot, there are no standard widths or thicknesses, and lengths are random.

More common is sheet paneling: 4' × 8' sheets with surface grooves to imitate the look of individual boards. Panel sheets are made of either

Walls and Ceilings

plywood or processed wood fibers. Plywood paneling is of higher quality. The best plywood paneling has a veneer of genuine hardwood. Thickness is generally $\frac{1}{4}''$, but sheets with channel grooves may be $\frac{5}{16}''$ or $\frac{7}{16}''$ thick. The less expensive plywood paneling has a photo finish imitation veneer of simulated wood grain and is only $\frac{5}{32}''$ thick.

Paneling made of wood fiber is less expensive than plywood paneling. Like the less expensive kinds of plywood paneling, it has simulated wood grain printed on a paper or vinyl facing.

Panels can be nailed to stud walls or furring strips or glued to plaster or drywall with panel adhesive applied with a caulking gun.

Wallpaper

The term *wallpaper* now includes a wide variety of wall coverings: regular wallpaper, vinyl papers, and special coverings such as fabrics, flocks (velvet look and texture), grass cloth, and metallics.

The vinyl papers are easier to maintain than regular wallpaper. Both the paper-backed and fabric-backed vinyls are not merely "washable" but "scrubbable"; the distinction means you can wash them repeatedly and vigorously, as opposed to an occasional swipe with sponge and mild detergent. The fabric-backed vinyls are the best for withstanding the humidity of bathrooms and the grease of kitchens.

Vinyl wallpaper can be slick and shiny, but it doesn't have to be. Vinyl choices include look-alikes of flannel, tweed, linen, sackcloth, silk, suede, and wood. There are, in fact, over 1,000 patterns, colors, textures, and finishes —more than can be stocked in any one store.

Fabrics, flocks, and grass cloth are more expensive than regular or vinyl wallpaper. Choices among fabrics range from burlap to silk. The specialty coverings may damage easily and can be difficult to clean. Use in low-traffic areas, such as bedrooms, and away from direct sunlight or moisture.

On some walls, you may need to put up a lining paper before the wallpaper. Liner is most often used over rough, damaged walls, over paneling, and under delicate papers. A special liner is available to cover cinder block.

Most papers today are available prepasted, so there's no need to mess with brushes and paste. Simply soak the paper in a trough and hang on the wall.

Wallpapers come in bolts, which contain one, two, or three rolls. As a rule, each roll contains 36 square feet, no matter what the width. Widths can vary from 18" (standard) to 54". When estimating your needs, however, remember that each roll has only about 30 square feet of *usable* paper. To estimate, merely figure the square footage of the wall area to be covered, then divide by 30 or use the accompanying chart. Deduct for windows and doors, but throw in an extra roll so you're not caught short.

Walls should be sealed with sizing before applying wallpaper. Also use a paste that allows you to peel the covering material off later, particularly in the case of vinyl wallpaper, as a new wallpaper cannot be applied over that.

Vinyl and foil wallpapers create a vapor barrier. This is good, unless you already have a vapor barrier under the dry wall and little or no insulation. Moisture entering from the living area through light fixtures and other penetrations may then collect and condense at dew point in the drywall, causing it to puddle and slump.

Wallpaper Estimating

Based on standard wallpaper rolls 8 yards long and 18″ wide. Deduct 1 roll for every 50 square feet of door or window opening.

Room Size (in feet)	No. of Rolls Ceiling Height 8′	9′	Yards of Border	Rolls for Ceiling
6 × 10	8	9	12	2
6 × 12	9	10	13	3
8 × 12	10	11	15	4
8 × 14	11	12	16	4
10 × 14	12	14	18	5
10 × 16	13	15	19	6
12 × 16	14	16	20	7
12 × 18	15	17	22	8
14 × 18	16	18	23	8
14 × 22	18	20	26	10
15 × 16	15	17	23	8
15 × 18	16	18	24	9
15 × 20	17	20	25	10
15 × 23	19	21	28	11
16 × 18	17	19	25	10
16 × 20	18	20	26	10
16 × 22	19	21	28	11
16 × 24	20	22	29	12
16 × 26	21	23	31	13
17 × 22	19	22	23	12
17 × 25	21	23	31	13
17 × 28	22	25	32	15
17 × 32	24	27	35	17
17 × 35	26	29	37	18
18 × 22	20	22	29	12
18 × 25	21	24	31	14
18 × 28	23	26	33	16
20 × 26	23	26	33	17
20 × 28	24	27	34	18
20 × 34	27	30	39	21

Note: Vinyl wall covering comes 27″ wide: to estimate, divide rolls given above by $\frac{1}{3}$.

Acoustical Ceilings

Add the noise of computer games to the stereo, blender, hair dryer, dishwasher, and trash compactor, and you have a sound justification for the cost of acoustical ceilings for your home.

Ceiling tiles and suspended ceiling panels stop sound reflection by absorbing the sound waves. Installing such a ceiling is easy. Flexible 2′ × 4′ panels are the easiest to install. More rigid types are fairly easy but require care to avoid breakage. As you turn them into position above the grid, be particularly careful of the hanging wires, which can act like knife blades. Dozens of designs, patterns, colors, and facings are available in the marketplace, so satisfying your esthetic demands should be easy. Fibrous materials have the best sound absorbency.

Walls and Ceilings

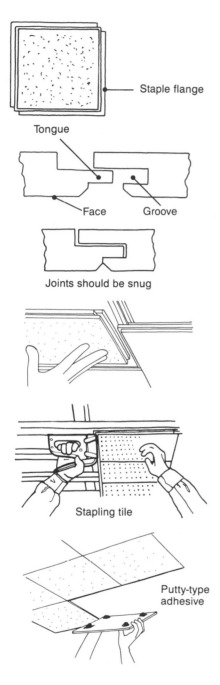

Staple flange

Tongue

Face   Groove

Joints should be snug

Stapling tile

Putty-type
adhesive

Permanent Ceiling Tiles

When it comes to tile installation methods, you may nail or staple to furring strips or glue to Gypsum Board or to the existing ceiling if it's level. Many have tongue-and-groove edges for easy installation. Use four walnut-sized daubs of adhesive per square foot and for square-edged tiles, and use splines between tiles for leveling. Standard tile face is 12" × 12" although 12" × 24", 16",18", 24" × 24", and 24" × 48" are available.

Ceiling panels, on the other hand, require a concealed or exposed suspension system. Buy the suspension system at the same store where you buy your ceiling panels, because there are variations between manufacturers' standards and not all panels fit all systems. Attach wall angles at desired ceiling height around the room, using a level. The main tees are hung on twist wires attached to screw eyes in the joists or rafters. Locate and install your light fixtures. Run main tees on 2' centers in same direction as joists. Cross tees fit into slots on main tee every 4' and have a twist tab for securing. Then you merely drop in panels. It's that easy.

Since you are buying the ceiling partially to reduce noise, it would be wise to compare the absorbency measurements, given as NRC (noise-reduction coefficient), for each product. The higher the number, the better the absorbency. Unfortunately, some manufacturers give neither the NRC nor the flame spread ratings, which leaves the customer to form his own conclusion.

Basically, the ½" painted wood fiber tile is at the low-priced end of the market, and the vinyl-faced fiberglass thermal ceilings are at the top end. The latter not only have the best of the published noise reduction coefficients but allow the addition of fiberglass insulation over the top. For example, a ceiling panel with an R-value of 12 can be top loaded with up to R-38 insulation to give a total R-50 value.

Facings are usually embossed vinyl in a choice of patterns—fissured, pebbled, striated, etc. Large fiberglass ceiling panels (4' x 16') allow the use of box beams every 4' so no breaks are visible in the ceiling surface—excellent for cathedral ceilings.

For installation, wear white cotton gloves to avoid marring the surfaces.

A suspended ceiling is also a good choice where a ceiling needs lowering, in basement rooms where easy access to pipes and wiring is important, and where an older ceiling is heavily damaged. It is generally not a good choice in formal rooms, such as a living or dining room.

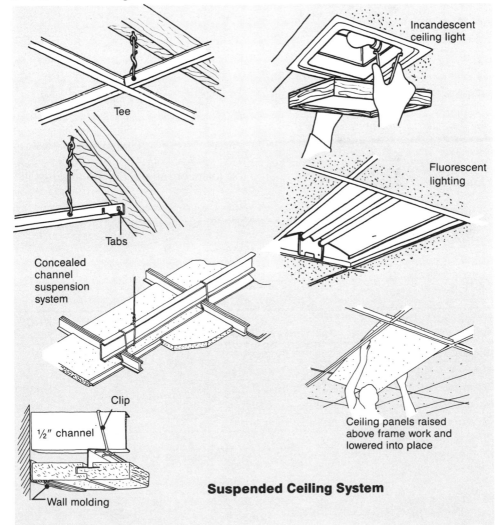

Tee

Tabs

Concealed channel suspension system

Incandescent ceiling light

Fluorescent lighting

Ceiling panels raised above frame work and lowered into place

Clip

½" channel

Wall molding

Suspended Ceiling System

Walls and Ceilings

Ceilings

Sound-Absorbing Type	Fastening Suspension System	Flame Spread†	Smoke Developed†	NRC Range‡	Light Reflection†
Fiberglas panels	Suspension system	25	50	.65-.75	1 or 2
		25	NA	.70	1 or 2
Fiberglass thermal ceilings	Suspension system	25	NA	.65-.80	1 or 2
Mineral fiber tile	Adhesive to gypsum or existing ceiling suspension system. Stapled to furring strips.	25	10	.50-.65	1
Mineral tile, fissured	Adhesive system as above	20	10	.45-.55	1
Mineral fiber panels	Suspension system	20	0	.50-.65	1

†The lower the number, the better the performance.
‡The higher the number, the better the performance.
*May be top loaded with addition of fiberglass insulation to achieve total R-value up to R-38.

Ceilings

Non-Sound-Absorbing Type	Fastening or Suspension System	NRC Range
Gypsum Board	Nail to furring strips	.05
Plank T & G board	Nail to furring strips	.15
Tempered tile board	Nail to furring strips	NA
Embossed metal ceilings	Nail to furring strips	NA
Plywood panels	Nail to furring strips	.10
Plaster & lath	Plaster to lath	.05
Mineral tile (unperforated)	Staple to lath or suspended ceiling	NA
Wood fiber tile (unperforated)	Staple to lath or suspended ceiling	NA

NOTE: NA means either not available or not applicable.

Approx. R-Value‡	Surfaces	Thickness	Standard Dimensions	Edge Cut	Adhesive (gal.) or Nails (lb.) per 100 Sq. Ft.
2.6	PVC film	5/8"	24" × 48"	Square	NA
8.0	PVC film	2"	48" × 16'	Square	NA
8.0-12.0*	PVC film	2"	24" × 48"	Square	NA
		3"	48" × 12.6'	Square	
1.5	CVA (vinyl acrylic), coated or painted.	5/8"	24" × 24" or 24" × 48"	Edge cut rabbeted or beveled. Kerfed & rabbeted long edges for concealed suspension or square cut.	1.5 gal.
1.5	Painted	5/8"	12" × 12"	Beveled, kerfed, & rabbeted	NA
1.5	Vinyl acrylic, coated or painted	5/8"	24" × 24" or 24" × 48" 24" × 60" 30" × 60"	Square	NA

Thickness	Standard Dimensions	Edge Cut	Nails (lb.) per 100 Sq. Ft.
1/2"	48" × 96"	Square	5 lb.
1/2", 3/4"	12" × 96"	Square	2 lb.
NA	48" × 48"	Square	1 lb.
NA	24" × 96"	Square	1 lb.
5/32", 1/4", 5/16"	48" × 96"	Square	1.25 lb.
	NA	NA	NA
5/8"	12" × 12" 24" × 24" 24" × 48"	Square	NA
1/2"	12" × 12" 24" × 48"	Square or tongue & grooved & beveled	NA

Walls and Ceilings

Walls and Ceilings—Uses, Sizes, and Installations

Facing Materials	Use on Ceilings	Use on Walls	Attachment Base
Tile			
Acoustical	●	●	Drywall plaster or furring strips
Ceramic		●	Exterior plywood, hardboard, plaster, moisture-resistant (blue) gypsum, lath
Cork	●	●	Any drywall material
Mirror	●	●	Any drywall material
Tin	●		Any drywall material
Vinyl	●	●	Any drywall material
Paint	●	●	Any clean, dry surface—use alkali-resistant paint or cementitious surfaces
Wallpapers			
Foil	●	●	Any drywall surface if primed
Paper	●	●	Any drywall surface if primed
Textile	●	●	Any drywall surface if primed
Vinyl	●	●	Any drywall surface if primed
Laminates	●	●	Oriented-strand board, particle board, plywood—also premounted
Decorative Gypsum	●	●	On furring strips, gypsum, or plaster walls.
Dimensional Panels—Brick, Stone, Tile		●	Studs or furring strips
Wood			
Boards, T&G	●	●	Studs, rafters, furring strips oriented-strand board, plywood
Hardboard	●	●	Studs, rafters, or furring strips
Paneling	●	●	Studs, rafters, or furring strips
Plywood	●	●	Studs, rafters, or furring strips

Standard Sizes	Fastening Method							
	Nails	Staples	Screws	Clips	Suspension System	Adhesive	Mortar	Brush Applied
12″ × 12″, 12″ × 24″, 24″ × 24″, 24″ × 28″		•		•		•		
3⁄8″ thick 4¼″ × 4¼″ & various						•	•	
1⁄8″ to 5⁄16″ thick 6″ × 12″, 12″ × 24″, 24″ × 48″						•		
2″ × 6″, 4¼″ × 4¼″, 6″ × 6″, 8″ × 8″, or cut to size					•	•		
2′ × 8′ sheets with embossed designs	•	•	•					
9″ × 9″, 12″ × 12″ tiles 1⁄16″, 3⁄32″, 1⁄8″ thick; sheet vinyl 6′, 9′, 12′ wide						•		
1 pint, 1 quart, ½ gal., 1 gal., 5 gal., & aerosol containers								•
27″, 53″, 54″ in rolls of 36, 72, or 108 sq. ft.						•		
27″, 53″, 54″ in rolls of 36, 72, or 108 sq. ft.						•		
27″, 53″, 54″ in rolls of 36, 72, or 108 sq. ft.						•		
27″, 53″, 54″ × 90′						•		
24″ to 60″ wide, 6′ to 12′ long						•		
¼″, 5⁄8″ thick, 4′ × 8′, 4′ × 9′	•	•				•		
Varies by manufacturer Approximately 2′ × 4′	•	•	•	•				
1″ thick; 2″ × 4″, 2″ × 6″ 2″ × 8″	•							
4′ × 8′, 9′, 10′ or 12′	•							
5⁄32″, 5⁄16″, ¼″ thick, 4′ × 8′, some 4′ × 9′	•	•	•			•		
5⁄32″, ¼″, 5⁄16″ thick; 4′ × 8′, 4′ × 9′, 4′ × 10′;	•	•	•			•		

Walls and Ceilings

Walls and Ceilings—Uses, Sizes, and Installations (Concluded)

Facing Materials	Use on Ceilings	Use on Walls	Attachment Base
Veneers	●	●	Any smooth, clean, drywall surface
Acoustical Panels	●		Wire-hung suspension system attached to joists or rafters

Noise Attenuation

When you take an afternoon nap, you want to keep the noise of lawn mowers, airplanes, jack hammers, and barking dogs out of your home. You may also want noise dividers within the home. This is easier and more effective if done during construction rather than after the fact.

To reduce noise requires the choice of sound-deadening construction materials, nonbridging construction, and the caulking of any voids in the walls. Ceilings with R-38 insulation or more and Gypsum Board or plaster will normally reduce overhead intrusion. Exterior wall constructions and the products you will need in the interior partitions to isolate your quiet room are indicated in the diagrams below.

In addition you will want to install well-weather stripped, insulated exterior doors and either thicker glazing or triple-glazed windows, also carefully weather stripped. Caulk all wall penetrations with a flexible caulking. To soundproof floors, use two layers of gypsum suspended by clips to the ceiling below, and fill joists with fiberglass or mineral wool insulation. Then add plywood floor and subfloor overlaid with carpet. Caulk all penetrations through floor and ceiling.

An investment in noise reduction will provide ceilings and walls that are energy saving, will reduce the size and cost of heating and cooling equipment, and may help reduce annual energy costs.

Exterior Wall

Good: 2" × 6", 24" o.c., R-19 fiberglass batts, 6 mil polyethylene vapor barrier and ½" Gypsum Board screwed to resilient metal channel inside. No. 15 felt building paper and 1" wire mesh with ⅞" stucco on exterior. Use single windows and a storm window or double-glazed windows and insulated exterior doors.

Exterior

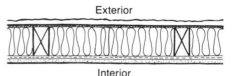

Interior

	Fastening Method							
Standard Sizes	Nails	Staples	Screws	Clips	Suspension System	Adhesive	Mortar	Brush Applied
Brick: ¾″ thick; 2¼″ × 8″ Wood: ¹⁄₂₈″ to ¹⁄₄₀″ thick by 4″ to 18″ wide and 3′ long. Available to 10′ in some species						●		
2′ × 4′					●			

Better: 2″ × 6″ studs, 24″ o.c., R-19 fiberglass batts, 6 mil polyethylene vapor barrier, and ½″ Gypsum Board screwed to resilient channel inside. Install sheathing board and a brick veneer exterior. Use double- or triple-glazed windows and insulated doors.

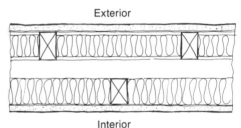

Exterior

Interior

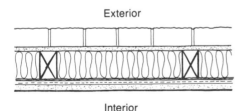

Exterior

Interior

Best: 2″ × 4″ double stud wall, studs staggered 16″ o.c. and plates spaced 4″ apart with R-11 fiberglass batts in exterior wall, R-19 fiberglass batts in interior wall, 6 mil polyethylene vapor barrier and ½″ Gypsum Board or ½″ plaster inside. Tyvek™ (DuPont) on exterior wall with ½″ sheathing and siding stucco or brick veneer of choice. Use double- or triple- glazed windows and insulated exterior doors.

Interior Wall

Good: Solid brick wall with ½″ plaster on each side.

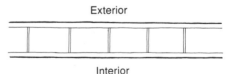

Exterior

Interior

Better: 2′ × 6″ studs, 24″ o.c., with ½″ gypsum on resilient channel both sides and R-19 fiberglass insulation between studs. Avoid back-to-back electric boxes and caulk all gaps. *Note:* Check if acceptable under local fire codes.

Walls and Ceilings

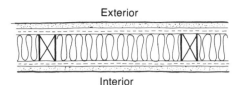

Exterior

Interior

Best: 2″ × 4″ studs, double wall construction, studs staggered, 16″ or 24″ o.c. with two layers ½″ gypsum wallboard on each side and R-11 fiberglass or mineral wool insulation in each wall. NOTE: In some localities fire codes require one layer of ½″ fire rated Gypsum Board to be attached directly to each side of each wall. Check with your code officials.

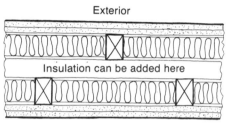

Exterior

Insulation can be added here

Interior

Other Decorative Ceilings

Other than acoustical ceilings, Gypsum Board, and plaster, there are a variety of ceiling materials you can choose for special effects. There has been a revival of interest in "tin" or embossed metal ceilings; eight manufacturers make hundreds of varieties. (Addresses are given at the end of this chapter.) You may want rustic pine planks or Pacific redwood boards. The easiest, least expensive way to construct a wood ceiling is with hardboard or plywood paneling. Stained corkboard with self-adhesive backing is easy to attach to a Gypsum Board ceiling and can provide a unique effect. If you wish to use wallpaper on a ceiling, choose a nondirectional design and consider bringing the paper down to the picture rail on the adjoining walls.

If the room is small, you may want to use a suspended ceiling with lighting panels. The edge may need filling out with acoustical panels, but the effect is dramatic for a dressing room, bathroom, or kitchen.

Another way to decorate a ceiling is with crown moldings around the perimeter and a medallion at the hanging point of your ceiling fan or chandelier. You'll usually find a wide selection of moldings and medallions at your home center store.

Moldings

While most moldings are made of wood, cove moldings and base moldings are available prefinished in brown or with a simulated wood grain surface made with vinyl or foamed polystyrene and at a much lower price. Recently, aluminum moldings have been developed for attaching paneling —peel-and-stick matching hardwood veneer strips are supplied to attach to the unfinished face. Moldings are normally attached with finishing nails, center-punched below the surface, and filled with colored scratch-repair putty sticks.

Tin Ceiling Suppliers

AA Abbingdon Ceiling Co., Dept. BV, 2149 Utica Avenue, Brooklyn, New York 11234

Ceilings, Walls and More, Inc., Box 494, 124 Walnut Street, Jefferson, Texas 75657

Chelsen Decorative Metal Co., 6115 Cheena Drive, Houston, Texas 77096

WF Norman Corporation, P.O. Box 323, Nevada, Missouri 64772

Remodelers & Renovators, 1503 North 11th, Dept. BV, Boise, Idaho 83702

Renovation Concepts, Inc., Dept. BV, 213 Washington Avenue North, Minneapolis, Minnesota 55401

Shanker-Glendale Steel Corp. Dept. BV, 70-32 83rd Street, Glendale, Queens, New York 11385

Steptoe and Wife Antiques Ltd., Dept. BV, 3626 Victoria Park Avenue, Willowdale, Ontario, Canada M2H 3B2

Typical Moldings

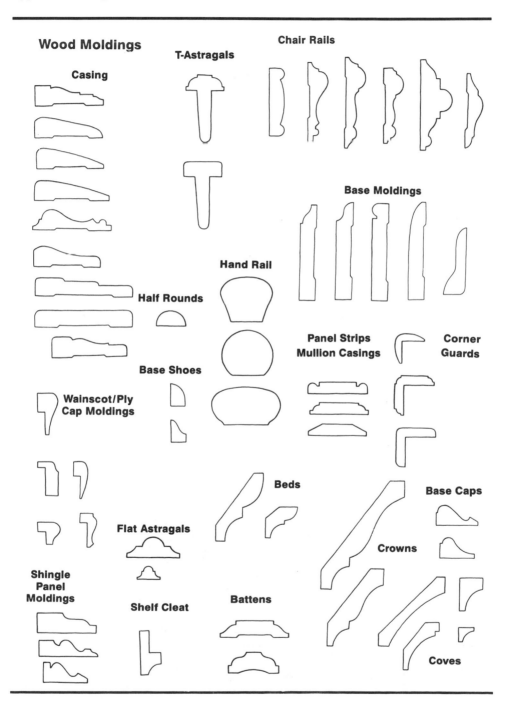

Wood Moldings

Casing

T-Astragals

Chair Rails

Base Moldings

Hand Rail

Half Rounds

Panel Strips
Mullion Casings

Corner
Guards

Base Shoes

Wainscot/Ply
Cap Moldings

Beds

Base Caps

Flat Astragals

Crowns

Shingle
Panel
Moldings

Shelf Cleat

Battens

Coves

Walls and Ceilings

Typical Moldings (Continued)

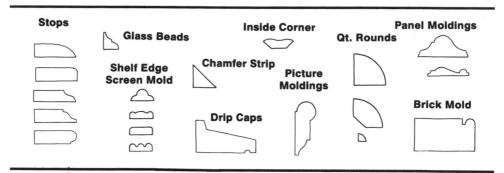

Stops

Glass Beads

Shelf Edge Screen Mold

Chamfer Strip

Drip Caps

Inside Corner

Picture Moldings

Qt. Rounds

Panel Moldings

Brick Mold

Wall and Ceiling Materials

Materials	Apply Over	Can Use on Walls	Can use on Ceilings	Available Surfaces	Finishes that Can be Applied	Standard Sizes Widths × Lengths	Standard Thicknesses (inches)
Gypsum Board Requires use of paper or glass fiber tape at joints.	Wood or metal studs, rafters, or joists (Furring required for concrete block or masonry walls. Can attach to studs through insulating boards) Can be installed vertically or horizontally as single or double layers.	●	●	• Paper & vinyl • Foil backed • Moisture resistant • Painted and textured • Wall and ceiling textures sold by 25# bag apply by spray or trowel.	Paint, wallpaper, plaster, vinyl, tile, lumber, plywood, mirror or tin tile. Photo-murals, paper backed fabrics and no-wax vinyl floor coverings.	4'×7, 8, 9, 10, 12, 14 & 16 feet.	1/4* 3/8 1/2 5/8 Decorative 3/8 in.*
Plaster and Lath Plaster available as ready-mix; just add water. Contains: gypsum, wood fibers, sand and perlite. Use Keene's cement for kitchens or bathrooms.	Metal lath: • Expanded metal lathe • 4 mesh Riblath • Stucco mesh • 3/4" riblath • self furring mesh or spaced wood lath. • Gypsum lath • Perforated gypsum lath • Fiberboard	●	●	Sand floated or smooth trowled by applicator. Sand can be added to finish coat for texture.	Alkali resistant paint. Wall paper after sizing.	Materials sold by the 25 lb. bag— add water Gypsum Lath††† 16"×4' 2'×4' 2'×6, 7, 8, 10, 12'	3 coats 1/2" 5/8" 1"
Building Board†† Special purpose (Made from cement non-asbestos fibers) Heavy material: 107.6 lbs/ft.³	Studs, joists or rafters. Particularly suitable for use in damp basements.	●	●	Natural mica flecked gray. No finish necessary.	Use only alkali resistant paints unless sealed with impermeable barrier. Needs sealing prior to application of wall paper. Good water proof wall board for tub surrounds and base for attaching tile.	4'×8' 4'×10'	3/16† 1/4 3/8

NOTES:
*For covering new or old gypsum only.
†For 16 in. stud spacing or less.
††Based on data for ULTRA-BOARD®
†††Sold 8 pieces per bundle

Typical Moldings (Concluded)

Plastic Stick On Moldings

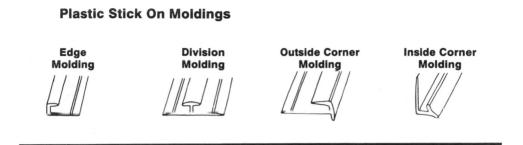

| Edge Molding | Division Molding | Outside Corner Molding | Inside Corner Molding |

R-Value Range	Available Fire Rated	Cost	Application Method						Cutting Method
			Nail	Screw	Staple	Trowel	Clips	Adhesives	
— .33 .44 .55 —	Standard 15-15-0 (ASTM E-84) also available with U.L. labels for 45 min. 1, 2 and 3 hour ratings.	Low for paper-faced low-med vinyl faced.	●	●	●		●	●	Score with knife and snap.

Edge Designs: T—Tapered Edge
S—Square Edge
RE—Tapered with Round Edge
B—Beveled Edge or HB—modified beveled.
T&G—Tongue and Groove

R-Value Range	Available Fire Rated	Cost	Nail	Screw	Staple	Trowel	Clips	Adhesives	Cutting Method
½" 0-32 .45 .56 .87	Fire retardant	Material—low Labor— Medium			● (lath)		●		Not applicable
— 0.03 0.05	Non-combustible per ASTM E 136	Med	●	●				●	Tungsten Carbide Saw

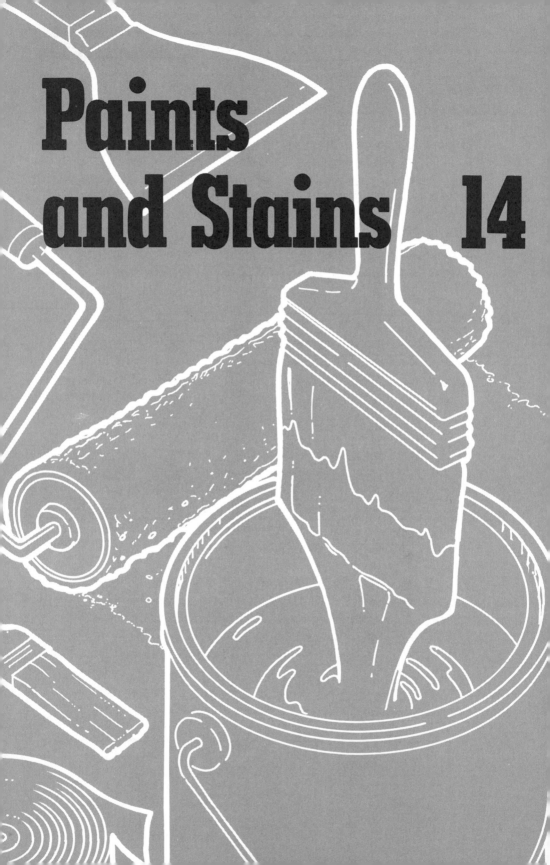

Paints
and Stains 14

14. Paints and Stains

The job of painting has never been easier. New paints advertise one-coat coverage, ceiling paints are dripless, and stains are now water-based for easy clean-up, just like latex paints. Aerosol spray cans and paint sprayers are being marketed to do-it-yourselfers to speed certain jobs.

All that is great, but don't be fooled. Painting is still no snap. The success or failure of a paint job rests largely upon the preparation you do—the sanding, scraping, washing, priming, and caulking that makes a surface dry, solid, clean, and paintable. Preparation is a pain, but it must be done. Naturally you should buy the right kind of paint for the job you're doing—and buy a high-quality paint. But that's just the first step.

Primers

A primer is applied to a new surface before painting. By sealing the surface it provides a nonporous base so the top coat will not penetrate to create uneven areas of gloss. It also provides a bond between the top coat and base. Additionally, it provides resistance to moisture, fills in cracks and crevices, and smooths the surface. Pigment-loaded top coats do not have enough fluidity to sink into and bond surfaces without the aid of a primer.

You don't need to know too much about undercoats or primers as you will normally prime the surface as recommended by the manufacturer of the top coat you are using. However, a little knowledge can save you money. In covering any alkali surface (cement, drywall, plaster) except basement walls and floors, the least expensive product to use is a cutback shellac mixed with alcohol. Next most economical is a latex primer. But latex primers will not bond to highly finished,

Approximate Drying Time for Primers

Primer	Time (hours)
Acrylic latex block filler	2 to 4
Alkyd flat enamel	2 to 4
Alkyd metal primer	4 to 5
Alkyd primer	2 to 4
Alkali-resistant enamel	2 to 4
Epoxy	5 to 8
Lacquer sealer	1
Latex flat	2 to 4
Latex primer	2 to 4
Liquid filler	24
Non-Grain-raising (NGR)	3 to 4
Oil-base	24
Paste wood filler	24
Polyurethane	12
Portland cement masonry primer	24
Primer sealer	¾ to 1
Sanding sealer	1
Shellac	3 to 4
Stain blocking primer	24
Stains	24
Varnish	24 to 36
Water-base	24
Zinc metal primer	24

NOTE: These indicate the time required before applying finishing coat. Times vary by product. Check the manufacturer label.

smooth, or glossy surfaces. For plaster, use a solution of phenolic varnish or other penetrating sealer to reinforce the bonding of the surface.

For metal, use a zinc chromate or alkyd resin primer. Zinc chromate seals out oxygen and moisture and contains minute quantities of alkali which neutralize any acid, effectively eliminating the causes of corrosion on metal surfaces.

Don't use alkyds on cementitious surfaces; use B-I-N made by William Zinsser & Co. (shellac primer) or latex. Do not use sealants that form a film or vapor barrier on basement walls; moisture back-up may cause the paint to peel off in sheets. Instead, use latex, masonry paint, or an alkali-resistant

Paints and Stains

primer. If using epoxy or urethane as a top coat, use a prime coat of the same resin.

Use polyvinyl acetate latex under oil or alkyd paints because it dries quickly and is odorless. Never use the old standby, sizing. Sizing is cheap but will detach from the wall if the slightest moisture is present.

Because some woods are oily (see lumber chapter) their surface should be scrubbed with tri-sodium phosphate or mineral spirits before applying primer or enamel undercoat. Stain-blocking primers should be used over redwood or other surfaces that leech color. For primer recommendations refer to the accompanying charts.

Oil or Latex?

Latex paints clean up with water; oil-base paints clean up with mineral spirits or paint thinner. Actually, true oil-base paint is all but extinct; what are called "oil-base" paints today are in fact alkyds. Alkyds give off less odor and dry faster (twelve to forty-eight hours) than the old oil paints but not as fast as latex paints (one to four hours).

The next section, "Special Problems," lists some troubles that may be cured better by either alkyd (oil) or latex, as the case may be. In general, however, the debate over oil versus latex comes down to a matter of personal preference and experience. Not all paints are created equal. A good latex will perform better than a poor alkyd and vice-versa. Most do-it-yourselfers prefer latex because it dries in a few hours, cleans up with soap and water, and can be applied outside earlier in the day and even in damp weather.

Professionals often favor the traditional oil-base paints, maintaining that clean-up is actually easier with them. Unlike latex paint, alkyds are less likely to clog spray guns if these are left uncleaned overnight (a bad practice in any case). At day's end, all you have to do with alkyds is stick your brush in paint thinner and leave it 'til the morning. Some do-it-yourselfers prefer oil-base for interior work because, in drying slower, it levels better and does not leave as many brush strokes. On the exterior, with the chance of dust, insects, and grass clippings blowing around and sticking to the surface, this slow drying can be a disadvantage.

There is general agreement that a good acrylic latex outdoor paint will outlast a good oil-base paint, but it does not provide as high a gloss. This has yet to prompt a great many defections from the ranks of alkyd advocates.

Contrary to conventional belief, you can apply latex paints over sound aged alkyd or oil-based paints, and vice-versa.

Special Problems

The prime cause of exterior paint failure is moisture. The moisture comes from a number of sources:

- from water vapor in household air that migrates through the siding, from dryers or bathrooms that are not vented to the outdoors
- from reversed vapor barriers on the outside instead of inside the wall, trapping condensation against the back of the siding
- from rain that hits cracks and bare spots, working its way under paint from there
- from overflowing gutters that have been incorrectly attached directly to the fascia board
- from rain that penetrates failed flashing and cracked caulking.

When the moisture tries to push its way through the paint film, it causes the paint, particularly alkyd, to blister and peel in a way that exposes the bare wood beneath. This is particularly bad on south-facing walls when the moisture is heated by the sun.

If your house suffers from excessive *peeling,* your problem is moisture, not paint. Start indoors by installing ventilation to disperse built-up moisture. Install attic vents, bathroom fans, and dryer vents. Consider painting the inside surfaces of exterior walls with a vapor barrier paint. But check first—someone may have installed the vapor barrier on the wrong side (outside) of the insulation, in which case you'll have to remove the errant vapor barrier first, an expensive job.

Latex paint is slightly more porous than oil-base paint, allowing more moisture to migrate through it. Thus, latex is a better choice of exterior finish coat to apply over a scraped-down peeling wall, if there is not already a heavy buildup of paint.

A heavy buildup, no matter what kind of paint, can result in cracks called *crazing* or, if severe, *alligatoring* (because the paint looks like an alligator's hide). When paint builds up past a thickness of $\frac{1}{64}$", moisture in the wall cannot pass through it. The paint also becomes inflexible, in contrast to the seasonal expansion and contraction of the wood beneath. In fact, the optimal thickness of exterior house paint is about the thickness of a sheet of newspaper. If crazing is caught in its early stages, the usual scraping or wire brushing and fresh paint may solve the problem. But if the old paint is really thick and the cracks go all the way down to the bare wood, it's probably time to remove the buildup and start anew.

Another common painting problem is *chalking.* Chalking is the buildup of dusty, talclike powder on the surface of exterior walls. That powder is actually pigment of the previous coat of paint that "got loose," perhaps because the paint was poor quality with no UV (ultraviolet) retardant to protect the binder—or the underlying surface should have been primed. Self-cleaning paints are actually designed to chalk or erode so a clean surface is continually exposed.

When painting over chalking, first wash the wall thoroughly with detergent and water, then use an oil-base primer or add "Emulsabond" (manufactured by the Flood Company) to any good latex exterior primer, one quart to the gallon. Emulsabond is also good for sealing T-III plywood and old weathered boards, but that takes a 50/50 (Emulsabond to primer) mixture. It's available at most home centers.

Washing any previously painted wall is a good idea before applying new paint, especially in urban areas. A detergent cleaner, such as Spic-and-Span or Mr. Clean, followed by a good hosing will generally suffice. Grease and dirt, if left on the surface, can keep the new coat from bonding to the old, and the new coat will soon peel. You can distinguish this from moisture-caused peeling because only the top coat will flake off. Sanding will also help the new coating adhere firmly to the old.

While washing, you may encounter patches of dirtlike brown dots. They may be *mildew.* Dab a little chlorine bleach on the area: Dirt won't clean away, but mildew will. If it is mildew, it must be scrubbed with chlorine bleach, borax, and detergent. Then apply mildew-resistant paint (or you can buy mildewcides to add to the paint—a small amount of di(phenylmercury)-dodecenyl succinate goes a long way). Otherwise the fungi will spread and the mildew will grow back, feed on the

Paints and Stains

fresh paint, and reappear at the surface of your new paint job.

In areas of heavy rain or wind, use a nonchalking paint—the self-cleaning paint will wear off too fast. Do not use a high-zinc-content paint, because the surface will not erode and dirt will pile up. (But zinc paints are less susceptible to fungi and mildew and are recommended for use on metal roofs.)

In marine and shore environments, use a salt-resistant exterior alkyd enamel over a thoroughly washed and primed surface.

When painting interiors, one common problem is the bleed-through of stains, such as water stains caused by a roof or plumbing leak. These stains should be primed with either latex primer containing 1 quart to the gallon of Emulsabond or a special stain sealer such as polyvinyl acetate latex sealer (Pal). Also, knots of bare wood will bleed through paint and should be similarly sealed with an alcohol-based primer (such as B-I-N).

Paint Contents

One way to shop for paint quality is to read and compare labels. Most good-quality paints will list the paint's contents, broken down into "pigment" and "vehicle." The pigment gives the paint its color, opacity, and durability. The vehicle contains the thinner—either water or mineral spirits—which evaporates, and a resin binder. The pigment and resin binder are the two ingredients to watch for. The more of each, the better.

Of course, you may need a calculator to figure out the true percentage of these ingredients. A sample can of exterior acrylic latex trim enamel, for instance, lists "vehicle" at 74.7 percent. It then lists "acrylic emulsion" as 65.7 percent of that 74.7 percent. What's not listed is some math: 65.7 percent of 74.7 percent is 49 percent. A footnote says the acrylic emulsion is 50 percent acrylic resin, and 50 percent water. So the binder resin is really 50 percent of 49 percent, or 24.5 percent of the can. Pigment volume concentrations in the range of 32 percent to 36 percent (with binder 68 to 64 percent) are generally held to be the most durable.

Safety Tips

While all paints sold to the public are essentially safe, they do contain aromatic and sometimes combustible solvents. When opening cans or painting, always extinguish all flames and pilot lights and turn off electric motors. Don't use cigarette lighters or matches while painting.

Be particularly careful to avoid skin or eye contact when using paint sprayers, aerosols, shellac, paint thinner, varnish remover, stains, brush cleaner, scale remover, epoxies or products containing alkaline or acid compounds.

Be careful when disposing of paint containers, bottles or cans that contain thinners, and, especially, aerosol cans. Aerosol cans should be turned upside down and the valve pressed to relieve all pressure. Even then the can must be discarded in a shaded place and in accordance with local regulations.

If the paint vehicle is combustible, have an appropriate fire extinguisher at hand.

Preparation—Exterior

The steps in preparing an exterior for new paint are:

1. Remove all loose paint with a scraper, sandpaper, or wire brush. If the paint film is heavy or alligatored, it must be removed. If there is just a little blistering or peeling you can use a motorized wire brush or a rotary or disc power sander with a carborundum disc. Avoid using a propane torch to burn off old paint. Old wood tends to be

tinder-dry. Also, the paint you remove may contain lead, which will result in toxic fumes. A hot air paint remover works well when removing layered paint buildup, without the combustion problems of an open flame. Wear goggles, gloves, and a face mask.

2. If you are installing new trim or siding, treat the wood with a paintable water-repellent preservative (NRP). This will give the wood some protection against decay, staining, fungus, shrinking, swelling, or warping. Window and door frames may already have been treated at the factory, ask your dealer or look for the WRP seal of the National Woodwork Manufacturers Association (NWMA).

NWMA Seal

3. Remove oil or grease with mineral spirits and wipe off or scrub with trisodium phosphates.

4. Sand any shiny old paint to give enough "tooth" for the new paint to grip.

5. Caulk joints; countersink nail heads in trim boards and fill with putty.

6. Paint spots of bare wood with a primer. If much of the wall is bare at this point, consider using two coats of primer. Manufacturer's directions on the top coat product selected should govern your choice of primer. Use a stain-blocking primer on woods that bleed, such as red cedar or redwood.

7. Coat any stains with B-I-N (a white pigmented alcohol-shellac-based primer made by Wm. Zinsser & Co., Somerset, NJ) or Emulsabond in latex primer.

8. Paint with finish coat. If the wall was in good shape, all it may need is a good washing and no primer coat. If

you're making a radical color change, you may need a primer-sealer to hide the old color completely.

The general advice about primers and finish coats is to consider them as a system. To some, this means that if you use an oil-base primer, you should finish with an oil-base paint. Others say you will get better adhesion if you use a polyvinyl acetate latex sealer as the prime coat. You can also apply latex over oil, but for compatibility buy both paints from the same manufacturer and follow top coat manufacturer's primer recommendations.

Primers—Exterior

Here is a summary of the types of primers available for exterior use and comments on their outstanding characteristics. (See also the accompanying chart.)

Alkali-resistant primers: Two coats of this primer are required over concrete, block, or stucco under alkali-sensitive top coats such as alkyd paints or enamels.

Alkyd-based metal primers: These dry harder and faster than oil-based primers and provide corrosion resistance.

Alkyd primers: These are also faster-drying and harder-surfaced than oil primers. They have greater resistance to bleeding and are less likely to dissolve stains that would show through the prime coat.

Latex metal primer: This type of primer is gaining in popularity because of its white color (allowing overcoating in any color), quick drying, and easy clean-up.

Latex primer: Formulated for use under latex or latex-acrylic top coats on wood surfaces, it requires thorough surface preparation. It can be used over nonglossy or weathered oil paint.

Paints and Stains

Oil-based metal primer: Used to help reduce corrosion on ferrous metal surfaces, this type primer is particularly suited for coating galvanized steel.

Oil primer: Oil primer contains bodied oil to control penetration into wood.

Exterior Primers

	Aluminum	Aluminum Gutters, Downspouts, or Siding	Asphalt Roofing	Brick, Block, Concrete, Stone, or Stucco	Brass, Bronze, or Copper	Galvanized Steel[2]	Iron or Steel (bright)	Metal Roofing	Plywood
Types[1]									
Alkyd-base metal primer	●	●			●	●	●		
Alkyd deck primer									
Alkyd primer									
Alkali-resistant coating				●					
Asphalt roof paint			●						
Iron oxide primer									
Latex metal primer					●	●	●		
Latex primer									
Masonry surface conditioner				●					
Oil-base metal primer	●	●			●	●	●		
Oil primer									
Portland cement masonry paint				●					
Portland cement metal paint						●	●		
*Stain-sealing primer									●
Use top coat as primer			●						
Water-repellent preservative									●
Zinc chromate primer						●	●	●	
Zinc-dust primer						●	●		

NOTE: Clear or transparent finish coats are penetrated more by the sun's ultraviolet light and are not as durable as opaque finishes.
[1]These may be alkyd or latex. Select on basis of top coat manufacturer's recommendations. Must be used instead of alkyd or latex or stain-leeching woods such as redwood or Western red cedar. Alcohol-based primer sealers can be used to spot-seal knotholes on exterior work but should not be used as a coating since they form a vapor barrier.
[2]Galvanized steel should be allowed to weather for six months or be given a vinegar wash and rinse.

Portland cement metal paint: This is something of a hybrid in that it can be used either as a primer or top coat system for galvanized steel.

Stain-blocking primers: Use B-I-N (white pigmented alcohol-shellac based primer), polyvinyl acetate latex primers, or latex primers to which you have

Surfaces

Porches and Decks	Pressure-Treated Lumber	Shakes, Shingles, Wood Clapboard, or Siding	Terne Roofing	Wood Trim	Finish Coat
					Alkyd house paint, alkyd trim enamel, aluminum paint, alkyd-base metal exterior enamel
●	●				Alkyd deck paint, (2-part epoxy, 2-part polyurethane)
				●	Alkyd house paint or alkyd trim enamel
					Alkali-resistant coating
					Aluminum or bituminous roof coating
			●		Alkyd, oil-based latex house or trim or exterior metal enamel
					Latex house and trim paint
		●		●	Latex house paint, latex trim enamel alkyd or oil-based paints
					Oil-base alkyd latex house, trim, or masonry paint; alkali-resistant coating
					Oil-base exterior metal paint; oil-base house and trim paint
●	●	●			Oil-base flat, semigloss, or gloss house paint barn paint
					Portland cement masonry paint
					Portland cement paint for metal
	●	●		●	Any alkyd, latex or oil-base house or trim paint for plywood use on acrylic-latex
					Aluminum or bituminous roof coating
					Stain (semi-transparent or solid color)
					Aluminum paint, bituminous roof coating
					Aluminum paint, bituminous roof coating

Paints and Stains

added Emulsabond under latex, oil, or alkyd paints. B-I-N is a particularly easy to apply and economical stain sealer. These primers seal underlying stain and knotholes, and stop water-soluble color extracts in Western red cedar or redwood from discoloring top coats.

Preparation—Interior

Preparing interiors for painting often involves less trouble than an exterior job. As a rule, surfaces in good shape need a simple washing. Interior woodwork almost always is painted with a gloss or semigloss, which means you must either sand the surface with fine-grit paper or wash the surface with one of the commercially available, abrasive liquid sanding products and rinse, to

Interior Finishes Selection Guide

	Acoustical Tile	Aluminum	Brick	Cement Blocks	Concrete	Concrete Floors	Drywall	Galvanized Steel
Interior Primers								
Acrylic latex block filler				●				
Alkali-resistant enamel				●	●			
Alkyd flat enamel								
Alkyd metal primer		●						
Alkyd primer	●				●			
Clear wood sealer								
Enamel undercoat								
Exterior masonry alkyd paint			●	●				
Latex flat wall paint	●						●	
Latex primer	●						●	
Latex metal primer		●						●
Portland cement masonry paint				●	●	●		
Portland cement metal primer								●
Surface conditioner			●		●			
Use top coat as primer							●	
Wood filler*								
Zinc metal primer								●

*Do not use under urethane finishes if it contains stearates.
NOTE: These are generalized recommendations. Read and follow specific directions on the manufacturer's label. Prime coat must provide complete coverage on cementitious surfaces before applying alkyds which can be damaged by alkalis.

give the new paint better adhesion.

The higher the gloss, the easier the surface is to clean. Manufacturers use different descriptions, which can be confusing. Here is a list of commonly used terms and their better understood description. With the exception of lacquers, the higher the gloss, the less the pigment and the less the hiding capacity (and durability outdoors).

Interior—Primers

While many interior painting jobs on non-porous surfaces require no application of a primer, in other instances, and when changing colors, you will achieve a more professional appearance and get better top coat hiding and coverage with use of the appropriate primer.

Surfaces

Iron and Steel	Paneling	Plaster	Wood Flooring	Wood Trim	
Finish Coats					
					Latex masonry paint or enamel
					Alkali-resistant enamel or latex paint
	●			●	Latex flat or alkyd semigloss or gloss enamel
●					Latex flat or alkyd semigloss or gloss enamel
		●			Only use latex flat paint on acoustical tile
			●	●	Any latex or alkyd paint or polyurethane over stain
	●			●	Any latex or alkyd paint
					Latex or alkyd masonry paint
		●			Latex flat wall paint
		●			Any latex or alkyd paint or enamel (only use latex flat on acoustical tile)
●					Any latex paint or enamel
					Portland cement masonry paint
					Portland cement metal paint
			●		Latex or alkyd semigloss or gloss enamel
			●		Same as primer: polyurethane, clear finish, epoxy enamel, moisture-cured urethane, 2-part epoxy, or polyurethane
	●		●	●	Clear wood sealer
					Any alkyd paint or enamel

Paints and Stains

Alkali-resistant primers. These are for use on damp cement block or concrete.

Alkyd. These are for use only on dry concrete or plaster.

Acrylic or latex block filler. This is characterized by a thick consistency for application by roller or brush to seal alkali (cementitious) surfaces. The latex material can be applied to damp or wet surfaces.

Latex. Formulated to seal drywall surfaces without raising the nap, it is also good on plastics or concrete. Latex primer is quick-drying. It is not adequate for protecting metal against moisture. Nails in the primed surface may rust if they are not first countersunk, caulked, and sealed.

Latex metal primer. Usually white, this gives good corrosion resistance if applied to a bright clear surface and covered by a moisture-impervious top coat.

Surface conditioner. A sealer for masonry (brick or concrete) surfaces, this may be used prior to top coating or, where label suggests, mixed with top-coat material as a prime coat.

Enamel undercoat. Use on wood when any type of gloss enamel is to be used.

Paint Color

The color wheels will help you judge which colors are compatible. Remember, colors will appear lighter on a large area than they do on a small chip. Always match color chips on a white background.

The conventional color wheel selector has been used for years but will give you only safe, ordinary combinations. Today there are no set rules in color schemes that are not successfully broken by interior decorators at times. Explore the opportunities: Experiment with color chips, carpet samples, textile swatches, and wallpapers until you find a combination that pleases you. Paint departments can custom-blend to give you any color, depth, or tone you desire.

Do you want your room bright or subdued? The table on page 375 shows the measured reflectance of various colors and surfaces.

Paint Finishes

Actual Gloss	Commonly Used Terms	Uses
Gloss	High gloss Gloss ¾ gloss	Kitchen and bathroom walls, or a playroom if it is subject to frequent washing; painted outdoor furniture
Semigloss	Semigloss Eggshell Velvet Satin	Hallways, bathrooms, and dens
Flat	Dull Flat Matte	Living and dining rooms

Here are a few decorating tips:

1. Use contrasts, not just in color but also in hue, shade, and texture.
2. Lighter colors, whites, and pastels expand space; dark colors make a room look smaller.
3. You can make a room brighter by using white or light yellows, dignified by using vertical lines or Williamsburg pastels, or contemporary and lively by contrasting bold colors.
4. Design the whole decor by using carpet samples, wallpaper swatches, upholstery fabrics, drapery samples, paint chips, and even the paintings you wish to hang.
5. Judge your color schemes by day and night using the same incandescent or fluorescent light you will use to illuminate your room.
6. Remember to consider the colors you are using in adjoining rooms, particularly those joined by large openings.
7. If all else fails, get the help of an interior decorator.

Triad harmony utilizes three equidistant colors on the color wheel, achieves variety by using different tints of principal colors.

Complementary colors are any two opposite each other on the color wheel. These are familiar contrasts, generally considered harmonious.

Split complementaries are a foolproof way to choose tri-color schemes. Turn the Y pointer 180° for opposite split complementary colors.

Double complementaries combine two pairs of opposite colors and are a sound basis for selecting harmonious four-way combinations.

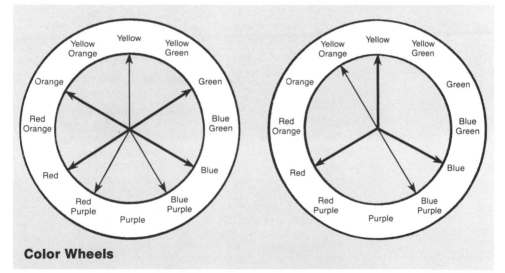

Color Wheels

Color Reflectances

Mirror	100%	Salmon	53%
White	80%	Pale apple green	51%
Ivory (light)	71%	Medium grey	43%
Apricot beige	66%	Light green	41%
Lemon yellow	65%	Pale blue	41%
Ivory	59%	Deep rose	12%
Light buff	56%	Dark green	9%
Peach	53%	Black (matte)	0%

Paints and Stains

Fading

Pigments used in paints and stain are most often inert, inorganic materials that are not changed by chemicals. However, some of them are changed in time by ultraviolet light, heat, or weathering. Their light wave absorbency is altered so they appear to fade, darken, or change color. The table here lists some common color pigments and indicates their resistance to fading.

Fade and Change Resistance in Paint Colors

Color	Pigment	Fade Resistance	Other
Blue	Prussian blue	Tends to develop streaky iridescence	These metallic blues have high hiding properties and do not bleed, but are not alkali-resistant. Don't use on masonry.
	Chinese blue	Good fade resistance	
	Milori blue	Good fade resistance	
	Ultramarine	Fades in sunlight	Alkali-resistant, but color is destroyed by acid.
	Phthalocyanine blue	Expensive but very fade resistant. The best of the blue pigments, with good exterior durability.	Acid-, alkali-, and heat-resistant
Green	Chromium oxide	Poor hiding power and tinting strength, but one of the better of the greens for fade resistance	Acid- and alkali-resistant; heat-resistant
	Chrome green	Excellent fade resistance and good hiding	Not alkali-resistant. (Never mix yourself. If put into an oxidant such as linseed oil, it will start spontaneous combustion!)
	Chromium hydrate	Expensive, but excellent fade resistance	Alkali-resistant
	Phthalocyanine green	Expensive but very fade resistant—the best of the green pigments, with good exterior durability	Acid, alkali-, and heat-resistant
	Organic greens (dyes)	Brilliant color but poor fade resistance—don't use out of doors. Not very durable.	Varies by specific dye
Red	Iron oxides	Varies by origin—Spanish oxide is one of the best; fade-resistant and durable.	Alkali-resistant
		Synthetic iron oxide has high hiding power and fade resistance.	Alkali-resistant

Fade and Change Resistance in Paint Colors (Concluded)

Color	Pigment	Fade Resistance	Other
Red (continued)		Venetian reds have poor fade resistance, are not durable.	Indoor use only
	Burnt/Sienna	Indoor use only.	
	Toluidine toners	Excellent fade resistance and hiding power. Non-bleeding in oil but bleed in lacquers.	Acid- and alkali-resistant
Orange	Cadmium orange	Fair fade resistance. Do not use in areas having acid rain.	Alkali-resistant but decomposed by acids
Brown	Pure iron oxide (metallic brown)	Durable, nonfading. A variety of formulations with various performance characteristics. Used in low-cost paints and primers.	Nonbleeding
	Vandyke brown and raw amber	Used only in stains.	
Yellow	Hydrated iron oxide	Often called French ochre, now made synthetically. Very durable and fade-resistant.	Alkali-resistant
	Toluidine yellows	Low hiding power. Used in interior water-based paints. Fades outdoors.	Alkali-resistant
	Cadmium yellow	Poor exterior durability and fade resistance.	Poor resistance to ultraviolet light, acids, and alkali

NOTE: Alkali-resistant pigments can be used on masonry. Paints with pigments that are neither acid- nor alkali-resistant should not be used on masonry or in bathrooms or kitchens. Those that are not acid-resistant should not be used outdoors in areas subject to acid rain or industrial pollution.

Specialty Paints

Masonry paints (portland cement paints) for block, stucco and cement come in two forms: oil based and powdered. The powdered paint must be mixed with water and applied to wet surfaces and is not as abrasion-resistant or durable as vehicle-based paints. They can be applied over surfaces previously painted with the same type paint and can be used for both primer or top coat. They must be kept damp until well cured and can be pigmented. Their chief advantage is low cost. (Do not confuse them with oil based masonry paint which is used chiefly as a primer-top coat system on weathered galvanized steel.)

Aluminum paint can be applied to all prepared metal, asphalt, and dry wood surfaces. Do not apply during freezing weather. Do not apply over damp porous surfaces. It is not considered appropriate for residential

Paints and Stains

Comparing Interior Paints

Paint	Uses	Features
Latex	Primed surfaces such as: drywall, ceilings, windowsills, trim, moldings, wallboard and plaster. Window frames and wrought iron.	Hardly any odor. Easy application. Nonflammable and quick-drying. Available in all glosses and flat. Easy touchup. Less durable and washable than alkyd paints. Will not adhere to polished surfaces. Available in nondrip formulation. Also available as one-coat paint.
Alkyd	Primed surfaces as shown for latex except for drywall and plaster.	Superior hiding power. Tough surface. Washable. Slight odor. Slower drying than latex. Excellent leveling. Also available as one-coat paint. Consider more expensive dripless formulation when painting ceiling.
Acrylic	Primed surfaces as shown for latex.	Clear, bright colors. Washable, with good hiding power.
Acrylic latex with Tetrafluoro ethylene	Primed surfaces as shown for latex	A nondrip one-coat paint. Clear, bright colors. Excellent leveling. Water-resistant and washable. Unaffected by grease or oil. Good hiding power. Available in nondrip formulation.
Oil	Rarely used except as authentic trim coating in restorations	Strong odor. Slow-drying, highly combustible, and not as durable as alkyds. If used, you cannot apply other types of paint over it later.
Urethane and polyurethane (two-part systems)	Use over any porous surface or existing finish. Particularly good on tables, counter tops, wood flooring, and stairs.	Somewhat tricky and difficult to apply but provides tough surface that resists alcohol, grease, dirt, and abrasion. Very deep appearing high gloss but also available in semigloss.
Epoxy (two-part system)	Adheres to nonporous surfaces but cannot be applied over other finishes	The strongest and toughest paint but must be applied immediately after adding and mixing hardening agent.

Primer	Thinning and Clean-up
Wood and Drywall Acrylic latex, latex primer, latex flat *Cementitious Surfaces* Acrylic latex block filler, alkyd masonry paint *Metals* Latex metal primer	Thin with potable water. Clean brushes and rollers with soap and water, then dry brushes or ferrule will rust.
As above. For cementitious surfaces see interior finishes selection guide	Mineral spirits or turpentine
Save as shown above for latex	Mineral spirits or turpentine
Same as shown above for latex	One-coat. Do not thin. Clean up with water.
On new wood use alkyd primer sealer or an alcohol based primer sealer. In repainting use an alcohol-shellac based primer sealer.	Mineral spirits or turpentine
Top coat used for primer	Most are thinned with mineral spirits, but check manufacturer's label.
Top coat used for primer	Can't be thinned and will only clean up with acetone while still liquid.

Paints and Stains

Comparing Interior Paints (Concluded)

Paint	Uses	Features
Epoxy (continued)		Sets up quickly and requires skill to apply.
Alcohol based primer sealer (white pigmented cutback shellac)	Seals surface both to stop resin and stains from reaching top coat and forms a vapor-barrier (Bin = 0.4 perms.)	Covers stains—such as marking pens and resinous knots in new wood—that would creep through most paints. Quick drying and lower cost than other options.
Alkyd primer sealer	Seals resinous, staining or porous surfaces	Easy to apply, practically odor-free.

use, because it gives an industrial appearance.

Textured paints are available in a variety of consistencies for special effects, such as creating a stucco appearance, and can be applied with brushes, rollers, putty knives, and trowels. They are not appropriate for historic houses and are difficult to clean. Other than to create special effects, their main use is to cover up cracks and imperfections in work areas or garages.

Acoustical paints have a flat porous film that does not harm the noise-reducing properties of acoustical tile. Never use glossy paints on acoustical tile as you will seal the holes that allow noise to penetrate the absorbent backing.

Aerosol paints are special-purpose enamels and lacquers for small jobs. Their labels identify their use—for model painting, high-temperature engine paint, furniture lacquer, automotive finishes, etc. Dozens of types and colors are available. They may be applied directly from aerosol cans, so there are no brushes or rollers to clean up. But note how little pigment there is in the can (2 to 3 percent), making their use expensive.

Buy cans with tamper-proof tops. It assures you the can is full and in working order. And read the label to compare the propellant versus paint content of each can. For example, "77%/23%" tells you about 12 ounces of a 16-ounce can is paint and vehicle and 4 ounces is hydrocarbon. Cans must be thoroughly shaken before use. Can must be kept upright. Clean the nozzle after every use by inverting the can and pressing the spray nozzle; then wipe clean. Keep your finger on the back of the spray nozzle to avoid splattering.

Miscellaneous coatings are available for such special purposes as painting table tennis tables, chalk boards, swimming pools, marine equipment, driveways, asphalt roofs, underground metal, and windows.

Floor paints. Where the existing surface is dry, hard, smooth, caulked, and sealed, a good-quality polyurethane, acrylic latex, or Lucite interior floor and deck paint can be used to resurface. Two-part polyurethane or epoxy paints, mixed before application, give a particularly hard-wearing surface. These paints can be used both as a primer or a top coat. Outdoors, use an alkali-resistant coating under porch and deck paint.

Concrete and stucco sealers and

Primer	Thinning and Clean-up
NA	Denatured alcohol
NA	Mineral spirits or turpentine

paints. Concrete may need a primer to tie down the chalking that occurs even while painting. The concrete or stucco must have cured for three weeks before sealing. Naturally the surface should be brushed, hosed down, or mopped with water (alone) before starting.

The sealers are available as powdered or ready-mixed masonry primer and are applied to wet concrete. The higher the Portland cement content, generally the greater the durability. Normally look for 65 percent portland cement; 85 to 90 percent if using it on a swimming pool.

The surface should be sprayed with water between coats and twelve hours after final application to help harden the portland cement. Never use below 40°F.

Apply by rigorous scrubbing with a coarse fiber scrubbing brush. Thirty days after sealer application the concrete can be coated with a good-quality acrylic latex or polystyrene latex paint to withstand washing and wear.

Lacquers are fast-drying, clear or pigmented, high-gloss coatings that dry by solvent evaporation. Having very low solid content, they form a very thin film and while they dry fast, a number of coats need to be applied. Most lacquers are sold in aerosol cans.

Indoors, concrete can be sealed with alkaline-resistant phenolic varnish, but it takes two coats. Aqua-thane (white), a polyurethane wall or floor coating is easy to use and also waterproofs. Of course, no coating on the inside can keep out water under a couple of feet of hydrostatic pressure for long. Waterproofing should be applied to the outside wherever such pressure is a factor.

Use only the recommended thinners and solvents in the proportion recommended on the label, and have a plentiful supply of rags and water or thinner on hand.

Air out used paint rags or leave in a pail of water until removed from the premises. Otherwise they can cause spontaneous combustion.

When painting beyond reach of the ground, use only sound, sturdy ladders securely based and supported. Never stand on the top two steps. Look for an inclination indicator on the side rail of the ladder and set the ladder at the correct angle. Ladders can be hazardous! Properly used ladders are safe. Read and believe the safety instructions printed on labels on the

Paints and Stains

side rail and think! If you are working on a ladder in front of a door, be sure to hang a sign on the other side of the door warning people not to open it.

Working with Stains

Exterior Stains

Houses built with wood siding these days are often meant to display the natural warmth and beauty of the material. So, too, are redwood decks— it would be a crime to cover that gorgeous wood with paint! To maintain their good looks, these woods are covered with clear finishes or semitransparent stains and preservatives.

Clear finishes are designed to be penetrating: They sink into the surface fibers of the wood. They maintain the warm, freshly cut hue of the wood and prevent it from turning the silver-gray color it would attain after a few years in the open weather without such protection. Many of the clear finishes contain water repellents, such as paraffin wax, or preservatives. Those with preservatives offer more protection, not only from weather but from mildew, fungi, and insects.

When a pigment is added to a clear finish, it becomes a semitransparent penetrating stain. However, these stains don't contain enough pigment to obscure the wood grain; most of the grain shows through. These stains are made in both oil and latex versions, although the latex kind forms a surface film and is not truly a penetrating stain. In both, the pigment improves the durability of the finish by blocking more ultraviolet light. Penetrating stains are ideal for rough-sawn or weathered wood.

These finishes may be applied by brush, roller, or sprayer. Brushing gets the best coverage and is essential on rough-sawn wood. Work in the shade, and apply a second coat before the first is dry to get maximum penetration of the wood.

Clear finishes and semitransparent stains may require new coats a little sooner than a properly done coat of paint, but reapplication is much less laborious. You don't have to sand, scrape, or prime. All you do is brush on a new coat, and you're done.

Interior With Stains

Four reasons for using stains on woodwork and furniture are: (1) to make one wood look like another, (2) to give new wood an aged appearance, (3) to make wood look natural, and (4) to make all wood used on a project match in color and grain.

The materials you'll use will depend on the type of wood grain and whether you want to pay for premixed materials or save by mixing your own. You have the following options:

Penetrating stains. They stain and seal in one coat. Some oil-penetrating stains may be applied over painted surface.

Latex stains. These are self-priming and quick-drying and age with the wood, but they are generally not water-repellent.

Oil stains. These commonly come premixed and are easy to use.

Water-base stains. The pigment is sold in 1-ounce packages that you mix with water. These are the lowest in cost and preferred by professionals but hard to locate.

Shellac stains. A package of pigment is mixed with a cup of shellac and a cup of alcohol to create a semiopaque wiping stain. By applying heavily and wiping off with a cloth you can create an artificial grain.

Urethane stains. These provide stain and finish in one coat. A second coat, if desired, should be applied before

Paints and Stains

Materials for Working with Stains

Useful Materials	Appropriate Thinners
Rubber gloves and apron	For shellac—alcohol
Bristle paintbrush	For varnish—turpentine
Foam brushes or a sponge	For polyurethane—turpentine
Lint-free wiping cloths	For penetrating oil stains—mineral spirits
Putty knife or scraper	For non-grain-raising stains—alcohol
0-grade steel wool	For latex stains—water
Old toothbrush	
Sander and 00-grade sandpaper	
Tack rag	
Cotton swabs	
Empty cans	

the first is completely dry. Test on a matching scrap of wood as once applied, these stains are impossible to remove.

Stains can be applied with a foam brush, bristle brush, or clean lint-free cloth. A real bristle brush works the best.

Five Rules to Staining

1. The surface must be free of all contaminants.
2. Test the stain on a similarly prepared sample of the wood before you begin.
3. Stir the stain often and thoroughly (do not shake) as you work.
4. Don't use exterior stains indoors.
5. Choose a well-ventilated, well-lighted room, free of dust, flame, children, and pets, where the work can cure without problems.

Preparing Wood for Finishing

If you want a smooth top coat you may need a filler coat. Apply your stain first. Close-grain woods such as maple, beech, and birch (see table) need only a thin filler. Oak and mahogany are open grain and will need several coats to penetrate and fill the open grain. Wood filler is available in paste or liquid form. For porous woods, the paste is best but will need thinning as directed

on the label. You may be able to use the stain to both tint and thin the filler. If no stain is used, a colored wood filler that matches the wood should be used. Fillers should be allowed to set five to ten minutes after diluting with mineral spirits. Applied with burlap, the stain should not be wiped off until it forms a ball by rubbing the surface with your finger.

After the wood filler has dried and been sanded, clean the surface with a tack-cloth. If no added stain is being used, wait twenty-four hours and apply the sealer over the sanded and cleaned filled surfaces. Another coat of stained filler may be necessary at this stage if stain raised the grain and required sanding. The sealer can be a penetrating sealer or a varnish. The penetrating sealer will be absorbed by the fibers in the wood and form a wear-resistant surface level with the wood. Touch-up is easier with a sealer that has a lower gloss than varnish. Sealers will generally require waxing.

Varnish is available in a variety of glosses, the high gloss being the most wear resistant. The first coat should be thinned with 10 percent mineral spirits or turpentine. You can use a clear lacquer, but it may be more difficult to apply.

Paints and Stains

Both the varnish and the lacquer should be applied in a dust-free location where they can be left to dry. Urethane or epoxy finishes are more expensive but offer the best abrasion resistance and require the least maintenance. An alkyd or latex floor enamel can be used for light or moderate use areas.

Gloss Finishes

Today's polymers—polyurethane, polyester, epoxy, and acrylics—don't require rubbing or polishing, cover fast, lay flat, and are so quick in drying that only the lower price will persuade some people to use hard-to-apply natural resin varnish. (In the thirty-six hours varnish takes to dry, a lot of dust, flies, and lawn clippings can ruin your work.)

Once dry, the polymer varnishes are spill- and stain-resistant and stay clear. They do go on thick, however, which may not be what you want on fine furniture. Shellac is a good sealer and dries fast, but it is brittle, has a short shelf life, and is stained by water or alcohol, so must have an additional protective coating. Shelf life is a problem with most polymers. Always run a test strip when using a new can to be sure it cures in the specified time.

Enhancing Specific Wood Finishes

If you are using an opaque paint or coating, you can use less costly wood or plywood. All you need is a smooth surface, and you can use sealers and fillers if the wood you are using contains knots or splices. However, if you want to bring out the beauty of the grain and enhance or change the coloring while providing a protective coating, you'll need to consider the particular wood you are using.

Here are some traditional methods:

Natural pine. Brush on boiled linseed oil; wipe off and wax. In several months the wood will acquire an attractive golden brown patina.

Antique pine. Sand, then apply a wash coat of 4 to 6 parts orange shellac diluted with 1 part alcohol. Stain, using a coat of raw sienna in

Filling Requirements of Wood

Hardwoods	Softwoods
Ash/require fillers	Apple/varnishes well
Aspen	Basswood/paints well
Beech/requires filler/paints poorly	Birch/requires filler/varnishes well
Butternut	Boxwood
Chestnut/paints poorly/requires filler	Cedar/varnishes well/paints well
Elm/paints poorly/requires fillers	Cherry/varnishes well
Hickory/requires filler	Cottonwood/paints well
Lauan	Cypress/varnishes well/paints well
Mahogany/requires filler	Ebony
Locust	Fir/paints poorly
Oak/requires filler	Gum/varnishes well
Rosewood	Maple/requires filler/varnishes well
Teak/requires filler	Pear
Walnut/requires filler	Pine
	Poplar
	Redwood/paints well
	Satinwood

linseed oil. Wipe off. If the article being finished is furniture, varnish; if a wood wall, use acrylic coat or wax.

Natural mahogany. To retain the original color, bleach briefly and rinse. Wipe dry, then sand lightly and dust. Apply resin penetrating sealer; add raw sienna to paste wood filler and apply.

Wood-Finishing Products

Type	Comments
Fillers **Liquid fillers**	Thickened varnish Sanding sealer It may take five coats and lots of sanding.
Paste filler	Available prestained. May need thinning with turpentine. One coat sufficient if surface has been presealed with shellac, varnish, primer sealer, or polyurethane. TIP: Need to raise shallow dents? Apply a medium-hot iron to a damp cloth covering the dent.
Stains **Water based stain:** (aniline dyes in water or alcohol)	Packet of dye is dissolved in boiling water. Brilliant transparent color without hiding grain of wood. Not bleached by sunlight. Require dampening the wood and sanding off grain before applying.
Wiping stains: (oil or shellac)	These are nonpenetrating oil stains or pigmented shellac and alcohol. Will darken, cover, and cloud grain. Used chiefly on poor wood. Applied heavily, they can be wiped off with a cloth to create artificial grain. Very economical compared to premixed stains.
Penetrating oil stains:	Easy to apply and control. May need several coats to achieve dark shades.
NGR (non-grain raising) **Water-based and latex stains**	Most water-based stains do raise the grain, particularly on soft woods. Do not use on softwoods. Work best on maple, oak and walnut. Some are ready mixed and easy to apply. The longer they are left on before wiping, the darker the effect.
Exterior stains:	These are oil- or latex-based with mildewcides and preservatives. More expensive than others and require special solvent. Some don't need a finish coat. Read label. Never use for indoor applications. Red stains are photosensitive and will turn brown-gray in sunlight.

Paints and Stains

Top Coat Selection Chart

Type	Characteristics	Application Tips
Polyester Resin (requires addition of activator).	Slight yellow cast but looks excellent on pine or redwood. Water-, stain-, scuff-, and scratch-resistant. Available pigmented in white and colors (called gel-coat). Recommended for outdoor furniture and other exterior jobs. Works best on soft-woods.	Do not apply over paint, sealers, fillers, oil stain, or shellac. Apply with natural bristle brush or spray gun. Maybe used when recommended on NGR water stains.
Polyurethane varnish	Clear transparent coating. Is both water- and mar-resistant as well as durable.	Do not apply over paint, shellac, sealers, thinners or oil stains. Apply with natural bristle brush, roller, or spray gun.
Two-part epoxy varnish	Provides hard surface with excellent abrasion resistance.	Use throwaway brush—impossible to wash out. Read manufacturer's label.
Shellac	Brittle and easily spotted by alcohol or water. Use only as undercoat. If used as finish apply several coats and wax heavily.	Use brush.
Lacquer	Fast-drying furniture finish. Lays smooth.	Sprayed. (Requires equipment.) Can be used over NGR stains that have been sealed with shellac or lacquer sealer.
Natural resin varnish	For indoor use. Available in colors. Use Spar varnish outdoors or on tables or counter tops that will get wet with water or alcohol (but they will need recoating annually).	Use natural-bristle brush or cheesecloth. Thin as necessary (see label).
Resin oil finish or tung oil	Penetrates into wood and hardens grain. Resists stains, burns, water, and alcohol. Good for counter tops.	Hand rubbed with cheesecloth. Takes 2 or 3 applications. Cannot be applied over sealer and thinners.

Sand lightly and varnish. If a darker color is acceptable, just apply several coats of clear lacquer. Use tinted filler if necessary.

Dark mahogany. Use mahogany tung oil as a wiping stain. Wipe off when the depth of color desired is achieved. Seal with shellac; fill with

Drying Time	Finish	Solvent/Clean-up
Depends on the amount of activator—read label. Normally 15 to 30 minutes.	Gloss	Acetone
1 to 2 hours. Allow 12 hours between coats.	High gloss to dull sheen	Acetone
3 hours for first coat; 5 to 8 hours for second coat.	High gloss	Not soluble. (Acetone may work if it hasn't cured.)
About 15 minutes to 2 hours. Allow 3 to 4 hours before covering.	High gloss, but may be rubbed down with steel wool	Alcohol
Dries quickly, but allow 2 to 3 days before rubbing down with very fine steel wool.	Selection of finishes	Lacquer thinner
24 to 36 hours; slower in damp weather	Low to high gloss.	See label.
8 to 12 hours	Darkens to give rich appearance	Alcohol

paste filler, adding vandyke brown or burnt sienna. Apply a transparent coating of choice or varnish.

Blond mahogany. Follow the same procedure as with natural mahogany, but bleach twice and use a neutral wood filler.

Paints and Stains

Natural oak. Oak is naturally variable in color so may need bleaching to get an even final appearance. Bleach, sand, and dust, then fill with neutral filler. Apply lacquer, acrylic, or varnish.

Bleached oak. Sand and dust. If the wood is mottled green in appearance, bleach. Fill with white-tinted paste filler. Use white wiping stain or white penetrating filler and varnish.

White grain oak. Sand and vacuum the surface to remove all dust. Brush on gloss enamel: black, dark brown, blue, or green. Again sand smooth and vacuum, then apply a second coat. Don't sand. Mix white enamel with paste wood filler to the desired tint. Brush on, then scrape off across the grain with stiff cardboard or a flexible plastic blade. Wipe with burlap across the grain. Sand very lightly and apply at least two coats of varnish.

Natural maple. Sand and dust. Apply synthetic sealer, lacquer, or white shellac. Finish with varnish.

Blond maple. Sand, then bleach. Sand, dust, and apply lacquer or acrylic transparent coating. (You can first use a white wiping stain, if desired.)

Colonial maple. Use wiping stain, then sand, dust, and varnish.

Pigment stain fir. Never sand fir. Brush on synthetic resin penetrating filler. Apply wiping stain by brush (you can make your own by diluting oil paint or enamel with turpentine) in the color desired. Wipe off. Apply two coats of varnish.

White stain fir. Apply turpentine-diluted white enamel and wipe off. Varnish.

Medium stain fir. Use synthetic resin sealer. Quickly apply and then remove a walnut oil stain. Varnish.

Natural and stained walnut. Bleach and use an all-lacquer finish. You can use wiping stain, but keep it light by wiping quickly.

Wood Finishing Aids

Sandpaper. Used to smooth. Use very fine 8-0, or at least 6-0 waterproof sandpaper wet.

Water. Used to raise grain. (Bleach will raise grain, too.)

Bleach. Used to compensate for darkening of wood by shellacs and varnishes.

Penetrating sealers. Used to retard penetration of stain (prevent over-darkening). Also used prior to painting to ensure even appearance of finish coat.

Stain. To impart color and intensify natural color.

Stain-seal. Used with shellac coat to prevent bleeding of oil stains.

Paste and liquid wood filler. Used to fill and smooth open grain woods. They are often pigmented and must always be sanded.

Finish Coat. Can be acrylic, urethane, polyester resin, varnish, rubbing oil, or silicone oil—choice depends on wood surface. Never finish with shellac, since it is easily stained by spilled alcohol or water.

Garnet paper. Use 6-0 grade garnet for finishing surface.

Steel wool. Use 3-0 grade for finish rubbing.

Pumice oil. Used sometimes instead of sandpaper, particularly on fluted or shaped objects.

Maintenance of Finished Wood

Surface	Protection	Cleaner
Resilient flooring: asphalt tile, linoleum, rubber vinyl, and terrazzo	Use liquid or paste floor wax with Carnuba base wax, or sponge on coat of clear acrylic or urethane protective coating.	Damp mop with soap and water.
Wood floors and lacquer, retardant spray varnish, enamel, or polyurethane finish	Use paste or spray wax. Polish.	Apply a silicone dust, and wipe furniture as directed.
Wood treated with penetrating resin	Add additional coat of resin.	Use soap and water.
Wood with shellac and French polish	Use paste or liquid wax and silicone spray wax.	Oiled cloth. Don't use water or alcohol.
Wood finished with rubbed oil	Never wax. Instead, use linseed-oiled cloth and rub in.	Clean with cloth and mixture of 3 parts turpentine to 1 part linseed oil.

NOTE: Read the labels. Some acrylic coatings should not be used on wood floors or paneling.

Paint Removal

Several new electric tools and paint strippers are now available to make this tedious chore easier.

Chemical paint removers now come with spray cans to make application easier. One is called Dad's Easy Spray. The time-proven products, such as UGL's Raizoff and Strip-Eze, are applied with a thick, broad brush in one direction and, after allowing time for the old paint to soften, are scraped off. Norton's Unpaint is a powder supplied in a bucket to which you add water and mix. Spread as a blanket over the paint, it sets and can be peeled off without a scraper. It doesn't contain hazardous methylene chloride, found in some other liquid strippers. Before you buy any chemical stripper read the label. Some contain a wax that comes to the surface and keeps the stripper liquid and working longer, but it requires latex removal with turpentine or mineral spirits. Liquid sandpaper is an abrasive cleaner that can be used to prepare glossy surfaces for painting.

If you choose to avoid chemical strippers, you have several other options. There is the Milwaukee heat gun stripper that combines a hot air blower with a scraper, several brands of electrical "iron" type paint softeners, an Allover air heat gun, and a new Pow'r Scraper with a reciprocating blade. While many do-it-yourselfers still favor the putty knife, there are new hand scrapers with comfort-designed hand grips, such as Warner's Pistol Grip, the Hyde scraper, and Allway's, that can make the job more comfortable.

Some people use propane or blowtorches, but there is a risk of charring the wood or starting a fire if you are not careful. Bernz-o-matic makes these.

Paints and Stains

Regardless of the method used, you'll need to finish the job with steel wool or a belt sander.

TIP: To save time and avoid the tedious and painstaking job of stripping down antique furniture, look in your Yellow Pages for a professional paint stripper who has the facility to dip and clean your furniture. However, this should not be done to really valuable furniture, as it may raise the grain and dissolve the glue in joints and wood pins.

The Right Tools to Remove Paint

Scrapers are made from polished spring steel. Only the most expensive have been milled, so you will want to file and prepare the edge on a sharpening stone before using. Make sure you have removed all burrs and have a flat edge. A hand scraper should be square and a cabinet scraper angled.

Hook scrapers provide a hooked blade, which is pulled along the work surface to scrape away paint. The scraper usually has replaceable blades, which can be removed by loosening a screw. Carbide blades are available for longer life. Most blades can be resharpened by filing. A new scraper called Black and Silver, by Hyde, has a computer-designed handle to fit the human hand and comes with a long-

Chemical Paint Strippers and Rust Removers

Type	Trade Names†	Uses
Paint Strippers		
Semi-Paste	Kwikeez	Brush cleaner only
Semi-Paste	Strypeeze	Paints, varnishes, enamels
Semi-Paste	Zipcleen	Brush cleaner only
Semi-Paste	Zip Strip	Paints, varnishes, enamels
Liquid	Zip Strip	Paints, varnishes, enamels
Liquid	Zip Strip Marine	Paints, varnishes, enamels
Liquid	Nasco	Paints, varnishes, enamels
Liquid	Nasco Brush Cleaner	Brushes—natural bristle (Not for synthetic brushes)
Liquid	Nasco Latex Brush Cleaner	Removes dried-on latex paint from brushes and rollers
Rust Removers		
Jelly	Duro Navy Jelly	Dissolves rust, coats metal with rust inhibitor
Jelly	Duro Aluminum Jelly	Cleans and brightens aluminum
Jelly	Trustan Rust Converter	Converts iron oxide to new metal paintable surface
Jelly	Woodhill Extend Rust Treatment	Converts rust into stable iron complex and coats with latex

+ This is an incomplete listing but demonstrates the variety of materials available.
*Removers that contain a wax to help retard evaporation of solvents need an afterwash of mineral spirits. Water-wash strippers may raise the grain of the wood and turn some woods, such as oak, black. Some removers are now sold with spray can for easier, more even application.
NOTE: You can extend the active time of a stripper by covering the coated surface with wax paper.

term warranty. Wagner offers a power scraper with a blade that moves back and forth 3,600 times a minute. Optional attachments include a wire brush for removing rust and a special scraper for removing adhesives.

Push scrapers resemble putty knives. Handle and blade widths vary and should be matched to the job. Push scrapers are best suited for flat surfaces and removing paint from corners. They are not as effective as hook scrapers, although they are normally cheaper.

Cabinet scrapers have a hooked blade and take a paper-thin scraping from the surface and leave a flatter surface than sandpaper. They are pushed, not pulled.

Molding scraper sets are easier to use and more effective than sandpaper. The scraper typically has a 10″ handle with 1½″ × 1½″ blades.

Scraper planes are designed like a plane. They allow you to set the depth of the blade and the angle with thumbscrew and brass lock nuts.

Blade burnishers enable you to put the necessary sharp hook on your hand scrapers. They have a hardened steel wheel.

Rotary strippers are electric drill attachments for professional use and consist of stiff wires bristling from a

		Packaging		
Rinse*	8 Oz.	Pt.	Qt.	Gal.
Mineral Spirits		●	●	●
Mineral Spirits		●	●	●
Water		●	●	
Water		●	●	●
None Required			●	●
Water		●	●	●
Water		●	●	●
Mineral Spirits			●	
Water			●	
Water	●	●	●	
Water	●	●	●	
None		(1 & 7 oz. only)		
	●			

Paints and Stains

hub. Paint or rust removal from metal surfaces is accomplished with relative ease. Be sure to wear safety goggles when using this tool. Fiber brushes and buffers are also available.

Heat guns are used to soften paint so that it can be scraped away easily. Most consist of an electric heating element, metal shield, and a handle. They are safer than propane torches and not nearly as messy or smelly as chemical paint strippers. They work more slowly than strippers but are less expensive on large jobs.

The electric putty softener is a 700-watt square electric iron that melts putty so you can remove glass without damaging the window sash. Make sure it has an on/off switch for temperature control and a UL label.

The electric paint softener is a 1,000-watt resistance heating iron with reflective shield and insulated phenolic handle. It comes with a stand for holding while turned on and not in use. Make sure it has a heavy-duty 3-wire cord and UL label. This is excellent for removing alligatored paint. Never use on varnish or combustible resin surfaces.

The Right Tools to Apply Paint

Paintbrushes

Bargain-shoppers, beware: The quality of the brush you buy will dictate the appearance of the finished surface and the speed of application. Here are the tips on judging quality and selecting the right brush.

Natural bristles. The best natural bristles are imported hog bristles, which get fine at the tip with split ends. For detail work, camel, sable, and badger are preferred, followed by squirrel and ox. Poor, in regard to holding paint and leaving brush marks, are horse hair and poor-quality hog hair. Neither of these has much "flagging" (multiple

sizes of tapered filaments), so they are often used in cheap throw-away brushes. Natural bristles should not be used in water-based paints, because the fibers will absorb moisture, causing them to soften and become limp.

Synthetics. Preferred among these are polyester fibers, which are chemically resistant and, if well flagged and tapered, give good service with any paint or varnish. Nylon should only be used with latex paints. It can be softened by solvents and become limp or even dissolve. Polypropylene brushes are durable and less likely to lose filaments while painting.

Construction. Quality brushes are thicker with fibers at the ferrule inserted via smaller wooden plugs. Also look for brushes with a high percentage of bristles with flagged (split) ends and filaments of varied length. The longer and thicker the brush, the faster the work and the quicker the job will be done.

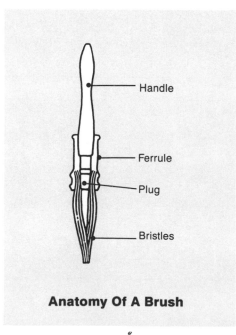

Anatomy Of A Brush

Testing. Before you buy a brush, there are several ways to evaluate its quality. (1) Squeeze the bristles—they should feel full and spongy. (2) They should be dense at the ferrule, with only a narrow wooden plug. (3) When pressed against a hard surface, the bristles should not fan out. (4) Shake the brush and tap it: Few loose filaments should fall out. (5) Make sure there is a reasonable length of bristles from ferrule to tip. (6) Make sure the ferrule is of stainless steel or aluminum so it won't rust. (7) Look at the tip and make sure the bristles are split. (8) The bristles should be of various lengths, and the brush length from ferrule to tip should be a minimum of 2¼", longer for wider brushes (see chart). (9) The tip should be cut evenly, without stray bristles sticking out. (10) Tap the brush against the back of your hand, it should bounce. (11) A sharp taper may indicate too many short bristles.

Before using a synthetic brush soak it in thinner (never water). A new natural bristle brush will work better after it has been soaked in linseed oil for a couple of days.

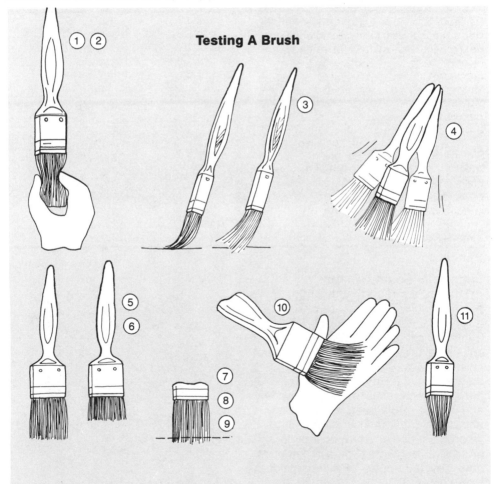

Testing A Brush

397

Paints and Stains

Brushes—Recommended Bristles by Paint/Vehicle

Type of Paint/Vehicle	Type of Bristle
Oil Paints and Oil Stains	Natural bristles or polyester
Alkyds, epoxies, enamels, varnishes, shellac, lacquer	Polyester
Latex, water-based paints, calcimine water-based stains	Synthetic bristles such as polyester, nylon, and polypropylene
Adhesive and paste	Stiff vegetable fiber brushes or trowels

Paintbrush Types and Sizes

Uses	Tips	Width (inches)	Length out of Ferrule (inches)
Ceilings	Square	4	3¼–4
Doors and shelves	Chiseled edge	2, 2½, 3	2½–3
Enamel and varnish	Chiseled edge	1, 1½	2–2¼
Floors	Square	4	3¼–4
Furniture	Square	1, 1½, 2, 2½	2¼–3
Masonry Walls	Square	6	3¼–4
Muntins and moldings	Chiseled or angular	1½	2¼–2¾
Sashes (round or flat)	Round square	1	2¼–2¾
	Flat beveled	1½	2–2¼
Siding	Square	4, 5	3¼–4
Trim	Chiseled or beveled	1	2¼
Walls (interior)	Square	4, 5	3¼–4
Walls (exterior)	Square	6	3¼–4
Window frames	Square	2	2¼–2¾
Wrought iron and metal furniture	Square	1, 1½	2¼–2¾

Sponge or Foam Brushes

These are a recent addition to painting tools. They can be used for all paints but not lacquer or shellac. Synthetic sponges are resistant to solvents and excellent for applying clear finishes. Available in brush shape, they are ideal for painting corners, curved objects, slats, serrated surfaces, and carved medallions. Mounted as pads, they provide an exceptionally smooth surface when applying gloss or semigloss paints. Some of the pads have beveled edges for painting close to moldings. They can be cleaned and

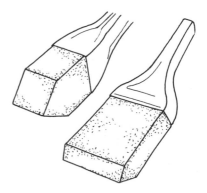

Foam Brushes

reused and cost much less than good brushes.

Paint Rollers

Paint rollers can speed application on walls and ceilings or other large, flat surfaces. You should select a roller based on the surface to be painted rather than by the paint you intent to apply. Basically, the smoother the surface, the shorter the nap. Lambs' wool covers are excellent for alkyds but not enamels, which are easier to apply with mohair. Most paints can be applied with synthetic rollers.

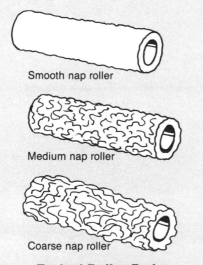

Smooth nap roller

Medium nap roller

Coarse nap roller

Typical Roller Pads

Smooth surfaces. Use a short-nap roller cover with a depth of $\frac{1}{8}''$ to $\frac{3}{8}''$—best for drywall, smooth plaster wallboard, plywood, and hardboard.

Slightly rough. Use $\frac{3}{8}''$ to $\frac{1}{2}''$ nap roller—best for concrete, sand-embedded or texturized plaster acoustical tile, and wood shakes.

Rough surfaces. Use $\frac{3}{4}''$ to $1\frac{1}{4}''$ nap roller—best for cinder block, brick, stucco, corrugated metal, and fencing.

Very rough or striated. Use $1\frac{1}{2}''$ nap roller—best for wood shingles.

Sizes. Regular rollers are normally 7″ to 9″ wide, but special rollers are available from 2″ to 18″ wide. Screw-in extension handles are available for some models for covering high walls and ceilings. Rollers are also available with a plastic splatter shield.

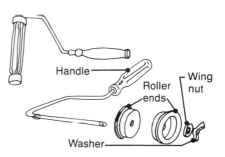

Handle

Roller ends

Wing nut

Washer

Roller Parts

Quality. A good roller cover is perfectly cylindrical without conspicuous seams and won't bend when you squeeze the end. The fabric must be glued to the core and the core treated against water penetration. Dense cover fibers will carry more paint. Rollers can also be used in applying stain to large areas. The fibers should be close and dense or they will tend to mat, producing a mottled finish.

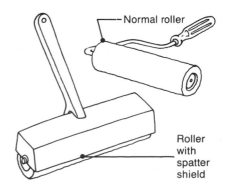

Normal roller

Roller with spatter shield

Typical Roller Assemblies

Paints and Stains

Painting Pads

These are a cross between a brush and roller and exhibit some of the qualities of each. Pads apply paint faster than a brush but slower than a similar-sized roller. They can be used for cut-in work, in corners, and on the bottom edges of clapboard siding, much like a brush. Their advantage over rollers is that they can produce a sharp, straight line and don't splatter the paint. However, pads require practice in applying paint evenly without leaving edge or fiber marks. Pads also drip more than brushes and rollers. Paint may have to be diluted with the appropriate water or mineral oil thinner to apply with a paint pad. Special paint trays are available to limit the amount of paint that is loaded on the pad. Get one with a large enough base area, or else you'll have to refill every few dips.

Pads come in sizes from 10″ to 1½″ across, with the standard width being 7″. Pads are replaceable. Sponge pads are easier to use, particularly on small areas or shaped articles.

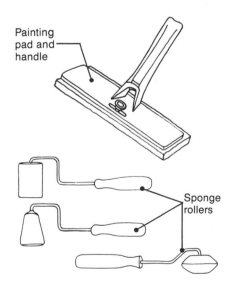

Painting pad and handle

Sponge rollers

Sponge Pads And Rollers

Paint Sprayers

There are two types: conventional air compressors and the "airless" type. The conventional type uses a spray gun connected to a separate air compressor by a rubber or plastic hose designed to carry air under pressure. The material being sprayed is housed in a glass, plastic, or metal reservoir attached to the bottom of the spray gun. Air pressure transforms the liquid into a sprayed mist.

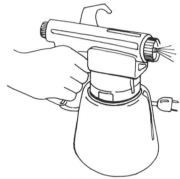

Airless sprayer

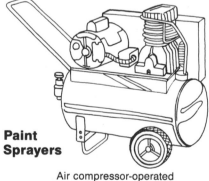

Paint Sprayers

Air compressor-operated sprayer

Two types of spray guns are used. Siphon or suction-feed spray guns are best suited for lacquer and other light-bodied compounds. Pressure-feed spray guns have the greater force needed to spray heavier liquids like enamel, varnish, or polyurethane.

Suction-feed spray guns normally use external-mix nozzles, and pressure-

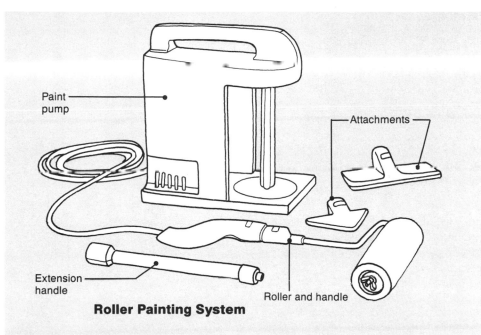

Paint pump

Attachments

Extension handle

Roller and handle

Roller Painting System

feed guns use internal-mix nozzles. The shape of the spray pattern can be changed by either changing the nozzle or setting adjustable nozzles to the required pattern.

Airless paint sprayers (self-contained spray guns) have the compressor built into the handle/nozzle assembly and are not recommended for amateurs. This type spray gun atomizes the paint by forcing it through a small opening under very high pressure (2,000 to 3,000 psi). Their potential danger is associated with accidentally injecting the paint into the flesh.

You can rent paint-spraying equipment.

Roller Painting System

This is a recent innovation using a pump that attaches directly to the paint can, tubing, a hollow handle, and a special porous roller to apply paint quickly. However, most units require a great deal of extra cleaning, so the total time saved may not be significant.

Fasteners 15

15. Fasteners

Nothing takes up more space on the home workbench than fasteners. There are so many different sizes of screws, kinds of nails, and types of glues, and each requires its own little box or jar. At first, you might think the world could get along nicely without nine-tenths of them. But you think differently after you've tried to reattach a broken handle to a coffee cup with a non-waterproof glue, or tried to hang a picture by pounding a nail into a plaster wall.

Most fasteners are suited to specific tasks, hence the size of this chapter. It identifies the most common kinds of adhesives, metal plates, nails, nuts and bolts, rivets, screws, staples, tapes, and wall anchors. It is by no means exhaustive. If you cannot find the perfect fastener in these pages or in the bins at your local hardware store or home center, another source is mail order catalogs of tool and hardware suppliers.

Adhesives

The right glue, in the right place, is stronger than the materials it bonds together. Today, most glues have a chemical base, and they are called "adhesives" to distinguish them from the glues of yesteryear that were made with an animal base, such as hide glues.

Choosing the right glue, however, can be a bewildering task. As the accompanying charts indicate, there is a sea of generic categories, and each category may be better known by several brand names. Look beyond the brand name on a label to see if the chemical ingredients are listed, and read the label to determine proper applications, as well as safety requirements and a "freshness date" if it's a glue with a short shelf life.

One currently popular adhesive is a hot-melt glue used in conjunction with an electric glue "gun." The gun heats the glue and is used to apply a bead of it to your project. This kind of glue is popular because it sets in about sixty seconds, is flexible enough to bind vinyl and fabrics, but is versatile and can bind wood, metal, and wood to plaster or concrete. It is also waterproof. The gun is low-priced.

Unlike hot-melt glue, most waterproof adhesives are two-part kinds—you mix ingredients from two separate containers to achieve a bond. Well-known two-part waterproof glues include resorcinol resin and many epoxies. Some acrylic, acrylonitrile, cellulose, and styrene-butadiene adhesives are also classified as waterproof; check the label.

A special category is construction adhesives. These are sold in tubes that fit into caulking guns, and are sold in nearly every home center in America. Different types of construction adhesive perform different jobs: adhering paneling to furring strips, subflooring to joists, foam insulation to concrete walls, or pressure-treated decking to its understructure. Be sure to pick up the right kind for your job.

Fasteners

Adhesive Job Guide

The letters in this chart refer to the adhesives listed in the accompanying chart "Glue Guide." Check manufacturer's label, as formulations and applications differ.

	Wood	Metal	Tile	Ceramics & Glass
Wood	A,B,C,E,I,J,N, O,P,R,U,V,Z	B,F,I,P,R,U,Y,Z	A,H,I,L,M, P,R,U,Y	B,I,P,R,Y
Metal	B,F,I,P,R,U,Y,Z	A,B,D,I,L,R,V,Z	B,I,L,R	B,I,R
Tile	A,H,I,L,M, P,R,U,V	B,I,R,Y,Z	F,R,Y	B,F,I,R,S,Y
Ceramics & Glass	B,I,P,R,Y	I,R,Z	B,F,I,R,S,Y,Z	B,F,I,R,Z
Vinyl	M,S,T,U,V	B,Y,Z	S,Y	B,Y
Leather	F,H,R,S,T,Y	F,H,R,S,T,Y	F,P,R,Y	F,I,P,R,Y
Phenolic Plastics	A,B,I,R,Y,Z	A,B,I,R,U,Y	A,B,I,R	A,B,I,R,Y
Fabrics	P,T,Y	P,Y	Y	P,Y
Paper	P,R,Y	P,R,Y	P,R,Y	P,R,Y

NOTE: Special applications—for attaching foil: casein, PVAC silicates; glass to glass: polyvinyl butyra; bonding PVC pipe: ABS CPVC. Substitute for urea formaldehyde indoors—isocyanurate. Asphalt cutbacks and emulsions are low-cost adhesives for resilient flooring and asphalt tile.

Glue Guide

This guide is reliable but not infallible: Because of the great variation between the formulations of various manufacturers, one may work, another fail. The manufacturer's label should help you in making your selection.

Type	Primary Use	Holding Power (in lbs/sq. in.)	Water Resistance
A. Acrylic adhesive (clear)	Bonds most surfaces, including oily or porous wood, china, masonry. Nonflammable. Can be used to seal nuts to bolts.	Excellent 6000	Good
B. Acrylonitrile (brown)	Carpet and fabrics. Will bond glass and metal. Poor as wood glue. Has good oil resistance.	Good 2000–3000	Good
C. Aliphatic (clear)	Excellent for bonding wood. Quick tack. Some creep.	Good 2000–3500	Low
D. Anaerobic adhesive (acrylic acid diester, colored by strength grades)	Sealing nuts to bolts. Cannot be used on polypropylene. Protects against corrosion.	Good 2000–3000	Excellent

Vinyl	Leather	Phenolic Plastics	Fabrics	Paper
M,S,T,U,Y	F,H,R,S,T	A,B,I,R,Y,Z	P,T,Y	P,R,Y
B,Y	F,P,R,Y	A,B,I,R,U,Y	P,Y	P,R,Y
S,Y	F,P,R,Y	A,B,I,R	Y	P,H,Y
B,Y	F,I,P,R,Y	A,B,I,R,Y	P,Y	P,R,Y
B,Y	Y	B	Y	Y
Y	F,P,R,T,Y	R,Y	T,Y	R,Y
B,Y	R,Y	B,I,R	Y	R,Y
Y	T,Y	Y	R,T,Y	T,W,Y
Y	R,T,Y	R,Y	T,W,Y	M,R,W,Y

Set Time	Cure Time	Adhesive Flex	Applicator or Clean-Up Solvent
30–60 seconds	45 minutes	None	Mix two parts with application stick or brush/Acetone
Depends on application	Variable	Good	Brush or tube/Acetone or MEK
Sets in 30 minutes	24 hours	Good	Squeeze bottle or use with applicator/ Warm water
Sets in absence of air	Variable	None	Brush or tube/Acetone or MEK

Fasteners

Glue Guide (Continued)

Type	Primary Use	Holding Power (in lbs/sq. in.)	Water Resistance
E. Casein glue (clear to brown)	Heavy wood gluing. Moisture-resistant but mold-susceptible. Stains.	Good, on hardwoods 2500	Good
F. Cellulose (clear or amber)	Repairs on furniture, ceramics, glass, fabrics and plastics.	Good 3500	Excellent
G. Clear cement (see Aliphatic)	Used chiefly for model making and requires air to set, so only bonds around edges.	Good 2000–3000	Excellent
H. Contact cement	Bonds veneer to cabinet or counter tops. Also bonds plastic, foam, hardboard, or metal to wood.	Good	Variable
I. Epoxy	Bonds nonporous materials, metal, pipes, ceramic, china, marble, glass, and masonry. Not good on wood. Available in clear, white, or metallic finish. Expensive.	Excellent 2000–3500	Excellent
J. Hide glue (liquid)	Conventional furniture maker's glue. Sensitive to high humidity and moisture.	Good 3200	Low
K. Hide glue (flake)	Furniture glue but must be mixed with water and heated to 130°F until smooth.	Good 3200	Good
L. Instant-set glue (cyanoacrylates)	Nonporous material, ceramics, plastic, rubber, metal, synthetics. Will not bond to Teflon or polyethylene. Binding to glass may not be permanent. Cannot be used on plastic foam.	Excellent 3900–8000 [maximum strength attained on cure after 48 hours then slowly (i.e., over years) loses strength]	Fair
M. Latex mastic	Ceiling tile, floor tile, paneling.	Low 50–500	Good
N. Plastic cement (model airplane glue)	Nonporous material, wood, fabric.	Good 500	Good
O. Plastic resin glue* (urea formaldehyde) (clear)	Furniture repair, wood, hardboard, chipboard, attaching paneling.	Excellent 3000	Excellent

Set Time	Cure Time	Adhesive Flex	Applicator or Clean-Up Solvent
3 hours at 70° or above	24 hours	Stiff	Powder mixed with water* ready to apply with brush or stick
2 hours	24–48 hours	Stiff	In tube or can spread with paddle or stick
At 70°F about 5 minutes to 1 hour	24 hours	Good	Brush or stick
Dry surfaces separately. Sets on contact.	30–48 hours to several weeks	Good	Brush with notched trowel or roller
4 minutes to 1 hour	4 minutes to 24 hours	Stiff	Mix two parts with stick applicator
1 hour	8 hours at 70°F	Stiff	One part liquid cans or bottles. Use brush or roll/Warm water
As soon as cool	8 hours at 70°F	Stiff	Comes in can or bottle. Apply hot; brush on/Warm water
Within seconds	12–48 hours	None—do not use for stressed joints	Squeeze tube. Avoid contact with skin. Sets instantly and is not soluble. Keep out of reach of children or pets/ Non-oily Acetone.
On contact to 2 hours	2–3 days	Very flexible	Use notched trowel or caulking gun. Apply to both surfaces/Warm water
5 minutes to 1 hour	6–24 hours	Good	Squeeze tube/Acetone
3–5 hours	10–30 hours at 70°F or above	Stiff	Electric melt sticks or powder mixed with water. Use stick or brush/Acetone

Fasteners

Glue Guide (Continued)

Type	Primary Use	Holding Power (in lbs/sq. in.)	Water Resistance
P. Polyvinyl acetate (PVA) ("White Glue") (white, dries clear)	All-purpose adhesive (except metal). The most popular furniture adhesive. Poor in heat or moisture. Low cost, quick-setting, temporary bond.	Good 3200–4000	Poor
Q. Resorcinol (Phenol) (red-brown)	Hard and medium-hard wood, plywood. Stains porous surfaces.	Excellent 135,000	Excellent
R. Silicone rubber (clear, white, bathroom white, paintable, black, natural wood, bronze, aluminum, metallic and masonry gray)	All-purpose adhesive—all woods, metals, plastics (including PVC pipe), masonry, ceramic tile, and glass. Very durable.	4500–9000	Excellent
S. Styrene-butadiene (rubber) (cream color)	Good for attaching hard flooring, gypsum board, quarry tiles and attaching fixtures to walls. Can be drilled, sanded, and painted. May not be freeze-resistant. Used for jointing PVC pipes.	Good to excellent	Excellent
T. Urethane adhesive (cream to brown)	Wood, plastic, metal, ceramics, and glass. Has strength of epoxy but takes longer to cure.	Excellent	Good
U. Polyvinyl chloride (PVC) (clear)	All-purpose.	Good 3200	Excellent
V. Woodworkers glue (animal glue) (tan)	Wood, paper, cork, plywood, and paneling. Initial set, or grab, is faster than white glue. Good water and heat resistance and easier to sand.	Excellent	Good
W. Wallpaper paste (methocel, glycerin and water or CME) (carboxymethyl) (white or clear)	Known as "peel paste," this is easier to put on and remove than old flour pastes.	Sufficient	Fair
X. Asphalt	Attaching acoustical, wall and flooring tile, rigid insulations, and vapor barriers.	Good	Excellent

Set Time	Cure Time	Adhesive Flex	Applicator or Clean-Up Solvent
20 minutes	8 hours at 70°F	Fair	Squeeze bottle, brush on/Soap and warm water
7–10 hours at 70°F or above	24–30 hours	Stiff	Two-part system. Small brush, stick/Cool water until hardened (then no longer soluble).
6–8 minutes	24–48 hours	Excellent	Cartridges or tubes. Use wood or plastic blade/If fresh try MEK or Acetone. If cured try Zylene.
1–3 hours	48 hours	Stiff	Tube, use stick/Mineral spirits or MEK
1–3 hours	24 hours	Good	Comes in can or tube. Use brush or stick. Also used in electric melt gun/Acetone
Within minutes but varies by manufacturer	8–24 hours	Flexible	Tube, use stick/Acetone
1–3 hours	18 hours	Good	Bottle with pour spout. Apply with brush/Warm water
NA	NA	NA	Roller or brush/Varies by products, read label
On contact	24 hours	Excellent	Cans, applied with paddle/Mineral spirits

Fasteners

Glue Guide (Concluded)

Type	Primary Use	Holding Power (in lbs/sq. in.)	Water Resistance
Y. Elastomerics (A grouping that includes rubber and neoprene)	Used for attaching paper, leather, vinyl, and rubber to other surfaces.	Excellent	Excellent
Z. Phenolic blends (A grouping that includes phenolic vinyls, phenolic nylon, phenolic neoprene— also see "B")	Attaches metal to metal, wood, tile, glass, and phenolic plastics (usually electrical components) and most nonporous materials.	Excellent	Excellent

*Read directions on label. Requires two periods of five-minute stirring with a couple of minutes pause in between.

Some Well-Known Brand Names by Resin Type

Type	Brand Name(s)
Acrylic	3-ton Adhesive, F-88 Adhesive
Acrylic latex with silicone	White Lightning
Acrylonitrile	Pliobond
Aliphatic	Elmer's Carpenter's Glue, Titebond, Se-Cur-It, Macco Woodworkers' Glue
Cellulose	Ambroid, Duco Cement
Cyanoacrylate	Duro Super Glue, Borden Wonderbond Plus, Krazy-Glue
Epoxy	On-the-Spot Epoxy, 5 Minute Epoxy Gel, Scotch Epoxy
Hide glue	Franklin Hide Glue
Latex tile adhesive	Contech Tile Adhesive, Color Tile Tile Adhesive
Polyurethane	OSI Quick Bond Panel Foam
Polyvinyl acetate (PVA)	Fas'n-it, Scotch Wood, Elmer's Paper Glue
Polyvinyl chloride (PVC)	Sheer Magic
Resorcinol	U.S. Polywood, Elmer's Waterproof Glue
Styrene-butadiene	Brite Magic, Black Magic
Thermoplastic (for glue guns)	Bostic All-Purpose Hot Melt
Synthetic rubber	Max Bond, Liquid Nail, Fix-and-Seal
Urea formaldehyde	Weldwood, Elmer's Plastic Resin Glue

Metal Fasteners

Essential to almost any frame construction, metal fasteners are available for securing, hanging, and holding down building materials. Some standard designs are shown, but many more are available. Their uses include brackets (for stairs, shelving, and bracing), joist or beam hangers, post or column caps and bases, hurricane hold-down anchors, bridging, and drywall backup clips. The last-mentioned permit two-stud house corners and the substitution of insulation in place of the third stud, which then is not needed for nailing drywall.

Use of some metal fasteners is required by code, and they will generally be identified on blueprints. Hurricane hold-downs tie trusses to

Set Time	Cure Time	Adhesive Flex	Applicator or Clean-Up Solvent
On contact	Stays flexible	Excellent	Apply by paddle or brush/See manufacturer's directions.
Varies	Varies	Stiff	Squeeze tube, brush, or stick/Acetone

studs, not to top plates, because the top plates are nailed into the end grain of the studs and have little uplift strength.

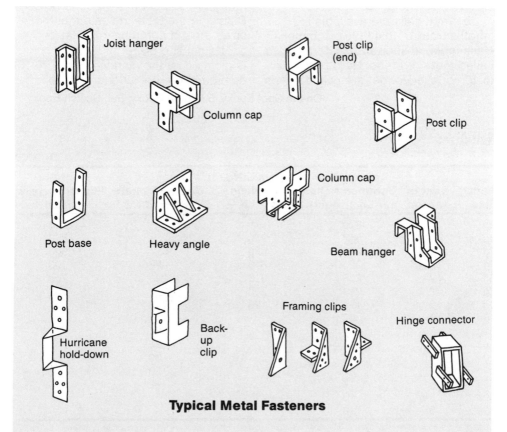

Joist hanger

Post clip (end)

Column cap

Post clip

Post base

Heavy angle

Column cap

Beam hanger

Hurricane hold-down

Back-up clip

Framing clips

Hinge connector

Typical Metal Fasteners

Fasteners

Nails

Over 300 pounds of nails are used in building the average 1,700-square-foot frame home. The many accompanying charts help you select the right nail size, point, head, shank, and metal for each job. In calculating quantities, add 10 percent for waste.

Local building codes should be consulted; they are quite specific as to which nail and how many should be used for each construction detail. The codes vary by location due to differing seismatic, snow, and wind loads. However, for many jobs around the home you can make your own selection. The explanations that follow will enable you to choose the best nail for each fastening job.

Common nails are available in lengths from 1″ to 4″ (see Common Nails table). If shorter than 1″ they are called tacks or brads. Nails from 4½″ to 18″ or even longer are called spikes and often require the drilling of a pilot hole before driving.

Nails have traditionally been described in "penny" sizes, with a small "d" written after the number. (The "d" stands for denarius, an ancient Roman coin.) The number did not originally refer to the length of the nail but to the number of denarii it once cost for 100 nails of that size. A 6d nail is 2″ long, as a rule. However, this system is on its way out because it can be misleading. Box nails are usually ⅛″ shorter than common nails of the same penny number.

The table "Nail Sizes" gives a quick reference for selecting the most common types of nails, showing how many you will get in a 1-pound box. Blanks in the table indicate that those sizes are not commonly available.

The holding power of a nail is dictated by the diameter and configuration, point (long, needle,

Nail Sizes

Penny Size	Length (inches)	Approx. No. Common Nails per Lb. (bright)	Approx. No. Box Nails per Lb.	Coated Sinkers per Lb.	Finishing Nails per Lb.
2d	1	870			1350
3d	1¼	543	950		850
4d	1½	290	680	527	600
5d	1⅝	254	510	387	300
6d	2	236	315	293	200
7d	2⅛	223	280	223	125
8d	2½	135	190	153	
10d	3	92		111	
12d	3¼	61		81	
16d	3½	47		64	
20d	4	29		39	
30d	4½	22		29	
40d	5	17		22	
50d	5½	13			
60d	6	10			

NOTE: Average count varies slightly by manufacturer. Lengths vary—box nails are generally ⅛″ shorter than common nails. The quantities per pound relate to penny size, not length.

diamond, chisel, sharp, or blunt) or coating of the shank, and by the grain direction and spacing, moisture content, and hardness of the wood.

In general, the holding power of mechanically deformed nails is better than coated nails.

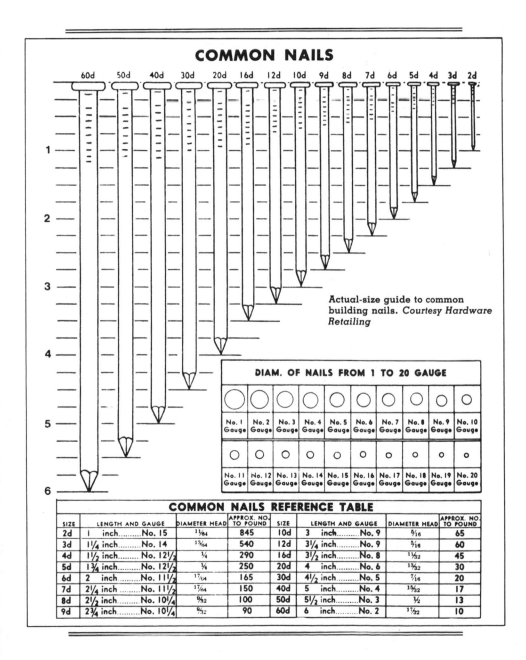

COMMON NAILS

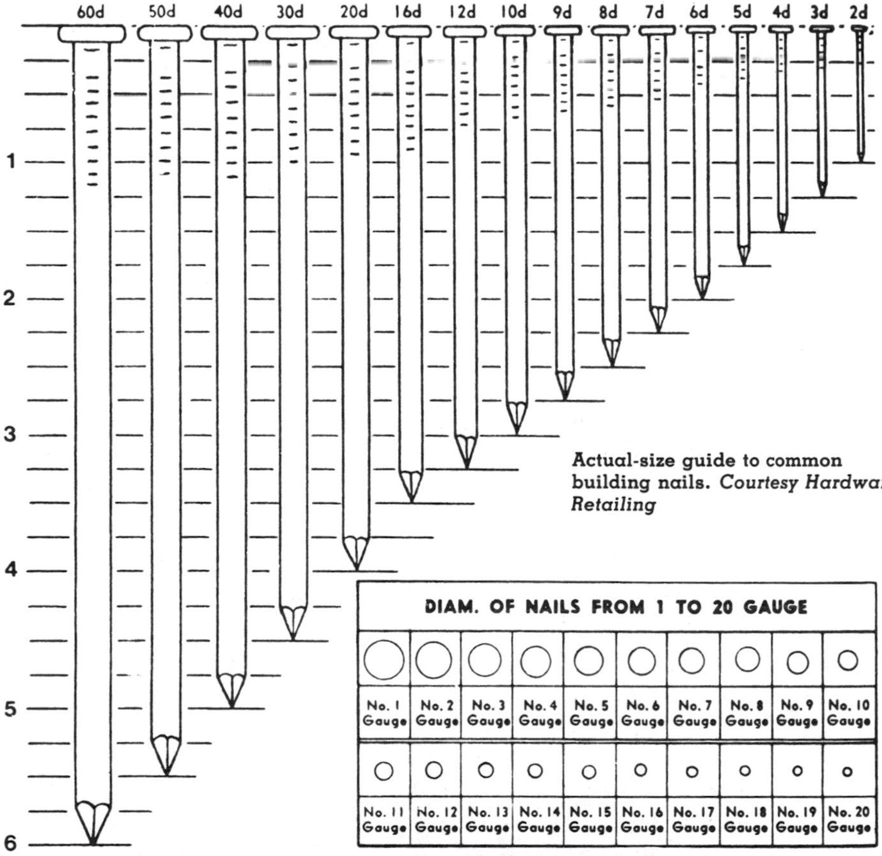
60d
50d
40d
30d
20d
16d
12d
10d
9d
8d
7d
6d
5d
4d
3d
2d
1
2
3
4
5
6
DIAM. OF NAILS FROM 1 TO 20 GAUGE
No. 1 Gauge
No. 2 Gauge
No. 3 Gauge
No. 4 Gauge
No. 5 Gauge
No. 6 Gauge
No. 7 Gauge
No. 8 Gauge
No. 9 Gauge
No. 10 Gauge
No. 11 Gauge
No. 12 Gauge
No. 13 Gauge
No. 14 Gauge
No. 15 Gauge
No. 16 Gauge
No. 17 Gauge
No. 18 Gauge
No. 19 Gauge
No. 20 Gauge

Actual-size guide to common building nails. *Courtesy Hardware Retailing*

COMMON NAILS REFERENCE TABLE

SIZE	LENGTH AND GAUGE	DIAMETER HEAD	APPROX. NO. TO POUND	SIZE	LENGTH AND GAUGE	DIAMETER HEAD	APPROX. NO. TO POUND
2d	1 inch.........No. 15	11/64	845	10d	3 inch.........No. 9	5/16	65
3d	1 1/4 inch.........No. 14	13/64	540	12d	3 1/4 inch.........No. 9	5/16	60
4d	1 1/2 inch.........No. 12 1/2	1/4	290	16d	3 1/2 inch.........No. 8	11/32	45
5d	1 3/4 inch.........No. 12 1/2	1/4	250	20d	4 inch.........No. 6	13/32	30
6d	2 inch.........No. 11 1/2	17/64	165	30d	4 1/2 inch.........No. 5	7/16	20
7d	2 1/4 inch.........No. 11 1/2	17/64	150	40d	5 inch.........No. 4	15/32	17
8d	2 1/2 inch.........No. 10 1/4	9/32	100	50d	5 1/2 inch.........No. 3	1/2	13
9d	2 3/4 inch.........No. 10 1/4	9/32	90	60d	6 inch.........No. 2	17/32	10

Fasteners

Nail Selection Chart

Type	Use	Size Range	Remarks
Common	All rough and heavy construction, such as wall and roof framing, concrete forms, etc.	2d (1″) to 60d (6″) lengths (13 standard lengths to 4″—nails longer than 4″ called spikes). Common spikes are made from 10d (3″) to 60d (6″) plus $\frac{5}{16}$″ (7″ long) and $\frac{3}{8}$″ (8½″ long)	Available with helical, annular, or annular with helix angle thread for increased holding power. 6d through 90d or 9″. Usually thinner than other common nails. Plain (bright), cemented, blued (heat treated), and polished finishes are available. Also available with rust-resistant treatments and in stainless steel.
Box	Constructing boxes and packing crates where thin, dry wood will be nailed close to its edge	3d (1¼″) to 20d (4″) (10d and above may require special ordering)	Point is dulled to prevent splitting wood.
Finishing	Used in cabinetry, paneling, or anywhere head must be concealed	2d (1″) to 6d (2″)	Has small round head with dimple in center for countersinking with a nail set.
Casing	Similar to finishing nail but hardened with dulled point to allow penetration of toe-strips and trim	4d (1½″) to 40d (5″)	Dipped or coated in colors to blend with trim or paneling. Available with ring shanks for more holding power.
Sheathing	Short wire nail with large flat head used to retain insulated sheathing or thin soft panels	4d (1½″) to 8d (2½″)	Nail heads often backed with washers. Available with resin coating.
Drywall	Attaching drywall. For ½″ drywall	4d (1½″) to 6d (2″)	Available plain and resin coated to retard popping.

414

Nail Selection Chart (Concluded)

Type	Use	Size Range	Remarks
SPECIALTY NAILS			
Masonry	Used to attach studs and furring strips to masonry walls and concrete floors	2d (1") to 16d (3½")	Hardened steel to withstand driving blows. Installed by hand using ball peen hammer or by power-operated or explosive stud-driving tools.
Double Headed	Used for temporary structures such as concrete forms or scaffolding	6d (1¾") to 20d (3½") (length under collar)	Drive flush with bottom head; pull out with top head.
Flooring	Used to secure hardwood floorboards	6d (2") to 8d (2½")	Have plain shank between head and threads. Thinner than common nail. Can be installed with floor-nailing machine.
Siding	For attaching shake siding or hardboard	5d (1⅝") to 8d (2½")	Available in steel, aluminum, and bronze.
Roofing	Use to secure shingles or roofing to the underlayment	2d (1") to 6d (2") with ⁷⁄₁₆" dia. head.	Available with spiral or helix-threaded shank for extra holding power or with hot-dipped galvanized finish to protect against rust.
Cut	Used to provide authenticity in historic buildings when restoring cabinetry, doors, and flooring. Four sides make them excellent choice to prevent movement	4d (1½") to 8d (2½")	Some are case hardened for concrete work. Nails are cut from high-carbon rolled sheet, are tempered to prevent bending. Available with decorative heads.

Fasteners

Coated nails may be called "cement-coated," but actually they are coated in a resin, not cement. Those coated with nylon seem to retain their friction longer. Their shanks provide a rough gripping surface that holds in softwoods, but gets rubbed off as they are driven into hardwoods. These nails are also called coolers, sinkers, or coated box nails. They'll provide the same holding power as a size larger bright (smooth) nail and, therefore, are about ⅛" shorter and of smaller diameter than the same penny size common nail. Since the thermoplastic coating is melted by the friction of being driven through the wood and quickly resets, these nails must be driven home with a few quick blows. Once the resin resets the nail can't be driven any farther.

Chemically etched nails are designed to provide a rougher, more tenacious shank surface. These are a little better than coated nails.

Annularly threaded nails have circular threads around the shank. Because they grip better than bright nails, they have smaller diameters than the same penny size common nail (you get more nails per pound).

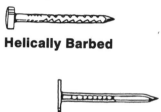

Annular Thread

The problem is, they exhibit greater withdrawal resistance than helical nails so they should be used only on permanent construction.

Helically threaded nails have a screwlike thread at a more gradual angle than does a screw, so they can be driven with a hammer. These have a 40 percent greater withdrawal resistance than do common nails and, where the wood later dries out, can

Helically Threaded Nail

exhibit four times the holding strength of bright nails under the same conditions. Where impact is expected, such as in attaching stair treads, they will hold better than annular shanks.

Helically barbed nails are designed for even greater friction. Like all the mechanically "deformed" nails (nails such as helical, annular or ridged), these are harder to drive.

Helically Barbed

Plain Barbed

Barbed nails are special purpose nails used for attaching shingles and other soft or flexible surfaces.

Zinc-coated nails do have added gripping strength compared to bright nails but are coated primarily to provide improved stain and corrosion resistance.

Square-cut nails are four-sided nails cut from high-carbon rolled sheet steel tempered to prevent bending. Invaluable for authenticity in restoring historic homes, these nails come in

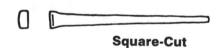

Square-Cut

twenty different patterns and various sizes. They have excellent lateral and holding strength due to their four surfaces. They are available with decorative nail heads for plank doors and cabinets.

The variety of nail points is shown here. While manufacturing methods have dictated some of the points, others are carefully designed for faster penetration or to reduce splitting. For example a smooth, round-shank nail will have greater holding strength, especially in softwoods, if it has a long sharp point. However, this is a disadvantage when nailing into dry wood because the sharp point will cause splitting. For dry wood you need a dull (or blunt) point, but then a blunt point destroys fibers, reducing withdrawal resistance except in heavy woods.

wood. If the green wood dries later, the holding strength will improve as much as 460 percent with the nail clinched across the grain.

The head of a nail is selected based on the material being attached. The softer the material, the larger the head.

While you will most often use a flat head, there are special jobs where, as in furniture upholstering, you will need special decorative heads. When building temporary forms or structures you will need double-headed smooth-shank nails that make disassembly easier. Finishing nails have a dimple in the top to permit countersinking with a punch. You may need to fill the countersink with caulking to prevent rusting. Power nailers use a strip of nails to facilitate loading of the magazine.

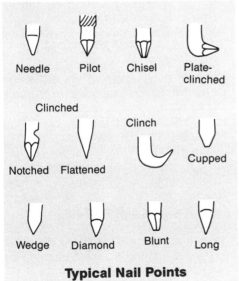

Typical Nail Points

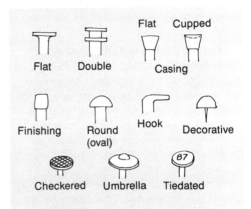

Nail Head Configurations

"Clinched" tips, which can be used where the complete penetration of the wood and bent-over tips will not be seen, are the most tenacious grippers. Clinching increases holding strength 45 to 170 percent in dry or green

Wherever there is humidity and two dissimilar metals come in contact, there exists the potential for galvanic corrosion of the metals. Thus, you should select nails compatible with any metal being attached to wood. Use aluminum spikes to attach aluminum gutters, aluminum nails for aluminum siding, and copper or brass nails for copper sheeting or to attach copper

Fasteners

pipe hangers. Noncorroding brass or bronze nails can be used for attaching leather or plastic to wood, or wood to wood in marine or damp locations.

Hot-dipped or hot-tumbled galvanized wire or stainless steel nails should be used where nails will be exposed to moisture. Zinc-coated, electro-galvanized, cadmium- or nickle-plated nails offer resistance to corrosion. Galvanized nails should be used in siding or shingling where staining could be a problem. Blue nails are sterilized by heat for temporary rust resistance but should not be used outdoors.

A galvanized nail driven by a do-it-yourselfer is more likely to rust than one driven by a professional carpenter. The carpenter drives the nail home in three to four taps. The weekend carpenter strikes five or six times, exposing the untreated steel on the head.

Masonry nails are made of a high-strength carbon steel. These have a graduated thread and may be driven into concrete or block. They are brittle and hard. They should only be driven with a ball peen hammer, and the carpenter must wear protective eye goggles. Masonry nails are also available for use with explosive or power fastening tools. Never use explosive fasteners unless you have taken training and have been awarded a license. Misuse can cause injury.

Nailing Tips

- When attaching hardwoods or nailing close to the edge of plywoods or paneling, pilot drilling is recommended. If drilling a pilot hole for a nail, drill a hole of slightly smaller diameter than the nail shank.
- Deformed (threaded) nails are difficult to withdraw and will damage the wood when pulled out. Use them only for permanent construction.
- Increased diameter increases holding strength, but beware: Large-diameter shanks will split dry wood.
- You should normally nail through the thinner into the thicker piece of wood. Attach plywood to wood, not wood to plywood.
- Softwoods have less holding power than dense woods, but since they are (unless very dry) less likely to split, you can use either more nails or nails of larger diameter to achieve equal withdrawal strength.
- There is little holding strength provided by nails driven into end grain. If this is the only option, "toe-nail" at an angle from either side.
- The backing out of driven nails (popping), particularly in drywall, is caused by wet lumber. Use of wet lumber is sometimes unavoidable. Your options are either to use barbed or resin-coated nails or to use screws. If nails still pop, pull them out and replace with screws.
- You will buy nails in cardboard boxes. It is highly recommended that you store them in glass jars or plastic boxes—even plastic milk jugs, if you have the tops. This will keep the nails from rusting.
- If you want to order more nails to match those you have and you don't know the penny size, just measure the length (add ⅛″ for box nails), subtract ½″, and multiply by 4. This will give you penny sizes up to 10d.
- When attaching plywood or paneling or doing cabinetwork, you can obtain stronger joints by using a combination of adhesives and nails.
- If you are doing any finish work that will be stained, coated, or painted with a water-based vehicle, countersink the nail and fill with putty or caulking to prevent rust stains.

418

- When nailing into hardwood you may reduce splitting by rubbing soap or candle wax on the shank of the nail.
- When nailing into softwoods you can reduce splitting by making the point of the nail blunt. Tap it on concrete or other hard surface, or buy preblunted nails.
- For finishing interior trim you can use enamel-coated casing nails. They are available in several colors to blend with your paneling.

Nailing Tables

The following tables give the nailing requirements specified in the CABO (Council of American Building Officials) 1983 code for one- and two-family dwellings. Ask your building inspector if there have been any amendments. If your region requires adherence to some other code, you will need to consult the code that is applicable (available at your local building inspector's office). As you can see, these tables describe the structural building material, nailing method, the nail size and type, and the required spacing. Be sure to read indicated footnote references for special points of information.

Flooring Nail Schedule

Tongue and groove flooring must always be blind-nailed, square-edge flooring face-nailed.

Size Flooring (inches)	Type and Size of Nails	Spacing
(Tongue & groove) $25/32 \times 3\frac{1}{4}$	7d or 8d screw-type, cut steel nails, or 2″ barbed fasteners*	10″–12″ apart
(Tongue & groove) $25/32 \times 2\frac{1}{4}$	Same as above	Same as above
(Tongue & groove) $25/32 \times 1\frac{1}{2}$	Same as above	Same as above
(Tongue & groove) $\frac{1}{2} \times 2$, $\frac{1}{2} \times 1\frac{1}{2}$	5d screw, cut, or wire nail, or $1\frac{1}{2}$″ barbed fasteners*	8″–10″ apart
Following flooring must be laid on a wood subfloor.		
(Tongue & groove) $\frac{3}{8} \times 2$, $\frac{3}{8} \times 1\frac{1}{2}$	4d bright casing, wire, cut, screw nail or $1\frac{1}{4}$″ barbed fasteners*	6″–8″ apart
(Square-edge) $\frac{5}{16} \times 2$, $\frac{5}{16} \times 1\frac{1}{2}$	1″, 15-gauge fully barbed flooring brad, preferably cement-coated	2 nails every 7″

*If steel wire flooring nails are used they should be 8d, preferably cement-coated. Newly developed machine-driven barbed fasteners, used as recommended by the manufacturer, are acceptable.

Fasteners

Plywood Thicknesses, Spans, and Nailing Recommendations

(Plywood continuous over two or more spans; grain of face plies across supports)

Plywood Floor Construction

Application	Recommended Thickness	Maximum Space of Supports (C. to C.)	Nail Size and Type	Nail Spacing Panel Edges	Intermediate
Subflooring	½" (a)	16" (b)	6d common (c) (e)	6"	10"
	⅝" (a)	20"	8d common (c) (e)	6"	10"
	¾" (a)	24"	8d common (c) (e)	6"	10"
		48"	8d ring-shank (c)	6"	6"
Underlayment	⅜" (d)		6d ring-shank or cement-coated	6"	8" each way
	⅝"		8d flathead		

(a) Provide blocking at panel edges for carpet, tile, linoleum, or other nonstructural flooring. No blocking required for $^{25}/_{32}$" strip flooring.
(b) If strip flooring is perpendicular to supports, ½" plywood can be used on 24" span.
(c) If resilient flooring is to be applied without underlayment, countersink nails $^{1}/_{16}$".
(d) FHA accepts ¼" plywood.
(e) If supports are not well seasoned, use ring-shank nails.

Plank Sheathing and Subflooring

(Horizontal application)

			Lbs. Nails Per 1000 Bd. Ft.			
		Bd. Ft. per Sq. Ft. of Area	Spacing of Framing Members			
Type	Size		12"	16"	20"	24"
	1" × 4"	1.32	66	52	44	36
	1" × 6"	1.23	43	33	28	23
T&G	1" × 8"	1.19	32	24	21	17
	1" × 10"	1.17	37	29	24	20
	1" × 4"	1.38	69	55	46	38
	1" × 6"	1.26	44	34	29	24
Shiplap	1" × 8"	1.21	32	25	21	17
	1" × 10"	1.18	37	29	25	20
	1" × 4"	1.19	60	47	40	33
	1" × 6"	1.15	40	31	26	22
545	1" × 8"	1.15	30	23	20	17
	1" × 10"	1.14	36	28	24	19

Wood Block Flooring

Size	Block per 100 Sq. Ft.	Adhesive per 100 Sq. Ft.	Nails per 100 Sq. Ft.
8" × 8"	225	1 gallon	4.0 pounds
9" × 9"	178	1 gallon	3.5 pounds
12" × 12"	100	1 gallon	2.8 pounds

Strip Flooring

Size	Bd. Ft. per 100 Sq. Ft.	1000 Bd. Ft. will lay Sq. Ft.	Nails per 100 Sq. Ft.
$^{25}/_{32}" \times 1^{1}/_{2}"$	155.0	645.0	3.7 pounds
$^{25}/_{32}" \times 2"$	142.5	701.8	3.0 pounds
$^{25}/_{32}" \times 2^{1}/_{4}"$	138.3	723.0	3.0 pounds
$^{25}/_{32}" \times 3^{1}/_{4}"$	129.0	775.2	2.3 pounds
$^{3}/_{8}" \times 1^{1}/_{2}"$	138.3	723.0	3.7 pounds
$^{3}/_{8}" \times 2"$	130.0	769.2	3.0 pounds
$^{1}/_{2}" \times 1^{1}/_{2}"$	138.3	723.0	3.7 pounds
$^{1}/_{2}" \times 2"$	130.0	769.2	3.0 pounds

Floor and Ceiling Joists

	Material				Nails
	Bd. Ft. Required for 100 Sq. Ft. of Surface Area				Lbs.
Size of Joist	12" O.C.	16" O.C.	20" O.C.	24" O.C.	per 1000 Bd. Ft.
Floor Joist					
2" × 6"	128	102	88	78	10
2" × 8"	171	136	117	103	8
2" × 10"	214	171	148	130	6
2" × 12"	256	205	177	156	5
Ceiling Joist					
2" × 4"	78	59	48	42	19
2" × 6"	115	88	72	63	13
2" × 8"	153	117	96	84	9
2" × 10"	194	147	121	104	7
2" × 12"	230	176	144	126	6

Exterior Wall Studs
(Studs including corner bracing)

Size of Studs	Spacing on Centers	Bd. Ft. per Sq. Ft. of Area	Lbs. Nails per 1000 Bd. Ft.
2" × 3"	12"	.83	30
	16"	.78	
	20"	.74	
	24"	.71	
2" × 4"	12"	1.09	22
	16"	1.05	
	20"	.98	
	24"	.94	
2" × 6"	12"	1.66	15
	16"	1.51	
	20"	1.44	
	24"	1.38	

Fasteners

Bevel Siding

| | Siding for 100 Sq. Ft. Wall | | | |
Size	Exposed to Weather	Add for Lap	Bd. Ft. per 100 Sq. Ft.	Nails per 100 Sq. Ft.
½″ × 4″	2¾″	46%	151	1½ pounds
½″ × 5″	3¾″	33%	138	1½ pounds
½″ × 6″	4¾″	26%	131	1 pound
½″ × 8″	6¾″	18%	123	¾ pound
⅝″ × 8″	6¾″	18%	123	¾ pound
¾″ × 8″	6¾″	18%	123	¾ pound
⅝″ × 10″	8¾″	14%	119	½ pound
¾″ × 10″	8¾″	14%	119	½ pound
¾″ × 12″	10¾″	12%	117	½ pound

NOTE: Quantities include 5 percent for end-cutting and waste. Deduct for all openings over 10 square feet.

Drop Siding

| | Siding for 100 Sq. Ft. Wall | | | |
Size	Exposed to Weather	Add for Lap	Bd. Ft. per 100 Sq. Ft.	Nails per 100 Sq. Ft.
1″ × 6″	5¼″	14%	119	2½ pounds
1″ × 8″	7¼″	10%	115	2 pounds

NOTE: Quantities include 5 percent for end-cutting and waste. Deduct for all openings over 10 square feet.

Built-Up Girders

Size	Bd. Ft. per Linear Ft.	Nails per 1000 Bd. Ft.
4″ × 6″	2.15	53
4″ × 8″	2.85	40
4″ × 10″	3.58	32
4″ × 12″	4.28	26
6″ × 6″	3.21	43
6″ × 8″	4.28	32
6″ × 10″	5.35	26
6″ × 12″	6.42	22
8″ × 8″	5.71	30
8″ × 10″	7.31	24
8″ × 12″	8.56	20

Partition Studs
(Studs including top and bottom plates)

Size of Studs	Spacing on Centers	Bd. Ft. per Sq. Ft. of Area	Lbs. Nails per 1000 Bd. Ft.
2" × 3"	12"	.91	
	16"	.83	25
	24"	.76	
2" × 4"	12"	1.22	
	16"	1.12	19
	24"	1.02	
2" × 6"	16"	1.48	
	24"	1.22	16

Furring

Size of Strips	Spacing on Centers	Bd. Ft. per Sq. Ft. of Area	Nails per 1000 Bd. Ft.
1" × 2"	12"	.18	
	16"	.14	
	20"	.11	55 pounds
	24"	.10	
1" × 3"	12"	.28	
	16"	.21	
	20"	.17	37 pounds
	24"	.14	
1" × 4"	12"	.36	
	16"	.28	
	20"	.22	30 pounds
	24"	.20	

Wall Boards

Material	Size	Fastened by	Adhesive (gal.) or Nails (lb.) per 100 Sq. Ft.
Gypsum board	48" × 96"	Nailing to studs	5 pounds
Plank T&G board	8" to 12" × 96"	Nailing to studs	2 pounds
Tempered tileboard	48" × 48"	Nailing to studs	1 pound
Tempered tileboard	48" × 48"	Adhesive to walls	1.5 gallons
Plywood panels	48" × 96"	Nailing to studs or wall	1.25 pounds
Rock lath	16" × 48"	Nailing to studs	5 pounds
Perforated hardboard	48" × 96"	Nailing to studs	4 pounds

Fasteners

Plywood Roof Sheathing

Recommended Thickness	Maximum Spacing of Supports (C. to C.) 20PSF	30PSF (b)	40PSF (b)	Nail Size and Type	Nail Spacing Panel Edge	Intermediate
5/16″	20″	20″	20″	6d common	6″	12″
3/8″	24″	24″	24″	6d common	6″	12″
1/2″(a)	32″	32″	30″	6d common	6″	12″
5/8″(a)	42″	42″	39″	8d common	6″	12″
3/4″(a)	48″	47″	42″	8d common	6″	12″

(a) Provide blocking or other means of suitable edge support when span exceeds 28″ for 1/2″ or 32″ for 3/4″.
(b) For special case of two-span continuous beams, plywood spans for 30 and 40 PSF can be increased 6 1/2%.

Insulating Sheathing

Walls
Galvanized roofing nails with 3/4″ diameter heads (or 16-gauge wire staples with 3/4″ crown).
Length: sheathing thickness plus 3/4″
 (Length of staple legs: sheathing thickness plus 1/2″)
 Fasteners on 24″ center on both field and perimeter
  (4′ × 8′, 24″ O.C.—15 nails
  4′ × 8′, 16″ O.C.—20 nails)
  4′ × 8′, 24″ O.C.—15 nails)

Frame Roof
Galvanized roofing nails with 3/8″ diameter heads.
Length: sheathing thickness plus 3/4″
Fasteners on 24″ centers on both field and perimeter
 (4′ × 8′, 24″ O.C.—15 nails
  4′ × 8′, 16″ O.C.—20 nails)

Interior Partitions
Secure sheathing to studs with galvanized roofing nails with 3/8″ heads.
Length: sheathing thickness plus 1/2″ (minimum)
Fasteners on 24″ centers on both field and perimeter
 (4′ × 8′, 24″ O.C.—15 nails)
Partitions: Fasten 8″ O.C. Add thickness of gypsum to thickness of sheathing plus 3/4″ (minimum).
Ceilings: Fasten 7″ O.C. Add thickness of gypsum to thickness of sheathing plus 3/4″ (minimum).

Selecting Shingle Nails

Application	Threading	Nail Sizes
Strip or individual shingle (new construction)	plain or helix	1 1/4″
Over asphalt roofing (reroofing)	helix or annular	1 1/2″
Over wood shingles (reroofing)	helix or barbed	1 3/4″

Fasteners

Wood Shingles

Laid to Weather	Shingles per 100 Sq. Ft.	Waste	Shingles per 100 Sq. Ft. with Waste	Nails per 100 Sq. Ft. 3d Nails	4d Nails
4″	900	10%	990	3¾ pounds	6½ pounds
5″	700	10%	792	3 pounds	5¼ pounds
6″	600	10%	660	2½ pounds	4¼ pounds

NOTE: Nails based on using 2 nails per shingle. Increase time factor 25 percent for hip roofs.

Nail*** Requirements for Asphalt Roofing Products

Type of Roofing	Shingles per Square	Nails per Shingle	Length of Nail*	Nails per Square	Pounds per Square (approximate) 12-gauge by 7⁄16″ head	11-gauge by 7⁄16″ head
Roll roofing on new deck			1″	252**	.73	1.12
Roll roofing over old roofing			1¾″	252**	1.13	1.78
19″ selvage over old shingle			1¾″	181	.83	1.07
3-tab sq. butt on new deck	80	4	1¼″	336	1.22	1.44
3-tab sq. butt reroofing	80	4	1¾″	504	2.38	3.01
Hex strip on new deck	86	4	1¼″	361	1.28	1.68
Hex strip reroofing	86	4	1¾″	361	1.65	2.03
Giant American	226	2	1¼″	479	1.79	2.27
Giant Dutch lap	113	2	1¼″	236	1.07	1.39
Individual hex	82	2	1¾″	172	.79	1.03

*Length of nail should always be sufficient to penetrate at least ¾″ into sound wood. Nails should show little, if any, below underside of deck.
**This is the number of nails required when spaced 2″ apart.
***Staples may be used instead of nails on a one for one basis. Use as a minimum 16-gauge zinc-coated staples with minimum 15⁄16″ crown and shank sufficient to penetrate ¾″ into deck lumber or plywood.

Fasteners

Wall Sheathing, Panel Siding and Floor Underlayment Attached to Wood Members

Description Attached Material	Attached Material Nominal Thickness	Spacing Specifications (in inches)		Fastener Specifications[1]	
		Edges	Intermediate	Leg Length (in inches)	Fastener Style[2]
Plywood	3/8"	6	12	1½	6d galv. casing nail *or* 6d galv. siding nail
Panel	1/2"	6	12	1⅝	6d galv. casing nail *or* 6d galv. siding nail
Siding 2 + 3	5/8"	6	12	1⅞	8d galv. casing nail *or* 8d galv. siding nail
Fiberboard wall sheathing	1/2"	6 / 4	12 / 10	1½	No. 14 gauge staple *or* No. 15 gauge staple *or* No. 16 gauge staple
	25/32"	6 / 4	12 / 10	1¾	No. 14 gauge staple *or* No. 15 gauge staple *or* No. 16 gauge staple
Gypsum wall sheathing	1/2"	6 / 4	12 / 10	1½	No. 14 gauge staple *or* No. 15 gauge staple *or* No. 16 gauge staple

Description Attached Material	Attached Material Nominal Thickness	Spacing Specifications (in inches)		Fastener Specifications[1]	
		Edges	Intermediate	Leg Length (in inches)	Fastener Style[2]
Floor underlayment: plywood, hardboard, flakeboard, particle board	1/4" & 5/16"	6 / 4	8-grid / 6-grid	1¼ / ⅞	3d ring-shank nail *or* No. 19 gauge staple (3/16" crown)
	3/8"	6 / 4	8-grid / 6-grid		3d ring-shank nail *or* No. 16 gauge staple
	1/2"	6 / 4	8-grid / 8-grid	1¼	6d box nail *or* 3d ring-shank nail *or* No. 16 gauge staple
	5/8"	6 / 4	8-grid / 6-grid		6d box nail *or* 4d ring-shank nail *or* No. 16 gauge staple

1. Except as noted above, all staples shall have a minimum O.D. crown width of 7/16".
2. Fasteners manufactured from steel wire exposed to the weather shall be zinc-coated by hot-dip galvanized zinc, mechanically deposited zinc, or electro-deposited zinc. Fasteners manufactured from aluminum alloy wire or other nonferrous alloys exposed to the weather do not require protective coatings.

Nuts and Bolts

Nuts and bolts used to hold metal to metal will usually stay tight on nonvibrating parts if enough torque is applied to stretch the shank slightly. Nuts and bolts attaching wood to wood or wood to metal will become loose as the wood loses moisture. A split washer on the metal side provides one method to take up the slack. The advantage of a nut and bolt over a screw or nail is that they permit removal and replacement as often as desired.

In the United States, nuts and bolts are classified by the American Standard for Unified Threads. There are two common bolt threads: UNC (coarse threads) and UNF (fine threads). A rarer type for close-tolerance jobs or attaching thin materials is UNEF (very fine threads).

Domestic bolts are measured in inches (from base of the head). Most imported bolts are metric and will not mesh with American Standard.

The threaded fasteners you buy at your hardware or home center store will almost always have coarse (American Standard) threads. These are deep cut and less likely to cross thread, but they are a trifle looser so you may need some type of thread locker. In critical applications, where you must have the maximum strength for a given diameter, use a bolt with the UNF threads. These are fine threads, so are not cut as deep into the shank, making the bolt less likely to break.

Where a permanent joint is involved and there is vibration, you can also use an anaerobic adhesive on the threads. Otherwise, you may choose to use a castle nut and cotter pin, lock washers, or two nuts tightened together on one bolt. You can also use torque locknuts, one of which has a plastic material inset into the top of the nut to act like a wedge (elastic stop nut). A nylon locknut has a nylon insert on one side that compresses when tightened, holding the nut securely. Both it and the elastic stop nut are reusable.

You can tell the strength of a bolt by looking at the SAE number on its head. Strongest are the high numbers. The SAE 8 and 7 bolts (marked with six segments for number 8 and five for number 7) are quenched and tempered carbon alloy steel with cold-rolled threads. (The Metric Property Class in high-strength steel will have a letter and a number on the head—the higher the number, the stronger the bolt.) SAE 5 is also tempered carbon steel but with hot-rolled threads. Grade 1 is low-carbon steel and if given a bright finish is graded as SAE 2.

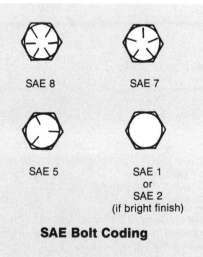

SAE 8   SAE 7

SAE 5   SAE 1
                or
              SAE 2
        (if bright finish)

SAE Bolt Coding

Nuts are available in hex or square shapes or as cap nuts in an acorn shape. Where finger tightening is desired, use knurled or wing nuts. Don't use square nuts in difficult-to-reach places—a greater than 90° turn is required for each twist with the wrench. With a hex nut you can turn 65° and get a new grip. Castle nuts permit locking with a cotter pin.

427

Fasteners

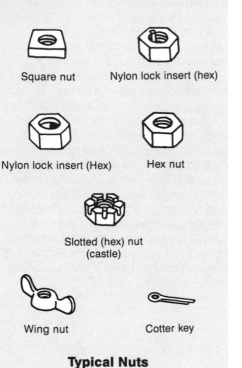

Square nut

Nylon lock insert (hex)

Nylon lock insert (Hex)

Hex nut

Slotted (hex) nut
(castle)

Wing nut

Cotter key

Typical Nuts

Tee nuts have angled prongs to secure the nut in wood and are ideal for joining legs to furniture. Tinnerman nuts are often found on the panels of large appliances. They allow for a large hole and eliminate the need for lock or flat washers.

Where corrosion could be a problem or there is a need to prevent any static electricity or electrical conduction, fiberglass-reinforced plastic or nylon nuts and bolts are available. Brass and aluminum corrosion-resistant nuts and bolts are available but may not be stocked at your hardware store.

If you have many uses for a given size bolt, you can save money by buying them in boxes of 100. If you need only a dozen and the rest will sit on your shelf for years, it won't be worth the larger purchase.

In buying nuts and bolts you will find them sized by diameter and threads per inch: e.g., $\frac{1}{4}'' \times 13$. They will be described by type (machine, stove, carriage, etc.) and head style as well as the SAE strength number.

It pays to store nuts and bolts in sealed containers with a light coating of oil to prevent rust.

Types of Bolts

Machine screws. Generally small bolts or self-tapping screws with diameters up to $\frac{1}{4}''$. Used for metal-to-metal fastening.

Round head

Flat head

Machine bolts. These come in diameters $\frac{1}{4}''$ and up. See head for guide to strengths.

Hex head

Studs and anchors. These come threaded at one or both ends. In small sizes they are used as a locking device on pulleys to fasten them to the axle or drive shaft.

Carriage bolts. These have a hexagonal shank under the head to lock into the part being fastened and permit tightening with a single wrench on the nut.

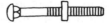

Stove bolts. Round- or flat-head bolts that come fully or partially threaded for noncritical assemblies.

Flat head   Round head

U and J bolts. Used for the temporary joining of components.

U-bolt

Eye bolts. These are designed for attaching rope, cable, or wire.

Lag screws. Often used in place of wood screws in wood frame construction when wood screws would be too short. Their hex heads can be driven with a socket wrench.

Hex lag screws

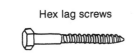

Washers

Washers are used as spacers; to cover oversized bolt holes; to protect a softer surface, such as wood, as the nut is tightened; as a slip surface so the bolt can turn without loosening; and, in the case of spring washers, to stop the nut from loosening on vibrating equipment. They are also used to make more secure electric contacts.

Palnuts consist of a washer attached to a nut—usually a self-tapping nut that cuts a sharp angular thread, speeding attachment. They were originally designed for the automotive industry but have become common in all types of manufactured construction. They are also made with a standard machine thread.

Push nuts look like washers but are actually fasteners that, pushed onto rods or axles, grip to hold on wheels or pulleys.

Washers are usually sold twenty-five to the box but may be purchased individually.

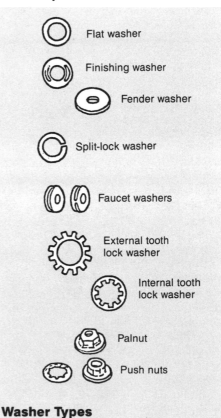

Washer Types

Fasteners

Washers

Description	Types of Metal	Sizes
Flat washers for carriage bolts	Zinc-plated steel	Bolt sizes: $1/4''$, $5/16''$, $3/8''$, $1/2''$
Flat washers, miniature, for use with screws	Brass	Screw gauge sizes: #00, #0, #1, #2, #3, #4
Flat washers for machine bolts	Grade 2 steel	Bolt sizes (metric): 3, 4, 5, 6, and 8 mm. Also British sizes: #6, #8, #10, $1/4''$, $7/16''$, $1/2''$, $5/16''$
Flat washers	Stainless steel	Screw and bolt sizes: #6, #8, #10, $1/4''$, $5/16''$, $3/8''$
Finishing washers (for use on housing)	Stainless steel	Bolt sizes: #6, #8, #10
Fender washers (for oversized holes)	Zinc-plated steel	Sizes: $1/4$–$1^1/4''$, $5/16$–$1^1/4''$, $1/4$–$1^1/2''$, $5/16$–$1^5/8''$, $3/8$–$1^5/8''$, $1/2$–$1^3/4''$
Split-lock (spring) washers	Grade 2 steel	Sizes: #6, #8, #10, $1/4''$, $5/16''$, $3/8''$, $7/16''$, $1/2''$ Metric sizes: 3, 4, 5, 6, and 8 mm.
Split-lock (spring) washers	Stainless steel	Sizes: #6, #8, #10, $1/4''$, $5/16''$, $3/8''$
Backup washers for riveting	Steel	Sizes ID: $1/8''$, $5/32''$, $3/16''$
Faucet washers*		Fiber sizes: 0, $1/4$S, $1/4$, $1/4$L Neoprene sizes: 00, 0, $1/4$S, $1/4$L, $3/8$, $3/8$M, $3/8$L, and $1/2''$
External-tooth lock washers		Sizes: #6, #8, #10, $1/4''$, $5/16''$, $3/8''$
Internal-tooth lock washers	Grade 2 steel	Same sizes as external-tooth lock washers above.
Palnuts for self-tapping or studs and for machine screws	Steel	Sizes: $1/8''$, $5/32''$, $3/16''$, $1/4''$, 6-32, 8-32, 10-32, $1/4$-20
Push nuts, flat round		Sizes: $3/16''$, $1/4''$, $5/16''$, $3/8''$, $1/2''$ Cod-type sizes: as above plus $5/8''$
Lock nuts (nuts with nylon insert that locks on bolt)	Steel	Sizes: 10-24, $1/4$-20, $1/4$-28, $5/16$-18, $3/8$-16, $1/2$-13

*While neoprene faucet washers are more durable, fiber washers seal better in worn faucet seats. Both materials resist swelling and distortion due to hot or cold water.

Pop Rivets

When facing a fastening job, few people consider riveting. Yet it is an excellent bonding method and very strong. Consider rivets when planning the permanent fastening of sheet materials of metal, plastic, or wood. If you're connecting soft materials you may need backup plates, which act as washers.

The most common household rivet is the blind rivet, also known as the pop rivet. It can fasten light metals and heavy fabrics. Its beauty is that it can fasten when you have access to one side only. A closed-end rivet is installed the same way but is watertight.

Common rivets can be set by hand or with special pliers. Threaded rivets work better than sheet metal screws where the metal is so thin it can't easily be tapped.

Gesipa Fasteners, Inc. has a new tool that allows hydraulic or pneumatic one-step installation of blind rivets.

Screws

Although more expensive and usually more time-consuming to drive, screws provide better holding power than nails. Besides general construction use, they may be used for built-in furniture, for holding wall brackets, or anywhere there may be a future need to disassemble a part.

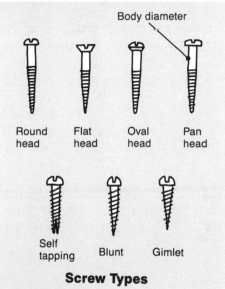

Screw Types

Screws are available in steel, brass, copper, and aluminum. Slotted thread screws are available for attaching to hardwoods—the cut-threads help cut through the wood and prevent cracking. Wax or soap the threads when screwing into hardwood.

Predrilling is recommended to provide a pilot hole in the entry stock and a starter hole in the holding stock; the table gives the appropriate drill sizes. You also need a countersink drill. Wood screws should be chosen in a length that allows two-thirds to penetrate into the holding stock.

Self-tapping screws, also known as sheet metal screws, are available for attaching to metal. Use sheet metal screws when attaching metal trim—their

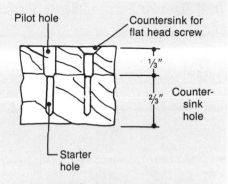

Predrilling Screw Holes

thread extends all the way to the head.

Headless set screws are used to lock parts onto rods or axles. They have recessed hex heads and are tightened with a hex wrench.

Headless Set Screws

These days, manufacturers have mostly converted to Phillip's head screws. This avoids damage. It's easy to get a flat-bladed screwdriver off center so you end up gouging the wood; a Phillip's head screwdriver is self-centering.

Screw diameter is dictated by the needed withdrawal strength. The larger the diameter, the better the holding strength.

When attaching wooden parts that will be exposed to the weather, use brass screws; countersink them and caulk the tops. Don't overdrive brass or aluminum screws—they break easily.

Fasteners

Drill Sizes for Standard Screw Shanks and Threads

No. of Screw	Maximum Head Dia. (inches)	Shank Diameter (inches)				Shank Wood Drill No.
		Decimal Size	Drill Size	Variation (oversize = +)		
0	.119	.060	1/16	+.002		2
1	.146	.073	5/64	+.005		(5/64")
2	.172	.086	3/32	+.007		3
3	.199	.099	7/64	+.010		(7/64")
4	.225	.112	7/64	−.003		(7/64")
5	.252	.125	1/8	Actual Size		4
6	.279	.138	9/64	+.002		(9/64")
7	.305	.151	5/32	+.005		5
8	.332	.164	5/32	−.007		(11/64")
9	.358	.177	11/64	−.005		6
10	.385	.190	3/16	−.002		(3/16")
11	.411	.203	13/64	Actual Size		(13/64")
12	.438	.216	7/32	+.003		7
14	.491	.242	1/4	+.008		8
16	.544	.268	17/64	−.002		9
18	.597	.294	19/64	+.003		10
20	.650	.320	5/16	−.001		11
24	.756	.372	3/8	+.003		12

To drill pilot hole use drill number (or size) given under thread diameter. In hardwoods you may need to drill a wider hole for depth of shank—see drill number (or size) under "Shank Diameter." You may also need to move up one drill size under "Thread Diameter" if a minus figure appears under "Variation."

Screw Hooks

Eight kinds of special-use screw hooks are shown here: The *cup hook* is also available plastic coated to help protect fine china. The *standard screw hook* has no stop and is normally screwed in to the depth of the thread. Large screw hooks are used to hang tools. *Eye and ring hooks* can be used with snap leashes or chains. The *eye hook* is frequently used in supporting lines or springs for curtains but has other uses. The *square-end hook* holds drapery rods or can be used for hanging kitchen utensils and pots.

Some of these, the screw hooks in particular, are available in large sizes for hanging overhead flowerpots and retaining the ends of working lines. For light duty—hanging car keys, caps,

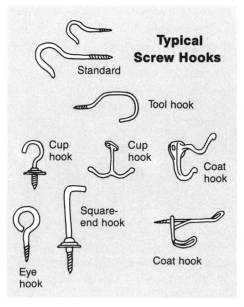

Typical Screw Hooks

Standard

Tool hook

Cup hook

Cup hook

Coat hook

Square-end hook

Eye hook

Coat hook

	Thread Diameter (inches)		Root Diameter	
Decimal Size	Drill Size	Variation (oversize = +)	Drill No.	Threads per Inch
.040	³⁄₆₄	+.007	(³⁄₆₄″)	32
.046	³⁄₆₄	Actual Size	(³⁄₆₄″)	28
.054	¹⁄₁₆	+.008	2	26
.065	¹⁄₁₆	−.002	2	24
.075	⁵⁄₆₄	+.003	(⁵⁄₆₄″)	22
.085	⁵⁄₆₄	−.007	(⁵⁄₆₄″)	20
.094	³⁄₃₂	Actual Size	3	18
.102	⁷⁄₆₄	+.007	(⁷⁄₆₄″)	16
.112	⁷⁄₆₄	−.003	(⁷⁄₆₄″)	15
.122	¹⁄₈	+.003	4	14
.130	¹⁄₈	−.005	4	13
.139	⁹⁄₆₄	+.001	(⁹⁄₆₄″)	12
.148	⁹⁄₆₄	−.007	(⁹⁄₆₄″)	11
.165	⁵⁄₃₂	−.009	5	10
.184	³⁄₁₆	+.003	6	9
.204	¹³⁄₆₄	−.001	7	8
.223	⁷⁄₃₂	−.004	7	8
.260	¹⁄₄	−.010	8	7

and kitchen utensils—there are also *magnetic, adhesive,* and *wire hooks.*

Corrugated Fasteners

Usually manufactured from 0.020″-thick steel 1″ × ½″ deep, these fasteners are used for fastening joints in wooden screen frames and picture frames.

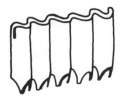

Corrugated Fastener

Staples

Staples are designed for hand-driven, pneumatic, or mechanical staplers. Some staples, such as fence or poultry netting staples and insulated staples, are typically hammer driven.

Pneumatic- and mechanical-stapler staples are made from steel wire, aluminum alloy wire, or copper-clad wire. Chemically etched staples are available for fastening wood or materials into wood. Bright finish and cement-coated staples are also available. Use zinc-coated staples for all exterior or damp locations.

Crowns from ³⁄₁₆″ to 1″ wide are commonly available in wire gauges 18 (for ³⁄₁₆″) to 14 (for 1″). Crown widths are 0.164″ to 0.5″. Hand-driven staples are preformed; those having chisel

Fasteners

points are called "common." They are sold by gauge, leg length, and crown width for hand-driven staples.

Type III, Style 3 flat-top crown staples are designed for pneumatic application to wood. Steel wire, aluminum alloy wire, or copper-clad wire with bright finishes, zinc-coated, cement-coated, or chemically etched finishes may be used as called for in building code or manufacturer's specifications. Use zinc-coated staples in any damp location.

For hand-driven applications, use Type III, Style 4 preformed steel wire, zinc-, or cement-coated staples. Copper-clad wire, tinned, or other plated finishes are available for hand-driven staples.

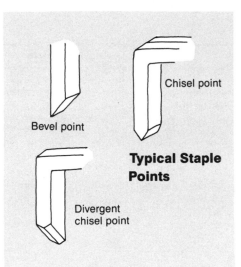

Typical Staple Points

Chisel-Point Staples ("Common")

Leg Length	Crown Width	Diameter (inches)	Flatten To (inches)	Point Length	Point Angle	No. per Lb.
3/8"	7/32"	.054	.040	3/16"	13°	1,920
13/32"	3/16"	.067	.048	3/16"	12°	1,376
7/16"	7/32"	.067	.048	1/4"	12°	1,248
1/2"	1/4"	.072	.057	1/4"	12°	864
9/16"	9/32"	.072	.057	5/16"	12°	800
5/8"	5/16"	.072	.057	5/16"	12°	672
11/16"	5/16"	.083	.060	11/32"	12°	544
3/4"	3/8"	.083	.060	11/32"	12°	410

Staples driven into shingles (roofing or other soft materials) should have underside of crown flush with the surface. Under-driving, tipping or over-driving will result in shingles being blown off the roof by winds.

Galvanized staples used in power staplers provide an alternative to nailing. We advise caution! Pneumatic staplers literally fire the staples into the base. Carelessly handled, they become a lethal weapon. We don't recommend the use of power staplers by anyone who has not been trained in their care and operation.

The tables that follow illustrate staple use and specifications for size and spacing.

Staple Recommendations for Plywood Subfloor and Roof Sheathing Attached to Wood Members

Subfloor or Sheathing Nominal Thickness (in inches)	Spacing Specifications (in inches)			Fastener Specifications[1,2]	
	Intermediate Edges	Roof	Floor[3]	Leg Length (in inches)	Fastener Style
$7/8$	6	12	10	$2\frac{3}{8}$	8d common *or* 8d ring-shank nail *or* 8d screw-shank nail
				2	13-gauge staple
				$2\frac{1}{8}$	14-gauge staple
	4	10	8	$2\frac{1}{8}$	15-gauge staple
				$2\frac{1}{2}$	16-gauge staple
1	6	12	10	$2\frac{1}{8}$	13-gauge staple
				$2\frac{1}{3}$	8d common nail *or* 8d ring-shank nail *or* 8d screw-shank nail
				$2\frac{1}{4}$	14-gauge staple
	4	10	8	$2\frac{3}{8}$	15-gauge staple
$1\frac{1}{8}-1\frac{3}{4}$	6	12	10	$2\frac{5}{8}$	13-gauge staple
				$2\frac{7}{8}$	10d common nail *or* 14-gauge staple
				$2\frac{1}{2}$	8d ring-shank nail *or* 8d screw-shank nail
	4	10	8	3	15-gauge staple
$1/4-5/16-3/8$	6	12	10	$1\frac{3}{8}$	14-gauge staple *or* 15-gauge staple
				$1\frac{5}{8}$	16-gauge staple *or* 6d common nail *or* 6d ring-shank nail *or* 6d screw-shank nail
$1/2$	6	12	10	$1\frac{1}{2}$	14-gauge staple *or* 15-gauge staple
				$1\frac{3}{4}$	16-gauge staple *or* 6d common nail *or* 6d ring-shank nail *or* 6d screw-shank nail
$5/8$	6	12	10	$1\frac{7}{8}$	14-gauge staple
				2	15-gauge staple
				$2\frac{1}{4}$	16-gauge staple
				$2\frac{1}{8}$	8d common nail
				$1\frac{7}{8}$	6d ring-shank nail *or* 6d screw-shank nail

Fasteners

Staple Recommendations for Plywood Subfloor and Roof Sheathing Attached to Wood Members (Concluded)

Subfloor or Sheathing Nominal Thickness (in inches)	Spacing Specifications (in inches)			Fastener Specifications[1,2]	
	Intermediate Edges	Roof	Floor[3]	Leg Length (in inches)	Fastener Style
¾	6	12	10	2	14-gauge staple
				2⅛	15-gauge staple
	6	10	8	2⅜	16-gauge staple
	6	12	10	2¼	8d common nail
				2	6d ring-shank nail *or* 6d screw-shank nail

1. Staples shall have a ⁷⁄₁₆" minimum O.D. crown width.
2. Fasteners exposed to weather shall be zinc-coated by hot-dip galvanized zinc, mechanically deposited zinc, or electro-deposited zinc.
3. Where subfloor spans 48" or more, fasteners shall be spaced 6" on center at all supports except where a closer spacing is indicated.

Staples for Attaching Wall, Ceiling, and Soffit Covering Materials to Metal Receiving Members Only

Wire Gauge No.	Leg Length (O.D., in inches)	Description of Covering Materials[3]	Staple[1,2] Spacing (in inches)	Receiving Member
16 or	1⅛	⅜" gypsum lath	5	Approved load- and non-load-bearing nailable studs "only" designed for receiving round staples or conventional nails
14			8	
16 or	1¼	½" gypsum lath, panels, & wallboard	5	
14			8	
16 or	1⅜	⅝" gypsum lath, panels, & wallboard	5	
14			8	
16	1¼	Metal lath & welded or woven wire lath & masonry veneer wire mesh, gun lath, Stucco-Rite & Aqua-K-Lath, heavy-duty furred, non-furred	6	
16	1⅜	⅜" high-rib metal lath		
16	1¾	¾" high-rib metal lath	At ribs	

1. Staples manufactured from round, semiround, or flat wire and shall have a minimum ⁷⁄₁₆" O.D. crown.
2. Staples required to be galvanized shall be zinc-coated by hot-dip galvanizing, mechanically deposited zinc, or electro-deposited zinc.
3. Wallboard requiring a smooth finish for appearance's sake shall be attached with an approved stapling tool that simultaneously drives the staple and dimples the surface of the wallboard without cutting the paper.

Staple Recommendations for Materials Attached to Wood Receiving Members
Subflooring, Wall Sheathing, Roof Sheathing (Solid or Spaced)

Nominal Thickness (inches)	Fastener Count per Board per Bearing	Minimum Length of Fastener Required (inches)	Staple Wire Gauge and Nail Size and Style[1]
1 × 4 or	2 Staples	1¾	16-gauge staple or 15-gauge staple or 14-gauge staple
1 × 6	2 Nails	2	6d common nail or 6d ring-shank nail or 6d screw-shank nail
1 × 8	4 Staples	1¾	16-gauge staple or 15-gauge staple
	3 Staples	1¾	14-gauge staple
	3 Nails	2	6d common nail or 6d ring-shank nail or 6d screw-shank nail

1. Staple crown width ⁷⁄₁₆" minimum T-nail, standard round head, clipped round head nail.

Staples for Attaching Wall, Ceiling, and Soffit Covering Materials to Wood Receiving Members Only

Staple Leg Length (O.D., in inches)	Description of Covering Materials[3]	Staple[1,2] Spacing (in inches)
⅞	⅜" gypsum lath—plain, perforated, Type X	
1	⅜" gypsum lath & metal or wire stripping (for one-hour fire-rated ceilings)	5
1⅛	½" gypsum lath—plain or Type X	4
	½" fiber insulation lath	
1¾	1" fiber insulation lath	
	Laminating ⅜" gypsum lath & ⅝" gypsum wallboard (for two-hour fire-rated wall)	5
⅞	⅜" gypsum lath panels, wallboard & backer board	
1⅛	½" gypsum lath panels, wallboard & backer board	
1¼	⅝" gypsum wallboard & backer board	7
1¾	Laminating ½" & ½" Type X wallboard (for one-hour fire rating)	
2	Laminating ⅝" & ⅝" Type X wallboard (for two-hour fire-rated wall)	

Fasteners

Staples for Attaching Wall, Ceiling, and Soffit Covering Materials to Wood Receiving Members Only (Concluded)

Staple Leg Length (O.D., in inches)	Description of Covering Materials[3]	Staple[1,2] Spacing (in inches)
$\frac{7}{8}$	Exterior self-furred stucco mesh[2] Expanded metal lath—furred and non-furred Welded or woven wire netting Welded wire fabric Flat rib metal lath Masonry veneer wire mesh (stucco mesh)	6
$1\frac{1}{4}$	Exterior self-furred stucco mesh[2] (attached on top of sheathing)	
$\frac{7}{8}$	Gun lath, Stucco-Rite, & Aqua-K-Lath, heavy	
$1\frac{3}{4}$	$\frac{3}{8}''$ high-rig metal lath	
$1\frac{3}{4}$	$\frac{3}{4}''$ high-rib metal lath	At ribs

1. Manufactured from 16-gauge round, semiround, or flattened wire and shall have a minimum $\frac{7}{16}''$ O.D. crown.
2. Manufactured from steel wire; if exposed to the weather shall be zinc-coated by hot-dip galvanized zinc, mechanically deposited zinc, or electro-deposited zinc. Fasteners manufactured from aluminum alloy wire or other nonferrous alloys exposed to the weather do not require coatings.
3. Wallboard requiring a smooth finish for appearance's sake shall be attached with an approved tool that simultaneously drives the staple and dimples surface area of the wallboard without cutting the paper.

Staples for Attaching Roof and Wall Covering Materials

Spacing Specifications[5,6]	Fastener Specifications[1,2]		
	Fastener Style	Min. O.D. Crown Width (in inches)	Leg Lengths[3] O.D. (in inches)
Asphalt—composition or fiberglass roof shingles and wall shingles			
A minimum of (4) staples per each 36" to 40" section of shingle	16-ga. staples	$\frac{15}{16}$	$\frac{3}{4}''$ penetration into the wood
Asphalt—composition, ridge, hip caps[4]			
A minimum of (4) staples are required		$\frac{3}{4}$	1
for ridge cap	16-ga. staples	$\frac{7}{16}$	$1\frac{1}{4}$
Roof and wall wood shingles[5]			
A minimum of (2) staples or nails per shingle	16-ga. staples	$\frac{7}{16}$	$1\frac{1}{4}$
Wood shakes[7]			
A minimum of (2) staples or nails per shake	16-ga. staples	$\frac{7}{16}$	$1\frac{3}{4}$

Staples for Attaching Roof and Wall Covering Materials (Concluded)

		Fastener Specifications[1,2]	
Spacing Specifications[5,6]	Fastener Style	Min. O.D. Crown Width (in inches)	Leg Lengths[3] O.D. (in inches)
Tin capping—roof felts			
All tin caps placed and stapled 12″ on center	16-ga. staples	$\frac{7}{16}$	$\frac{7}{8}$
Tin cap roofing felts to gypsum decks	16-ga. staples	$\frac{3}{4}$ $\frac{7}{16}$	$1\frac{5}{8}$
Aluminum siding[6]			
Staple spacing maximum of 32″ on center	16-ga. staples	$\frac{7}{16}$	$\frac{3}{4}$

1. Shingles and shakes attached to roof sheathing having the underside of the sheathing exposed to visual view may be attached in these locations with staples or nails having shorter lengths than specified so as not to penetrate the exposed side of the sheathing.
2. All fasteners are manufactured from steel wire zinc-coated (by hot-dip galvanized zinc, mechanically deposited zinc, or electro-deposited zinc). Fasteners manufactured from aluminum alloy wire or other nonferrous alloys do not require coatings.
3. For reroofing or recover applications, the staples leg length shall be long enough to penetrate the opposite side of sheathing ⅛″ or penetrate sheathing ¾″; all other provisions of this table will prevail.
4. Asphalt composition shingles attached with staples are driven so that the staple crown bears tightly against the shingle but does not cut the shingle surface. The crown is parallel to the long dimension of the shingle course.
5. Wood shingles and shakes attached with staples are driven so that the staple crown is parallel to the butt-edge, compressing the wood surface no more than the total thickness of the staple crown wire.
6. Staples shall be aluminum and have a minimum penetration of ¾″ into the wood supporting member. One leg of the staple shall be driven through the prepunched hole in the sealing rib, with the crown perpendicular to the width of the siding.
7. 18-gauge staples with ⁷⁄₁₆″ crown may be used to attach roof and wall shingles, provided the butt ends do not exceed ¾″. The staple leg lengths shall be long enough to penetrate into the sheathing ¾″ or through the thickness of the sheathing, whichever is less. Two staples shall be used to attach each shingle or shake.

Staple Recommendations for Plywood Wall Sheathing Attached to Wood Members

Nominal Thickness (inches)	Spacing Specifications (in inches)		Fastener Specifications[1,2]	
	Edges	Intermediate	Leg Length (in inches)	Fastener Style[3]
$\frac{1}{4}$ & $\frac{5}{16}$	6	12	$1\frac{3}{8}$	14-gauge staple *or* 15-gauge staple *or* 16-gauge staple
			$1\frac{1}{2}$	6d box nail
$\frac{3}{8}$	6	12	$1\frac{3}{8}$	14-gauge staple *or* 15-gauge staple *or* 16-gauge staple
			$1\frac{5}{8}$	6d common nail *or* 6d ring-shank nail *or* 6d screw-shank nail
			$1\frac{1}{2}$	6d box nail

Fasteners

Staple Recommendations for Plywood Wall Sheathing Attached to Wood Members (Concluded)

Nominal Thickness (inches)	Spacing Specifications (in inches)		Fastener Specifications[1,2]	
	Edges	Intermediate	Leg Length (in inches)	Fastener Style[2]
$\frac{1}{2}$	6	12	$1\frac{1}{2}$	14-gauge staple or 15-gauge staple or 16-gauge staple
			$1\frac{3}{4}$	6d common nail or 6d ring-shank nail or 6d screw-shank nail
			$1\frac{5}{8}$	6d box nail
$\frac{5}{8}$	6	12	$1\frac{5}{8}$	14-gauge staple or 15-gauge staple or 16-gauge staple
			$1\frac{7}{8}$	6d common nail or 6d ring-shank nail or 6d screw-shank nail or 8d cooler nail or 8d box nail

1. Staples shall have a $\frac{7}{16}$″ minimum O.D. crown width.
2. Fasteners exposed to weather shall be zinc-coated by hot-dip galvanized zinc, mechanically deposited zinc, or electro-deposited zinc.
3. Nails may have T-heads, modified round heads, or standard round heads.

Tapes

While one generally thinks of tape as a temporary or package-sealing material, there are some tapes that have much more permanent uses.

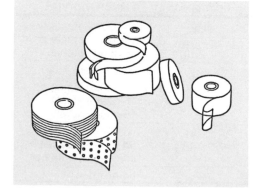

Fiberglass-reinforced filament tape. Having a high tensile (pull) strength, this tape can be used instead of steel strapping. It can be used to hold together stacks of panels or bundles of pipes and will keep cabinet doors and drawers closed during transportation. Remember, its strength is greatest lengthwise. Used two or three layers thick, it can permanently secure pipes and cables.

Double-faced carpet tape. This tape has two sticky sides and is available in different widths and types. Double-faced tape is excellent for applying wall tiles or for holding down carpet edges. It can also be used at the workbench to secure blocks you are sanding or chiseling. It will hold clean, dry, smooth materials together while you drill, nail, saw, rivet, or screw them. Used on the face of a sander, it will keep the sandpaper smooth and prevent slippage.

Duct tape. This plastic-coated cloth tape can repair most plastic and fabric articles. It can be used to hold panels in place and tape temporary extension cords to the floor so people won't trip. It can be used to seal air leaks in sheet metal ducts and to seal insulated sheathing joints—but do the latter only if you have a tightly sealed inside poly vapor barrier. Taped across windows, it can be used to reduce damage during hurricanes. Duct tape comes in gray, black, safety yellow, or aluminized colors.

Electric tape. Beyond its obvious electric wire-insulating applications, this type tape can be used temporarily to stop leaks in plumbing pipes and garden hoses. You'll often see carpenters use it to wrap hammer and plier handles in order to provide a better cushioned grip.

Plaster tape. This plaster-of-Paris coated cotton scrim is soaked in water, wrung out, and applied by smoothing along a joint or seam in Gypsum Board walls or ceilings. Used for fire-resistant construction, this material sets hard and rigid—it's the same tape used by doctors for making casts. Its use is only limited by the imagination, as it can be molded and will quickly set into any desired shape. When several layers are used, it will become very rugged and can be used to form planters, masks, and other unusually shaped decorative items that are then finished with fiberglass cloth and polyester resin and painted.

Masking tape. This type tape is primarily used to protect woodwork while painting. Automotive body shops use plastic masking tape to mask decorative stripes on cars or trucks. It's less likely to "bridge" and cause the paint to peel off when removed and adheres better so paint doesn't bleed under it. Paper masking tape, torn in short strips, is handy to label parts, write reminders, or stick on glazing during construction to inform people there is glass in the door or window.

Aluminum foil tape. Use this tape to patch ducts and gutters.

Plastic decorative tape. Available in many colors, this tape may be used to patch torn plastic or fabrics and provide stripes of accent color when decorating.

Drywall tapes, Velcro carpet tape, and Teflon plumbing tape are covered in chapters 13, 11, and 8, respectively.

Wall Anchors

There are many kinds of wall anchors, but all fall into one of two main categories: (1) those to be used in solid walls and (2) those to be used in frame walls with hollow stud cavities.

The anchors for solid walls include plastic and nylon anchors, lead anchors, and lag screw expansion shields. They are installed by drilling a (continued on p. 444)

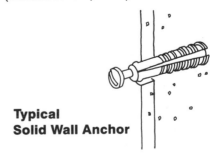

**Typical
Solid Wall Anchor**

Fasteners

Fasteners

Fasteners	Wedge Anchors	Plastic Anchors	Nylon Anchors	Screw Anchors	Toggle Bolts
Brick	M	M	L	H	M
Concrete	H	M	L	H	M
Concrete Block	O	M	L	H	M
Cinder Block	O	M	L	H	H
Fiberboard Siding-Decking	O	M	L	H	H
Glass	O	O	O	H	H
Gypsum	O	H	L	H	H
Marble	H	M	L	H	M
Plaster	O	L	L	H	H
Plasterboard	O	M	L	H	H
Stone	H	M	L	H	M
Stucco	O	M	L	H	M
Terrazzo	H	M	L	H	M
Terra-Cotta	H	M	L	H	M
Tile (Building)	O	M	L	H	M
Tile (Ceramic)	O	M	L	H	M
Accessories—Bolt or Screw Required	None Anchor Complete	Sheet Metal or Wood Screw	None Anchor Complete	Sheet Metal or Wood Screw	None Anchor Complete
Method Tools	Drill Hammer Wrench	Drill Screwdriver Wrench	Drill Hammer	Drill Screwdriver	Drill Screwdriver
Comments	Fastest growing anchor for heavy loads	Works in any material Excellent all purpose anchor	Works in all materials All-purpose light duty—fast installation anchor with threaded or unthreaded nail	Works in any material Excellent all-purpose anchor	Will work on all material backed by a hollow ☐ See legend

LEGEND
H—Best of heaviest duty anchor for this material
M—Good anchor for this material
L—Light duty for this material

☐—Anchor will work if material contains hollow
O—Not recommended

442

Zinc or Aluminum Drive Anchors	Machine Screw Anchors	Lead Anchors	Steel Expansion Anchors	Zinc Lag Shield	Hollow Wall Anchors
H	H	M	H	M	H
H	H	M	H	M	H
H	H	M	H	M	H
M	M	M	M	M	H
O	O	O	O	O	H
O	O	O	O	O	H
O	O	O	O	O	H
H	H	M	H	O	H
O	O	O	O	O	H
O	O	O	O	O	H
H	H	M	H	M	H
O	O	M	O	O	H
H	H	M	H	O	H
O	O	M	O	O	H
O	O	M	O	O	H
O	O	M	O	O	H
None Anchor Complete	Machine Screw	Sheet Metal or Wood Screw	None Anchor Complete	Lag Screw	None Anchor Complete
Drill Hammer	Drill, Hammer, Screwdriver, Wrench Setting Tools	Drill Hammer Screwdriver	Drill Wrench Screwdriver	Drill Wrench	Drill Screwdriver
Will work on all hard materials	Will work on all hard materials	Will work on all hard materials	Will work on all hard materials	Will work on all hard materials	Will work on all material backed by a hollow ☐ See legend

Fasteners

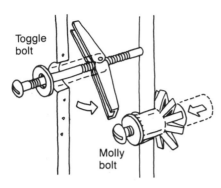

Hollow Wall Anchors

pilot hole into the wall, then tapping the anchor into the hole until the head is flush with the wall surface. When you thread a screw into the anchor, the anchor expands and grips tightly by pressing against the sides of the hole.

The plastic anchors serve to hang light objects like pictures on drywall or plaster walls. The metal anchors are for heavy-duty loads on concrete, brick, or stone walls.

The anchors for hollow walls include expansion bolts (often called Molly bolts) and toggle bolts. These bolts have a section that expands in the cavity on the "blind" side of the drywall or paneling.

The selection chart indicates which anchor is best for each job.

Packaging labels will help you select the right anchor size, depending on the weight being supported and the nature of the supporting material.

If vibration will be experienced, you will need special vibration-proof anchors. Neoprene sleeves or polypropylene screw anchors should be used for mounting window fans, stereo speakers, or shelves on which blenders, mixers, or other vibrating equipment will be mounted. Self-drilling expandable anchors and drive (or split)

anchors of high-strength steel or aluminum are also available. Some have a stainless steel pin for hard materials. They come with round, countersunk, or stud heads—the last-named where later removal is anticipated.

The Right Tools for Fasteners

Staplers. You will want to own both a double-leverage-action staple tacker and a hammer stapler for small to medium-sized jobs; for large jobs it pays to rent an electric stapler. For installing insulated sheathing, you will need a stapler that can handle 16-gauge wire staples having a minimum ¾" crown and legs at least ½" long. In some locations a license is required to operate a power stapler because it can be misused.

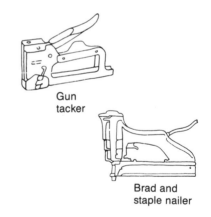

Gun tacker

Brad and staple nailer

Hand Staplers

Powder-activated stud driver (PASD). Activated by a .22 caliber charge, the PASD drives case-hardened masonry nails into block, concrete, mortar, metal, or wood. This driver requires careful handling and should be used only by a trained applicator. Again, a license may be required to use this tool.

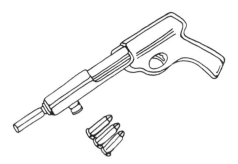

Powder-Activated Stud Driver

Riveters. Standard hand-riveters are available in sets containing interchangeable nose pieces for $\frac{1}{8}"$, $\frac{5}{32}"$, and $\frac{3}{16}"$ diameter rivets of various lengths. The rivet, steel or aluminum, is attached to a mandrel inserted into the riveter. The rivet is inserted into a predrilled hole through both pieces to be joined. The riveter "pops" the rivet as you squeeze the handle and nips off the mandrel, which is thrown away. You can also buy solid split rivets, which are set with a ball peen hammer and a center punch by driving them against a solid piece of steel.

Hand-Operated Blind Riveter

Nail gun. On large projects you can save time by renting a nail gun. This drives and countersinks nails into paneling, carpeting, and molding with a single stroke. It will not mar, scratch, or dent work surfaces. The nails come in wood tones to match paneling.

Pneumatic power nailer. This tool feeds and drives a roll of glued or wired-together nails at speeds up to 4,000 nails per hour (requires an air compressor). It can handle twenty-six different nails, between $2"$ to $3\frac{1}{2}"$ long, and weighs less than 10 pounds. If you have an air compressor and the job is large enough, this tool is a real labor saver.

Floor-nailing machine. This tool is designed to drive $2" \times 0.105"$ spiral-threaded flooring nails at the correct $45°$ angle from above the tongue, while holding each flooring strip tight against its neighbor. A good piece of equipment to assure a well-laid floor, the floor nailer is well worth its rental cost.

Floor-Nailing Machine

Glue gun. This electrically heated gun is loaded with thermoplastic glue or caulking sticks, which it melts, allowing you to trigger a bead or spot on the parts to be joined or sealed. It normally takes about a minute for the adhesive to cool and set, so the parts being joined must be held tight with a C clamp or vise. Thrust-pushed or automatic-feeding models are available.

Heavy-duty glues are available for wood joints. Light-duty glues can be used for attaching veneers and thin materials.

The caulking sticks can be used to waterproof a crack.

Hardware   16

16. Hardware

This chapter gives you a general idea of the hardware that's available in the home marketplace today. But to select among all the styles, shapes, colors, and treatments, you'll have to go out and see them for yourself. The choice is wide indeed. Visit at least two or three stores.

Hardware in this chapter includes cabinet knobs and catches, drawer hardware, hasps, latches, hinges, locks for entry doors, French doors and sliding glass doors, and shelf brackets.

Cabinet Knobs

Cabinet knobs are usually attached with one screw from the back of the door. They may be made from glass, cast iron, brass, bronze, ceramic, wood, or plastic. Round knobs are usually comfortable to use. For sliding doors, inset round or scalloped handles are used. Matching switch plates are available for decorative accents.

Solid brass or bronze are the most elegant and durable and hence the most expensive.

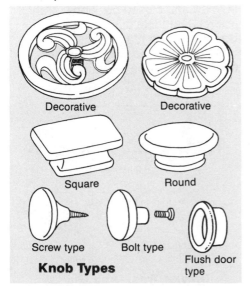

Decorative   Decorative

Square   Round

Screw type   Bolt type

Flush door type

Knob Types

Catches

There are nine standard types of cabinet drawer and door catches. Since noise can be annoying, the rubber roller or plastic friction types are often preferred. On doors, the catch should be installed on a centerline through the handle. Where there is a likelihood of pans or other stored or stacked items falling against the door, a spring-loaded twist latch can be used with an inset door. Where there is a need to keep children from opening a drawer or door, a child safety latch with finger access can be installed inside.

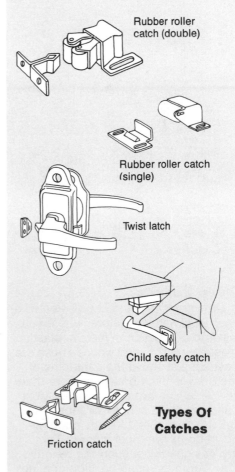

Rubber roller catch (double)

Rubber roller catch (single)

Twist latch

Child safety catch

Friction catch

Types Of Catches

Hardware

Push or touch catches are mounted inside the cabinet and have no knobs or pulls. By simply pushing on the door the catches release and the door swings open, but beware of kids' palm prints and sticky fingers. Elbow catches are for latching the first closed of a pair of doors. They mount inside on the shelf or frame and are released by a push of the finger.

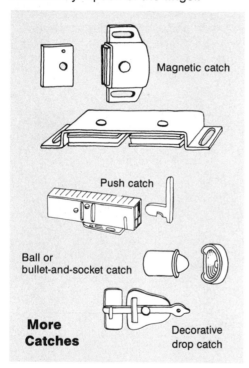

Magnetic catch

Push catch

Ball or bullet-and-socket catch

More Catches

Decorative drop catch

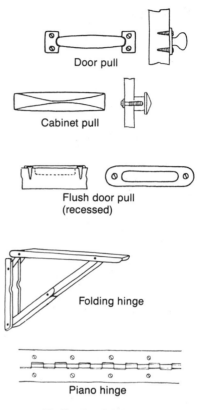

Door pull

Cabinet pull

Flush door pull (recessed)

Folding hinge

Piano hinge

Pulls And Hinges

in open and closed positions. A shelf or drop-leaf table support is similar. Use with piano hinges.

Rail drawer glides come in one- and two-track versions. A drawer with a

Drawer Hardware

Drawer pulls can best be selected at your local hardware store, where you will find a selection in metals, plastics, glass, ceramics, and wood. These are best set just above the centerline of the drawer. If the drawer is more than 18″ wide, use two drawer pulls. Most pulls use No. 8 screws for mounting.

Folding supports for lids and pull-down doors are triple-hinged. They are designed to support the weight of the door in the open position and lock

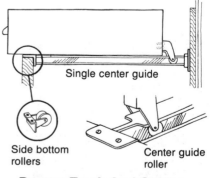

Single center guide

Side bottom rollers

Center guide roller

Drawer Track And Guides

monorail bottom center guide has a single bottom rail with drawer rollers left and right, but it may permit too much side-to-side movement. You may prefer a side-mounted version. Each track has rollers on which the drawer rides and a stop so it won't surprise you by falling out. If you rely on wooden drawers sliding on wooden rails, humidity may cause a drawer to stick. Regular usage may result in wear and make them loose. However, you can use soap or paraffin wax to keep the runners slippery.

Hasps

Surpisingly strong and secure when padlocked, a safety hasp folds back over the fastening screws and covers the screws on the clasp, making them tamperproof. These are the "thing-a-majigs" everyone uses on toolsheds, barn doors, and chests. They are available in galvanized steel, wrought iron, or bronze in a variety of sizes. NOTE: They can only be opened from one side.

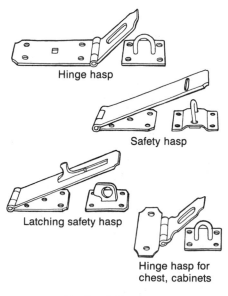

Hinge hasp

Safety hasp

Latching safety hasp

Hinge hasp for chest, cabinets

Typical Hasps

Latches

For doors and gates there are latches which can be opened from two sides. When used on doors, these can be locked with a nail by drilling a hole through the latch guide. Gate latches are designed to be reached over the top of the gate and cannot be locked. Sliding bolts are designed with a retrieval chain. Gate hinges have long post pivots to allow for width of gate; you can use a double post hinge that pivots.

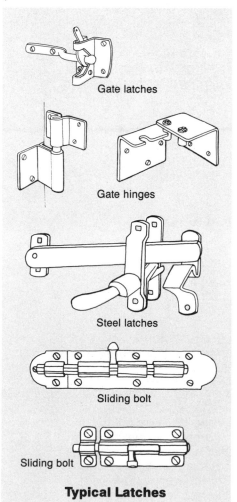

Gate latches

Gate hinges

Steel latches

Sliding bolt

Sliding bolt

Typical Latches

Hardware

Hinges

Here are fourteen of the most common kinds of hinges for doors and cabinets:

Flush Door Hinge

A concealed hinge— only the barrel shows.

Ball Bearing Hinge

Excellent for heavy doors. These are permanently lubricated.

Knuckle Hinge

Only a decorative knuckle shows.

Rising Butt Hinge

Door lifts as it opens to clear carpet. Self-closing.

Butt Hinge

Simple hinge installed in rabbeted slot. Door cannot be taken off without unscrewing hinge.

Lift-Joint Hinge

Permits door to be lifted off without unscrewing hinge.

Loose-Pin Hinge

Permits removal of door without unscrewing hinge— just remove hinge pins. The most common door hinge.

Decorative H Hinge

Available in flat black, wrought iron, copper, brass, or bronze finishes for rustic effect. Comes with pyramid head screws.

HL Hinge

A variation of the rustic H hinge.

Lacquered Cabinet Hinge

A decorative hinge in brass or flat black. There are many design variations.

Piano Hinge

Sold in lengths up to 7 feet with holes spaced 2″ apart. These continuous hidden hinges give full support for lids and can be used for doors. They will support considerable weight.

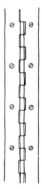

Semi-Concealed Hinge

Particularly attractive on raised panel doors, this hinge is attached to the stile in front and bends around a rabbeted joint to be attached to the back of the door.

Spring Hinge

This has a spring in the barrel so the opened door will close when released.

Cabinet Pivot

Attached to the top and bottom of the door, this provides a concealed closure system.

Locksets

Locksets are doorknobs and locks sold in sets with keys. You have a choice of standard cylinder locks, mortise locks, dead bolt locks, or rim locks.

Cylinder locks are always installed after the door is hung. In some prehung doors the doorknob holes are predrilled and strike plate recesses are premortised. Keep in mind that with predrilled doors your choice of locks is more limited. If they aren't drilled, you will find a cardboard template in the box with the door handle set for locating them.

Locks are usually located 36″ from the floor. Dead bolts are located above the doorknob, except for the type that combines the bolt with a dead bolt. Dead bolts usually have a hardened steel shaft that slides through the hole in a strike plate, through the casing, and into a hole in the trimmer stud. Mortise locks combine both a regular bolt and a dead bolt (each with its own handle or latch inside), but only a key will open the dead bolt from outside. Wraparound strike plates help prevent the use of a screwdriver or wrecking bar to retract the bolt.

Dead bolts are available with keylocks on one or both sides. Dead

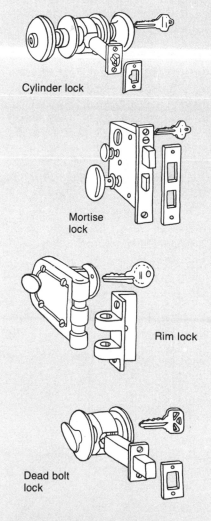

Cylinder lock

Mortise lock

Rim lock

Dead bolt lock

Typical Locksets

bolts with two keylocks are often used with glass sidelighted doors for security reasons. (The lock can't be opened without a key by breaking sidelight.) *Caution:* Be sure guests and children know where key is stored in case of an emergency.

Most cylinder locks have a spring-latch locking mechanism. This kind of latch gives the least security among

Hardware

door locks—burglars can easily pop the latch out of the hole in the strike plate, foiling the lock. If you have any entry door with only a spring-latch lock, add a dead bolt lock.

One of the strongest door locks is a diagonal-bar lock, also known as a "city lock." Designed for inward-opening doors, its steel brace prevents the door from being shouldered open from the outside. When unlocked with a key from the outside, the top of the bar is displaced into a slot, permitting entry.

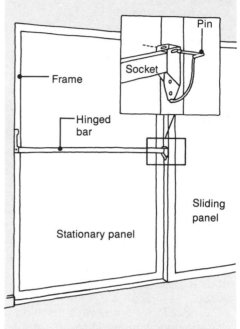

Hinged Bar Installation

- A *hinged bar lock* swings down into a socket to prevent moving door from opening.

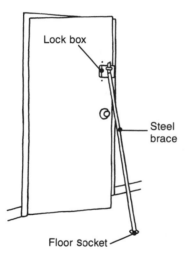

Diagonal-Bar Lock

Locks for Sliding and French Doors

There are several styles of locks to add to sliding glass doors:
- The *bar lock* fits into the inside of the track, preventing the sliding door from being pushed open. When not in use, the bar can be pivoted up and out of the way.
- A *screw-threaded telescoping rod* can be adjusted to the door width and dropped in the track.

Telescoping Rod (Similar To Hinged Rod Above)

- A special *dead bolt lock* for *sliding glass doors* can be attached at center bottom. The lock mechanism is screwed into the bottom of the inner door's center stile, and its dead bolt enters a hole in the bottom rail of the outer (fixed) door. A key operates the lock. There is also a similar lock that can be attached to the bottom track to serve the same purpose.

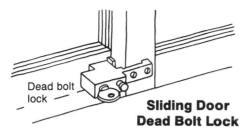

Dead bolt lock

**Sliding Door
Dead Bolt Lock**

- A special *mortised lock for French doors* makes one of the doors immovable. The locks insert a bolt into the threshold and the top jamb.
- A similar lock called a *sliding bar lock* can be used on bottom panelled French doors. A special cam-operating handle, mounted in the center of the door, thrusts bars into receivers installed on either side of the doorjamb.

None of the locks can be operated from outside.

Shelf Brackets

There's more than one way to hang a shelf. In fact, there are at least eleven. A selection guide to eleven types of angles, brackets, and hangers is given here.

Do you want adjustable spacing? If so, focus on pin clips, bracket clips, or adjustable clips, all of which can be

moved to other holes. The supporting metal sides with horizontal holes are called pilasters; three-sided metal supports with vertical holes are called standards.

Shelves supported in a dado cut or cleats may serve your purpose better, and with these you will need no hardware at all, which is worth mentioning because sometimes the hardware costs more than the shelves.

The rigidity of a shelf can be dramatically increased by nailing and gluing a 1½" x 2½" rail along the front edge of the shelf.

Board thicknesses are provided in the following chart.

Shelving Spans

Material	Maximum Span
¾" plywood or oriented-strand board	36"
¾" particle board or waferboard	28"
1" x 12" solid lumber	24"
½" acrylic	22"
⅜" glass	18"

NOTE: For shelves that will be heavily loaded with can goods, appliances, or heavy books the span should be reduced 33%, the thickness increased or a brace ¾" x 1" or thicker should be laminated to both front and back underside of shelf.

Selection Guide for Shelf Supports

Type	Comments
Rigid pressed-steel angle bracket	Rigid pressed-steel angle brackets are not adjustable but will hold medium-weight loads. They may be installed as pairs at each end at the back. For heavier weights select brackets with triangular gussets. NOTE: Always mount brackets with the longer leg against the wall.

Selection Guide for Shelf Supports (Continued)

Type	Comments
Cleats 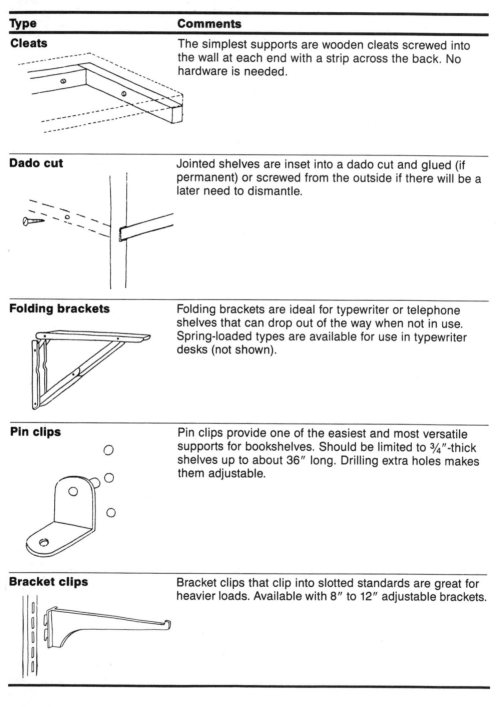	The simplest supports are wooden cleats screwed into the wall at each end with a strip across the back. No hardware is needed.
Dado cut	Jointed shelves are inset into a dado cut and glued (if permanent) or screwed from the outside if there will be a later need to dismantle.
Folding brackets	Folding brackets are ideal for typewriter or telephone shelves that can drop out of the way when not in use. Spring-loaded types are available for use in typewriter desks (not shown).
Pin clips	Pin clips provide one of the easiest and most versatile supports for bookshelves. Should be limited to ¾"-thick shelves up to about 36" long. Drilling extra holes makes them adjustable.
Bracket clips	Bracket clips that clip into slotted standards are great for heavier loads. Available with 8" to 12" adjustable brackets.

Selection Guide for Shelf Supports (Concluded)

Type	Comments
Adjustable clips	Adjustable clips are used with pilasters. The clips are available in a variety of styles and finishes.
Freestanding brackets	Freestanding brackets fit into standards with spring-loaded caps that force the pole against the ceiling.
Pegboard brackets	Light-duty pegboard brackets come in sizes up to 12″ and are particularly useful for garage shelving.
Shelf clamps	These panel clips are each attached with two screws and hold ⅝″ particle board shelving. Three attached to studs on back wall will hold a 3′-long, 10″-wide shelf and, with load evenly divided, support up to 100 pounds.
Dowel supports	Decorative dowel supports, often made with lathed designs, have wooden threads at top and female at bottom to go through precut holes in shelves. The succeeding dowels have one recessed and one threaded end. Decorative newels are available for the top; ball feet for the bottom. These are available in light or dark stained wood.

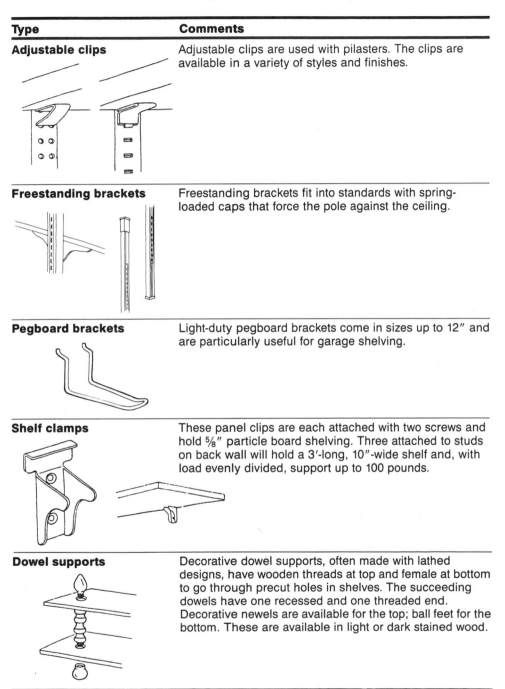

Weatherizers

17

17. Weatherizers

Insulation is a major tool in reducing your energy bills, but it is not the only tool. Although it stems heat loss by radiation, conduction, and convection, most insulation, foams excepted, do nothing about infiltration. And infiltration —drafts of outside air that sneak through the cracks and gaps in your home—is now believed to be the cause of 20 to 50 percent of total household heat loss.

Fortunately, the tools to fight infiltration are inexpensive: caulking and weather stripping. The right materials in the right places will not only lower your utility bills but make your home more comfortable and waterproof.

Also in this chapter are some other energy-saving tools that have proven their effectiveness and are commonly available on the shelves of home centers and hardware stores.

Caulks

The hardest part of a caulking job is choosing which caulk to buy. The store display racks usually have a wide variety, and they all come in the 11-ounce cartridges that fit your caulking gun. Should you purchase the high-priced silicone or go with the low-priced latex? Answer: It all depends on the location of the crack you're filling.

If you're using the caulk indoors, say to fill in a gap between a wall and window trim molding before painting a room, all you need is a paintable caulk like acrylic latex or a thermoplastic melt caulk. (Latex has the advantage of cleaning up with soap and water.)

But if you're filling a crack outside, as between siding and chimney or window trim, you need a caulk with flexibility, water resistance, and a long life. Flexibility is required because outdoor temperature swings cause

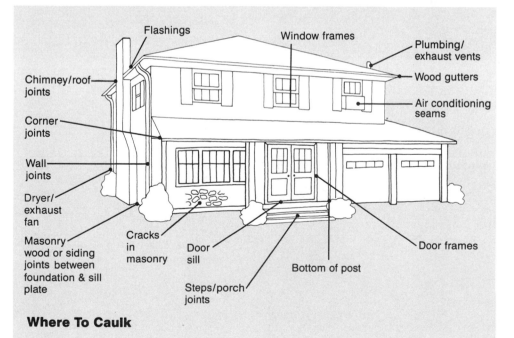

Where To Caulk

Flashings · Window frames · Plumbing/exhaust vents · Wood gutters · Air conditioning seams · Door frames · Bottom of post · Door sill · Cracks in masonry · Steps/porch joints · Masonry wood or siding joints between foundation & sill plate · Dryer/exhaust fan · Wall joints · Corner joints · Chimney/roof joints

Weatherizers

your home's building materials to expand and contract—and at different rates, if the materials are different. For jobs like this, you need caulks like siliconized acrylic latex, silicone, or the ethylene elastomeric copolymer caulk made by Geocel.

Not all caulks can be painted—polysulfide and a few silicones among them—so it's advisable to choose the clear formulation if you want to use an unpaintable kind. At least two premium silicone caulks, Red Devil "Lifetime II"

and GE "Silicone II Paintable," can be painted.

Clean surfaces before caulking, and don't try to fill too large a gap. Any gap more than ½" wide or deep should be filled with fiberglass insulation or oakum before you caulk. When caulking, most people "pull" the cartridge along the crack. Instead, it should be pushed along, forcing the caulk into the crack.

The illustration "Where to Caulk" on p. 457 shows the major places on

Caulking Selection Guide*

Type	Container	Uses	Service Temperature Range
Acrylic Latex	cartridges: 6, 10, 10.5 & 11 oz. aerosol cans: 12 oz. squeeze tubes: 4 & 6 oz.	Indoor cracks.	−20 to 180°F
Asphalt Based Caulks	cartridges: 10.5 & 11 oz. cans: 2½, 10, 30, 38, 40 & 50 lb.	Cementing and waterproofing chimneys, dormer flashings, skylights, roof seams, and for bonding polyethylene to studs, sills, and sealing overlaps.	40 to 150°F

Pushing The Cartridge—The Preferred Method

a house's exterior to caulk for waterproofing and reduction of infiltration. The chart on caulks gives details of specific types. If you have a special problem such as finding a caulk that will not dissolve polystyrene foam, or caulking that can be installed in freezing weather, one that will adhere to glass, or a caulk that will withstand high temperatures around a fireplace, you'll find suitable candidates by reading the "benefits" and "other considerations" columns.

Benefits	Other Considerations	Relative Cost	Representative Registered Trade Names
Dries quickly. Can be painted with oil or latex paint. Many colors. Up to 20-year life.	Avoid use outdoors in areas subject to wetting. Some brands are not mildew resistant or resistant to household chemicals—read labels. High-performance types are suitable for kitchen and bath applications, others for windows and doors.	Moderate	Bostik Chem-Calk 600 Contech D.A.P. Rely-On Easy Caulker Geocel Sempra H.B. Fuller Caulk-In-Color Macco Acrylic-Latex 137 Metylan All Purpose Miracle Acrylic-Latex OSI Acrylic-Latex Caulk Plio-Calk Red Devil Life Time I Seamseal 2002 Acrylic-Latex Caulk Synko UGL Acrylic-Latex Caulk
Waterproof and have good bonding. Some are designed for bonding acoustical tile and vapor barriers. 10 to 15 year life. Stay resilient.	These are actually cut-back asphalts. Check estimated resilient life as shown in manufacturer's data sheet.	Low	Champion Int. Acoustical Caulk D.A.P. Black Tite Caulking H.B. Fuller Roof/Shingle Caulk Kool Seal Instant Patch OSI Roofing & Flashing Sealant Tremco Instant Patch Tremco Non-skinning Acoustical Sealant UGL Nudeck Roof Cement

Weatherizers

Caulking Selection Guide* (Continued)

Type	Container	Uses	Service Temperature Range
Butyl Sealant	cartridges: 10.3 & 30 oz. cans: 1 qt. & 1 gal. pails: 5 gal.	Outdoor sealant for driveway cracks, gutters, etc.	−20 to 200°F
Ethylene Elastomeric Copolymer	cartridges: 10 oz.	Exterior applications to all surfaces. Plastics need priming.	−30 to 180°F
Neoprene	cartridges: 10.5 oz. cans: 2 & 5 gal.	Metal and mortar joints, flashing and seams; adheres to any surface.	−40 to 250°F
Nitrile	cartridges: 10.6 oz. cans: ½ pt., 1 pt. & quart tubes: 1 & 4 oz.	Outdoor use. Adheres to metal, wood, plastics, glass, ceramics, plaster, drywall, and concrete.	40 to 210°F

Benefits	Other Considerations	Relative Cost	Representative Registered Trade Names
10 to 20 year life. Resistant to heat, oil, and chemicals. Good water resistance.	Shrinks: Use only for narrow openings no wider or deeper than ¼″. Stringy. Does not dry quickly. Can be used to caulk windows.	Moderate	Bostik Chem-Calk 300 Butyl Plio-Calk Contech Butyl D.A.P. Butyl Flex H.B. Fuller Butyl Caulk Macco Guard House Nankee Butyl Caulk Ohio Sealants Butyl Red Devil Butyl Caulk Synco Butyl Caulk UGL Butyl Caulk
UV resistant. May be applied below freezing point. Good elasticity. 20 to 25 year life.	24 hour cure. Paintable. Available in clear, white, gray, brown, bronze, aluminum and black.	Moderate	Brush Grade Flexible Seal Flexible Seal Geocel Construction 2000 Geocel Exterior Caulking Sealant H.B. Fuller Clear Max Sealer Macco Fix-N-Seal FS145 (colors) Macco All Purpose Caulk AP 138 (white) Macco All Purpose Caulk AP 139 (clear) Non-Flam Flex Seal (bulk) 60
15 to 20 year life expectancy. Resistant to heat, oil, and chemicals. Use between driveway and foundation slab and for driveway sealing.	Good resistance to movement. Won't run or sag. Chemical resistant. Surface dries in 4 hours. Resilient.	High	Elmer's Neoprene Caulk Flexon Neoprene Caulk
Long life expectancy. Excellent for narrow cracks and joints in gutters, metal frames, and flashings.	Resists movement and vibration. Will not soften and cavitate polystyrene foamboard. Fast setting.	Very high	Non-Sag Sealing Compound 1 OSI Nitrile Gutter Sealant Ruscoe's Permanent Sealer Seam Sealer 12-1 Self-Leveling Sealant 12-3

Weatherizers

Caulking Selection Guide* (Continued)

Type	Container	Uses	Service Temperature Range
Oil-Based (Made using linseed oil, whiting, talc, kerosene)	cartridges: 10.5 oz.	Fills holes in metal, wood, or masonry. Use indoors.	−20 to 180°F
Polybutane Rope Caulk	packaged coils: 30', 45' & 90'	Indoors or outdoors to seal openings, cracks, and gutters. Caulks windows.	−20 to 200°F
Polysulphides	cartridges: (1 part) $\frac{1}{12}$ gal. aerosol cans: (1 part) 11 oz. kits: (2 part) $1\frac{1}{2}$ gals. pails: (2 part) $\frac{1}{2}$ & 1 gal.	Excellent for caulking between glass and frame.	−40 to 250°F
Polyurethane (foam sealant)	cartridges: 10.3 oz. aerosol cans: 12 & 26 oz. disposable cylinders: 10 lb. pails: 2 gal.	Around vents, ducts, and pipes. Good for sealing sill plates, top plates, T-joints and wood-to-wood joints. Polyurethane foam sealant comes in two types: a high-foaming (HF) variety and a minimum expansion foam (MEF). Use MEF around windows and doors as the HF foam will push out frames and cause binding.	−40 to 120°F (Apply above 40°F.)

Benefits	Other Considerations	Relative Cost	Representative Registered Trade Names
Inexpensive.	Not flexible. Has a 1-year to 3-year life. Allow to cure before painting.	Low	Miracle Oil-Based Caulk UGL Therma King
Easy to apply—less mess to clean up. Resistant to heat, oil, and chemicals. Good water resistance. 10 to 20 year life.	Shrinks. Use only on openings 1/4″ or less, wide or deep. Dries slowly. Can be used to caulk windows or doors.	Moderate	FrostKing Rope Caulk Myro Rope Caulk Thermwell Finger-Tip Caulk Thermwell Press-and-Seal Caulk
Excellent flexibility, stretch, and bonding. Can be used in high movement joints. Life expectancy 20 years.	Two-part formulation has superior performance. One-part formulation is easier to use but is not recommended for joints over 3/4″ wide or 3/8″ deep. Must be applied to dry surfaces.	High	Bostik Chem-Calk 100 Pecora Synthacaulk PRC Permapol Sealants
Excellent adhesion. HF expands 100-200% rapidly to fill deep voids. MEF expands before it leaves wand, so will only expand 10-20% in crack. Can be trimmed within 10 minutes, cures in 8 hours. Greatly improves thermal efficiency of building—approximately R-5 per inch and stops drafts.	May turn brown if not protected from ultraviolet radiation. Thermal effectiveness depends on deep joint penetration. Aerosol cans have 2-year shelf life and 10-lb. cylinders have indefinite shelf life. Store in cool place. Requires application skill to avoid waste. Read caution notices on label before using or disposing. Keep out of the reach of children. Combustible; use only in well-ventilated area. Estimated 20-year life. Moisten dry, porous surfaces before application. Shake aerosol cans before using.	High by the can, but low for the coverage provided.	*High foaming* Bostik Chem-Calk 900 Geocel Expanding Foam Sealant Henkel Metylan OSI Wonderfoam Polycel One Insulating Foam Sealant Red Devil Foam Sealant Touch'n foam *Minimum Expansion Foam* Instafoam's Great Stuff

Weatherizers

Caulking Selection Guide* (Continued)

Type	Container	Uses	Service Temperature Range
Rubber Caulk	cartridges: 10.6 & 11 oz. tube: 4 oz.	Around windows and doors.	0 to 100°F
	cartridge: 11 oz. square tube: 8 oz.	Gutters and down spouts.	0 to 100°F
Silicone (fluorosilicone)	cartridges: 11 oz. squeeze tubes: 7/8, 3, 4.7 & 5 oz. drums: 1, 4.5 & 52 gal.	Almost universal use. Can be used to coat, protect, and seal components from water and chemicals.	Extended −75 to 450°F Intermittent −80 to 500°F

Benefits	Other Considerations	Relative Cost	Representative Registered Trade Names
Never stringy or course. Extrudes consistently. Does not collect dirt.	Available in 13 colors, aluminum, bronze, black, white and clear.	Moderate	OSI SBR Rubber Siding and Window Caulk Plio-Seam Elastomeric Rubber Sealant
Can be painted.	Available in white or aluminum.	Moderate	OSI SBR Gutter and Seam Sealant
Seals, bonds, and insulates. Top performer among sealants and priced accordingly. It is the most water- and weather-resistant, most flexible caulk (Life Time II stretches 2500% without breaking). Outstanding bond to wood, metals, glass, concrete tile, and most plastics but may need primer (will not bond to tetrachlorethylene). Unaffected by movement; does not crack or become brittle with age. Does not sag, slump, run, or drip. Some types are resistant to and can be immersed in fuels, oils, or solvents. Good dielectric properties.	Some manufacturers offer a 50-year limited warranty on their silicone sealants. Make sure the type you are using for bathrooms, kitchens, or outdoors is recommended for high-moisture areas. Work time 3–10 minutes, vulcanizes in 24 hours. Cure 4–7 days. Requires moist air to cure. Do not use heat—it delays cure. Most silicone caulks can be used as sealants, caulks or adhesives—consult label and manufacturer's data sheet. Not recommended for subgrade masonry applications. Most will not accept paint. Solvents: naptha, xylene, or toluene. Shelf life (stored at 40°F) 12 months. Available white or clear.	Expensive (for most wood-to-wood cracks). Acrylic latex, polysulphides or polyurethanes provide satisfactory performance at less cost.	Bostik Chem-Calk 1000 Bostik Chem-Calk 1200 Bostik 9700 Bathroom Caulk Contech Dow-Corning Silicone Rubber General Purpose Sealant Dow-Corning Bath/Tub Caulk Dow-Corning Clear Sealer Dow-Corning 786 (Mildew Resistant Sealant) Dow-Corning Silicone Rubber Concrete Sealant Dow-Corning Silicone Rubber Paintable Sealant Dow-Corning Plus Silicone Sealant Dow-Corning Silastic RTV Dow-Corning Silicone Paint Sealant Easy Caulk GE 1200 GE Silicone Rubber A1 GE Silicone Bath Tub Caulk Lucas Tiger Grip Macco Silicone Miracle Bathroom & Kitchen Caulk Miracle White or Clear Caulk OSI Ultrasil Stauffer-Wacker "SWS" Surebond SB-188

Weatherizers

Caulking Selection Guide* (Continued)

Type	Container	Uses	Service Temperature Range
Siliconized Acrylic Latex	cartridges: 11 oz.	Indoor and outdoor cracks.	−20 to 180°F
Solvent-Based Acrylics	cartridges: 10 oz.	Adhesive and sealant. Caulking around windows, doors, sinks, bathtubs and showers. Adheres to ceramic tiles. Fills holes and cracks in wood, plaster and drywall.	−40 to 300°F
Thermoplastic Caulking Sticks (for applications using electric glue guns)	Shrink-pak cards holding 12 sticks 2″ or 6 sticks 4″. Boxes add 60 2″ sticks or 30 4″ sticks.	General use and where extra tight bonded seal is required.	0 to 350°F

Benefits	Other Considerations	Relative Cost	Representative Registered Trade Names
New on market. Easy to use. 20+ year life. For use outdoors. Dries fast. Available in colors.	Good flexibility.	High	Contech "Siliconized" Caulk Cuprinol Outdoor Caulk D.A.P. Acrylic Latex with Silicone Dow-Corning Silicone "Plus" GE Silicone II Geotech Construction 1100 "Life Time II" Macco Insul Caulk Macco Super Caulk Macklanburg-Duncan Wet or Dry OSI Siliconized Acrylic Latex Red Devil "Life Time II" Synco Siliconized Acrylic Latex UGL 25 Year Lasticaulk
Anticipated 20-year life. All-purpose caulk for both inside and outdoor use. Can be painted. Mildew resistant.	Some types require preheating before use. Does not adhere to Teflon, polyethylene, silicone, or wet surfaces. Difficult to apply.	High	Bostik Chem-Calk 800 H.B. Fuller Maxseal (clear) Henkel Metylan All-Purpose Caulk UGL AC-88
No mess, sets quickly and adheres firmly.	Electric glue guns to apply this caulk are inexpensive.	Moderate	Bostik Sealer Emhart Sealer

Weatherizers

Caulking Selection Guide* (Concluded)

Type	Container	Uses	Service Temperature Range
Urethane	pails: (2 part) ½ & 1 gal. froth paks: (2 part with applicators) 9 lb. (⅝ gal.) & 36 lb. (2½ gal.)	General use. Adheres tenaciously to almost any surface except some plastics.	0 to 250°F
Vinyl Caulk	cartridges: 10 & 30 oz. pails: 1 gal. squeeze tubes: 6 oz.	All-purpose adhesive caulk. Bonds to wood, masonry, ceramics, glass, and metal.	20 to 180°F
Vinyl Foam Tape	coils: 25'	As above. Tape is easier to apply. Just press into crack.	As above.

*Formulations may vary—read manufacturer's product data sheets.

Outlet Seals

Several manufacturers make sealing pads to install behind the faceplates of electrical switches and outlets.

Judging by their size, you may think these sealers play an insignificant role in controlling home heat loss. Actually, their role is important: They reduce drafts into your rooms. And when the electrical boxes are located on the inside of exterior walls, the seals reduce the flow of household air into the wall cavities, thus reducing the amount of moisture that could potentially condense within the wall and lower the insulation's R value. (The higher the R value, the greater the insulating power.) Electrical boxes are a major pathway of moisture into walls.

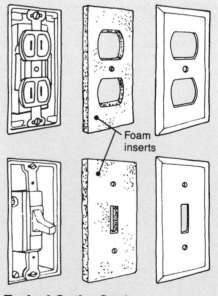

Foam inserts

Typical Outlet Seals

Benefits	Other Considerations	Relative Cost	Representative Registered Trade Names
20-year life expectancy. Tough and abrasion-resistant. Can be used in high-movement joints.	Two-part formulation has superior performance over one-part systems. Aged R-value of 6.25 claimed.	Expensive	Bostik Chem-Calk 500 Froth Pak Geocel Spec 3000 Insta-Foam OSI General Purpose Foam Polycel Foam Kit (FK 220) Vulkem Sealant
Resilient, mildew-resistant, water-resistant, and paintable.	Nontoxic, nonflammable. Permits water cleanup.	Moderate	Cloucester Company Phenoseal Polyseamseal All Purpose Adhesive Caulk
As above.	As above.	Moderate	Mortell Mortite Press-to-Seal

Setback Thermostats

New thermostats are equipped with timers that can turn down the heat while you're asleep or away and set it back up to a comfortable temperature just before you awaken or return.

Many tests have shown that these thermostats, if used regularly, are effective in reducing heating costs. An eight-hour, 10-degree nighttime setback will reduce a home's heating bill by 9 to 15 percent, depending on your climate. Thus, their high cost (often just under $100) will usually be paid back in a year or less.

Some models also save money on summertime central air-conditioning bills; read the labels carefully to be sure the model you buy fits this need.

Most setback thermostats have microchip memories that you "program" by means of buttons on the thermostat face. The better models allow you to program multiple setback periods each day and to change or override your routine setback times without a lot of extra programming.

Most models are designed to allow homeowners to replace their existing thermostat with ease and without professional help. But most models will not function properly if hooked up to heat pumps, new gas-fired furnaces with electric ignition instead of pilot lights, electric baseboards, or a millivolt

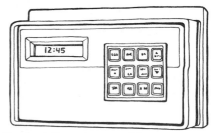

Typical Programmable Thermostat

Weatherizers

instead of 24-volt connection to the furnace. If that's your case, call a heating contractor for advice.

Water Heater Jackets

According to the Washington State electric utility Puget Sound Power and Light, a water heater insulation jacket on an electric water heater can save about 650 kilowatt hours a year. That's an annual savings of $52 for someone with an average electricity cost of 8 cents per kilowatt hour.

A Jacketed Water Heater

There are two types of water heater insulation jackets: one for gas heaters, the other for electric heaters. The gas heater jackets leave air intake space at the bottom and have no insulation on top so they won't interfere with the heater's flue vent. Be sure to buy the right type for your water heater.

Weather Stripping—Doors

Weather stripping is necessary to seal the gaps around doors. An ⅛" crack between a door bottom and the threshold is the same as a 2″ × 2″ hole in your wall.

Illustrated below are the various types of weather stripping available.

Magnetic
1. Vinyl-covered
2. Direct contact

Used on insulated steel doors. Attach to both head and strike jamb. (Compression strip has to be used on hinge jamb.) Provides a tight seal, is not affected by slight door warpage, and stays flexible in cold.

V-Spring Strip

Attaches to head and both side jambs. Strips are made of metal or plastic—both are very efficient and durable; plastic is less likely to catch on clothing and get bent out of shape. This type of strip will accommodate minor door warpage.

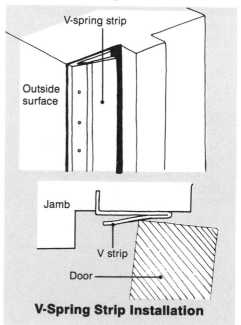

V-Spring Strip Installation

Foam Strip

These rubber or plastic foam strips are self-adhesive, with peel-off backing. They are easy to install but need replacing every year or so.

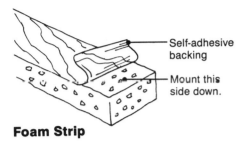

Self-adhesive backing

Mount this side down.

Foam Strip

Rolled Vinyl Tack Strip

This is a vinyl bulbous tube with tacking strip that is attached to the outside doorstop. The door compresses the bulb for a tight seal. It must be carefully installed for a proper fit and will need relocating if the door warps. This type of weather stripping is frequently used for hinge jambs. Stapling may be easier than tacking for attachment.

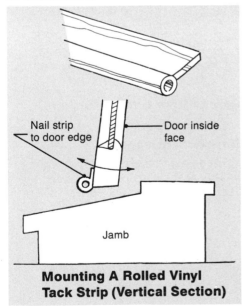

Nail strip to door edge

Door inside face

Jamb

Mounting A Rolled Vinyl Tack Strip (Vertical Section)

Felt Strip

This is tacked on the doorstop. It is not as resilient as foam but lasts longer and is very effective. Felt strip should not be used on unsheltered doors where passing people and pets can abrade or strip off the surface.

Felt Strip

PVC Draftshield

A weather stripping product made by Enpro, of Minneapolis. It has a pressure-sensitive adhesive foam tape backing.

Metal Interlocking Channels

Because these have to mesh, they are tricky to install. The channel metal protrudes from the doorstop so can catch on clothing or on articles being carried in or out of the door. Properly installed, this type of weather stripping provides a very effective infiltration barrier.

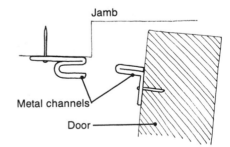

Jamb

Metal channels

Door

Interlocking Channel Mounting

Weatherizers

Metal J Strips

These make a professional-looking and effective seal but can only be used on wood doors because they require a channel to be routed in the door edge. Probably the most difficult seal to install but the most durable.

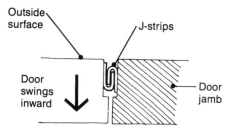

J Strip Mounting

Metal Drip Cap

This is attached to the outside bottom of the door and rides over a bulb threshold. When the door is closed it rests against the bulb.

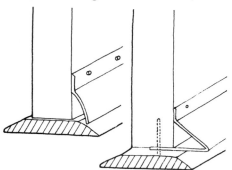

Metal Drip Caps

Automatic Sweep

This contains a spring-loaded hoist. An extended rod presses against a strike plate on the hinge jamb so the sweep drops as the door closes. The spring automatically raises the sweep as the door opens to clear high-pile carpeting.

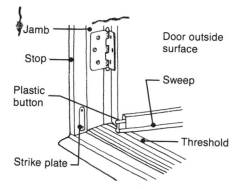

Automatic Sweep

Garage Door Bottom Gasket

This rubber or plastic cupped strip spreads out against the floor inside and out as the door is lowered to effectively keep out water and wind.

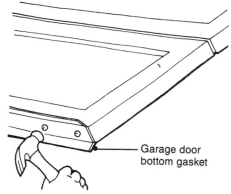

Garage Door Bottom Gasket

Threshold Sweeps

These all attach to the door with or without a show and press against the threshold.

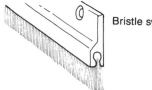

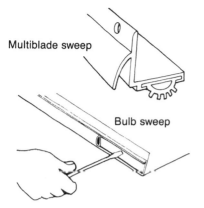

Multiblade sweep

Bulb sweep

Bulb Threshold

This works well and is easy to replace. A rubber bulb fits in a track in the aluminum threshold. The bottom of the door has to be beveled.

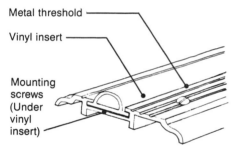

Metal threshold

Vinyl insert

Mounting screws (Under vinyl insert)

Bulb Threshold

Storm Door Sweeps

This is a plastic sweep that attaches to the outside bottom edge of the door with a screwed-on aluminum strip (use aluminum screws). It brushes against the threshold.

Door opens this way

Sweep

Storm Door Sweep

Threshold

Weather Stripping—Windows

Double-hung windows can be weatherstripped with spring metal, PVC (self-adhesive), or polypropylene seals. They are tacked inside sash channels (A, C), under the bottom of lower sash (D), and to the outside of the bottom rail of the upper sash (B).

Vinyl tubular or foam-filled bulbous strips or vinyl weather stripping is tacked to the exterior of parting strips that divide the channel (E, G) and also against the bottom rail of the lower sash (H). These can also be used extending out from under the bottom rail of the top sash (F).

Foam rubber with adhesive backing is applied in the same locations as vinyl weather stripping. It's easier to install and costs less but catches dirt and needs annual replacement.

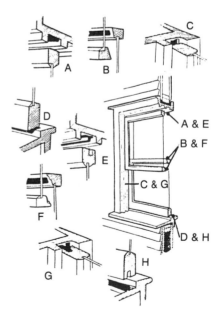

A   B   C

D

A & E

B & F

E

C & G

F

D & H

G   H

Weather Stripping Double-Hung Window

Weatherizers

Casement windows generally seal tight, but if not, attach foam rubber to the inside of the stop.

On **metal windows** use foam rubber at joints or wrap a transparent vinyl tape (sold for the purpose) over all edges.

For weather stripping that requires tacking, use only rustproof tacks or brass brads.

Window Shading Devices

In the Sunbelt, summer heat creates the costliest energy bills. A proven way to trim air-conditioning costs is to reduce the amount of sunlight that enters through the home's windows.

There are a variety of strategies, as shown in the accompanying chart. You can choose to suit your esthetic taste and budget. Some devices are more effective than others. In general, those outside the window block more heat than shades inside.

The Florida Solar Energy Center studied seven kinds of window shading devices and ranked them according to kilowatt hours saved. Found most effective were metal awnings with sidewalls, followed closely by canvas awnings with sidewalls, and woven fiberglass solar screens. Next most effective were reflective films and metal awnings without sidewalls (Bahama shutters). Tinted glass trailed the list; it was only half as effective as the films and Bahama shutters.

The most important windows to shade are those facing east or west—they allow the direct penetration of the morning and afternoon sun.

Shading for Energy Conservation

Outside	Types Available	Comments
Awnings	Fixed aluminum Pull-down rolled fabric Fiberglass panels	Come in stripes and colors. Effectively shade interior but may restrict solar gain in winter unless fully retractable. Attractive and effective. Tend to sag and collect dirt and water near bottom. Those with side panels are more efficient.
Structures (either as shading for windows or to cover porch)	Frames can be erected and covered in a variety of ways: a. Spaced vertical 2 x 8 boards b. Fiberglass paneling c. Shingle roof	Provide shade without sacrificing light. Attractive and easy to maintain. Permit light transmission but reduce glare. Very durable. Provide shade, keep porch dry, but may make rooms dark.
Lattice Wall or Fence	Specially shaped decorative concrete blocks to provide a setting sun barrier in the west. Can also be accomplished with trees, bushes, or a fence.	

Shading for Energy Conservation (Concluded)

Outside	Types Available	Comments
Solar Screens	Used instead of insect screening in windows. Allow see-through visibility from inside, privacy from outside. Available in over 20 colors. Use in summer, take down in wintor.	Reject 70% of solar radiation. When used on east, south, and west of home will noticeably reduce air-conditioning costs.

Inside	Types Available	Comments
Venetian Blinds	Mini-blinds—available installed between double glazing in a sash; effective in reflecting solar radiation. Regular venetian blinds—available in aluminum or plastic.	Like all manually operated energy-saving devices, these only work if used. They will reduce air-conditioning costs and can be opened to admit solar heat when wanted in winter. But reflecting the sun's rays after they have entered the home is only partially effective.
Shades	The opaque variety will reflect solar radiation. Operate on spring rollers.	Not as effective as exterior shading. Since they are not sealed around sides, they will not stop convective heat loss or gain.
Drapes	Come in every variety of fabric, some with insulated liners.	Too often the heat register ends up on the window side of the drapes, since it is located too close to the window. That wastes energy. If no register is involved, drapes will help keep heat in in winter, out in summer. However, keeping the windows cooler in winter can increase condensation.
Films (Consult window section p. 203 for information on low emissivity glass)	Silver or bronze reflective. Affix to inside face of window glass.	Effective and do not block view. But do cut window solar gain. Some brands, such as 3M's Scotchtint, are removable for winter.

Index